Object Oriented Programming with C++

SECOND EDITION

Sourav Sahay
Lead Consultant
Capgemini
Detroit, Michigan

OXFORD

UNIVERSITY PRESS

OXFORD
UNIVERSITY PRESS

Oxford University Press is a department of the University of Oxford.
It furthers the University's objective of excellence in research, scholarship,
and education by publishing worldwide. Oxford is a registered trade mark of
Oxford University Press in the UK and in certain other countries.

Published in India by
Oxford University Press
22 Workspace, 2nd Floor, 1/22 Asaf Ali Road, New Delhi 110 002

© Oxford University Press 2006, 2012

The moral rights of the author/s have been asserted.

First Edition Published in 2006
Second Edition Published in 2012

ISBN-13: 978-0-19-806530-2
ISBN-10: 0-19-806530-2

Typeset in Times New Roman
by Recto Graphics, Delhi 110096
Printed in India by Repro India Limited

Preface to the Second Edition

The object-oriented programming system (OOPS) enables a programmer to model real-world objects. It allows the programmer to add characteristics like data security, data encapsulation, etc.

In the procedure-oriented programming system, procedures are dissociated from data and are not a part of it. Instead, they receive structure variables, or their addresses, and then work upon them. The code design is centered around procedures. While this may sound obvious, this programming pattern has its drawbacks, a major one being that the data is not secure. It can be manipulated by *any* procedure.

It is the lack of data security of the procedure-oriented programming system that led to OOPS, in which, with the help of a new programming construct and new keywords, associated functions of the data structure can be given exclusive rights to work upon its variables.

There is another characteristic of real-world objects—a guaranteed initialization of data. Programming languages that implement OOPS enable library programmers to incorporate this characteristic of real-world objects into structure variables. Library programmers can ensure a guaranteed initialization of data members of structure variables to the desired values. For this, application programmers do not need to write code explicitly.

OOPS further supports the following concepts:

- **Inheritance** This feature allows a class to inherit the data and function members of an existing class.
- **Data abstraction** Data abstraction is a virtue by which an object hides its internal operations from the rest of the program.
- **Modularity** This feature supports dividing a program into small segments and implement those segments using different functions.
- **Polymorphism** Through polymorphism, functions with different set of formal arguments can have the same name.

The first edition had covered the fundamentals of the object oriented programming system in depth. These explanations in the first edition hold true for any programming language that supports OOPS. This second edition enhances coverage, as listed below.

New to this Edition

- New chapter on data structures containing new and original algorithms, especially an elegant and simple recursive algorithm for inserting nodes into trees. The explanations are elaborate and full of diagrams.
- New sections on explicit constructors, command line arguments, and re-throwing exceptions.

- Expanded glossary.

Key Features

- Simple and concise language eases the understanding of complex concepts that have made C++ powerful but enigmatic.
- Plenty of solved examples with complete program listings and test cases to reinforce learning.
- Review questions and program writing exercises at the end of each chapter to provide additional practice.
- Self-tests at the end of the book to prepare the students for examinations.

Organization of the Book

A brief knowledge of C language is a prerequisite for this book. The readers need to know how programs are written in C, data types, decision-making and looping constructs, operators, functions, header files, pointers, and structures.

Chapter 1 contains an explanation of the procedure-oriented programming system, the role played by structures in this system, its drawbacks and how these drawbacks led to the creation of OOPS. The meaning and method of modelling real-world objects by the object-oriented programming system have been clearly explained. The chapter includes a study of the non-object-oriented features of C++.

Chapter 2 is devoted to the study of objects and classes. It gives a thorough explanation of the class construct of C++. Superiority of the class construct of C++ over the structure construct of C language is explained. A description of the various types and features of member functions and member data is included. Other concepts included are namespaces, arrays of objects, arrays in objects, and nested classes.

Chapter 3 deals with dynamic memory management. It explains the use of the new and the delete operators. It also explains the method of specifying our own new handler for handling out-of-memory conditions.

Chapter 4 explains constructors and destructors. It discusses their importance, their features, and the method of defining them.

Chapter 5 is devoted to inheritance. Concepts like base class, derived class, base class pointer, and derived class pointer are covered. The protected keyword and the implications of deriving by different access specifiers are explained. This chapter describes various types of inheritance.

Chapter 6 gives a detailed explanation of one of the most striking features of C++—dynamic polymorphism. This chapter describes the virtual functions and how it enables C++ programmers to extend class libraries. The importance of pure virtual functions and clone functions is also explained.

Chapter 7 describes the standard C++ library for handling streams. It explains the two types of input and output—text mode and binary mode. Input and output from disk files are explained. The chapter also describes the use of error-handling routines of the standard C++ stream library and manipulators.

Chapter 8 is devoted to operator overloading, type conversion, new style casts, and RTTI. This chapter explains the various intricacies and the proper use of operator overloading. This chapter also explains how a C++ programmer can implement conventional style type conversions. New style casts for implementing type conversions are explained next. This chapter ends with a treatment of run time type information (RTTI).

Chapter 9 explains and illustrates the most important data structures—linked lists and trees. It includes full-fledged programs that can be used to create various data structures.

Chapter 10 contains a detailed description of templates. The importance of function templates and class templates and their utilization in code reuse is explained. This chapter also provides an overview of the Standard Template Library (STL) of C++.

Chapter 11 explains the concept of exception handling. It begins with a section on conventional methods and their drawbacks. This is followed by an explanation of the try-catch-throw mechanism provided by C++ and its superiority over the conventional methods.

The appendices in the book include a case study, comparison of C++ with C, comparison of C++ with Java, an overview of object-oriented analysis and design, and self tests.

Acknowledgements

The blessings of my parents continue to give me the courage I need to overcome the obstacles that are associated with difficult ventures like writing books. Every achievement of my life, including this book, is because of the valuable education they gave me early in my life. Thanks to my wife Madhvi against whose wishes I decided to spend most of the weekends over the last 2 years on my laptop writing this edition. My daughters Surabhi and Sakshi continue to inspire and motivate me.

Thanks to Professor Shanmuka Swamy, Assistant Professor in the Sridevi Institute of Engineering and Technology, Tumkur, for pointing out a couple of printing mistakes in the first edition. These have been corrected.

The editorial staff members of the Oxford University Press deserve a special mention for its support and prompt responses.

Please continue to send your valuable feedback and questions to my e-mail id sourav1903@yahoo.com.

Sourav Sahay

Preface to the First Edition

C++ made its advent in the early 1980s and enabled programmers to write their programs the object-oriented way. For this reason, the language quickly gained popularity and became a programming language of choice. Despite the development of a number of competing object-oriented languages including Java, C++ has successfully maintained its position of popularity.

C++ starts where C stops. C++ is a superset of C. All the language features of C language appear in C++ with little or no modification. Over and above such features, C++ provides a number of extra features, which provide the language its object-oriented character.

About the Book

The continued popularity of C++ has led to considerable literature. Innumerable books, journals, magazines, and articles have been written on C++. So, why another book on C++?

The aim of the book is to thoroughly explain all aspects of the language constructs provided by C++. While doing full justice to the commonly explained topics of C++, the book does not neglect the advanced and new concepts of C++ that are not widely taught.

This book is a power-packed instruction guide for Object-Oriented Programming and C++. The purpose of this book is two-fold:

- To clarify the fundamentals of the Object-Oriented Programming System
- To provide an in-depth treatment of each feature and language construct of C++

This book emphasizes the Object-Oriented Programming System—its benefits and its superiority over the conventional Procedure-Oriented Programming System.

This book starts directly with C++ since the common features of C and C++ are anyway covered in books on C language. Each feature of C++ is covered from the practical point of view. Instead of brief introductions, this book gives an in-depth explanation of the rationale and proper use of each object-oriented feature of C++.

To help the readers assimilate the large volume of knowledge contained in this book, an adequate number of example programs, well-designed diagrams, and analogies with the real world have been given. Some program examples given in this book are abstract in nature to help readers focus on the concept being discussed.

Acknowledgements

First, I thank my parents for teaching me a number of valuable lessons of life including the value of hardwork and the value of good education (neither of which I have learnt yet!). I also thank my wife Madhvi for her patience, her encouragement, and also for having tolerated my long periods of silence and temper tantrums! Thanks (rather apologies) to my little daughters, Surabhi and Sakshi, who tolerated Papa's frequent refusals to take them on outings.

I thank Dr David Mulvaney and Dr Sekharjit Datta of the University of Loughborough for their valuable guidance, encouragement, and inspiration. My teachers always encouraged me to think big and to think independently. My sincerest gratitude to each one of them.

The editorial team of Oxford University Press deserves my heartfelt thanks for their guidance and for their timely reminders about the deadlines I would have definitely missed otherwise!

Feedback about the book is most welcome. Readers are requested and encouraged to send their feedback to the author's mail id sourav1903@yahoo.com.

Sourav Sahay

Brief Contents

Detailed Contents

1

Introduction to C++

**O
V
E
R
V
I
E
W**

This chapter introduces the reader to the fundamentals of object-oriented programming systems (OOPS).

The chapter begins with an overview of structures, the reasons for their inclusion as a language construct in C language, and their role in procedure-oriented programming systems. Use of structures for creating new data types is described. Also, the drawbacks of structures and the development of OOPS are elucidated.

The middle section of the chapter explains OOPS, supplemented with suitable examples and analogies to help in understanding this tricky subject.

The concluding section of the chapter includes a study of a number of new features that are implemented by C++ compilers but do not fall under the category of object-oriented features. (Language constructs of C++ that implement object-oriented features are dealt with in the next chapter.)

1.1 A Review of Structures

In order to understand procedure-oriented programming systems, let us first recapitulate our understanding of structures in C. Let us review their necessity and use in creating new data types.

1.1.1 The Need for Structures

There are cases where the value of one variable depends upon that of another variable.

Take the example of date. A date can be programmatically represented in C by three different integer variables taken together. Say,

```
int d,m,y; //three integers for representing dates
```

Here 'd', 'm', and 'y' represent the day of the month, the month, and the year, respectively. Observe carefully. Although these three variables are not grouped together in the code, they actually belong to the same group. *The value of one variable may influence the value of the other two.* In order to understand this clearly, consider a function next_day() that accepts the addresses of the three integers that represent a date and changes their values to represent the next day. The prototype of this function will be

```
void next_day(int *,int *,int *); //function to calculate
                                   //the next day
```

Suppose,

```
d=1;
m=1;
y=2002;                              //1st January, 2002
```

Now, if we write

```
next_day(&d,&m,&y);
```

'd' will become 2, 'm' will remain 1, and 'y' will remain 2002.

But if

```
d=28;
m=2;
y=1999; //28th February, 1999
```

and we call the function as

```
next_day(&d,&m,&y);
```

'd' will become 1, 'm' will become 3, and 'y' will remain 1999.
Again, if

```
d=31;
m=12;
y=1999;                              //31st December, 1999
```

and we call the function as

```
next_day(&d,&m,&y);
```

'd' will become 1, 'm' will become 1, and 'y' will become 2000.

As you can see, 'd', 'm', and 'y' actually belong to the same group. A change in the value of one may change the value of the other two. *But there is no language construct that actually places them in the same group.* Thus, members of the wrong group may be accidentally sent to the function (Listing 1.1)!

Listing 1.1 Problem in passing groups of programmatically independent but logically dependent variable

```
d1=28;  m1=2;   y1=1999;        //28th February, 1999
d2=19;  m2=3;   y2=1999;        //19th March, 1999
next_day(&d1,&m1,&y1);          //OK
next_day(&d1,&m2,&y2);          //What? Incorrect set passed!
```

As can be observed in Listing 1.1, there is nothing in the language itself that prevents the wrong set of variables from being sent to the function. Moreover, integer-type variables that are not meant to represent dates might also be sent to the function!

Let us try arrays to solve the problem. Suppose the next_day() function accepts an array as a parameter. Its prototype will be

```
void next_day(int *);
```

Let us declare date as an array of three integers.

```
int date[3];
date[0]=28;
date[1]=2;
date[2]=1999;        //28th February, 1999
```

Now, let us call the function as follows:

```
next_day(date);
```

The values of 'date[0]', 'date[1]', and 'date[2]' will be correctly set to 1, 3, and 1999, respectively. Although this method seems to work, it certainly appears unconvincing. After all *any* integer array can be passed to the function, even if it does not necessarily represent a date. There is no data type of date itself. Moreover, this solution of arrays will not work if the *variables are not of the same type*. The solution to this problem is to create a data type called date itself using structures

```
struct date                          //a structure to represent dates
{
    int d, m, y;
};
```

Now, the next_day() function will accept the address of a variable of the structure date as a parameter. Accordingly, its prototype will be as follows:

```
void next_day(struct date *);
```

Let us now call it as shown in Listing 1.2.

Listing 1.2 The need for structures

```
struct date d1;
d1.d=28;
d1.m=2;
d1.y=1999;
next_day(&d1);
```

'd1.d', 'd1.m', and 'd1.y' will be correctly set to 1, 3, and 1999, respectively. Since the function takes the address of an entire structure variable as a parameter at a time, there is no chance of variables of the different groups being sent to the function.

Structure is a programming construct in C that allows us to put together variables that should be together.

Library programmers use structures to create new data types. Application programs and other library programs use these new data types by declaring variables of this data type.

```
struct date d1;
```

They call the associated functions by passing these variables or their addresses to them.

```
d1.d=31;
d1.m=12;
d1.y=2003;
next_day(&d1);
```

Finally, they use the resultant value of the passed variable further as per requirements.

```
printf("The next day is: %d/%d/%d\n", d1.d, d1.m, d1.y);
```

Output
The next day is: 01/01/2004

1.1.2 Creating a New Data Type Using Structures

Creation of a new data type using structures is loosely a three-step process that is executed by the library programmer.

Step 1: Put the structure definition and the prototypes of the associated functions in a header file, as shown in Listing 1.3.

Listing 1.3 Header file containing definition of a structure variable and prototypes of its associated functions

```
/*Beginning of date.h*/
/*This file contains the structure definition and
prototypes of its associated functions*/

struct date
{
    int d,m,y;
};
void next_day(struct date *);       //get the next date
void get_sys_date(struct date *);   //get the current
                                    //system date
/*
   Prototypes of other useful and relevant functions to
   work upon variables of the date structure
*/
/*End of date.h*/
```

Step 2: As shown in Listing 1.4, put the definition of the associated functions in a source code and create a library.

Listing 1.4 Defining the associated functions of a structure

```
/*Beginning of date.c*/
/*This file contains the definitions of the associated
functions*/
#include "date.h"

void next_day(struct date * p)
{
//calculate the date that immediately follows the one
//represented by *p and set it to *p.
}
void get_sys_date(struct date * p)
{
//determine the current system date and set it to *p
}
/*
   Definitions of other useful and relevant functions to work upon variables
   of the date structure
*/
/*End of date.c*/
```

Step 3: Provide the header file and the library, in whatever media, to other programmers who want to use this new data type.

Creation of a structure and creation of its associated functions are two separate steps that together constitute one complete process.

1.1.3 Using Structures in Application Programs

The steps to use this new data type are as follows:

Step 1: Include the header file provided by the library programmer in the source code.

```
/*Beginning of dateUser.c*/
#include"date.h"
void main( )
{
    . . . .
    . . . .
}
/*End of dateUser.c*/
```

Step 2: Declare variables of the new data type in the source code.

```
/*Beginning of dateUser.c*/
#include"date.h"
void main( )
{
    struct date d;
    . . . .
    . . . .
}
/*End of dateUser.c*/
```

Step 3: As shown in Listing 1.5, embed calls to the associated functions by passing these variables in the source code.

Listing 1.5   Using a structure in an application program

```
/*Beginning of dateUser.c*/
#include"date.h"
void main()
{
    struct date d;
    d.d=28;
    d.m=2;
    d.y=1999;
    next_day(&d);
    . . . .
    . . . .
}
/*End of dateUser.c*/
```

Step 4: Compile the source code to get the object file.

Step 5: Link the object file with the library provided by the library programmer to get the executable or another library.

1.2 Procedure-Oriented Programming Systems

In light of the previous discussion, let us understand the procedure-oriented programming system. The foregoing pattern of programming divides the code into functions. Data (contained in structure variables) is passed from one function to another to be read from or written into. The focus is on procedures. This programming pattern is, therefore, a feature of the procedure-oriented programming system.

In the procedure-oriented programming system, procedures are dissociated from data and are not a part of it. Instead, they receive structure variables or their addresses and work upon them. The code design is centered around procedures. While this may sound obvious, this programming pattern has its drawbacks.

The drawback with this programming pattern is that the data is not secure. It can be manipulated by *any* procedure. Associated functions that were designed by the library programmer do not have the exclusive rights to work upon the data. They are not a part of the structure definition itself. Let us see why this is a problem.

Suppose the library programmer has defined a structure and its associated functions as described above. Further, in order to perfect his/her creation, he/she has rigorously tested the associated functions by calling them from small test applications. Despite his/her best efforts, he/she cannot be sure that an application that uses the structure will be bug free. The application program might modify the structure variables, not by the associated function he/she has created, but by some code inadvertently written in the application program itself. Compilers that implement the procedure-oriented programming system do not prevent unauthorized functions from accessing/manipulating structure variables.

Now, let us look at the situation from the application programmer's point of view. Consider an application of around 25,000 lines (quite common in the real programming world), in which variables of this structure have been used quite extensively. During testing, it is found that the date being represented by one of these variables has become 29th February 1999! The faulty piece of code that is causing this bug can be anywhere in the program. Therefore, debugging will involve a visual inspection of the entire code (of 25000 lines!) and will not be limited to the associated functions only.

The situation becomes especially grave if the execution of the code that is likely to corrupt the data is conditional. For example,

```
if(<some condition>)
    d.m++;    //d is a variable of date structure… d.m may
              //become 13!
```

The condition under which the bug-infested code executes may not arise during testing. While distributing his/her application, the application programmer cannot be sure that it would run successfully. Moreover, every new piece of code that accesses structure variables will have to be visually inspected and tested again to ensure that it does not corrupt the members of the structure. After all, compilers that implement procedure-oriented programming systems do not prevent unauthorized functions from accessing/manipulating structure variables.

Let us think of a compiler that enables the library programmer to assign exclusive rights to the associated functions for accessing the data members of the corresponding structure. If this happens, then our problem is solved. If a function which is not one of the intended associated functions accesses the data members of a structure variable, a compile-time error will result. To ensure a successful compile of his/her application code, the application programmer will be forced to remove those statements that access data members of structure variables. Thus, the application that arises out of a successful compile will be the outcome of a piece of code that is free of any unauthorized access to the data members of the structure variables used therein. Consequently, if a run-time error arises, attention can be focused on the associated library functions.

It is the lack of data security of procedure-oriented programming systems that led to object-oriented programming systems (OOPS). This new system of programming is the subject of our next discussion.

1.3 Object-Oriented Programming Systems

In OOPS, we try to model real-world objects. But, what are real-world objects? Most real-world objects have internal parts and interfaces that enable us to operate them. These interfaces *perfectly* manipulate the internal parts of the objects. They also have the *exclusive rights* to do so.

Let us understand this concept with the help of an example. Take the case of a simple LCD projector (a real-world object). It has a fan and a lamp. There are two switches—one to operate the fan and the other to operate the lamp. However, the operation of these switches is necessarily governed by rules. If the lamp is switched on, the fan should automatically switch itself on. Otherwise, the LCD projector will get damaged. For the same reason, the lamp should automatically get switched off if the fan is switched off. In order to cater to these conditions, the switches are suitably linked with each other. The interface to the LCD projector is perfect. Further, this interface has the exclusive rights to operate the lamp and fan.

This, in fact, is a common characteristic of all real-world objects. *If a perfect interface is required to work on an object, it will also have exclusive rights to do so.*

Coming back to C++ programming, we notice a resemblance between the observed behaviour of the LCD projector and the desired behaviour of data structure's variables. In OOPS, with the help of a new programming construct and new keywords, associated functions of the data structure can be given exclusive rights to work upon its variables. In other words, all other pieces of code can be prevented from accessing the data members of the variables of this structure.

Compilers that implement OOPS enable data security by diligently enforcing this prohibition. They do this by throwing compile-time errors against pieces of code that violate the prohibition. This prohibition, if enforced, will make structure variables behave like real-world objects. Associated functions that are defined to perfectly manipulate structure variables can be given exclusive rights to do so.

There is still another characteristic of real-world objects—a guaranteed initialization of data. After all, when you connect the LCD projector to the mains, it does not start up in an invalid state (fan off and lamp on). By default, either both the lamp and the fan are off or both are on. Users of the LCD projector need not do this explicitly. The same characteristic is found in all real-world objects.

Programming languages that implement OOPS enable library programmers to incorporate this characteristic of real-world objects into structure variables. Library programmers can ensure a guaranteed initialization of data members of structure variables to the desired values. For this, application programmers do not need to write code explicitly.

Two more features are incidental to OOPS. They are:
- Inheritance
- Polymorphism

Inheritance allows one structure to inherit the characteristics of an existing structure.

As we know from our knowledge of structures, a variable of the new structure will contain data members mentioned in the new structure's definition. However, because of inheritance, it will also contain data members mentioned in the existing structure's definition from which the new structure has inherited.

Further, associated functions of the new structure can work upon a variable of the new structure. For this, the address/name of a variable of the new structure is passed to the associated functions of the new structure. Again, as a result of inheritance, associated functions of the existing structure from which the new structure has inherited will also be able to work upon a variable of the new structure. For this, the address/name of a variable of the new structure is passed to the associated functions of the existing structure.

In inheritance, data and interface may both be inherited. This is expected as data and interface complement each other. The parent structure can be given the general common characteristics while its child structures can be given the more specific characteristics. This allows code reusability by keeping the common code in a common place—the base structure. Otherwise, the code would have to be replicated in all of the child structures, which will lead to maintenance nightmares. Inheritance also enables code extensibility by allowing the creation of new structures that are better suited to our requirements as compared to the existing structures.

Polymorphism, as the name suggests, is the phenomena by virtue of which the same entity can exist in two or more forms. In OOPS, functions can be made to exhibit polymorphic behaviour. Functions with different set of formal arguments can have the same name. Polymorphism is of two types: static and dynamic. We will understand how this feature enables C++ programmers to reuse and extend existing code in the subsequent chapters.

1.4 Comparison of C++ with C

C++ is an extension of C language. It is a proper superset of C language. This means that a C++ compiler can compile programs written in C language. However, the reverse is not true. A C++ compiler can understand all the keywords that a C compiler can understand. Again, the reverse is not true. Decision-making constructs, looping constructs, structures, functions, etc. are written in exactly the same way in C++ as they are in C language. Apart from the keywords that implement these common programming constructs, C++ provides a number of additional keywords and language constructs that enable it to implement the object-oriented paradigm.

The header file given in Listing 1.6 shows how the structure Date, which has been our running example so far, can be rewritten in C++.

Listing 1.6   Redefining the Date structure in C++

```
/*Beginning of Date.h*/
class Date    //class instead of structure
{
   private:
      int d,m,y;
   public:
      Date();
      void get_sys_date();        //associated functions appear
                                  //within the class definition
      void next_day();
};
/*End of Date.h*/
```

The following differences can be noticed between Date structure in C (Listing 1.3) and C++ (Listing 1.6):
- The keyword class has been used instead of struct.
- Two new keywords—private and public—appear in the code.
- Apart from data members, the class constructor also has member functions.
- A function that has the same name as the class itself is also present in the class. Incidentally, it has no return type specified. This is the class constructor and is discussed in Chapter 4 of this book.

The next chapter contains an in-depth study of the above class construct. It explains the meaning and implications of this new feature. It also explains how this and many more new features implement the features of OOPS, such as data hiding, data encapsulation, data abstraction, and a guaranteed initialization of data. However, before proceeding to Chapter 2, let us digress slightly and study the following:

- Console input/output in C++
- Some non-object-oriented features provided exclusively in C++ (reference variables, function overloading, default arguments, inline functions)

Remember that C++ program files have the extension '.cpp' or '.C'. The former extension is normally used for Windows or DOS-based compilers while the latter is normally used for UNIX-based compilers. The compiler's manual can be consulted to find out the exact extension.

1.5 Console Input/Output in C++

This section discusses console input and output in C++.

1.5.1 Console Output

The output functions in C language, such as `printf()`, can be included in C++ programs because they are anyway defined in the standard library. However, there are some more ways of outputting to the console in C++. Let us consider an example (see Listing 1.7).

Listing 1.7 Outputting in C++

```
/*Beginning of cout.cpp*/
#include<iostream.h>
void main()
{
   int x;
   x=10;
   cout<<x;      //outputting to the console
}
/*End of cout.cpp*/
```

Output

10

The third statement in the `main()` function (Listing 1.7) needs to be understood.

`cout` (pronounce see-out) is actually an object of the class `ostream_withassign` (you can think of it as a variable of the structure `ostream_withassign`). It stands as an alias for the console **out**put device, that is, the monitor (hence the name).

The << symbol, originally the left shift operator, has had its definition extended in C++. In the given context, it operates as the `insertion` operator. It is a binary operator. It takes two operands. The operand on its left must be some object of the `ostream` class. The operand on its right must be a value of some fundamental data type. The value on the right side of the `insertion` operator is 'inserted' (hence the name) into the stream headed towards the device associated with the object on the left. Consequently, the value of 'x' is displayed on the monitor.

The file `iostream.h` needs to be included in the source code to ensure successful compilation because the object `cout` and the `insertion` operator have been declared in that file.

Another object endl allows us to insert a new line into the output stream. Listing 1.8 illustrates this.

Listing 1.8 Inserting new line by 'endl'

```
/*Beginning of endl.cpp*/
#include<iostream.h>
void main()
{
    int x,y;
    x=10;
    y=20;
    cout<<x;
    cout<<endl;          //inserting a new line by endl
    cout<<y;
}
/*End of endl.cpp*/
```

Output
10
20

One striking feature of the **insertion** operator is that it works equally well with values of all fundamental types as its right-hand operand. It does not need the format specifiers that are needed in the printf() family of functions. Listing 1.9 exemplifies this.

Listing 1.9 Outputting data with the **insertion** operator

```
/*Beginning of cout.cpp*/
#include<iostream.h>
void main()
{
    int iVar;
    char cVar;
    float fVar;
    double dVar;
    char * cPtr;
    iVar=10;
    cVar='x';
    fVar=2.3;
    dVar=3.14159;
    cPtr="Hello World";
    cout<<iVar;
    cout<<endl;
    cout<<cVar;
    cout<<endl;
    cout<<fVar;
    cout<<endl;
    cout<<dVar;
    cout<<endl;
    cout<<cPtr;
    cout<<endl;
}
/*End of cout.cpp*/
```

Output
10
x
2.3
3.14159
Hello World

Just like the arithmetic addition operator, it is possible to cascade the `insertion` operator. Listing 1.10 is a case in point.

Listing 1.10 Cascading the `insertion` operator

```
/*Beginning of coutCascade.cpp*/
#include<iostream.h>
void main()
{
    int x;
    float y;
    x=10;
    y=2.2;
    cout<<x<<endl<<y;                //cascading the insertion operator
}
/*End of coutCascade.cpp*/
```

Output
10
2.2

It is needless to say that we can pass constants instead of variables as operands to the `insertion` operator, as shown in Listing 1.11.

Listing 1.11 Outputting constants using the `insertion` operator

```
/*Beginning of coutMixed.cpp*/
#include<iostream.h>
void main()
{
    cout<<10<<endl<<"Hello World\n"<<3.4;
}
/*End of coutMixed.cpp*/
```

Ouput
10
Hello World
3.4

In Listing 1.11, note the use of the new line character in the string that is passed as one of the operands to the `insertion` operator.

It was mentioned in the beginning of this section that `cout` is an object that is associated with the console. Hence, if it is the left-hand side operand of the `insertion` operator, the value on the right is displayed on the monitor. You will learn in the chapter on stream handling that it is possible to pass objects of some other classes that are similarly associated with disk files as the left-hand side operand to the insertion operator. In such cases, the values on the right get stored in the associated files.

1.5.2 Console Input

The input functions in C language, such as scanf(), can be included in C++ programs because they are anyway defined in the standard library. However, we do have some more ways of inputting from the console in C++. Let us consider an example.

Listing 1.12 Inputting in C++

```
/*Beginning of cin.cpp*/
#include<iostream.h>
void main()
{
    int x;
    cout<<"Enter a number: ";
    cin>>x;                              //console input in C++
    cout<<"You entered: "<<x;
}
/*End of cin.cpp*/
```

Output
Enter a number: **10**<*enter*>
You entered: 10

The third statement in the main() function of Listing 1.12 needs to be understood.

cin (pronounce see-in) is actually an object of the class istream_withassign (you can think of it as a variable of the structure istream_withassign). It stands as an alias for the console input device, that is, the keyboard (hence the name).

The >> symbol, originally the right-shift operator, has had its definition extended in C++. In the given context, it operates as the extraction operator. It is a binary operator and takes two operands. The operand on its left must be some object of the istream_withassign class. The operand on its right must be a variable of some fundamental data type. The value for the variable on the right side of the extraction operator is *extracted* (hence the name) from the stream originating from the device associated with the object on the left. Consequently, the value of 'x' is obtained from the keyboard.

The file iostream.h needs to be included in the source code to ensure successful compilation because the object cin and the extraction operator have been declared in that file.

Again, just like the insertion operator, the extraction operator works equally well with variables of all fundamental types as its right-hand operand. It does not need the format specifiers that are needed in the scanf() family of functions. Listing 1.13 exemplifies this.

Listing 1.13 Inputting data with the extraction operator

```
/*Beginning of cin.cpp*/
#include<iostream.h>
void main()
{
    int iVar;
```

```
    char cVar;
    float fVar;
    cout<<"Enter a whole number: ";
    cin>>iVar;
    cout<<"Enter a character: ";
    cin>>cVar;
    cout<<"Enter a real number: ";
    cin>>fVar;
    cout<<"You entered: "<<iVar<<" "<<cVar<<" "<<fVar;
}
/*End of cin.cpp*/
```

Output

Enter a whole number: **10**<*enter*>

Enter a character: **x**<*enter*>

Enter a real number: **2.3**<*enter*>

You entered: 10 x 2.3

Just like the `insertion` operator, it is possible to cascade the `extraction` operator. Listing 1.14 is a case in point.

Listing 1.14   Cascading the `extraction` operator

```
/*Beginning of cinCascade.cpp*/
#include<iostream.h>
void main()
{
    int x,y;
    cout<<"Enter two numbers\n";
    cin>>x>>y; //cascading the extraction operator
    cout<<"You entered "<<x<<" and "<<y;
}
/*End of cinCascade.cpp*/
```

Output

Enter two numbers

10<*enter*>

20<*enter*>

You entered 10 and 20

It was mentioned in the beginning of this section that `cin` is an object that is associated with the console. Hence, if it is the left-hand side operand of the `extraction` operator, the variable on the right gets its value from the keyboard. You will learn in the chapter on stream handling that it is possible to pass objects of some other classes that are similarly associated with disk files as the left-hand side operand to the `extraction` operator. In such cases, the variable on the right gets its value from the associated files.

1.6 Variables in C++

Variables in C++ can be declared anywhere inside a function and not necessarily at its very beginning. For example, see Listing 1.15.

Listing 1.15   Declaring variables in C++

```
#include<iostream.h>
void main()
{
    int x;
    x=10;
    cout<<"Value of x= "<<x<<endl;
    int * iPtr;                          //declaring a variable in the middle of a
                                         //function

    iPtr=&x;
    cout<<"Address of x= "<<iPtr<<endl;
}
```

Output
Value of x=10
Address of x= 0x21878163

1.7   Reference Variables in C++

First, let us understand the basics. How does the operating system (OS) display the value of variables? How are assignment operations such as 'x=y' executed during run time? A detailed answer to these questions is beyond the scope of this book. A brief study is, nevertheless, possible and necessary for a good understanding of reference variables. What follows is a simplified and tailored explanation.

The OS maintains the addresses of each variable as it allocates memory for them during run time. In order to access the value of a variable, the OS first finds the address of the variable and then transfers control to the byte whose address matches that of the variable.

Suppose the following statement is executed ('x' and 'y' are integer type variables).

```
x=y;
```

The steps followed are:
1. The OS first finds the address of 'y'.
2. The OS transfers control to the byte whose address matches this address.
3. The OS reads the value from the block of four bytes that starts with this byte (most C++ compilers cause integer-type variables to occupy four bytes during run time and we will accept this value for our purpose).
4. The OS pushes the read value into a temporary stack.
5. The OS finds the address of 'x'.
6. The OS transfers control to the byte whose address matches this address.
7. The OS copies the value from the stack, where it had put it earlier, into the block of four bytes that starts with the byte whose address it has found above (address of 'x').

Notice that addresses of the variables on the left as well as on the right of the assignment operator are determined. However, the value of the right-hand operand is also determined. The expression on the right must be capable of being evaluated to a value. This is an important point and must be borne in mind. It will enable us to understand a number of concepts later.

Especially, you must remember that the expression on the left of the `assignment` operator must be capable of being evaluated to a valid address at which data can be written.

Now, let us study reference variables. *A reference variable is nothing but a reference for an existing variable*. It shares the memory location with existing variable. The syntax for declaring a reference variable is as follows:

```
<data-type> & <ref-var-name>=<existing-var-name>;
```

For example, if 'x' is an existing integer-type variable and we want to declare iRef as a reference to it the statement is as follows:

```
int & iRef=x;
```

iRef is a reference to 'x'. This means that although iRef and 'x' have separate entries in the OS, their addresses are actually the same!

Thus, a change in the value of 'x' will naturally reflect in iRef and vice versa. Listing 1.16 illustrates this.

Listing 1.16   Reference variables

```
/*Beginning of reference01.cpp*/
#include<iostream.h>
void main()
{
    int x;
    x=10;
    cout<<x<<endl;
    int & iRef=x;                  //iRef is a reference to x
    iRef=20;                       //same as x=10;
    cout<<x<<endl;
    x++;                           //same as iRef++;
    cout<<iRef<<endl;
}
/*End of reference01.cpp*/
```

Output
10
20
21

Reference variables must be initialized at the time of declaration (otherwise the compiler will not know what address it has to record for the reference variable).

Reference variables are variables in their own right. They just happen to have the address of another variable. After their creation, they function just like any other variable.

We have just seen what happens when a value is written into a reference variable. The value of a reference variable can be read in the same way as the value of an ordinary variable is read. Listing 1.17 illustrates this.

Listing 1.17   Reading the value of a reference variable

```
/*Beginning of reference02.cpp*/
#include<iostream.h>
void main()
{
```

```
      int x,y;
      x=10;
      int & iRef=x;
      y=iRef;                          //same as y=x;
      cout<<y<<endl;
      y++;                             //x and iRef unchanged
      cout<<x<<endl<<iRef<<endl<<y<<endl;
   }
   /*End of reference02.cpp*/
```

Output
```
10
10
10
11
```

A reference variable can be a function argument and thus change the value of the parameter that is passed to it in the function call. Listing 1.18 is an illustrative example.

Listing 1.18   Passing by reference

```
/*Beginning of reference03.cpp*/
#include<iostream.h>
void increment(int &);               //formal argument is a reference
                                     //to the passed parameter

void main()
{
   int x;
   x=10;
   increment(x);
   cout<<x<<endl;
}
void increment(int & r)
{
   r++;                              //same as x++;
}
/*End of reference03.cpp*/
```

Output
```
11
```

Functions can return by reference also. See Listing 1.19.

Listing 1.19   Returning by reference

```
/*Beginning of reference04.cpp*/
#include<iostream.h>
int & larger(int &, int &);
int main()
{
   int x,y;
   x=10;
   y=20;
   int & r=larger(x,y);
   r=-1;
   cout<<x<<endl<<y<<endl;
}
```

```
int & larger(int & a, int & b)
{
    if(a>b) //return a reference to the larger parameter
        return a;
    else
        return b;
}
/*End of reference04.cpp*/
```

Output

10

−1

In the foregoing listing, 'a' and 'x' refer to the same memory location while 'b' and 'y' refer to the same memory location. From the `larger()` function, a reference to 'b', that is, reference to 'y' is returned and stored in a reference variable 'r'. The `larger()` function does not return the value 'b' because the return type is `int&` and not `int`. Thus, the address of 'r' becomes equal to the address of 'y'. Consequently, any change in the value of 'r' also changes the value of 'y'. Listing 1.19 can be shortened as illustrated in Listing 1.20.

Listing 1.20   Returning by reference

```
/*Beginning of reference05.cpp*/
#include<iostream.h>
int & larger(int &, int &);
int main()
{
    int x,y;
    x=10;
    y=20;
    larger(x,y)=-1;
    cout<<x<<endl<<y<<endl;
}
int & larger(int & a, int & b)
{
    if(a>b) //return a reference to the larger parameter
        return a;
    else
        return b;
}
/*End of reference05.cpp*/
```

Output

10

−1

The name of a non-constant variable can be placed on the left of the `assignment` operator because a valid address—the address of the variable—can be determined from it. A call to a function that returns by reference can be placed on the left of the `assignment` operator for the same reason.

If the compiler finds the name of a non-constant variable on the left of the `assignment` operator in the source code, it writes instructions in the executable to

• determine the address of the variable,

• transfer control to the byte that has that address, and

- write the value on the right of the assignment operator into the block that begins with the byte found above.

A function that returns by reference primarily returns the address of the returned variable. If the call is found on the left of the assignment operator, the compiler writes necessary instructions in the executable to

- transfer control to the byte whose address is returned by the function and
- write the value on the right of the assignment operator into the block that begins with the byte found above.

The name of a variable can be placed on the right of the assignment operator. A call to a function that returns by reference can be placed on the right of the assignment operator for the same reason.

If the compiler finds the name of a variable on the right of the assignment operator in the source code, it writes instructions in the executable to

- determine the address of the variable,
- transfer control to the byte that has that address,
- read the value from the block that begins with the byte found above, and
- push the read value into the stack.

A function that returns by reference primarily returns the address of the returned variable. If the call is found on the right of the assignment operator, the compiler writes necessary instructions in the executable to

- transfer control to the byte whose address is returned by the function,
- read the value from the block that begins with the byte found above, and
- push the read value into the stack.

A constant cannot be placed on the left of the assignment operator. This is because constants do not have a valid address. Moreover, how can a constant be changed? Functions that return by value, return the value of the returned variable, which is a constant. Therefore, a call to a function that returns by value cannot be placed on the left of the assignment operator.

You may notice that the formal arguments of the larger() function in the foregoing listing have been declared as constant references because they are not supposed to change the values of the passed parameters even accidentally.

We must avoid returning a reference to a local variable. For example, see Listing 1.21.

Listing 1.21   Returning the reference of a local variable

```
/*Beginning of reference06.cpp*/
#include<iostream.h>
int & abc();
void main()
{
    abc()=-1;
}
int & abc()
{
    int x;
    return x;                        //returning reference of a local variable
}
/*End of reference06.cpp*/
```

The problem with the above program is that when the abc() function terminates, 'x' will go out of scope. Consequently, the statement

```
abc()=-1;
```

in the main() function will write '–1' in an unallocated block of memory. This can lead to run-time errors.

1.8 Function Prototyping

Function prototyping is necessary in C++. A prototype describes the function's interface to the compiler. It tells the compiler the return type of the function as well as the number, type, and sequence of its formal arguments.

The general syntax of function prototype is as follows:

```
return_type function_name(argument_list);
```

For example,

```
int add(int, int);
```

This prototype indicates that the add() function returns a value of integer type and takes two parameters both of integer type.

Since a function prototype is also a statement, a semicolon must follow it.

Providing names to the formal arguments in function prototypes is optional. Even if such names are provided, they need not match those provided in the function definition. For example, see Listing 1.22.

Listing 1.22   Function prototyping

```
/*Beginning of funcProto.cpp*/
#include<iostream.h>
int add(int,int);                    //function prototype

void main()
{
   int x,y,z;
   cout<<"Enter a number: ";
   cin>>x;
   cout<<"Enter another number: ";
   cin>>y;
   z=add(x,y);                       //function call
   cout<<z<<endl;
}
int add(int a,int b)                 //function definition
{
   return (a+b);
}
/*End of funcProto.cpp*/
```

Output

Enter a number: **10**<*enter*>
Enter another number: **20**<*enter*>
30

Why is prototyping important? By making prototyping necessary, the compiler ensures the following:

- The return value of a function is handled correctly.
- Correct number and type of arguments are passed to a function.

Let us discuss these points.

Consider the following statement in Listing 1.22:

```
int add(int, int);
```

The prototype tells the compiler that the add() function returns an integer-type value. Thus, the compiler knows how many bytes have to be retrieved from the place where the add() function is expected to write its return value and how these bytes are to be interpreted.

In the absence of prototypes, the compiler will have to assume the type of the returned value. Suppose, it assumes that the type of the returned value is an integer. However, the called function may return a value of an incompatible type (say a structure type). Now, suppose an integer-type variable is equated to the call to a function where the function call precedes the function definition. In this situation, the compiler will report an error against the function definition and not the function call. This is because the function call abided by its assumption, but the definition did not. However, if the function definition is in a different file to be compiled separately, then no compile-time errors will arise. Instead, wrong results will arise during run time as Listing 1.23 shows.

Listing 1.23   Absence of function prototype produces weird results

```
/*Beginning of def.c*/
/*function definition*/
struct abc
{
   char a;
   int b;
   float c;
};

struct abc test()
{
   struct abc a1;
   a1.a='x';
   a1.b=10;
   a1.c=1.1;
   return a1;
}
/*End of def.c*/

/*Beginning of driver.c*/
void main()
{
   int x;
   x=test();                          //no compile time error!!
   printf("%d",x);
}
/*End of driver.c*/
```

Output
1688

A compiler that does not enforce prototyping will definitely compile the above program. But then it will have no way of knowing what type of value the test() function returns.

Therefore, erroneous results will be obtained during run time as the output of Listing 1.23 clearly shows.

Since the C++ compiler necessitates function prototyping, it will report an error against the function call because no prototype has been provided to resolve the function call. Again, if the correct prototype *is* provided, the compiler will still report an error since this time the function call does not match the prototype. The compiler will not be able to convert a `struct abc` to an integer. *Thus, function prototyping guarantees protection from errors arising out of incorrect function calls.*

What happens if the function prototype and the function call do not match? Such a situation cannot arise. Both the function prototype and the function definition are created by the same person, that is, the library programmer. The library programmer puts the function's prototype in a header file. He/she provides the function's definition in a library. The application programmer includes the header file in his/her application program file in which the function is called. He/she creates an object file from this application program file and links this object file to the library to get an executable file.

The function's prototype also tells the compiler that the `add()` function accepts two parameters. If the program fails to provide such parameters, the prototype enables the compiler to detect the error. A compiler that does not enforce function prototyping will compile a function call in which an incorrect number and/or type of parameters have been passed. Run-time errors will arise as in the foregoing case.

Finally, *function prototyping produces automatic-type conversion wherever appropriate.* We take the case of compilers that do not enforce prototyping. Suppose, a function expects an integer-type value (assuming integers occupy four bytes) but a value of double type (assuming doubles occupy eight bytes) is wrongly passed. During run time, the value in only the first four bytes of the passed eight bytes will be extracted. This is obviously undesirable. However, the C++ compiler automatically converts the double-type value into an integer type. This is because it inevitably encounters the function prototype before encountering the function call and therefore knows that the function expects an integer-type value. However, it must be remembered that such automatic-type conversions due to function prototypes occur only when it makes sense. For example, the compiler will prevent an attempted conversion from a structure type to integer type.

Nevertheless, can the same benefits not be realized without prototyping? Is it not possible for the compiler to simply scan the rest of the source code and find out how the function has been defined? There are two reasons why this solution is inappropriate. They are:

- It is inefficient. The compiler will have to suspend the compilation of the line containing the function call and search the rest of the file.
- Most of the times the function definition is not contained in the file where it is called. It is usually contained in a library.

Such compile-time checking for prototypes is known as *static-type-checking*.

1.9 Function Overloading

C++ allows two or more functions to have the same name. For this, however, they must have different signatures. *Signature of a function means the number, type, and sequence of formal arguments of the function.* In order to distinguish amongst the functions with the same name, the compiler expects their signatures to be different. Depending upon the type of parameters that are passed to the function call, the compiler decides which of the available definitions will be invoked. For this, function prototypes should be provided to the compiler for matching the function calls. Accordingly, the linker, during link time, links the function call with the correct function definition. Listing 1.24 clarifies this.

Listing 1.24 Function overloading

```
/*Beginning of funcOverload.cpp*/
#include<iostream.h>
int add(int,int);                    //first prototype
int add(int,int,int);                //second prototype

void main()
{
    int x,y;
    x=add(10,20);                    //matches first prototype
    y=add(30,40,50);                 //matches second prototype
    cout<<x<<endl<<y<<endl;
}

int add(int a,int b)
{
    return(a+b);
}

int add(int a,int b,int c)
{
    return(a+b+c);
}
/*End of funcOverload.cpp*/
```

Output
30
120

Just like ordinary functions, the definitions of overloaded functions are also put in libraries. Moreover, the function prototypes are placed in header files.

The two function prototypes at the beginning of the program tell the compiler the two different ways in which the add() function can be called. When the compiler encounters the two distinct calls to the add() function, it already has the prototypes to satisfy them both. Thus, the compilation phase is completed successfully. During linking, the linker finds the two necessary definitions of the add() function and, hence, links successfully to create the executable file.

The compiler decides which function is to be called based upon the number, type, and sequence of parameters that are passed to the function call. When the compiler encounters the first function call,

```
x=add(10,20);
```

it decides that the function that takes two integers as formal arguments is to be executed. Accordingly, the linker then searches for the definition of the add() function where there are two integers as formal arguments.

Similarly, the second call to the add() function

```
y=add(30,40,50);
```

is also handled by the compiler and the linker.

Note the importance of function prototyping. Since function prototyping is mandatory in C++, it is possible for the compiler to support function overloading properly. The compiler is able to not only restrict the number of ways in which a function can be called but also support more than one way in which a function can be called. *Function overloading is possible because of the necessity to prototype functions.*

By itself, function overloading is of little use. Instead of giving exactly the same name for functions that perform similar tasks, it is always possible for us to give them similar names. However, function overloading enables the C++ compiler to support another feature, that is, function overriding (which in turn is not really a very useful thing by itself but forms the basis for dynamic polymorphism—one of the most striking features of C++ that promotes code reuse).

Function overloading is also known as *function polymorphism* because, just like polymorphism in the real world where an entity exists in more than one form, the same function name carries different meanings.

Function polymorphism is static in nature because the function definition to be executed is selected by the compiler during compile time itself. Thus, an overloaded function is said to exhibit *static polymorphism.*

1.10 Default Values for Formal Arguments of Functions

It is possible to specify default values for some or all of the formal arguments of a function. If no value is passed for an argument when the function is called, the default value specified for it is passed. If parameters are passed in the normal fashion for such an argument, the default value is ignored. Listing 1.25 is an illustrative example.

Listing 1.25   Default values for function arguments

```
/*Beginning of defaultArg.cpp*/
#include<iostream.h>
int add(int,int,int c=0);            //third argument has default value

void main()
{
    int x,y;
    x=add(10,20,30);                 //default value ignored
    y=add(40,50);                    //default value taken for the
                                     //third parameter
    cout<<x<<endl<<y<<endl;
}

int add(int a,int b,int c)
{
    return (a+b+c);
}
/*End of defaultArg.cpp*/
```

Output
60
90

In the above listing, a default value—zero—has been specified for the third argument of the add() function. In the absence of a value being passed to it, the compiler assigns the default value. If a value is passed to it, the compiler assigns the passed value. In the first call

```
x=add(10,20,30);
```

the values of 'a', 'b', and 'c' are 10, 20, and 30, respectively. But, in the second function call

```
y=add(40,50);
```

the values of 'a', 'b', and 'c' are 10, 20, and 0, respectively. The default value—zero—for the third parameter 'c' is taken. This explains the output of the above listing.

Default values can be assigned to more than one argument. Listing 1.26 illustrates this.

Listing 1.26   Default values for more than one argument

```
/*Beginning of multDefaultArg.cpp*/
#include<iostream.h>
int add(int,int b=0,int c=0);            //second and third arguments
                                         //have default values

void main()
{
   int x,y,z;
   x=add(10,20,30);                      //all default values ignored
   y=add(40,50);                         //default value taken for the
                                         //third argument
   z=add(60);                            //default value taken for
                                         //the second and the third
                                         //arguments
   cout<<x<<endl<<y<<endl<<z<<endl;
}

int add(int a,int b,int c)
{
   return (a+b+c);
}
/*End of multDefaultArg.cpp*/
```

Output
60
90
60

There is no need to provide names to the arguments taking default values in the function prototypes.

```
int add(int,int=0,int=0);
```

can be written instead of

```
int add(int,int b=0,int c=0);
```

Default values must be supplied starting from the rightmost argument. Before supplying default value to an argument, all arguments to its right must be given default values. Suppose you write

```
int add(int,int=0,int);
```

you are attempting to give a default value to the second argument from the right without specifying a default value for the argument on its right. The compiler will report an error that the default value is missing (for the third argument).

Default values must be specified in function prototypes alone. They should not be specified in the function definitions.

While compiling a function call, the compiler will definitely have its prototype. Its definition will probably be located after the function call. It might be in the same file, or it will be in a different file or library. Thus, to ensure a successful compilation of the function calls where values for arguments having default values have not been passed, the compiler must be aware of those default values. Hence, default values must be specified in the function prototype.

You must also remember that the function prototypes are placed in header files. These are included in both the library files that contain the function's definition and the client program files that contain calls to the functions. While compiling the library file that contains the function definition, the compiler will obviously read the function prototype before it reads the function definition. Suppose the function definition also contains default values for the arguments. Even if the same default values are supplied for the same arguments, the compiler will think that you are trying to supply two different default values for the same argument. This is obviously unacceptable because the default value can be only one in number. Thus, *default values must be specified in the function prototypes and should not be specified again in the function definitions.*

If default values are specified for the arguments of a function, the function behaves like an overloaded function and, therefore, should be overloaded with care; otherwise ambiguity errors might be caused. For example, if you prototype a function as follows:

```
int add(int,int,int=0);
int add(int,int);
```

This can confuse the compiler. If only two integers are passed as parameters to the function call, both these prototypes will match. The compiler will not be able to decide with which definition the function call has to be resolved. This will lead to an ambiguity error.

Default values can be given to arguments of any data type as follows:

```
double hra(double,double=0.3);
void print(char='a');
```

1.11 Inline Functions

Inline functions are used to increase the speed of execution of the executable files. C++ inserts calls to the normal functions and the inline functions in different ways in an executable.

The executable program that is created after compiling the various source codes and linking them consists of a set of machine language instructions. When a program is started, the operating system loads these instructions into the computer's memory. Thus, each instruction has a particular memory address. The computer then goes through these instructions one by one. If there are any instructions to branch out or loop, the control skips over instructions and jumps backward or forward as needed. When a program reaches the function call instruction, it stores the memory address of the instruction immediately following the function call. It then jumps to the beginning of the function, whose address it finds in the function call instruction itself, executes the function code, and jumps back to the instruction whose address it had saved earlier.

Obviously, an overhead is involved in
- making the control jump back and forth and

- storing the address of the instruction to which the control should jump after the function terminates.

The C++ inline function provides a solution to this problem. *An inline function is a function whose compiled code is 'in line' with the rest of the program.* That is, the compiler replaces the function call with the corresponding function code. With inline code, the program does not have to jump to another location to execute the code and then jump back. Inline functions, thus, run a little faster than regular functions.

However, there is a trade-off between memory and speed. If an inline function is called repeatedly, then multiple copies of the function definition appear in the code (see Figures 1.1 and 1.2). Thus, the executable program itself becomes so large that it occupies a lot of space in the computer's memory during run time. Consequently, the program runs slow instead of running fast. Thus, inline functions must be chosen with care.

For specifying an inline function, you must:

- prefix the definition of the function with the `inline` keyword and
- define the function before all functions that call it, that is, define it in the header file itself.

The following listing illustrates the inline technique with the inline `cube()` function that cubes its argument. Note that the entire definition is in one line. That is not a necessary condition. But if the definition of a function does not fit in one line, the function is probably a poor candidate for an inlne function!

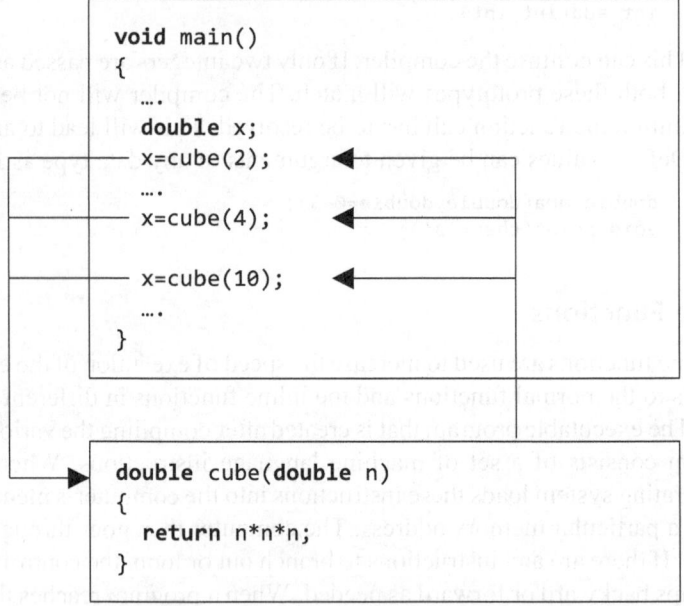

```
void main()
{
    ....
    double x;
    x=cube(2);
    ....
    x=cube(4);
    x=cube(10);
    ....
}
```

```
double cube(double n)
{
    return n*n*n;
}
```

The control is transferred to the function definition in case of a non-inline function

Figure 1.1   Transfer of control in a non-inline function

```
void main()
{
    ….
    double x;
    {
        double n;
        n=2;
        x=n*n*n;
    }
    ….
    {
        double n;
        n=4;
        x=n*n*n;
    }
    ….
    {
        double n;
        n=10;
        x=n*n*n;
    }
    ….
}
```

The control is not transferred to the function definition in case of an inline function since the call is replaced by the definition itself

Figure 1.2   Control does not get transferred in an inline function

Listing 1.27   Inline functions

```
/*Beginning of inline.cpp*/
#include<iostream.h>

inline double cube(double x) { return x*x*x; }

void main()
{
    double a,b;
    double c=13.0;
    a=cube(5.0);
    b=cube(4.5+7.5);
    cout<<a<<endl;
    cout<<b<<endl;
    cout<<cube(c++)<<endl;
    cout<<c<<endl;
}
/*End of inline.cpp*/
```

Output
125
1728
2197
14

However, under some circumstances, the compiler, despite your indications, may not expand the function inline. Instead, it will issue a warning that the function could not be expanded inline and then compile all calls to such functions in the ordinary fashion. Those conditions are:

- The function is recursive.
- There are looping constructs in the function.
- There are static variables in the function.

Let us briefly compare macros in C and inline function in C++. Macros are a poor predecessor to inline functions. For example, a macro for cubing a number is as follows:

```
#define CUBE(X) X*X*X
```

Here, a mere text substitution takes place with 'X' being replaced by the macro parameter.

```
a=CUBE(5.0);                    //replaced by a=5.0*5.0*5.0;
b=CUBE(4.5+7.5);                //replaced by
                                //b=4.5+7.5*4.5+7.5*4.5+7.5;
c=CUBE(x++);                    //replaced by c=x++*x++*x++;
```

Only the first statement works properly. An intelligent use of parentheses improves matters slightly.

```
#define CUBE(X) ((X)*(X)*(X))
```

Even now, CUBE(c++) undesirably increments 'c' thrice. But the inline cube() function evaluates 'c', passes the value to be cubed, and then correctly increments 'c' once.

It is advisable to use inline functions instead of macros.

Summary

Variables sometimes influence each other's values. A change in the value of one may necessitate a corresponding adjustment in the value of another. It is, therefore, necessary to pass these variables together in a single group to functions. Structures enable us to do this.

Structures are used to create new data types. This is a two-step process.

Step 1: Create the structure itself.

Step 2: Create associated functions that work upon variables of the structure.

While structures do fulfil the important need described above, they nevertheless have limitations. They do not enable the library programmer to make variables of the structure that he/she has designed to be safe from unintentional modification by functions other than those defined by him/her. Moreover, they do not guarantee a proper initialization of data members of structure variables.

Both of the above drawbacks are in direct contradiction with the characteristics possessed by real-world objects. A real-world object has not only a perfect interface to manipulate its internal parts but also exclusive rights to do so. Consequently, a real-world object never reaches an invalid state during its lifetime. When we start operating a real-world object, it automatically assumes a valid state. In object-oriented programming systems (OOPS), we can incorporate these features of real-world objects into structure variables.

Inheritance allows a structure to inherit both data and functions of an existing structure. Polymorphism allows different functions to have the same name. It is of two types: static and dynamic.

Console output is achieved in C++ with the help of `insertion` operator and the `cout` object. Console input is achieved in C++ with the help of `extraction` operator and the `cin` object.

In C++, variables can be defined anywhere in a function. A reference variable shares the same memory location as the one of which it is a reference. Therefore, any change in its value automatically changes the value of the variable with which it is sharing memory. Calls to functions that return by reference can be placed on the left of the `assignment` operator.

Function prototyping is necessary in C++. Functions can be overloaded. Functions with different signatures can have the same name. A function argument can be given a default value so that if no value is passed for it in the function call, the default value is assigned to it. If a function is declared inline, its definition replaces its call, thus, speeding up the execution of the resultant executable.

Key Terms

creating new data types using structures
lack of data security in structures
no guaranteed initialization of data in structures
procedure-oriented programming system
object-oriented programming system
data security in classes
guaranteed initialization of data in classes
inheritance
polymorphism
console input/output in C++
  - cout
  - ostream_withassign class
  - insertion operator

  - cin
  - istream_withassign class
  - extraction operator
  - iostream.h header file
  - endl
reference variable
  - passing by reference
  - returning by reference
importance of function prototyping
function overloading
default values for function arguments
inline functions

Exercises

1. Which programming needs do structures fulfill? Why does C language enable us to create structures?

2. What are the limitations of structures?

3. What is the procedure-oriented programming system?

4. What is the object-oriented programming system?

5. Which class is 'cout' an object of?

6. Which class is 'cin' an object of?

7. What benefits does a programmer get if the compiler forces him/her to prototype a function?

8. Why will an ambiguity error arise if a default value is given to an argument of an overloaded function?

9. Why should default values be given to function arguments in the function's prototype and not in the function's definition?

10. State true or false.
    (a) Structures enable a programmer to secure the data contained in structure variables from being changed by unauthorized functions.
    (b) The `insertion` operator is used for outputting in C++.
    (c) The `extraction` operator is used for outputting in C++.
    (d) A call to a function that returns by reference cannot be placed on the left of the `assignment` operator.
    (e) An inline function cannot have a looping construct.

11. Think of some examples from your own experience in C programming where you felt the need for structures.

Do you see an opportunity for programming in OOPS in those examples?

12. Structures in C do not enable the library programmers to guarantee an initialization of data. Appreciate the implications of this limitation by taking the date structure as an example.

13. Calls to functions that return by reference can be put on the left-hand side of the `assignment` operator. Experiment and find out whether such calls can be chained. Consider the following:

```
f(a, b) = g(c, d) = x;
```

where 'f' and 'g' are functions that return by reference while 'a', 'b', 'c', 'd', and 'x' are variables.

2

Classes and Objects

The previous chapter refreshed the reader's knowledge of the structure construct provided by C language—its use and usage. It also dealt with a critical analysis of structures along with their pitfalls and limitations. The reader was made aware of a strong need for data security and for a guaranteed initialization of data that structures do not provide.

This chapter is a logical continuation to the previous one. It begins with a thorough explanation of the class construct of C++ and the ways by which it fulfils the above-mentioned needs. Superiority of the class construct of C++ over the structure construct of C language is emphasized in this chapter.

This chapter also deals with how classes enable the library programmer to provide exclusive rights to the associated functions.

A description of various types and features of member functions and member data finds a prominent place in this chapter. This description covers:

- Overloaded member functions
- Default values for the arguments of member functions
- Inline member functions
- Constant member functions
- Mutable data members
- Friend functions and friend classes
- Static members

A section in this chapter is devoted to namespaces. They enable the C++ programmer to prevent pollution of the global namespace that leads to name clashes.

Example code to tackle arrays of objects and arrays inside objects form the penultimate portion of this chapter.

The chapter ends with an essay on nested classes—their need and use.

2.1 Introduction to Classes and Objects

Classes are to C++ what structures are to C. Both provide the library programmer a means to create new data types.

Let us briefly recapitulate the issues faced while programming in C described in the previous chapter. In C, the library programmer creates structures. He/she also provides a set of tested bug-free functions that correctly manipulate the data members of structure variables.

The Date structure and its accompanying functions may be perfect. However, there is absolutely no guarantee that the client programs will use only these functions to manipulate the members of variables of the structure. See Listing 2.1.

Listing 2.1   Undesirable manipulation of structures not prevented in C

```
struct Date d1;
setDate(&d1);     //assign system date to d1.
printf("%d",d1.month);
d1.month = 13;    //undesirable but unpreventable!!
```

The bug arising out of the last line of the `main()` function above is easily detected even by a visual inspection. Nevertheless, the same will certainly not be the case if the code is around 25,000 lines long. Lines similar to the last line of the `main()` function above may be scattered all over the code. Thus, they will be difficult to hunt down.

Notice that the absence of a facility to bind the data and the code that can have the exclusive rights to manipulate the data can lead to difficult-to-detect run-time bugs. C does not provide the library programmer with the facilities to encapsulate data, to hide data, and to abstract data.

The C++ compiler provides a solution to this problem. Structures (the `struct` keyword) have been redefined to allow member functions also. Listing 2.2 illustrates this.

Listing 2.2   C++ allows member functions in structures

```cpp
/*Beginning of structDistance01.cpp*/
#include<iostream.h>

struct Distance
{
    int iFeet;
    float fInches;
    void setFeet(int x)
    {
        iFeet=x;
    }
    int getFeet()
    {
        return iFeet;
    }
    void setInches(float y)
    {
        fInches=y;
    }
    float getInches()
    {
        return fInches;
    }
};

void main()
{
    Distance d1,d2;
    d1.setFeet(2);
    d1.setInches(2.2);
    d2.setFeet(3);
    d2.setInches(3.3);
    cout<<d1.getFeet()<<" "<<d1.getInches()<<endl;
    cout<<d2.getFeet()<<" "<<d2.getInches()<<endl;
```

```
}
/*End of structDistance01.cpp*/
```

Output

2 2.2

3 3.3

First, we must notice that functions have also been defined within the scope of the structure definition. This means that not only the member data of the structure can be accessed through the variables of the structures but also the member functions can be invoked. The `struct` keyword has actually been redefined in C++. This latter point is illustrated by the `main()` function in Listing 2.2 above. We must make careful note of the way variables of the structure have been declared and how the member functions have been invoked.

Member functions are invoked in much the same way as member data are accessed, that is, by using the variable-to-member access operator. In a member function, one can refer directly to members of the object for which the member function is invoked. For example, as a result of the second line of the `main()` function in Listing 2.2, it is `d1.iFeet` that gets the value of 2. On the other hand, it is `d2.iFeet` that gets the value of 3 when the fourth line is invoked. This is explained in the section on the `this` pointer that follows shortly.

Each structure variable contains a separate copy of the member data within itself. However, only one copy of the member function exists. Again, the section on the `this` pointer explains this.

However, in the above example, note that the member data of structure variables can still be accessed directly. The following line of code illustrates this.

```
d1.iFeet=2; //legal!!
```

2.1.1 Private and Public Members

What is the advantage of having member functions also in structures? We have put together the data and functions that work upon the data but we have not been able to give exclusive rights to these functions to work upon the data. Problems in code debugging can still arise as before. Specifying member functions as public but member data as private obtains the advantage. The syntax for this is illustrated by Listing 2.3.

Listing 2.3 Making members of structures private

```
/*Beginning of structDistance02.cpp*/
#include<iostream.h>
struct Distance
{
   private:
      int iFeet;
      float fInches;
   public:
      void setFeet(int x)
{
   iFeet=x;        //LEGAL: private member accessed by
                   //member function
}
int getFeet()
```

```
    {
        return iFeet;
    }
    void setInches(float y)
    {
        fInches=y;
    }
    float getInches()
    {
        return fInches;
    }
};
    void main()
    {
        Distance d1,d2;
        d1.setFeet(2);
        d1.setInches(2.2);
        d2.setFeet(3);
        d2.setInches(3.3);
        d1.iFeet++;                          //ERROR!!: private member accessed by
                                             //non-member function
        cout<<d1.getFeet()<<" "<<d1.getInches()<<endl;
        cout<<d2.getFeet()<<" "<<d2.getInches()<<endl;
    }
    /*End of structDistance02.cpp*/
```

First, let us have a close look at the modified definition of the structure Distance. Two new keywords, private and public have been introduced in the definition of the structure. Their presence in the foregoing example tells the compiler that iFeet and fInches are private data members of variables of the structure Distance and the member functions are public. Thus, values of iFeet and fInches of each variable of the structure Distance can be accessed/ modified only through member functions of the structure and not by any non-member function in the program (again note that it is the iFeet and fInches of the *invoking object* that are accessed/modified by the member functions). Any attempt to violate this restriction is prevented by the compiler because that is how the C++ compiler recognizes the private keyword. Since the member functions are public, they can be invoked from any part of the program.

As we can observe from Listing 2.3, the compiler refuses to compile the line in which a private member of a structure variable is accessed from a non-member function (the main() function in Listing 2.3).

The keywords private and public are also known as access modifiers or access specifiers because they control the access to the members of structures.

C++ introduces a new keyword class as a substitute for the keyword struct. *In a structure, members are public by default.* See the definition in Listing 2.4.

Listing 2.4   Structure members are public by default

```
struct Distance
{
    private:
        int iFeet;
        float fInches;
```

```
    public:
        void setFeet(int x)
        {
            iFeet=x;
        }
        int getFeet()
        {
            return iFeet;
        }
        void setInches(float y)
        {
            fInches=y;
        }
        float getInches()
        {
            return fInches;
        }
    };
```

can also be written as

```
struct Distance
{
    void setFeet(int x)            //public by default
    {
        iFeet=x;
    }
    int getFeet()                  //public by default
    {
        return iFeet;
    }
    void setInches(float y)        //public by default
    {
        fInches=y;
    }
    float getInches()              //public by default
    {
        return fInches;
    }
    private:
        int iFeet;
        float fInches;
};
```

In Listing 2.4, the member functions have not been placed under any access modifier. Therefore, they are public members by default.

On the other hand, *class members are private by default*. This is the only difference between the class keyword and the struct keyword.

Thus, the structure Distance can be redefined by using the class keyword as shown in Listing 2.5.

Listing 2.5 Class members are private by default

```
class Distance
{
        int iFeet;                 //private by default
        float fInches;             //private by default
```

```
public:
    void setFeet(int x)
    {
        iFeet=x;
    }
    int getFeet()
    {
        return iFeet;
    }
    void setInches(float y)
    {
        fInches=y;
    }
    float getInches()
    {
        return fInches;
    }
};
```

The struct keyword has been retained to maintain backward compatibility with C language. A header file created in C might contain the definition of a structure, and structures in C will have member data only. A C++ compiler will easily compile a source code that has included the above header file since the new definition of the struct keyword allows, not mandates, the inclusion of member functions in structures.

Functions in a C language source code access member data of structures. A C++ compiler will easily compile such a source code since the C++ compiler treats members of structures as public members by default.

2.1.2 Objects

Variables of classes are known as objects.

An object of a class occupies the same amount of memory as a variable of a structure that has the same data members. This is illustrated by Listing 2.6.

Listing 2.6 Size of a class object is equal to that of a structure variable with identical data members

```
/*Beginning of objectSize.cpp*/
#include<iostream.h>

struct A
{
    char a;
    int b;
    float c;
};

class B                              //a class with the same data members
{
    char a;
    int b;
    float c;
};

void main()
{
```

```
            cout<<sizeof(A)<<endl<<sizeof(B)<<endl;
        }
        /*End of objectSize.cpp*/
```

Output

9

9

Introducing member functions does not influence the size of objects. The reason for this will become apparent when we study the `this` pointer. Moreover, making data members private or public does not influence the size of objects. The access modifiers merely control the accessibility of the members.

2.1.3 Scope Resolution Operator

It is possible and usually necessary for the library programmer to define the member functions *outside* their respective classes. The scope resolution operator makes this possible. Listing 2.7 illustrates the use of the scope resolution operator (::).

Listing 2.7   The scope resolution operator

```
/*Beginning of scopeResolution.cpp*/
class Distance
{
        int iFeet;
        float fInches;
    public:
        void setFeet(int);              //prototype only
        int getFeet();                  //prototype only
        void setInches(float);          //prototype only
        float getInches();              //prototype only
};

void Distance::setFeet(int x)           //definition
{
    iFeet=x;
}

int Distance::getFeet()                 //definition
{
    return iFeet;
}

void Distance::setInches(float y)       //definition
{
    fInches=y;
}

float Distance::getInches()             //definition
{
    return fInches;
}
/*End of scopeResolution.cpp*/
```

We can observe that the member functions have been only prototyped within the class; they have been *defined* outside. The scope resolution operator signifies the class to which they belong. The class name is specified on the left-hand side of the scope resolution operator. The name of the function being defined is on the right-hand side.

2.1.4 Creating Libraries Using the Scope Resolution Operator

As in C language, creating a new data type in C++ using classes is also a three-step process that is executed by the library programmer.

Step 1: Place the class definition in a header file.

```
/*Beginning of Distance.h*/
/*Header file containing the definition of the Distance class*/

class Distance
{
    int iFeet;
    float fInches;
  public:
    void setFeet(int);              //prototype only
    int getFeet();                  //prototype only
    void setInches(float);          //prototype only
    float getInches();              //prototype only
};
/*End of Distance.h*/
```

Step 2: Place the definitions of the member functions in a C++ source file (the library source code). A file that contains definitions of the member functions of a class is known as the implementation file of that class. Compile this implementation file and put in a library.

```
/*Beginning of Distlib.cpp*/
/*Implementation file for the class Distance*/
#include"Distance.h"

void Distance::setFeet(int x)       //definition
{
    iFeet=x;
}

int Distance::getFeet()             //definition
{
    return iFeet;
}

void Distance::setInches(float y)   //definition
{
    fInches=y;
}

float Distance::getInches()         //definition
{
    return fInches;
}
/*End of Distlib.cpp*/
```

Step 3: Provide the header file and the library, in whatever media, to other programmers who want to use this new data type.

2.1.5 Using Classes in Application Programs

The steps followed by programmers for using this new data type are:

Step 1: Include the header file provided by the library programmer in their source code.

```
/*Beginning of Distmain.cpp*/
#include"Distance.h"

void main()
{
    . . . . .
    . . . . .
}
/*End of Distmain.cpp*/
```

Step 2: Declare variables of the new data type in their source code.

```
/*Beginning of Distmain.cpp*/
#include"Distance.h"

void main()
{
    Distance d1,d2;
    . . . . .
    . . . . .
}
/*End of Distmain.cpp*/
```

Step 3: Embed calls to the associated functions by passing these variables in their source code. See Listing 2.8.

Listing 2.8 Using classes in application programs

```
/*Beginning of Distmain.cpp*/
/*A sample driver program for creating and using objects of the class Dis-
tance*/
#include<iostream.h>
#include"Distance.h"

void main()
{
    Distance d1,d2;
    d1.setFeet(2);
    d1.setInches(2.2);
    d2.setFeet(3);
    d2.setInches(3.3);
    cout<<d1.getFeet()<<" "<<d1.getInches()<<endl;
    cout<<d2.getFeet()<<" "<<d2.getInches()<<endl;
}
/*End of Distmain.cpp*/
```

Step 4: Compile the source code to get the object file.

Step 5: Link the object file with the library provided by the library programmer to get the executable or another library.

Output of Listing 2.8
2 2.2
3 3.3

Implementation files are compiled and converted into static and dynamic libraries in the usual manner.

Again, we notice that there is no obvious connection between the member data being accessed within the member function and the object that is invoking the function.

2.1.6 this Pointer

The facility to create and call member functions of class objects is provided by the C++ compiler. You have already seen how this facility is to be used. However, how does the compiler support this facility? The compiler does this by using a unique pointer known as the this pointer. A thorough understanding of the this pointer is vital for understanding many concepts in C++.

The this pointer is always a constant pointer. The this pointer always points at the object with respect to which the function was called. An explanation that follows shortly explains why and how it functions.

After the compiler has ascertained that no attempt has been made to access the private members of an object by non-member functions, it converts the C++ code into an ordinary C language code as follows:

1. It converts the class into a structure with only data members as follows.

    Before

    ```
    class Distance
    {
        int iFeet;
        float fInches;
    public:
        void setFeet(int);          //prototype only
        int getFeet();              //prototype only
        void setInches(float);      //prototype only
        float getInches();          //prototype only
    };
    ```

    After

    ```
    struct Distance
    {
        int iFeet;
        float fInches;
    };
    ```

2. It puts a declaration of the this pointer as a leading formal argument in the prototypes of all member functions as follows.

    Before

    ```
    void setFeet(int);
    ```

    After

    ```
    void setFeet(Distance * const, int);
    ```

    Before

    ```
    int getFeet();
    ```

<u>After</u>

```
int getFeet(Distance * const);
```

<u>Before</u>

```
void setInches(float);
```

<u>After</u>

```
void setInches(Distance * const, float);
```

<u>Before</u>

```
float getInches();
```

<u>After</u>

```
float getInches(Distance * const);
```

3. It puts the definition of the this pointer as a leading formal argument in the definitions of all member functions as follows. It also modifies all the statements to access object members by accessing them through the this pointer using the pointer-to-member access operator (->).

<u>Before</u>

```
void Distance::setFeet(int x)
{
    iFeet=x;
}
```

<u>After</u>

```
void setFeet(Distance * const this, int x)
{
    this->iFeet=x;
}
```

<u>Before</u>

```
int Distance::getFeet()
{
    return iFeet;
}
```

<u>After</u>

```
int getFeet(Distance * const this)
{
    return this->iFeet;
}
```

<u>Before</u>

```
void Distance::setInches(float y)
{
    fInches=y;
}
```

<u>After</u>

```
void setInches(Distance * const this, float y)
```

```
    {
        this->fInches=y;
    }
```

Before

```
float Distance::getInches()
{
    return fInches;
}
```

After

```
float getInches(Distance * const this)
{
    return this->fInches;

}
```

We must understand how the scope resolution operator works. The scope resolution operator is also an operator. Just like any other operator, it operates upon its operands. The scope resolution operator is a *binary* operator, that is, it takes two operands. The operand on its left is the name of a pre-defined class. On its right is a member function of that class. Based upon this information, the scope resolution operator inserts a constant operator of the correct type as a leading formal argument to the function on its right. For example, if the class name is `Distance`, as in the above case, the compiler inserts a pointer of type `Distance * const` as a leading formal argument to the function on its right.

4. It passes the address of invoking object as a leading parameter to each call to the member functions as follows.

Before

```
d1.setFeet(1);
```

After

```
setFeet(&d1,1);
```

Before

```
d1.setInches(1.1);
```

After

```
setInches(&d1,1.1);
```

Before

```
cout<<d1.getFeet()<<endl;
```

After

```
cout<<getFeet(&d1)<<endl;
```

Before

```
cout<<d1.getInches()<<endl;
```

<u>After</u>

```
cout<<getInches(&d1)<<endl;
```

In the case of C++, the dot operator's definition has been extended. It not only takes data members as in C but also member functions as its right-hand side operand. If the operand on its right is a data member, then the dot operator behaves just like it does in C language. However, if the operand on its right is a member function, then the dot operator causes the address of the object on its left to be passed as an implicit leading parameter to the function call.

Clearly, members of the *invoking object* are referred to when they are accessed without any qualifiers in member functions. It should also be obvious that multiple copies of member data exist (one inside each object) but only one copy exists for each member function.

It is evident that the this pointer should continue to point at the same object—the object with respect to which the member function has been called—throughout its lifetime. For this reason, the compiler creates it as a constant pointer.

The accessibility of the implicit object is the same as that of the other objects passed as parameters in the function call and the local objects inside that function. Listing 2.9 illustrates this. A new function—add()—has been added to the existing definition of the Distance class.

Listing 2.9 Accessing data members of local objects inside member functions and of objects that are passed as parameters

```
/*Beginning of Distance.h*/
class Distance
{
   /*
     rest of the class Distance
   */
     Distance add(Distance);
};
/*End of Distance.h*/

/*Beginning of Distlib.cpp*/
#include"Distance.h"

Distance Distance::add(Distance dd)
{
   Distance temp;
   temp.iFeet=iFeet+dd.iFeet;          //legal to access both
                                       //temp.iFeet and
                                       //dd.iFeet
   temp.fInches=fInches+dd.fInches;    //ditto
   return temp;
}
/*
   definitions of the rest of the functions of class
   Distance
*/
/*End of Distlib.cpp*/

/*Beginning of Distmain.cpp*/
#include<iostream.h>
#include"Distance.h"
```

```
    void main()
    {
        Distance d1,d2,d3;
        d1.setFeet(1);
        d1.setInches(1.1);
        d2.setFeet(2);
        d2.setInches(2.2);
        d3=d1.add(d2);
        cout<<d3.getFeet()<<"'-"<<d3.getInches()<<"'"'\n";
    }
    /*End of Distmain.cpp*/
```

Output
3'-3.3'

The definition of `Distance :: add()` function, after the previously described conversion by the compiler is carried out, will appear as follows.

```
    Distance add(Distance * const this, Distance dd)
    {
        Distance temp;
        temp.iFeet=this->iFeet+dd.iFeet;
        temp.fInches=this->fInches+dd.fInches;
        return temp;
    }
```

When this function is called from the `main()` function with respect to 'd1', the `this` pointer points at 'd1'. Thus, it is the private data member of 'd1' that is being accessed in the second and third lines of the `add()` function.

So, now we can
- Declare a class
- Define member data and member functions
- Make members private and public
- Declare objects and call member functions with respect to objects

What advantages does all this lead to? The advantage that library programmers can now derive from this arrangement is epitomized in the following observation:

An executable file will not be created from a source code in which private data members of an object have been accessed by non-member functions.

Once again, the importance of compile-time errors over run-time errors is emphasized. Suppose, an if block exists in a function that is not intended by the library programmer to access the data members of a structure. This if block contains a bug (say 'd1.month' has been assigned the value of 13, where 'd1' is a variable of the structure 'date').

A pure C compiler would not recognize this statement as an invalid access. During testing, the if condition of this if block might never become true. The bug would remain undetected; the executable will get created with bugs. Thus, *creating bug-free executables is difficult and unreliable in C*. This is due to the absence of language constructs that enforce data security.

On the other hand, a C++ compiler that also detects invalid access of private data members would immediately throw an error during compile time itself and prevent the creation of the executable. Thus, *creating bug-free executables is easier and more reliable in C++ than in C*. This is due to the presence of language constructs that enforce data security.

2.1.7 Data Abstraction

The class construct provides facilities to implement data abstraction. Data abstraction is an important concept and should be understood properly. Let us take up the example of the LCD projector from the previous chapter. It has member data (light and fan) as well as member functions (switches that operate the light and the fan). This real-world object hides its internal operations from the outside world. It, thus, obviates the need for the user to know the possible pitfalls that might be encountered during its operation. During its operation, the LCD projector never reaches an invalid state. Moreover, the LCD projector does not start in an invalid state.

Data abstraction is a virtue by which an object hides its internal operations from the rest of the program. It makes it unnecessary for the client programs to know how the data is internally arranged in the object. Thus, it obviates the need for the client programs to write precautionary code upon creating and while using objects.

Now, in order to understand this concept, let us take an example in C++. The library programmer, who has designed the Distance class, wants to ensure that the fInches portion of an object of the class should never exceed 12. If a value larger than 12 is specified by an application programmer while calling the Distance::setInches() function, the logic incorporated within the definition of the function should automatically increment the value of iFeet and decrement the value of fInches by suitable amounts. A modified definition of the Distance::setInches() function is as follows.

```
void Distance::setInches(float y)
{
    fInches=y;
    if(fInches>=12)
    {
        iFeet+=fInches/12;
        fInches-=((int)fInches/12)*12;
    }
}
```

Here, we notice that an application programmer need not send values less than 12 while calling the Distance::setInches() function. The default logic within the Distance::setInches() function does the necessary adjustments. This is an example of data abstraction.

The above restriction may not appear mandatory. However, very soon we will create classes where similar restrictions will be absolutely necessary (and also complicated).

Similarly, the definition of the Distance::add() function should also be modified as follows by the library programmer. Here, it can be assumed that the value of fInches portion of neither the invoking object nor the object appearing as formal argument ('dd') can be greater than 12.

```
Distance Distance::add(Distance dd)
{
    Distance temp;
    temp.iFeet=iFeet+dd.iFeet;
    temp.setInches(fInches+dd.fInches);
    return temp;
}
```

Now, if we write the statements shown in Listing 2.10

Listing 2.10   Enforcing restrictions on the data members of a class

```
d1.setFeet(1);
d1.setInches(9.5);
d2.setFeet(2);
d2.setInches(5.5);
d3=d1.add(d2);
```

then the value of d3.fInches will become 3 (not 15) and the value of d3.iFeet will become 4 (not 3).

It has already been mentioned that real-world objects never attain an invalid state. They also do not start in an invalid state. Does C++ enable the library programmer to implement this feature in class objects?

Let us continue with our earlier example—the Distance class. Recollect that it is the library programmer's intention to ensure that the value of fInches portion of none of the objects of the class Distance should exceed 12. Now, let us consider Listing 2.11.

Listing 2.11   Object gets created with improper values

```
/*Beginning of DistJunk.cpp*/
#include<iostream.h>
#include"Distance.h"

void main()
{
    Distance d1;
    cout<<d1.getFeet()<<" "<<d1.getInches()<<endl;
}

/*End of DistJunk.cpp*/
```

Output
297 34.56

As you can see, the value of fInches of 'd1' is larger than 12! This happened because the value of both iFeet and fInches automatically got set to junk values when 'd1' was allocated memory and the junk value is larger than 12 for d1.fInches. Thus, the objective of the library programmer to keep the value of fInches less than 12 has not yet been achieved.

It would be unrealistic to expect that an application programmer will explicitly initialize each object that is declared.

```
Distance d1;
d1.setFeet(0);              //initialization
d1.setInches(0.0);          //initialization
```

Obviously, the library programmer would like to add a function to the Distance class that gets called automatically whenever an object is created and sets the values of the data members of the object properly. Such a function is the *constructor*. The concept of constructor and a related function, the *destructor*, is discussed in one of the later chapters.

But we may say that even if Distance was an ordinary structure and setInches() function was a non-member function just as in C, data abstraction would still be in place. Nevertheless, in the case of C, the library programmer cannot force calls to only those functions that have been defined. He/she cannot prevent calls to those functions that he/she has not defined. *Data abstraction is effective due to data hiding only* (recall the case of the overhead projector systems discussed earlier).

On the other side of the coin, in C language, life becomes difficult for an application programmer also. If a certain member of a structure variable acquires an invalid or a wrong value, he/she has to hunt through the entire source code to detect the bug. This problem rapidly gains significance as the code length increases. In actual practice, it is common to have code of more than 25,000 lines.

Let us now sum up as follows:

Perfect definitions of the member functions are guaranteed to achieve their objective because of data hiding.

This is the essence of the object-oriented programming system. Real-world objects have not only working parts but also an exclusive interface to these inner-working parts. A perfect interface is guaranteed to work because of its exclusive rights.

2.1.8 Explicit Address Manipulation

An application programmer can manipulate the member data of any object by explicit address manipulation. Listing 2.12 illustrates the point.

Listing 2.12   Explicit address manipulation

```
/*Beginning of DistAddrManip.cpp*/
#include"Distance.h"
#include<iostream.h>

void main()
{
   Distance d1;
   d1.setFeet(256);
   d1.setInches(2.2);
   char * p=(char *)&d1;              //explicit address manipulation
   *p=1;                             //undesirable but unpreventable
   cout<<d1.getFeet()<<" "<<d1.getInches()<<endl;
}
/*End of DistAddrManip.cpp*/
```

Output
257 2.2

However, such explicit address manipulation by an application programmer cannot be prevented. It is left as an exercise for the readers to explain the output of the above program (Listing 2.12).

2.1.9 Arrow Operator

Member functions can be called with respect to an object through a pointer pointing at the object. The arrow operator (->) does this. An illustrative example is shown in Listing 2.13.

Listing 2.13   Accessing members through pointers

```
/*Beginning of PointerToMember.cpp*/
#include<iostream.h>
#include"Distance.h"
```

```
void main()
{
    Distance d1;                            //object
    Distance * dPtr;                        //pointer
    dPtr=&d1;                               //pointer initialized
    /*Same as d1.setFeet(1) and d1.setInches(1.1)*/
    dPtr->setFeet(1);                       //calling member functions
    dPtr->setInches(1.1);                   //through pointers
    /*Same as d1.getFeet() and d1.getInches()*/
    cout<<dPtr->getFeet()<<" "<<dPtr->getInches()<<endl;
}
/*End of PointerToMember.cpp*/
```

Output
1 1.1

It is interesting to note that just like the dot (.) operator, *the definition of the arrow (->)
operator has also been extended in C++*. It takes not only data members on its right as in C,
but also member functions as its right-hand side operand. If the operand on its right is a data
member, then the arrow operator behaves just as it does in C language. However, if it is a
member function of a class where a pointer of the same class type is its left-hand side operand,
then the compiler simply passes the value of the pointer as an implicit leading parameter to
the function call. Thus, the statement

```
dPtr->setFeet(1);
```

after conversion becomes

```
setFeet(dPtr,1);
```

Now, the value of dPtr is copied into the this pointer. Therefore, the this pointer also
points at the same object at which dPtr points.

2.1.10 Calling One Member Function from Another

One member function can be called from another. An illustrative example is shown in
Listing 2.14.

Listing 2.14   Calling one member function from another

```
/*Beginning of NestedCall.cpp*/
class A
{
    int x;
  public:
    void setx(int);
    void setxindirect(int);
};

void A::setx(int p)
{
    x=p;
}

void A::setxindirect(int q)
{
    setx(q);
```

```
}
void main()
{
   A A1;
   A1.setxindirect(1);
}
/*End of NestedCall.cpp*/
```

It is relatively simple to explain the above program. The call to the A::setxindirect() function changes from

```
A1.setxindirect(1);
```

to

```
setxindirect(&A1,1);
```

The definition of the A::setxindirect() function changes from

```
void A::setxindirect(int q)
{
   setx(q);
}
```

to

```
void setxindirect(A * const this, int q)
{
   this->setx(q);                    //calling function through a pointer
}
```

which, in turn, changes to

```
void setxindirect(A * const this, int q)
{
   setx(this,q);                     //action of arrow operator
}
```

2.2 Member Functions and Member Data

Let us study the various kinds of member functions and member data that classes in C++ have.

2.2.1 Overloaded Member Functions

Member functions can be overloaded just like non-member functions. Listing 2.15 illustrates this point.

Listing 2.15 Overloaded member functions

```
/*Beginning of memFuncOverload.cpp*/
#include<iostream.h>

class A
{
   public:
      void show();
      void show(int);                //function show() overloaded!!
};
```

```
void A::show()
{
    cout<<"Hello\n";
}

void A::show(int x)
{
    for(int i=0;i<x;i++)
        cout<<"Hello\n";
}

void main()
{
    A A1;
    A1.show();                        //first definition called
    A1.show(3);                       //second definition called
}
/*End of memFuncOverload.cpp*/
```

Output
Hello
Hello
Hello
Hello

Function overloading enables us to have two functions of the same name and same signature in two different classes. The class definitions given in Listing 2.16 illustrate the point.

Listing 2.16 Facility of overloading functions permits member functions of two different classes to have the same name

```
class A
{
    public:
        void show();
};
class B
{
    public:
        void show();
};
```

A function of the same name show() is defined in both the classes—'A' and 'B'. The signature also appears to be the same. But with our knowledge of the this pointer, we know that the signatures are *actually* different. The function prototypes in the respective classes are actually as follows.

```
void show(A * const);
void show(B * const);
```

Without the facility of function overloading, it would not be possible for us to have two functions of the same name in different classes. Without the facility of function overloading, choice of names for member functions would become more and more restricted. Later, we will find that function overloading enables function overriding that, in turn, enables dynamic polymorphism.

2.2.2 Default Values for Formal Arguments of Member Functions

We already know that default values can be assigned to arguments of non-member functions. Default values can be specified for formal arguments of member functions also. An illustrative example follows in Listing 2.17.

Listing 2.17 Giving default values to arguments of member functions

```
/*Beginning of memFuncDefault.cpp*/
#include<iostream.h>

class A
{
   public:
      void show(int=1);
};

void A::show(int p)
{
   for(int i=0;i<p;i++)
      cout<<"Hello\n";
}

void main()
{
   A A1;
   A1.show();                    //default value taken
   A1.show(3);                   //default value overridden
}
/*End of memFuncDefault.cpp*/
```

Output
Hello
Hello
Hello
Hello

Again, it has to be kept in mind that a member function should be overloaded with care if default values are specified for some or all of its formal arguments. For example, the compiler will report an *ambiguity error* when it finds the second prototype for the show() function of class A in Listing 2.18.

Listing 2.18 Giving default values to arguments of overloaded member functions can lead to ambiguity errors

```
class A
{
   public:
      void show();
      void show(int=0);           //ambiguity error
};
```

Reasons for such ambiguity errors have already been explained in the section on function overloading in Chapter 1. As in the case of non-member functions, if default values are specified for more than one formal argument, they must be specified from the right to the left. Similarly, default values must be specified in the function prototypes and not in function definitions. Further, default values can be specified for a formal argument of any type.

2.2.3 Inline Member Functions

Member functions are made inline by either of the following two methods.
- By defining the function within the class itself (as in Listing 2.5)
- By only prototyping and not defining the function within the class. The function is defined outside the class by using the scope resolution operator. The definition is prefixed by the `inline` keyword. As in non-member functions, the definition of the inline function must appear before it is called. Hence, the function should be defined in the same header file in which its class is defined. Listing 2.19 illustrates this.

Listing 2.19 Inline member functions

```
/*Beginning of memInline.cpp*/
class A
{
  public:
    void show();
};

inline void A::show()          //definition in header file itself
{
                               //definition of A::show() function
}
/*End of memInline.cpp*/
```

2.2.4 Constant Member Functions

Let us consider this situation. The library programmer desires that one of the member functions of his/her class should not be able to change the value of member data. This function should be able to merely read the values contained in the data members, but not change them. However, he/she fears that while defining the function he/she might accidentally write the code to do so. In order to prevent this, he/she seeks the compiler's help. If he/she declares the function as a *constant function*, and thereafter attempts to change the value of a data member through the function, the compiler throws an error.

Let us consider the class `Distance`. The `Distance::getFeet()`, `Distance::getInches()`, and the `Distance::add()` functions should obviously be constant functions. They should not change the values of `iFeet` or `fInches` members of the invoking object even by accident.

Member functions are specified as constants by *suffixing the prototype and the function definition header with the* `const` *keyword*. The modified prototypes and definitions of the member functions of the class `Distance` are illustrated in Listing 2.20.

Listing 2.20 Constant member functions

```
/*Beginning of Distance.h*/
/*Header file containing the definition of the Distance
class*/
class Distance
{
```

```
        int iFeet;
        float fInches;
    public:
        void setFeet(int);
        int getFeet() const;                        //constant function
        void setInches(float);
        float getInches() const;                    //constant function
        Distance add(Distance) const;               //constant function
};
/*End of Distance.h*/

/*Beginning of Distlib.cpp*/
/*Implementation file for the class Distance*/
#include"Distance.h"

void Distance::setFeet(int x)
{
    iFeet=x;
}

int Distance::getFeet() const                       //constant function
{
    iFeet++;              //ERROR!!
    return iFeet;
}

void Distance::setInches(float y)
{
    fInches=y;
}

float Distance::getInches() const                   //constant function
{
    fInches=0.0;          //ERROR!!
    return fInches;
}

Distance Distance::add(Distance dd) const           //constant
                                                    //function
{
    Distance temp;
    temp.iFeet=iFeet+dd.iFeet;
    temp.setInches(fInches+dd.fInches);
    iFeet++;              //ERROR!!
    return temp;
}
/*End of Distlib.cpp*/
```

For constant member functions, the memory occupied by the invoking object is a read-only memory. How does the compiler manage this? For constant member functions, the this pointer becomes 'a constant pointer to a constant' instead of only 'a constant pointer'. For example, the this pointer is of type const Distance * const for the Distance::getFeet(), Distance::getInches(), and Distance::add() functions. For the other member functions of the class Distance, the this pointer is of type Distance * const.

Clearly, only constant member functions can be called with respect to constant objects. Non-constant member functions cannot be called with respect to constant objects. However, constant as well as non-constant functions can be called with respect to non-constant objects.

2.2.5 Mutable Data Members

A mutable data member is *never* constant. It can be modified inside constant functions also. Prefixing the declaration of a data member with the keyword `mutable` makes it `mutable`. Listing 2.21 illustrates this.

Listing 2.21   Mutable data members

```
/*Beginning of mutable.h*/
class A
{
    int x;                    //non-mutable data member
    mutable int y;            //mutable data member

  public:

    void abc() const          //a constant member function
    {
      x++;     //ERROR: cannot modify a non-constant data
               //member in a constant member function
      y++;     //OK: can modify a mutable data member in a
               //constant member function

    }
    void def()                        //a non-constant member function
    {
      x++;     //OK: can modify a non-constant data member
               //in a non-constant member function
      y++;     //OK: can modify a mutable data member in a
               //non-constant member function

    }
};
/*End of mutable.h*/
```

We frequently need a data member that can be modified even for constant objects. Suppose, there is a member function that saves the data of the invoking object in a disk file. Obviously, this function should be declared as a constant to prevent even an inadvertent change to data members of the invoking object. If we need to maintain a flag inside each object that tells us whether the object has already been saved or not, such a flag should be modified within the above constant member function. Therefore, this data member should be declared a mutable data member.

2.2.6 Friends

A class can have global non-member functions and member functions of other classes as friends. Such functions can directly access the private data members of objects of the class.

Friend non-member functions

A friend function is a non-member function that has special rights to access private data members of any object of the class of whom it is a friend. In this section, we will study only those friend functions that are not member functions of some other class.

A friend function is prototyped within the definition of the class of which it is intended to be a friend. The prototype is prefixed with the keyword `friend`. Since it is a non-member function, it is defined without using the scope resolution operator. Moreover, it is not called with respect to an object. An illustrative example is shown in Listing 2.22.

Listing 2.22 Friend functions

```
/*Beginning of friend.cpp*/
class A
{
     int x;
   public:
        friend void abc(A&);        //prototype of the friend function
};
void abc(A& AObj)     //definition of the friend function
{
    AObj.x++;            //accessing private members of the object
}

void main()
{
   A A1;
   abc(A1);
}
/*End of friend.cpp*/
```

A few points about the friend functions that we must keep in mind are as follows:

- `friend` keyword should appear in the prototype only and not in the definition.

- Since it is a non-member function of the class of which it is a friend, it can be prototyped in either the private or the public section of the class.

- A friend function takes one extra parameter as compared to a member function that performs the same task. This is because it cannot be called with respect to any object. Instead, the object itself appears as an explicit parameter in the function call.

- We need not and should not use the scope resolution operator while defining a friend function.

There are situations where a function that needs to access the private data members of the objects of a class cannot be called with respect to an object of the class. In such situations, the function must be declared as a friend. We will encounter one such situation in Chapter 8.

Friend functions do not contradict the principles of OOPS. Since it is necessary to prototype the friend function inside the class itself, the list of functions that can access the private members of a class's object remains well defined and restricted. The benefits provided by data hiding are not compromised by friend functions.

Friend classes

A class can be a friend of another class. *Member functions of a friend class can access private data members of objects of the class of which it is a friend.* If class B is to be made a friend of class A, then the statement

```
friend class B;
```

should be written within the definition of class A. Listing 2.23 illustrates this.

Listing 2.23   Declaring friend classes

```
class A
{
   friend class B;                    //declaring B as a friend of A
   /*
      rest of the class A
   */
};
```

It does not matter whether the statement declaring class B as a friend is mentioned within the private or the public section of class A. Now, member functions of class B can access the private data members of objects of class A. Listing 2.24 exemplifies this.

Listing 2.24   Effect of declaring a friend class

```
/*Beginning of friendClass.cpp*/
class B;  //forward declaration… necessary because
          //definition of class B is after the statement
          //that declares class B a friend of class A.
class A
{
     int x;
   public:
     void setx(const int=0);
     int getx()const;
     friend class B;                    //declaring B as a friend of A
};
class B
{
     A * APtr;
   public:
     void Map(A * const);
     void test_friend(const int);
};
void B::Map(A * const p)
{
   APtr = p;
}
void B::test_friend(const int i)
{
   APtr->x=i;                          //accessing the private data member
}
/*End of friendClass.cpp*/
```

As we can see, member functions of class B are able to access private data member of objects of the class A although they are not member functions of class A. This is because they are member functions of class B that is a friend of class A.

Friendship is not transitive. For example, consider Listing 2.25.

Listing 2.25   Friendship is not transitive

```cpp
class B;
class C;

/*Beginning of friendTran.cpp*/
class A
{
   friend class B;
   int a;
};

class B
{
   friend class C;
};

class C
{
   void f(A * p)
   {
      p->a++;                      //error: C is not a friend of A
                                   //despite being a friend of a friend
   }
};
/*End of friendTran.cpp*/
```

Friend member functions

How can we make some specific member functions of one class friendly to another class? For making only B::test_friend() function a friend of class A, replace the line

```cpp
friend class B;
```

in the declaration of the class A with the line

```cpp
friend void B::test_friend();
```

The modified definition of the class A is

```cpp
class A
{
   /*
     rest of the class A
   */
      friend void B::test_friend();
};
```

However, in order to compile this code successfully, the compiler should first see the definition of the class B. Otherwise, it does not know that test_friend() is a member function of the class B. This means that we should put the definition of class B before the definition of class A.

However, a pointer of type A * is a private data member of class B. So, the compiler should also know that there is a class A before it compiles the definition of class B. This problem of *circular dependence* is solved by forward declaration. This is done by inserting the line

```cpp
class A;                          //Declaration only! Not definition!!
```

before the definition of class B. Now, the declarations and definitions of the two classes appear as shown in Listing 2.26.

Listing 2.26   Forward declaring a class that requires a friend

```
/*Beginning of friendMemFunc.h*/
class A;

class B
{
    A * APtr;
  public:
    void Map(const A * const);
    void test_friend(const int=0);
};

class A
{
    int x;
  public:
    friend void B::test_friend(const int=0);
};
/*End of friendMemFunc.h*/
```

Another problem arises if we try to define the `B::test_friend()` function as an inline function by defining it within class B itself. See Listing 2.27.

Listing 2.27   Problem in declaring a friend member function inline

```
class B
{
  /*
    rest of the class B
  */
  public:
    void test_friend(const int p)
    {
        APtr->x=p;                   //will not compile
    }
};
```

But how will the code inside `B::test_friend()` function compile? The compiler will not know that there is a data member 'x' inside the definition of class A. For overcoming this problem, merely prototype `B::test_friend()` function within class B; *define it as inline* after the definition of class A in the header file itself. The revised definitions appear in Listing 2.28.

Listing 2.28   Declaring a friend member function inline

```
/*Beginning of friendMemFuncInline.h*/
class A;

class B
{
    A * APtr;
  public:
    void Map(const A * const);
    void test_friend(const int=0);
};
```

```
class A
{
    int x;
  public:
    friend void B::test_friend(const int=0);
};

inline void B::test_friend(const int p)
{
    APtr->x=p;
}
/*End of friendMemFuncInline.h*/
```

Friends as bridges

Friend functions can be used as bridges between two classes.

Suppose there are two unrelated classes whose private data members need a simultaneous update through a common function. This function should be declared as a friend to both the classes. See Listing 2.29.

Listing 2.29 Friends as bridges

```
class B;                        //forward declaration

class A
{
    /*
      rest of the class A
    */
    friend void ab(const A&, const B&);
};
class B
{
    /*
      rest of the class B
    */
    friend void ab(const A&, const B&);
};
```

2.2.7 Static Members

Static member data

Static data members hold global data that is common to all objects of the class. Examples of such global data are
• count of objects currently present,
• common data accessed by all objects, etc.

Let us consider class Account. We want all objects of this class to calculate interest at the rate of say 4.5%. Therefore, this data should be globally available to all objects of this class (Listing 2.30).

This data cannot and should not be a member of the objects themselves. Otherwise, multiple copies of this data will be embedded within the objects taking up unnecessary space. Same value would have to be maintained for this data in all objects. This is very difficult. Thus, this data cannot be stored in a member variable of class `Account`.

At the same time, this data should not be stored in a global variable. Then the data is liable to be changed by even non-member functions. It will also potentially lead to name conflicts. However, this means that it should be stored in a member variable of class `Account`!

How can this conflict be resolved? Storing the data in a *static variable* of the class resolves this conflict. Static data members are members of the *class* and not of any *object* of the class, that is, they are not contained inside any object.

We prefix the declaration of a variable within the class definition with the keyword `static` to make it a static data member of the class. See Listing 2.30.

Listing 2.30   Declaring a static data member

```
/*Beginning of Account.h*/
class Account
{
   static float interest_rate;                    //a static data member
   /*
     rest of the class Account
   */
};
/*End of Account.h*/
```

A statement declaring a static data member inside a class will obviously not cause any memory to get allocated for it. Moreover, memory for a static data member will not get allocated when objects of the class are declared. This is because a static data member is not a member of any object. Therefore, we must not forget to write the statement to define (allocate memory for) a static member variable. Explicitly defining a static data member outside the class is necessary. Otherwise, the linker produces an error. The following statement allocates memory for `interest_rate` member of class `Account`.

```
float Account::interest_rate;
```

The above statement initializes `interest_rate` to zero. If some other initial value (say 4.5) is desired instead, the statement should be rewritten as follows.

```
float Account::interest_rate=4.5;
```

Static data members should be defined in the implementation files only. The header file is included in both the implementation file and the driver program. If a static data member is defined in the header file, the static data member's definition would be in two files—the library file created from the implementation file and the object file created from the driver program. But in order to get the executable, the linker will have to link these files. Upon finding two definitions of the static data member, the linker would throw an error.

Making static data members private prevents any change from non-member functions as only member functions can change the values of static data members.

Introducing static data members does not increase the size of objects of the class. Static data members are not contained within objects. There is only one copy of the static data member in the memory. Let us try the following program (Listing 2.31) to find out.

Listing 2.31   Static data members are not a part of objects

```cpp
/*Beginning of staticSize.cpp*/
#include<iostream.h>
class A
{
   int x;
   char y;
   float z;
   static float s;
};
float A::s=1.1;
void main()
{
   cout<<sizeof(A)<<endl;
}
/*End of staticSize.cpp*/
```

Output
9

Static data members can be of any type. For example, name of the bank that has the accounts can be stored as a character array in a static data member of the class as illustrated in Listing 2.32.

Listing 2.32   Static data member can be of any type

```cpp
/*Beginning of Account.h*/

class Account
{
   static float interest_rate;
   static char name[30];
   /*
      rest of the class Account
   */
};

/*End of Account.h*/

/*Beginning of Account.cpp*/
#include"Account.h"

float A::interest_rate=4.5;
char A::name[30]="The Rich and Poor Bank";
/*
   definitions of the rest of the functions of class Account
*/
/*End of Account.cpp*/
```

Static data members of integral type can be initialized within the class itself if the need arises. For example, see Listing 2.33.

Listing 2.33   Initializing integral static data members within the class itself

```
/*Beginning of Account.h*/

class Account
{
   static int nameLength=30;
   static char name[nameLength];
   /*
      rest of the class Account
   */
};

/*End of Account.h*/

/*Beginning of Account.cpp*/
#include"Account.h"

int A::nameLength;
char A::name[nameLength]="The Rich and Poor Bank";
/*
   definitions of the rest of the functions of class Account
*/
/*End of Account.cpp*/
```

We must notice that the static data member that has been initialized inside the class must be still defined outside the class to allocate memory for it. Once the initial value has been supplied within the class, the static data member must not be re-initialized when it is defined.

Non-integral static data members cannot be initialized like this. For example, see Listing 2.34.

Listing 2.34   Non-integral static data members cannot be initialized within the class

```
/*Beginning of Account.h*/

class Account
{
   static char name[30]="The Rich and Poor Bank";      //error!!
   /*
      rest of the class Account
   */
};
/*End of Account.h*/
```

In Listing 2.33, the variable nameLength is referred to directly without the class name and the scope resolution operator while defining the variable name. One static data member can directly refer to another without using the scope resolution operator.

Member functions can refer to static data members directly. An example follows (Listing 2.35).

Listing 2.35   Accessing static data members from non-static member functions

```
/*Beginning of Account.h*/

class Account
{
     static float interest_rate;
   public:
```

```
                void updateBalance();
                /*
                   rest of the class Account
                */
        };

        /*End of Account.h*/

        /*Beginning of Account.cpp*/
        #include"Account.h"

        float Account::interest_rate=4.5;
        void Account::updateBalance()
        {
          if(end_of_year)
             balance+=balance*interest_rate/100;
        }
        /*
           definitions of the rest of the functions of class Account
        */
        /*End of Account.cpp*/
```

The object-to-member access operator can be used to refer to the static data member of a class with respect to an object. The class name with the scope resolution operator can do this directly.

```
        f=a1.interest_rate;                //a1 is an object of the class Account
        f=Account::interest_rate;
```

There are some things static data members can do but non-static data members cannot.

- A static data member can be of the *same type* as the class of which it is a member. See Listing 2.36.

Listing 2.36 Static data members can be of the same type as their class

```
class A
{
    static A A1;          //OK : static
    A * APtr;             //OK : pointer
    A A2;                 //ERROR!! : non-static
};
```

- A static data member can appear as the *default value* for the formal arguments of member functions of its class. See Listing 2.37.

Listing 2.37 A static data member can appear as the default argument in the member functions

```
class A
{
    static int x;
    int y;
  public:
    void abc(int=x);           //OK
    void def(int=y);           //ERROR!! : object required
};
```

A static data member can be declared to be a constant. In that case, the member functions will be able to only read it but not modify its value.

Static member functions

How do we create a member function that need not be called with respect to an existing object? This function's sole purpose is to access and/or modify static data members of the class. Static member functions fulfill the above criteria. Prefixing the function prototype with the keyword `static` specifies it as a static member function. However, the keyword `static` should not reappear in the definition of the function.

Suppose there is a function `set_interest_rate()` that sets the value of the `interest_rate` static data member of class `Account`. The application programmer should be able to call this function even if no objects have been declared. As discussed previously, this function should be static. Its definition can be as shown in Listing 2.38.

Listing 2.38   Static member function

```
/*Beginning of Account.h*/
class Account
{
      static float interest_rate;
   public:
      static void set_interest_rate(float);
   /*
      rest of the class Account
   */
};
/*End of Account.h*/

/*Beginning of Account.cpp*/
#include"Account.h"

float Account::interest_rate = 4.5;

void Account::set_interest_rate(float p)
{
   interest_rate=p;
}
/*
   definitions of the rest of the functions of class Account
*/
/*End of Account.cpp*/
```

Now, the `Account::set_interest_rate()` function can be called directly without an object.

```
Account::set_interest_rate(5);
```

Static member functions do not take the `this` pointer as a formal argument. Therefore, accessing non-static data members through a static member function results in compile-time errors. *Static member functions can access only static data members of the class.*

Static member functions can still be called with respect to objects.

```
a1.set_interest_rate(5);          //a1 is an object of the class
                                  //Account
```

2.3 Objects and Functions

Objects can appear as local variables inside functions. They can also be passed by value or by reference to functions. Finally, they can be returned by value or by reference from functions. Listings 2.39 and 2.40 illustrate all this.

Listing 2.39 Returning class objects

```
/*Beginning of Distance.h*/
class Distance
{
  public:
    /*function to add the invoking object with another
    object passed as a parameter and return the resultant
    object*/
    Distance add(Distance);
    /*
       rest of the class Distance
    */
};
/*End of Distance.h*/

/*Beginning of Distance.cpp*/
#include"Distance.h"

Distance Distance::add(Distance dd)
{
   Distance temp;
   temp.iFeet=iFeet+dd.iFeet;
   temp.setInches(fInches+dd.fInches);
   return temp;
}
/*
   definitions of the rest of the functions of class
   Distance
*/

/*End of Distance.cpp*/

/*Beginning of Distmain.cpp*/
#include<iostream.h>
#include"Distance.h"

void main()
{
   Distance d1,d2,d3;
   d1.setFeet(5);
   d1.setInches(7.5);
   d2.setFeet(3);
   d2.setInches(6.25);
   d3=d1.add(d2);
   cout<<d3.getFeet()<<" "<<d3.getInches()<<endl;
}

/*End of Distmain.cpp*/
```

Output
9 1.75

Listing 2.40   Returning class objects by reference

```
/*Beginning of Distance.h*/
/*Header file containing the definition of the Distance
class*/
class Distance
{
/*definition of the class Distance*/
};
Distance& larger(Distance&, Distance&);
/*End of Distance.h*/

/*Beginning of Distance.cpp*/
#include"Distance.h"
Distance& larger(Distance& dd1, Distance& dd2)
{
   float i,j;
   i=dd1.getFeet()*12+dd1.getInches();
   j=dd2.getFeet()*12+dd2.getInches();
   if(i>j)
      return dd1;
   else
      return dd2;
}
/*
definitions of the rest of the functions of class Distance
*/
/*End of Distance.cpp*/

/*Beginning of Distmain.cpp*/
#include<iostream.h>
#include"Distance.h"
void main()
{
   Distance d1,d2;
   d1.setFeet(5);
   d1.setInches(7.5);
   d2.setFeet(5);
   d2.setInches(6.25);
   Distance& d3=larger(d1,d2);
   d3.setFeet(0);
   d3.setInches(0.0);
   cout<<d1.getFeet()<<» «<<d1.getInches()<<endl;
   cout<<d2.getFeet()<<» «<<d2.getInches()<<endl;
}
/*End of Distmain.cpp*/
```

Output
0 0.0
5 6.25

2.4 Objects and Arrays

Let us understand how arrays of objects and arrays inside objects are handled in C++.

2.4.1 Arrays of Objects

We can create arrays of objects. The following program shows how.

Listing 2.41   Array of objects

```
/*Beginning of DistArray.cpp*/
#include"Distance.h"
#include<iostream.h>
#define SIZE 3

void main()
{
  Distance dArray[SIZE];
  int a;
  float b;
  for(int i=0;i<SIZE;i++)
  {
    cout<<"Enter the feet : ";
    cin>>a;
    dArray[i].setFeet(a);
    cout<<"Enter the inches : ";
    cin>>b;
    dArray[i].setInches(b);
  }
  for(int i=0;i<SIZE;i++)
  {
      cout<<dArray[i].getFeet()<<" "
          <<dArray[i].getInches()<<endl;
  }
}

/*End of DistArray.cpp*/
```

Output

Enter the feet : **1**<*enter*>
Enter the inches : **1.1**<*enter*>
Enter the feet : **2**<*enter*>
Enter the inches : **2.2**<*enter*>
Enter the feet : **3**<*enter*>
Enter the inches : **3.3**<*enter*>
1 1.1
2 2.2
3 3.3

2.4.2 Arrays Inside Objects

An array can be declared inside a class. Such an array becomes a member of all objects of the class. It can be manipulated/accessed by all member functions of the class. The class definition shown in Listing 2.42 illustrates this.

Listing 2.42   Arrays inside objects

```
#define SIZE 3
/*A class to duplicate the behaviour of an integer array*/
class A
{
     int iArray[SIZE];
   public:
     void setElement(unsigned int,int);
     int getElement(unsigned int);
};
/*function to write the value passed as second parameter at the position passed
as first parameter*/
void A::setElement(unsigned int p,int v)
{
   if(p>=SIZE)
      return;              //better to throw an exception
   iArray[p]=v;
}
/*function to read the value from the position passed as parameter*/
int A::getElement(unsigned int p)
{
   if(p>=SIZE)
      return -1;           //better to throw an exception
   return iArray[p];
}
```

The class definition is self-explanatory. However, the comments indicate that it is better
to throw exceptions rather than terminate the function. What are exceptions? How are they
thrown? What are the benefits of using them? All these questions are answered in the chapter
on Exception Handling.

2.5 Namespaces

*Namespaces enable the C++ programmer to prevent pollution of the global namespace that
leads to name clashes.*

The term 'global namespace' refers to the entire source code. It also includes all the directly
and indirectly included header files. By default, the name of each class is visible in the entire
source code, that is, in the global namespace. This can lead to problems.

Suppose a class with the same name is defined in two header files.

```
/*Beginning of A1.h*/
class A
{
};
/*End of A1.h*/

/*Beginning of A2.h*/
class A //a class with an existing name
{
};
/*End of A2.h*/
```

Now, let us include both these header files in a program and see what happens if we declare
an object of the class. See Listing 2.43.

Listing 2.43   Referring to a globally declared class can lead to ambiguity error

```
/*Beginning of multiDef01.cpp*/
#include"A1.h"
#include"A2.h"
void main()
{
    A AObj;                             //ERROR: Ambiguity error due to multiple
                                        //definitions of A

}
/*End of multiDef01.cpp*/
```

The scenario in Listing 2.43 is quite likely in large programs. The global visibility of the definition of class A makes the inclusion of the two header files mutually exclusive. Consequently, this also makes use of the two definitions of class A *mutually exclusive*.

How can this problem be overcome? How can we ensure that an application is able to use both definitions of class A simultaneously? Enclosing the two definitions of the class in separate namespaces overcomes this problem.

```
/*Beginning of A1.h*/
namespace A1                            //beginning of a namespace A1
{
    class A
    {
    };
}                                       //end of a namespace A1
/*End of A1.h*/

/*Beginning of A2.h*/
namespace A2                            //beginning of a namespace A2
{
    class A
    {
    };
}                                       //end of a namespace A2
/*End of A2.h*/
```

Now, the two definitions of the class are enveloped in two different namespaces. The corresponding namespace, followed by the scope resolution operator, must be prefixed to the name of the class while referring to it anywhere in the source code. Thus, the ambiguity encountered in the above listing can be overcome. A revised definition of the main() function from Listing 2.43 illustrates this (Listing 2.44).

Listing 2.44   Enclosing classes in namespaces prevents pollution of the global namespace

```
/*Beginning of multiDef02.cpp*/
#include"A1.h"
#include"A2.h"
void main()
{
    A1::A AObj1;                        //OK: AObj1 is an object of the class
                                        //defined in A1.h
    A2::A AObj2;                        //OK: AObj2 is an object of the class
                                        //defined in A2.h

}
/*End of multiDef02.cpp*/
```

Qualifying the name of the class with that of the namespace can be cumbersome. The `using` directive enables us to make the class definition inside a namespace visible so that qualifying the name of the referred class by the name of the namespace is no longer required. Listing 2.45 shows how this is done.

Listing 2.45   The `using` directive makes qualifying of referred class names by names of enclosing namespaces unnecessary

```
/*Beginning of using.cpp*/
#include"A1.h"
#include"A2.h"
void main()
{
    using namespace A1;
    A AObj1;                    //OK: AObj1 is an object of the class
                                //defined in A1.h
    A2::A AObj2;                //OK: AObj2 is an object of the class
                                //defined in A2.h

}
/*Beginning of using.cpp*/
```

However, we must note that the `using` directive brings back the global namespace pollution that the namespaces mechanism was supposed to remove in the first place! The last line in the above listing compiles only because the class name was qualified by the name of the namespace.

Some namespaces have long names. Qualifying the name of a class that is enclosed within such a namespace, with the name of the namespace, is cumbersome. See Listing 2.46.

Listing 2.46   Cumbersome long names for namespace

```
/*Beginning of longName01.cpp*/
namespace a_very_very_long_name
{
    class A
    {
    };
}

void main()
{
    a_very_very_long_name::A A1;     //cumbersome long name
}
/*End of longName01.cpp*/
```

Assigning a suitably short alias to such a long namespace name solves the problem as illustrated in Listing 2.47.

Listing 2.47   Providing an alias for a namespace

```
/*Beginning of longName02.cpp*/
namespace a_very_very_long_name
{
    class A
    {
    };
```

```
}
namespace x = a_very_very_long_name;    //declaring an
                                        //alias
void main()
{
   x::A A1;                             //convenient short name
}
/*End of longName02.cpp*/
```

Aliases provide an incidental benefit also. Suppose an alias has been used at a number of places in the source code. Changing the alias declaration so that it stands as an alias for a different namespace will make each reference of the enclosed class refer to a completely different class. Suppose an alias X refers to a namespace 'N1'.

```
namespace X = N1;                       //declaring an alias
```

Further, suppose that this alias has been used extensively in the source code.

```
X::A AObj;         //AObj is an object of class A that is
                   //enclosed in namespace N1.
AObj.f1();         //f1() is a member function of the above
                   //class.
```

If the declaration of alias X is modified as follows ('N2' is also a namespace)

```
namespace X = N2;                       //modifying the alias
```

then, all existing qualifications of referred class names that use X would now refer to class A that is contained in namespace 'N2'. Of course, the lines having such references would compile only if *both* of the namespaces, 'N1' and 'N2', contain a class named A, and if these two classes have the *same* interface.

For keeping the explanations simple, classes that have been given as examples in the rest of this book are not enclosed in namespaces.

2.6 Nested Inner Classes

A class can be defined inside another class. Such a class is known as a *nested class*. The class that contains the nested class is known as the *enclosing class*. Nested classes can be defined in the private, protected, or public portions of the enclosing class (protected access specifier is explained in the chapter on inheritance).

In Listing 2.48, class B is defined in the private section of class A.

Listing 2.48 Nested classes

```
/*Beginning of nestPrivate.h*/
class A
{
   class B
   {
      /*
         definition of class B
      */
   };
   /*
      definition of class A
   */
```

```
};
/*End of nestPrivate.h*/
```

In Listing 2.49, class B is defined in the public section of class A.

Listing 2.49   A public nested class

```
/*Beginning of nestPublic.h*/
class A
{
  public:
    class B
    {
      /*
        definition of class B
      */
    };
    /*
      definition of class A
    */
};
/*End of nestPublic.h*/
```

A nested class is created if it does not have any relevance outside its enclosing class. By defining the class as a nested class, we avoid a *name collision*. In Listings 2.48 and 2.49, even if there is a class B defined as a global class, its name will *not* clash with the nested class B.

The size of objects of an enclosing class is not affected by the presence of nested classes. See Listing 2.50.

Listing 2.50   Size of objects of the enclosing class

```
/*Beginning of nestSize.cpp*/
#include<iostream.h>

class A
{
    int x;
  public:
    class B
    {
        int y;
    };
};

void main()
{
    cout<<sizeof(int)<<endl;
    cout<<sizeof(A)<<endl;
}
/*End of nestSize.cpp*/
```

Output
```
4
4
```

How are the member functions of a nested class defined? Member functions of a nested class can be defined outside the definition of the enclosing class. This is done by prefixing the function name with the name of the enclosing class followed by the scope resolution operator. This, in turn, is followed by the name of the nested class followed again by the scope resolution operator. This is illustrated by Listing 2.51.

Listing 2.51   Defining member functions of nested classes

```
/*Beginning of nestClassDef.h*/
class A
{
    public:
    class B
    {
        public:
            void BTest();                //prototype only
    };
    /*
        definition of class A
    */
};
/*End of nestClassDef.h*/

/*Beginning of nestClassDef.cpp*/
#include"nestClassDef.h"
void A::B::BTest()
{
    //definition of A::B::BTest() function
}
/*
    definitions of the rest of the functions of class B
*/
/*End of nestClassDef.cpp*/
```

A nested class may be only prototyped within its enclosing class and defined later. Again, the name of the enclosing class followed by the scope resolution operator is required. See Listing 2.52.

Listing 2.52   Defining a nested class outside the enclosing class

```
/*Beginning of nestClassDef.h*/
class A
{
    class B;                         //prototype only
};

class A::B
{
    /*
        definition of the class B
    */
};
/*End of nestClassDef.h*/
```

Objects of the nested class are defined outside the member functions of the enclosing class in much the same way (by using the name of the enclosing class followed by the scope resolution operator).

```
A::B B1;
```

However, the above line will compile only if class B is defined within the `public` section of class A. Otherwise, a compile-time error will result.

An object of the nested class can be used in any of the member functions of the enclosing class without the scope resolution operator. Moreover, an object of the nested class can be a member of the enclosing class. In either case, only the public members of the object can be accessed unless the enclosing class is a friend of the nested class. See Listing 2.53.

Listing 2.53 Declaring objects of the nested class in the member functions of the enclosing class

```
/*Beginning of nestClassObj.h*/
class A
{
    class B
    {
      public:
                                        void BTest();       //prototype only
    };
      B B1;
  public:
      void ATest();
};
/*End of nestClassObj.h*/

/*Beginning of nestClassObj.cpp*/
#include"nestClassObj.h"

void A::ATest()
{
   B1.BTest();
   B B2;
   B2.BTest();
}
/*End of nestClassObj.cpp*/
```

Member functions of the nested class can access the non-static public members of the enclosing class through an object, a pointer, or a reference only. An illustrative example follows in Listing 2.54.

Listing 2.54 Accessing non-static members of the enclosing class in member functions of the nested class.

```
/*Beginning of enclClassObj.h*/
class A
{
  public:
      void ATest();
      class B
      {
        public:
                                        void BTest(A&);
                                        void BTest1();
      };
};
/*End of enclClassObj.h*/
```

```
/*Beginning of enclClassObj.cpp*/
#include"enclClassObj.h"

void A::B::BTest(A& ARef)
{
    ARef.ATest();                        //OK
}

void A::B::BTest1()
{
    ATest();                             //ERROR!!
}
/*End of enclClassObj.cpp*/
```

It can be observed that an error is produced when a direct access is made to a member of the enclosing class through a function of the nested class. This is as it should be. After all, *creation of an object of the nested class does not cause an object of the enclosing class to be created*. The classes are nested to merely control the visibility. Since 'A::B::BTest()' function will be called with respect to an object of class B, a direct access to a member of the enclosing class A can be made through an object of that class only.

By default, the enclosing class and the nested class do not have any access rights to each other's private data members. They can do so only if they are friends to each other.

Summary

Classes have both member data and member functions. Member functions can be given *exclusive rights* to access data members. Member functions and member data can be private, protected, or public. The **struct** keyword has been redefined in C++. Apart from member data, structures in C++ can have member functions also. In a class, members are *private* by default. In a structure, members are *public* by default.

The scope resolution operator is used to separate the class definition from the definitions of the member functions. The class definition can be placed in a header file. Member functions, with the aid of scope resolution operator, can be placed in a separate implementation file.

The **this** pointer is implicitly inserted by the compiler, as a leading formal argument, in the prototype and in the definition of each member function of each class. When a member function is called with respect to an object, the compiler inserts the address of the calling object as a leading parameter to the function call. Consequently, the **this** pointer, which exists as the implicit leading formal argument in all member functions, always points at the object with respect to which the member function has been called.

Access to member data and member functions from within member functions is resolved by the **this** pointer. The **this** pointer is a *constant pointer in case of non-constant member functions* and a *constant pointer to a constant in case of constant member functions*.

If the operand on its right is a data member, then the object-to-member access operator (.) behaves just as it does in C language. However, if it is a member function of a class whereas an object of the same class is its left-hand side operand, then the compiler simply passes the *address of the object* as an implicit leading parameter to the function call.

Similarly, if the operand on its right is a data member, then the pointer-to-member access operator (->) behaves just as it does in C language. However, if it is a member function of a class whereas a pointer to an object of the same class is its left-hand side operand, then the compiler simply passes *the value of the pointer* as an implicit leading parameter to the function call. Member functions can call each other. Calls are resolved through the **this** pointer. Member functions can be overloaded. Default values can be given to the formal arguments of member functions.

Programs having inline functions tend to run faster than equivalent programs with non-inline functions. A function is declared inline either by defining it inside a class or by declaring it inside a class and defining it outside with the keyword `inline`. This feature should be used sparingly. Otherwise, the increased size of the executable can slow it down.

If required, member functions can be declared as constant functions to prevent even an inadvertent change in the data members. A function can be declared as a constant function by suffixing its prototype and the header of its definition by the keyword `const`.

A mutable data member is never constant. It is modifiable inside constant functions also. A friend function is a non-member function that has a special right to access private data members of objects of the class of which it is a friend. This does not really negate the philosophy of OOPS. A friend function still needs to be declared inside the class of which it is a friend. The advantage that a friend function provides is that it is not called with respect to an object.

A global non-member function can be declared as a friend to a class. Member function of one class can be declared as a friend function of another. An entire class can be declared as a friend of another too. A class or a function is declared friend to a desired class by prototyping it in the class and prefixing the prototype with the keyword `friend`.

Only *one* copy of a static data member exists for the entire class. This is in contrast to non-static data members that exist separately in *each* object. Static data members are used to keep data that relates to the entire set of objects that exist at any given point during the program's execution. A data member is declared as a static member of a class by prefixing its declaration in the class by the keyword `static`.

Static member functions can access *static data members only*. They can be called without declaring any objects. A member function is declared as a static member of a class by prefixing its declaration in the class by the keyword `static`.

Objects can appear as local variables inside functions. They can also be passed by value or by reference to functions. Finally, they can be returned by value or by reference from functions.

Arrays of objects can be created. Arrays can be created inside classes also. One class can be defined inside another class. Such a class is known as a *nested class*. The class that contains the nested class is known as the *enclosing class*. Nested classes can be defined in the private, protected, or public portions of the enclosing class.

Namespaces enable the C++ programmer to prevent pollution of the global namespace. They help prevent name classes.

Key Terms

class
private access specifier
public access specifier
objects
scope resolution operator
the `this` pointer
data abstraction
arrow operator
overloaded member functions
default values for formal arguments of member functions

inline member functions
constant member functions
mutable data members
friend non-member functions
friend classes
friend member functions
friends as bridges
static member data
static member functions
namespaces
nested classes

Exercises

1. How does the class construct enable data security?
2. What is the use of the scope resolution operator?
3. What is the `this` pointer? Where and why does the compiler insert it implicitly?
4. What is data abstraction? How is it implemented in C++?
5. Which operator is used to access a class member with respect to a pointer?

6. What is the difference between a mutable data member and a static data member?

7. Describe the two ways in which a member function can be declared as an inline function.

8. How can a global non-member function be declared as a friend to a class?

9. What is the use of declaring a class as a friend of another?

10. Explain why friend functions do not contradict the principles of OOPS.

11. Explain why static data members should be explicitly declared outside the class.

12. Why should static data members be defined in the implementation files only?

13. What is the use of static member functions?

14. How do namespaces help in preventing pollution of the global namespace?

15. What is a nested class? What is its use?

16. How are the member functions of a nested class defined outside the definition of the enclosing class?

17. State true or false.

(a) Structures in C++ can have member functions also.

(b) Structure members are private by default.

(c) The this pointer is always a constant pointer.

(d) Member functions cannot be overloaded.

(e) Default values can be given to the formal arguments of member functions.

(f) Only constant member function can be called for constant objects.

(h) The keyword friend should appear in the prototype as well as the definition of the function that is being declared as a friend.

(i) A friend function can be prototyped in only the public section of the class.

(j) Friendship is not transitive.

(k) A static data member can be of the same type as the class of which it is a member.

(l) The size of objects of an enclosing class is affected by the presence of nested classes.

(m) An object of the nested class can be used in any of the member functions of the enclosing class without the scope resolution operator.

(n) An object of the nested class cannot be a member of the enclosing class.

(o) Public members of the nested class's object

which have been declared in a function of the enclosing class can always be accessed.

18. Your compiler should provide a structure and associated functions to fetch the current system date. Suppose the name of the structure is date_d and the name of the associated functions to fetch the current system date is getSysDate().

Create a class with a name that is similar to the above structure. This class should contain a variable of the above structure as its private data member. Introduce a member function in the class that calls the associated function of the date structure. Thus, create a wrapper class and make an available structure safe to use.

```
class date_D    //a wrapper class
{
    date_d d;
  public:
    void getSysDate();
};

void date_D::getSysDate()
{
getSysDate(&d); //calling the associ-
                    ated function from
                    //the member function
}
```

Also, write a small test program to test the above class.

19. Create a class named Distance_mks. This class should be similar to the class Distance, except for the following differences:

- The data members of this new class would be iMeters (type integer; for representing the meters portion of a distance) and fCentimeters (type float; for representing the centimeters portion of a distance) instead of iFeet and fInches.

- Suitably designed member functions to work upon the new data members should replace the ones that we have seen for the class Distance. The member functions should ensure that the fCentimeters of no object should ever exceed 100.

3

Dynamic Memory Management

O
V
E
R
V
I
E
W

This chapter explains the use of tools that are available in C++ for dynamic memory management. It begins with a brief explanation of static memory management and its limitation. This is followed by an elucidation of the mechanism of dynamic memory management.

The middle portion of the chapter deals with the use and usage of the new operator and the delete operator. Methods for allocating and deallocating memory for single objects and array of objects are explained.

The chapter also explains how the size of a dynamically allocated memory block is stored.

The last portion of the chapter explains the use of the set_new_handler() function for specifying our own new handler.

3.1 Introduction

Let us have an overview of static memory management. Memory for program variables gets allocated and deallocated during run time only. For example, we write

```
int x;
```

in some function in the source code. When the source code containing this statement (apart from the other statements) is compiled and linked, an executable file is generated. Besides containing equivalent instructions for the other statements, the executable file also contains the equivalent instructions for this statement. When the executable file is executed, all the instructions contained inside it, including the ones to allocate memory for 'x', are executed. *Thus, memory gets allocated for 'x' during run time*. This is known as static memory allocation (although memory gets allocated during run time only).

The compiler writes instructions in the executable to deallocate the memory previously allocated for 'x' when it encounters the end of the function, in which 'x' was declared, in the source code. When the executable file is executed, all instructions contained inside it including the ones to deallocate memory for 'x' are executed. *Thus, memory for 'x' gets deallocated during run time*. This is known as static memory deallocation (although memory gets deallocated during run time only).

Static allocation and deallocation of memory has a limitation. It is rigid. The programmers are forced to predict the total amount of data the program will utilize. They write statements to declare pre-calculated amounts of memory. During run time, if more memory is required, static memory allocation cannot fulfill the need. Once a certain memory block is no longer of any use to the program, memory allocated to it cannot be released immediately. The memory will continue to be held up until the end of the block in which the variable was created.

Dynamic memory management is a feature provided and supported in C and C++. It overcomes the drawbacks of static memory allocation. Just like in static memory allocation and deallocation, in dynamic memory allocation and deallocation also, memory gets allocated and deallocated during *run time* only. However, the decisions to do so can be taken *dynamically in response to the requirements arising during run time itself.*

If the program is running and the user indicates the need to feed in more data, a memory block sufficient to hold the additional amount of data is immediately allocated. For this, code utilizing the relevant functions and operators provided by C and C++ has to be explicitly written in the source code. Again, once a certain block of memory is no longer required, it can immediately be returned to the OS. For this again, code utilizing the relevant functions and operators provided by C and C++ has to be explicitly written in the source code. The OS can then allocate the deallocated memory block if the need arises.

3.2 Dynamic Memory Allocation

Dynamic memory allocation is achieved in C through the `malloc()`, `calloc()`, and `realloc()` functions. In C++, it is achieved through the `new` operator. An illustrative example (Listing 3.1) and its explanation follow.

Listing 3.1   Using the new operator for dynamic memory allocation

```
/*Beginning of dynamic.cpp*/
#include<iostream.h>
void main()
{
    int * iPtr;
    iPtr=new int;
    *iPtr=10;
    cout<<*iPtr<<endl;
}
/*End of dynamic.cpp*/
```

Output

10

The word `new` is a keyword in C++. It is an operator. It takes a predefined data type as an operand (`int` in Listing 3.1). It then allocates memory to hold one value of the data type that is passed as a parameter to it in the heap (four bytes in Listing 3.1). Finally, it returns the address of the allocated block. This address need not be explicitly typecast since the `new` operator returns the address with the correct cast (`int *` in this case). This address can then be stored in a pointer of an appropriate type (`iPtr` in this call). The allocated block of memory can then be accessed through the pointer. See Figure 3.1(a).

Statement: int * iptr;

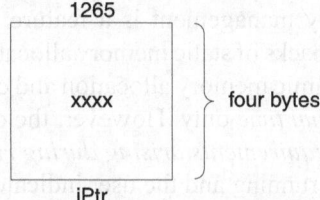

Four bytes get allocated for **iPtr** containing junk
value at the bytes with addresses from **1265** to **1268** (say).

Figure 3.1(a)   Dynamic memory allocation

Statement: iptr = new int;

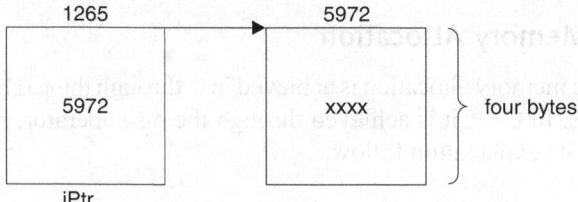

Figure 3.1(b)   Dynamic memory allocation

The new operator allocates memory in the heap to hold one integer-type value. Suppose, the block from the byte with address 5972 to the byte with address 5975 gets allocated. The new operator returns the base address of the block (5972). This value gets stored in iPtr. See Figure 3.1(b).

Statement: *iPtr = 10;

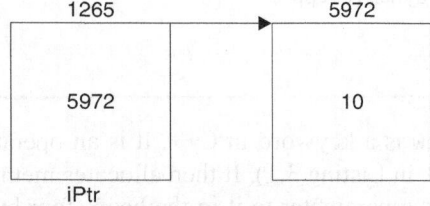

Figure 3.1(c)   Dynamic memory allocation

iPtr is dereferenced and the value 10 gets written into the memory block of four bytes at which iPtr points (5972 to 5975).

Statement: `cout<<*iPtr<<endl;`

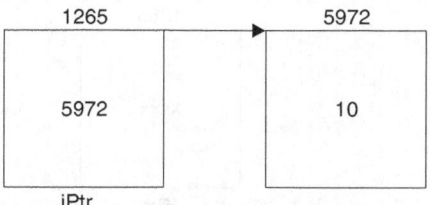

iPtr is again dereferenced and the value (10) stored in the
memory block to which iPtr points (5972 to 5975) is read.

Figure 3.1(d) Dynamic memory allocation using the new operator

The general syntax of the new operator is

    <pointer> = new <data_type>;

The new operator can be used to create multiple blocks of memory also. This is shown in Listing 3.2. Figures 3.2(a) and (b) explain the statements.

Listing 3.2 Creating an array dynamically using the new operator

```
/*Beginning of DynArray1.cpp*/
#include<iostream.h>
#define SIZE 10
void main()
{
   int * iPtr;
   iPtr = new int[SIZE];
   for(int i=0;i<SIZE;i++)
      iPtr[i]=i;                    //can write cin>>iPtr[i]; also
   for(int j=0;j<SIZE;j++)
      cout<<iPtr[j]<<endl;
}
/*End of DynArray1.cpp*/
```

Output
0
1
2
3
4
5
6
7
8
9

Statement: int * iPtr;

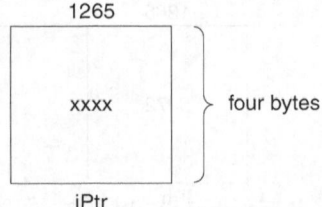

Four bytes get allocated for **iPtr** containing junk value at the bytes with addresses from, say, 1265 to 1268.

Figure 3.2(a) Memory allocation for an array using **iPtr**

Statement: iPtr = new int[SIZE]; //SIZE=10

The new operator allocates memory in the heap to hold ten integer type values [see Figure 3.2(b)]. If the block from the byte with address 5972 to the byte with address 6012 gets allocated, the new operator returns the base address of the block 5972. This value gets stored in iPtr. After this, iPtr is simply dereferenced within the for loop by using the subscript operator. All the elements of the array at whose first element the pointer is pointing are accessed. The syntax for using the new operator to create an array is as follows:

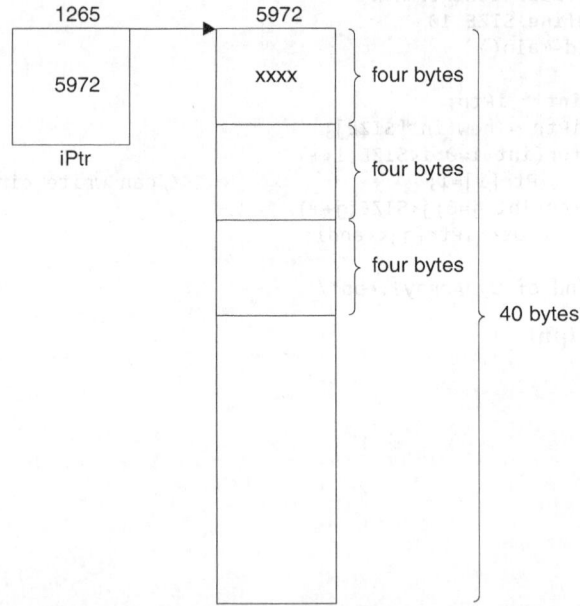

Figure 3.2(b) Dynamically allocating memory for an array using the new operator

```
<pointer> = new <data_type>[<number_of_elements>];
```

Now, let us make the program interactive to exploit the power of the new operator. The value that we passed inside the subscript while allocating the memory using the new operator can be that of a variable. In Listing 3.3, we will first ask the user to enter the size of the array and store it in a variable. Next, we will pass the variable into the subscript while using the new operator to allocate memory. The address returned by the new operator will then be stored in a pointer. Finally, we will access the array thus created through the pointer. The program is shown in Listing 3.3.

Listing 3.3 Creating an array dynamically when its size is specified during run time

```cpp
/*Beginning of DynArray2.cpp*/
#include<iostream.h>
void main()
{
    int * iPtr;
    unsigned int iSize;
    cout<<"Enter the size of the array : ";
    cin>>iSize;
    iPtr = new int[iSize];
    for(int i=0;i<iSize;i++)
    {
        cout<<"Enter the value for element "<<i+1<<" : ";
        cin>>iPtr[i];
    }
    for(int j=0;j<iSize;j++)
        cout<<iPtr[j]<<endl;
}
/*End of DynArray2.cpp*/
```

Output
Enter the size of the array : **3**<*enter*>
Enter the value for element 1 : **12**<*enter*>
Enter the value for element 2 : **7**<*enter*>
Enter the value for element 3 : **19**<*enter*>
12
7
19

We must note that the new operator has enabled us to allocate memory *dynamically*. In Listing 3.3, memory is getting allocated during run time (just like in static memory allocation). However, the amount of memory to be allocated is being decided during run time itself.

Same methodology can be applied for dynamically creating arrays of the other predefined fundamental data types. Arrays of class objects can also be created dynamically in the same way. Listing 3.4 is a case in point.

Listing 3.4 Creating an array of objects dynamically during run time

```cpp
/*Beginning of DynDist.cpp*/
#include<iostream.h>
#include"Distance.h"
void main()
{
    Distance * dPtr;
    unsigned int iSize;
    cout<<"Enter the number of elements : ";
    cin>>iSize;
    dPtr = new Distance[iSize];
    for(int i=0;i<iSize;i++)
```

```
    {
        cout<<"Enter the feet : ";
        cin>>a;
        cout<<"Enter the inches : ";
        cin>>b;
        dPtr[i].setFeet(a);
        dPtr[i].setInches(b);
    }
    for(int j=0;j<iSize;j++)
    {
        cout<<dPtr[j].getFeet()<<" "
            <<dPtr[j].getInches()<<endl;
    }
}
/*End of DynDist.cpp*/
```

Output
Enter the number of elements : **3**<*enter*>
Enter the feet : **1**<*enter*>
Enter the inches : **1.1**<*enter*>
Enter the feet : **2**<*enter*>
Enter the inches : **2.2**<*enter*>
Enter the feet : **3**<*enter*>
Enter the inches : **3.3**<*enter*>
1 1.1
2 2.2
3 3.3

In Listings 3.3 and 3.4, the user is explicitly asked to enter the size of the array he/she wants to create. This is a little abrupt. Requirements for more memory may arise during run time in a more subtle fashion (say, while creating data structures such as linked lists, trees, etc.). Nevertheless, the basic technique of using the new operator remains the same.

3.3 Dynamic Memory Deallocation

We already know that a block of memory allocated dynamically can be deallocated dynamically. Once it is not in use any more, a dynamically allocated block of memory should definitely be returned to the OS.

In C, dynamic memory deallocation is achieved through the free() function. Dynamically allocated blocks of memory can be returned to the OS in C++ through the delete operator.

What is the need to deallocate a dynamically allocated block of memory? What will happen if a dynamically allocated block of memory is not returned to the OS? These questions are answered by Listing 3.5 and the explanatory figure (Figure 3.3) that follows.

Listing 3.5 Memory leak

```
/*Beginning of memleak.cpp*/
#include<iostream.h>
void abc();
void main()
{
    abc();                              //call to the abc() function
    /*
        rest of the main() function
```

```
        */
}
void abc()
{
    int * iPtr;
    iPtr = new int;
    /*
        rest of the abc() function
    */
}
/*End of memleak.cpp*/
```

The following statement executes from within the abc() function which is called from the main() function.

Statement: iPtr = new int;

As a result, the following scenario emerges.

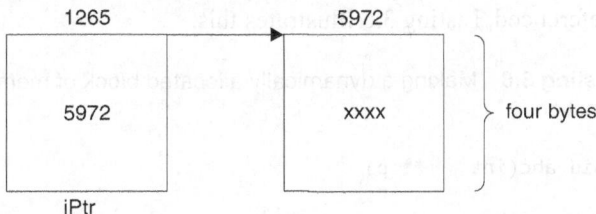

The new operator allocates memory in the heap to hold one integer type value. Suppose the block from the byte with address 5972 to the byte with address 5975 gets allocated. The new operator returns the base address of the block 5972. This value gets stored in iPtr.

After abc() finishes execution, memory for iPtr itself is deallocated. But, the memory in the heap area remains locked up as an orphan (unreferenced) locked up block of memory.

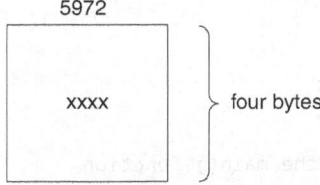

Figure 3.3   Memory leak

As it can be seen from Figure 3.3, after the abc() function terminates, four bytes of memory are lost. Since they have not been returned to the OS, they remain locked up. This is known as a *memory leak*. If more memory is required, the OS will *not* allocate this block of memory. Moreover, this block of memory cannot be accessed since the only pointer (iPtr) that was pointing at it has itself been removed from the stack.

This block of memory that is no longer of any use can and should be returned to the OS. A dynamically allocated block of memory can be deallocated by passing the pointer pointing to it as an operand to the delete operator. For example, the following statement should be inserted before the end of the abc() function in Listing 3.5.

```
delete iPtr;
```

The foregoing statement is executed just before the abc() function terminates. The memory block at which iPtr points gets deallocated (it becomes available for the OS). Next, the memory allocated for iPtr itself is deallocated. Finally, the function terminates. Thus, memory leak is prevented.

When the new operator is used, the OS blocks a block of memory of the requested size. The OS never allocates this particular block of memory in response to subsequent requests for memory blocks as long as this block of memory is not deallocated. When the delete operator is used on the pointer that points at this block of memory, the memory block gets deallocated, that is, freed and made available for the OS. In other words, the OS, in response to subsequent requests for memory blocks, may allocate this freed block of memory.

A dynamically allocated block of memory remaining locked up is frequently a blessing. The fact that the block of memory locked up by the code in a certain function persists even after the function terminates is frequently desirable. A called function may allocate a memory block and a pointer local to the calling function can be made to point at it. Even after the called function terminates, the dynamically allocated block of memory will remain persistent, but not unreferenced. Listing 3.6 illustrates this.

Listing 3.6   Making a dynamically allocated block of memory available to the calling function

```
void abc(int    ** p)
{
    /*
        some complex algorithm
    */
    *p = new int;
    /*
        rest of the abc() function
    */
}
void main()
{
    int * iPtr;
    abc(&iPtr);
    /*
        rest of the main() function
    */
}
```

In Listing 3.6, the address of iPtr that is local to the calling function (main() function) is passed as a parameter to the called function (abc() function). Its value needs to be changed by the abc() function. Its address is stored in a double pointer (a pointer to a pointer has to be a double pointer). A block of memory is allocated and its address is stored in iPtr by dereferencing the pointer that points at it. It is our obvious desire that the dynamically allocated block of memory persists even after the abc() function terminates. After the abc() function terminates, iPtr that is a local variable in the calling function will point at the dynamically allocated block of memory.

The general syntax of the delete operator to deallocate a single block of memory is:

```
delete <pointer>;
```

In the foregoing listings, the memory block was deallocated only at the end of the functions that allocated it. However, dynamic memory deallocation is usually conditional (Listing 3.7).

Listing 3.7   C++ allows deallocation of memory as and when required

```
void abc(int ** p)
{
    if(memory_not_required)
    {
        delete *p;
        *p = NULL;
    }
    /*
        rest of the abc() function
    */
}
```

A misconception about the delete operator is due to the commonly used phrase 'deleting the pointer'. An uninitiated reader may think that the memory being occupied by the pointer itself gets removed if the delete operator is used on the pointer. In reality, nothing of this sort happens.

When the delete operator is used on a pointer, the pointer continues to occupy its own block of memory and continues to have the same value that is the address of the first byte of the block of memory that has just got deallocated. Thus, the pointer continues to point at the same block of memory. This will lead to run-time errors if the pointer is dereferenced.

We can see in Listing 3.7 that the pointer being pointed at by 'p' was deliberately nullified after the memory that the pointer was pointing at had been deallocated. This is a very common practice to indicate that the pointer (the pointer whose address is passed from the calling function in this case) no longer points at a valid dynamically allocated block of memory. In other words, it is highly desirable that *either the pointer points at a valid block of memory or be NULL*. It is not possible to ensure this due to the low level of representation of pointers. A pointer is unlikely to be NULL at the time of its creation. But that does *not* mean that the value it contains is the address of some valid allocated block of memory. *There is no guaranteed initialization of data*. This problem is solved by the use of constructors, which have been discussed in Chapter 4.

A multiple block of memory is deallocated by suffixing the delete operator with an empty pair of square brackets followed by the pointer that points at the multiple block of memory, as shown in Listing 3.8.

Listing 3.8   Deallocating memory that was allocated for an array

```
int * iPtr;
….
iPtr = new int[10];
….
delete[] iPtr;
```

If we write delete iPtr instead of delete[] iPtr, only the first four bytes of the block of 40 bytes at which iPtr is pointing, will be deallocated. Using delete[] deallocates the entire block of 40 bytes. The syntax for using the delete operator to deallocate an array is as follows:

```
delete [] <pointer>;
```

The size of the array to be created is passed as a parameter to the new operator. But while deallocating the memory allocated for the array, the size is not passed (the square brackets are empty). Then how does the compiler know how much of memory is to be deallocated? The answer is that when the new operator executes to allocate a block of array, the OS stores the size passed. Figure 3.4 shows the size of the memory block, which is captured during run time, is prefixed to the memory block itself. When the delete operator is used followed by the empty pair of square brackets, the compiler uses the size stored and deallocates the entire block correctly.

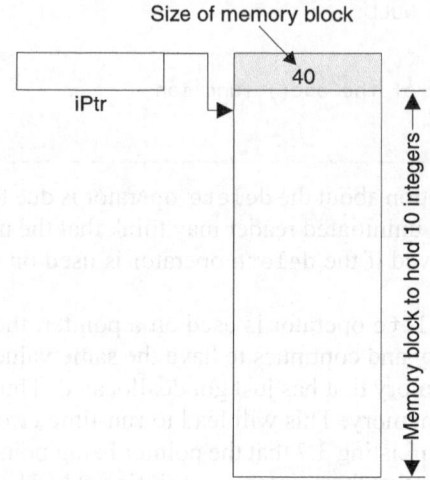

Figure 3.4   Size of the allocated memory is prefixed to the memory block

Blocks of memory containing arrays of other types can also be deallocated similarly. For example, see Listing 3.9.

Listing 3.9   Deallocating memory that was allocated for an array of objects

```
Distance * dPtr;
dPtr = new Distance[5];           //creates an array of 5 objects of
                                  //the class Distance
….

….
delete[] dPtr;                    //de-allocates the memory
                                  //allocated for the entire array
```

3.4 set_new_handler() Function

We already know that the new operator attempts to capture more chunks of memory from the heap during run time. But, what happens if no more memory is available to satisfy this attempt? We get an out-of-memory condition.

The new operator, when faced with an out-of-memory condition, calls a global function and then throws an exception of type bad_alloc (the chapter on exception handling deals with the mechanism of throwing and catching exceptions). This global function is known as the *new handler function*.

We can specify our own new handler function also! We can specify that the new operator, upon encountering an out-of-memory condition, calls a function of our choice. We can do this by calling the `set_new_handler()` function and passing the name of the desired function as a parameter to it. The prototype of the `set_new_handler()` function clarifies this. This prototype is in the `new.h` header file.

```
new_handler set_new_handler(new_handler);
```

Obviously, `new_handler` is a data type. It is a function pointer type. The formal argument of the `set_new_handler()` function is a function pointer. If we pass the name of our desired function as a parameter to the `set_new_handler()` function, all subsequent out-of-memory conditions cause the new operator to call it. Our desired function becomes the new handler. Moreover, when the `set_new_handler()` function is called, it returns a pointer to the *previous new handler function*.

An illustrative example follows in Listing 3.10.

Listing 3.10 Specifying a new handler function

```cpp
/*Beginning of newHandler.cpp*/
#define BIG_NUMBER 9999999
#include<new.h>                          //for set_new_handler() function
void myNewHandler()
{
   /*
      code to handle out-of-memory condition
   */
}
void main()
{
new_handler oldHandler;
//set the function myNewHandler as the new handler

oldHandler = set_new_handler(myNewHandler);
int * p = new int[BIG_NUMBER];      //probably cause out-of-
                                    //memory condition

}
/*End of newHandler.cpp*/
```

If the OS is unable to allocate the requested amount of memory, which is quite likely in Listing 3.10, the new operator fails. The new handler function gets called. The call to the `set_new_handler()` function, just prior to the call to the new operator, has already set the function `myNewHandler` as the new handler. Therefore, the function `myNewHandler` gets called.

An important characteristic of the new operator is that when its request for memory fails, it calls the new handler function *repeatedly* until its request is satisfied. This fact helps in meaningfully defining the new handler function (Listing 3.11).

We can make the new handler function log an error message and then call the `abort()` function.

Listing 3.11 Defining the new handler function

```cpp
void myNewHandler()
{
   //statement to log a suitable error message
   abort();
}
```

The `abort()` function simply terminates the program. We can also throw an exception from within the new handler function. The chapter on exception handling explains the syntax for throwing exceptions and its superiority over calling the `abort()` function.

Another course of action is to replace the existing new handler function by another one. For this, we can call the `set_new_handler()` function from within the existing new handler function and pass the name of the new handler as a parameter to it. Of course, such a call should be preceded by the code that attempts to resolve the out-of-memory condition first. The new handler should be replaced only if this attempt fails. See Listing 3.12.

Listing 3.12   Replacing the existing new handler function

```
#include<new.h>
void myNewHandler()
{
    //make an attempt to resolve the out-of-memory
    //condition
    if(above_attempt_fails)
        set_new_handler(myAnotherNewHandler);
}
```

An interesting way of defining the new handler is to allocate some buffer memory in advance and free it part by part as the need arises.

Summary

Memory is allocated for program variables during *run time* only. In static memory allocation, the amount of memory to be allocated is decided during *compile time* itself. The instance at which each statically allocated variable would get created during the program's execution is also decided during the program's compilation.

On the other hand, the amount of memory to be allocated is decided during *run time* in case of dynamic memory allocation. Moreover, memory can be allocated in response to conditions that arise during *run time*.

C++ provides the `new` operator for allocating memory dynamically. The syntax of the `new` operator for allocating memory for a single block is

`<pointer> = new <data_type>;`

The `new` operator allocates enough memory in the heap area to accommodate one variable of the data type that is passed as its right-hand-side operand. Further, it returns the address of the first byte of this allocated block of memory that can be stored in the pointer on the left-hand-side of the assignment operator as shown in the above statement.

Memory for an array can be allocated by using the `new` operator. The syntax is as follows:

`<pointer> = new <data_type>[<number_of_elements>];`

Again, dynamically allocated memory can be dynamically deallocated in response to conditions that arise during *run time*. Dynamically allocated memory must be deallocated, that is, returned to the Operating System. Otherwise, memory leak would occur.

C++ provides the `delete` operator for deallocating dynamically allocated memory. The syntax of the `delete` operator for deallocating memory earlier allocated for a single block is

`delete <pointer>;`

The `delete` operator deallocates the memory in the heap area that the pointer that is passed as its right-hand-side operand points at.

Memory allocated dynamically for an array can also be deallocated by using the `delete` operator. The syntax is as follows:

`delete [] <pointer>;`

This version is similar to the previous one with the difference that an empty pair of square brackets appears between the **delete** keyword and the name of the pointer. C++ knows the exact number of bytes to be returned. It stores the *size* of the dynamically allocated block in a block of memory that it prefixes to the allocated block of memory itself. The **set_new_handler()** function enables us to set a function of our choice as the new handler function.

Key Terms

static memory allocation
static memory deallocation
dynamic memory allocation
dynamic memory deallocation

new operator
delete operator
set_new_handler() function
new handler function

Exercises

1. What is static memory allocation?
2. When is memory allocated and deallocated in static memory allocation—during compile time, link time, or run time?
3. Under what conditions does static memory allocation become unsuitable?
4. What is dynamic memory allocation? How is it different from static memory allocation?
5. When is memory allocated and deallocated in dynamic memory allocation— during compile time, link time, or run time?
6. Under what conditions does the use of dynamic memory allocation become mandatory?
7. What is the syntax of the **new** operator for
   (a) allocating memory for a single variable?
   (b) allocating memory for an array?
8. Describe how additional blocks of memory can be captured in C++ during run time based upon existing run-time conditions?
9. What is the syntax of the **delete** operator for
   (a) deallocating memory that has been allocated for a single variable?
   (b) deallocating memory that has been allocated for an array?
10. The size of the array, whose memory is to be deallocated, is not passed to the **delete** operator. How does the compiler determine this size?
11. What is memory leak?
12. How can the **delete** operator be used to prevent a memory leak?
13. What is an out-of-memory condition?
14. What is the **new handler**? How is the **set_new_handler()** function used to set our own new handler?

4

Constructors and Destructors

**O
V
E
R
V
I
E
W**

We are already aware of the need to include a member function in our class that initializes the data members of its class to desired default values and gets called automatically for each object that has just got created. Constructors fulfill this need and the first portion of this chapter deals with constructors. Various types of constructors are described in the middle portion of this chapter.

There is also the need to include a member function in our class that gets called automatically for each object that is going out of scope. Destructors fulfill this need and the penultimate portion of this chapter deals with destructors.

Along with the class construct and the access specifiers, constructors and destructors complete the requirements needed to created new data type—safe and efficient data types. This is discussed in the last portion of this chapter.

4.1 Constructors

The constructor gets called automatically for each object that has just got created. It appears as member function of each class, whether it is defined or not. It has the same name as that of the class. It may or may not take parameters. It does not return anything (not even void). The prototype of a constructor is

```
<class name> (<parameter list>);
```

The need for a function that guarantees initialization of member data of a class was felt in Chapter 2. Constructors fulfill this need. Domain constraints on the values of data members can also be implemented via constructors. For example, we want the value of data member finches of each object of the class Distance to be between 0.0 and 12.0 at all times within the lifetime of the object. But this condition may get violated in case an object has just got created. However, introducing a suitable constructor to the class Distance can enforce this condition.

The compiler embeds a call to the constructor for each object when it is created. Suppose a class A has been declared as follows:

```
/*Beginning of A.h*/
class A
{
    int x;
  public:
    void setx(const int=0);
    int getx();
};
/*End of A.h*/
```

Consider the statement that declares an object of a class A in Listing 4.1.

Listing 4.1   Constructor gets called automatically for each object when it is created

```
/*Beginning of AMain.cpp*/
#include"A.h"
void main()
{
   A A1;                          //object declared … constructor called
}
/*End of AMain.cpp*/
```

The statement in the function `main()` in Listing 4.1 is transformed into the following statements.

```
A A1;          //memory allocated for the object (4 bytes)
A1.A();        //constructor called implicitly by compiler
```

The second statement above is then transformed to

```
A(&A1); //see Chapter 2
```

Similarly, the constructor is called for each object that is created dynamically in the heap by the new operator.

```
A * APtr;
APtr = new A;   //constructor called implicitly by compiler
```

The second statement above is transformed into the following two statements.

```
APtr = new A;   //memory allocated
APtr->A();      //constructor called implicitly by compiler
```

The second statement above is then transformed into

```
A(APtr);        //see Chapter 2
```

The foregoing explanations make one thing very clear. Unlike their name, constructors do not actually allocate memory for objects. They are member functions that are called for each object immediately after memory has been allocated for the object.

The constructor is called in this manner separately for each object that is created. But did we prototype and define a public function with the name 'A()' inside the class A? The answer is 'no'. Then how did the above function call get resolved? The compiler prototypes and defines the constructor for us. But what statements does the definition of such a constructor have? The answer is 'nothing'.

Before

```
class A
{
    . . . .
    . . . .
  public:
    . . . .
    . . . .
      //no constructor
};
```

<u>After</u>

```
class A
{
    . . . .
    . . . .
    public:
        A();        //prototype inserted implicitly by compiler
    . . . .
    . . . .
};

A::A()
{
    //empty definition inserted implicitly by compiler
}
```

As we can see, the name of the constructor is the same as the name of the class. Also, the constructor does not return anything. The compiler defines the constructor in order to resolve the call to the constructor that it compulsorily places for the object being created.

For reasons that we will discuss later, it is forbidden to call the constructor explicitly for an existing object as follows.

```
A1.A(); //not legal C++ code!
```

4.1.1 Zero-argument Constructor

We can and should define our own constructors if the need arises. If we do so, the compiler does not define the constructor. However, it still embeds implicit calls to the constructor as before.

The constructor is a non-static member function. It is called for an object. It, therefore, takes the this pointer as a leading formal argument just like other non-static member functions. Correspondingly, the address of the invoking object is passed as a leading parameter to the constructor call. This means that the members of the invoking object can be accessed from within the definition of the constructor.

Let us add our own constructor to class A defined in Listing 4.1 and verify whether the constructor is actually called implicitly by the compiler or not. See Listing 4.2.

Listing 4.2 Constructor gets called for each object when the object is created

```
/*Beginning of A.h*/
class A
{
    int x;
    public:
    A();                            //our own constructor
    void setx(const int=0);
    int getx();
};
/*End of A.h*/

/*Beginning of A.cpp*/
#include"A.h"
#include<iostream.h>
A::A()                              //our own constructor
```

```
{
    cout<<"Constructor of class A called\n";
}
/*
definitions of the rest of the functions of class A
*/
/*End of A.cpp*/

/*Beginning of AMain.cpp*/
#include<iostream.h>
#include"A.h"
void main()
{
    A A1;
    cout<<"End of program\n";
}
/*End of AMain.cpp*/
```

Output

Constructor of class A called
End of program

Let us now define our own constructor for the class `Distance`. What should the constructor do to the invoking object? We would like it to set the values of the `iFeet` and `fInches` data members of the invoking object to 0 and 0.0, respectively. Accordingly, let us add the prototype of the function within the class definition in the header file and its definition in the library source code. See Listing 4.3.

Listing 4.3 A user-defined constructor to implement domain constraints on the data members of a class

```
/*Beginning of Distance.h*/
class Distance
{
    public:
        Distance();              //our own constructor
        /*
            rest of the class Distance
        */
};
/*End of Distance.h*/

/*Beginning of Distance.cpp*/
#include"Distance.h"
Distance::Distance()             //our own constructor
{
    iFeet=0;
    fInches=0.0;
}
/*
    definitions of the rest of the functions of class
    Distance
*/
/*End of Distance.cpp*/

/*Beginning of DistTest.cpp*/
#include<iostream.h>
```

```
#include"Distance.h"
void main()
{
   Distance d1;                         //constructor called
   cout<<d1.getFeet()<<" "<<d1.getInches();
}
/*End of DistTest.cpp*/
```

Output

0 0.0

Now, due to the presence of the constructor within the class `Distance`, there is a guaranteed initialization of the data of all objects of the class `Distance`. Our objective of keeping the `fInches` portion of all objects of the class `Distance` within 12.0 is now fulfilled.

The constructor that we have defined in Listing 4.2 does not take any arguments and is called the zero-argument constructor. The constructor provided by default by the compiler also does not take any arguments. Therefore, the terms 'zero-argument constructor' and 'default constructor' are used interchangeably.

Now, let us start the study of a class that will enable us to abstract character arrays and overcome many of the drawbacks that exist in them. This class will be our running example for explaining most of the concepts of this book. We will define it incrementally. Our purpose is to ultimately define a class that can be used instead of character arrays.

Let us call the class `String`. It will have two data members. Both these data members will be private. The first data member will be a character pointer. It will point at a dynamically allocated block of memory that contains the actual character array. The other data member will be a long unsigned integer that will contain the length of this character array.

```
/*Beginning of String.h*/
class String
{
     char * cStr;             //character pointer to point at
                              //the character array

     long unsigned int len;   //to hold the length of the
                              //character array

     /*
        rest of the class String
     */

};
/*End of String.h*/
```

Suppose 's1' is an object of the class `String` and the string 'abc' has been assigned to it. Diagrammatically this situation can be depicted in Figure 4.1.

The address of the first byte of the memory block containing the string is 101. This value is stored in the 'cStr' portion of 's1'. The address of 's1' is 27.

Also, we would religiously implement the following two conditions on all objects of the class `String`.

- 'cStr' should either point at a dynamically allocated block of memory exclusively allocated for it (that is, no other pointer should point at the block of memory being pointed at by 'cStr') or 'cStr' should be NULL.
- There should be no memory leaks.

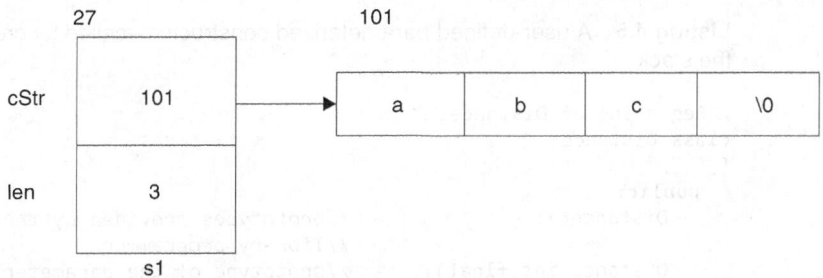

Figure 4.1   Memory layout of an object of the class `String`

Obviously, when an object of the class `String` is created, the 'cStr' portion of the object should be initially set to NULL (and 'len' should be set to 0). Accordingly, the prototype and the definition of the constructor are as shown in Listing 4.4.

Listing 4.4   A user-defined constructor

```
/*Beginning of String.h*/
class String
{
    char * cStr;
    long unsigned int len;
  public:
    String();                       //prototype of the constructor
    /*
       rest of the class String
    */
};
/*End of String.h*/

/*Beginning of String.cpp*/
#include"String.h"
String::String()                    //definition of the constructor
{                                   //When an object is created …
   cStr=NULL;                       //…nullify its pointer and…
   len=0;                           //…set the length as zero.
}
/*
   definitions of the rest of the functions of class String
*/
/*End of String.cpp*/
```

4.1.2 Parameterized Constructors

Constructors take arguments and can, therefore, be overloaded. Suppose, for the class `Distance`, the library programmer decides that while creating an object, the application programmer should be able to pass some initial values for the data members contained in the object. For this, he/she can create a parameterized constructor as shown in Listing 4.5.

Listing 4.5   A user-defined parameterized constructor—called by creating an object in the stack

```
/*Beginning of Distance.h*/
class Distance
{
   public:
      Distance();                   //prototypes provided by the
                                    //library programmer
      Distance(int,float);          //prototype of the parameterized
                                    //constructor
      /*
         rest of the class Distance
      */
};
/*End of Distance.h*/

/*Beginning of Distance.cpp*/
#include"Distance.h"
Distance::Distance()
{
   iFeet=0;
   fInches=0.0;
}
Distance::Distance(int p, float q)
{
   iFeet=p;
   setInches(q);
}
/*
   definitions of the rest of the functions of class
Distance
*/
/*End of Distance.cpp*/

/*Beginning of DistTest1.cpp*/
#include<iostream.h>
#include"Distance.h"
void main()
{
   Distance d1(1,1.1);                   //parameterized constructor called
   cout<<d1.getFeet()<<" "<<d1.getInches();
}
/*End of DistTest1.cpp*/
```

Output
1 1.1

Listing 4.5 demonstrates a user-defined parameterized costructor being called by creating an object in the stack while Listing 4.6 demonstrates a user-defined parameterized constructor being called in the heap.

Listing 4.6   A user-defined parameterized constructor—called by creating an object in the heap

```
/*Beginning of DistTest2.cpp*/
#include<iostream.h>
#include"Distance.h"
```

```
void main()
{
   Distance * dPtr;
   dPtr = new Distance(1,1.1);      // parameterized
                                    //constructor called Output
   cout<<dPtr->getFeet()<<" "<<dPtr->getInches();
}
/*End of DistTest2.cpp*/
```

Output

1 1.1

The first line of the function `main()` in Listing 4.5 and the second line of the `main()` function in Listing 4.6 show the syntax for passing values to the parameterized constructor. The parameterized constructor is prototyped and defined just like any other member function except for the fact that it does not return any value.

We must remember that if the parameterized constructor is provided and the zero-argument constructor is not provided, the compiler will not provide the default constructor. In such a case, the following statement will not compile.

```
Distance d1;                        //ERROR: No matching constructor
```

Just like in other member functions, the formal arguments of the parameterized constructor can be assigned default values. But in that case, the zero-argument constructor should be provided. Otherwise, an ambiguity error will arise when we attempt to create an object without passing any values for the constructor. See Listing 4.7.

Listing 4.7 Default values given to parameters of a parameterized constructor make the zero-argument constructor unnecessary

```
/*Beginning of Distance.h*/
class Distance
{
   public:
      //Distance();zero-argument constructor commented out
      Distance(int=0,float=0.0);    //default values given
      /*
         rest of the class Distance
      */
};
/*End of Distance.h*/
```

If we write,

```
Distance d1;
```

an ambiguity error arises if the zero-argument constructor is also defined. This is because both the zero-argument constructor and the parameterized constructor can resolve this statement.

Let us now create a parameterized constructor for the class `String`. We will also assign a default value for the argument of the parameterized constructor. The constructor would handle the following statements.

```
String s1("abc");
OR
```

```
char * cPtr = "abc";
String s1(cPtr);
OR
char cArr[10] = "abc";
String s1(cArr);
```

In each of these statements, we are essentially passing the base address of the memory block in which the string itself is stored to the constructor.

In the first case, base address of the memory block of four bytes in which the string "abc" is stored is passed as a parameter to the constructor. But the constructor of the class String should be defined in such a manner that 's1.cStr' is made to point at the base of a different memory block of four bytes in the heap area that has been exclusively allocated for the purpose. Only the contents of the memory block, whose base address is passed to the constructor, should be copied into the memory block at which 's1.cStr' points. Finally, 's1.len' should be set to 3. The formal argument of the parameterized constructor for the class String will obviously be a character pointer because the address of a memory block containing a string has to be passed to it. Let us call this pointer 'p'. Then, after the statements String s1 ("abc"); executes, the scenario shown in Figure 4.2 should emerge.

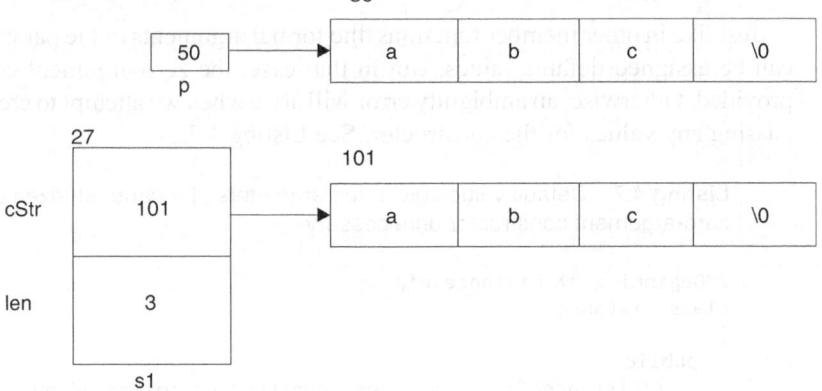

Figure 4.2   Assigning a string to an object of the class String

In Figure 4.2, 'p' is the formal argument of the constructor. The address of the memory block that contains the passed string is 50. This address is passed to the constructor and stored in 'p'. Therefore, the value of 'p' is 50. But the constructor should execute in such a manner that a different block that is sufficiently long to hold the string at which 'p' is pointing should also be allocated dynamically in the heap area (see Figure 4.2). This memory block extends from byte numbers 101 to 104. The base address of this block of memory is then stored in the pointer embedded in 's1'. The string is copied from the memory block at which 'p' points to the memory block at which 's1.cStr' points. Finally, 's1.len' is appropriately set to 3.

In the second case

```
char * cPtr = "abc";
String s1(cPtr);
```

the value of 'cPtr' is passed as a parameter to the constructor. This value is stored in 'p'. Thus, both 'p' and 'cPtr' point at the same place. As in the previous case, the constructor of the class String should be defined in such a manner that 's1.cStr' should be made to point

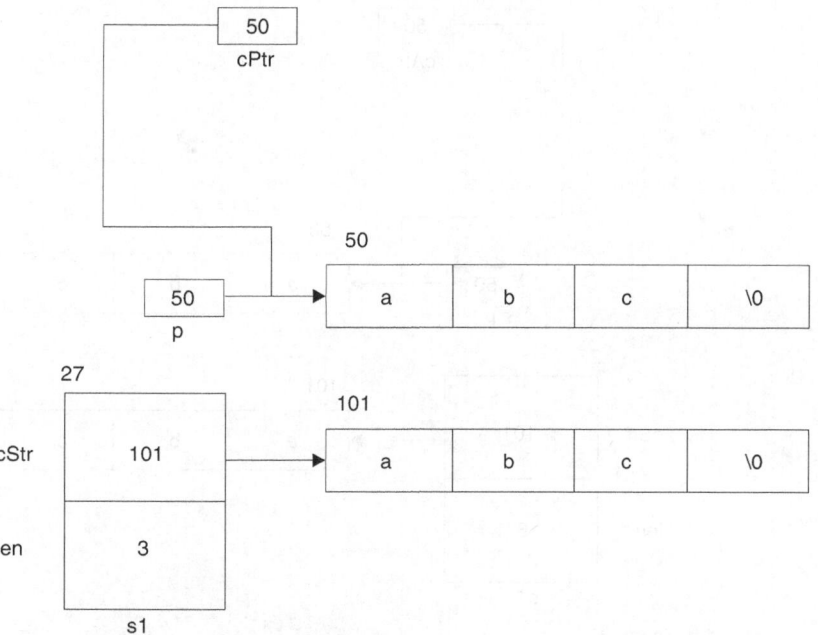

Figure 4.3   Assigning a string to an object of the class `String`

at the base of a different memory block of four bytes that has been exclusively allocated for the purpose. Only the contents of the memory block whose base address is passed to the constructor should be copied into the memory block at which 's1.cStr' points.

In Figure 4.3, 'cPtr' points at the memory block containing the string. In other words, the value of 'cPtr' is the address of the memory block containing the string.

The third case

```
char cArr[10] = "abc";
String s1(cArr);
```

is very similar to the second. In this, we are passing the name of the array as a parameter to the constructor. But we know that the name of an array is itself a fixed pointer that contains the base address of the memory block containing the actual contents of the array. This can be seen in Figure 4.4.

Let us now define the constructor that produces these effects. We must realize that 'p' (the formal argument of the constructor) should be as follows:

```
const char * const
```

First, it should be a constant pointer because throughout the execution of the constructor, it should continue to point at the same memory block. Second, it should be a pointer to a constant because even inadvertently, the library programmer should not dereference it to change the contents of the memory block at which it is pointing. Additionally, we would like to specify a default value for 'p' (NULL) so that there is no need to separately define a zero-argument constructor.

The definition of the class `String` along with the prototype of the constructor and its definition are shown in Listing 4.8.

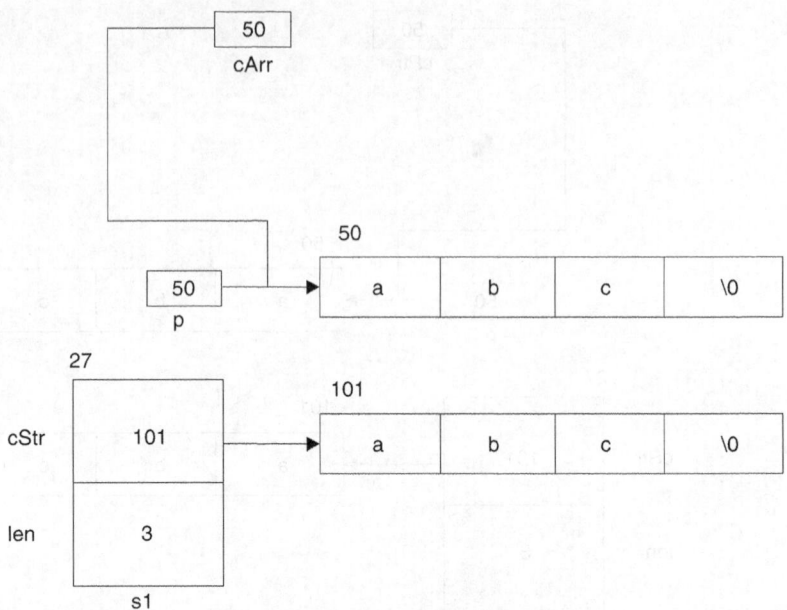

Figure 4.4   Assigning an array to an object of the class `String`

Listing 4.8   A user-defined parameterized constructor for acquiring memory outside the object

```
/*Beginning of String.h*/
class String
{
    char * cStr;
    long unsigned int len;
  public:
    /*no zero-argument constructor*/
    String(const char * const p = NULL);
    const char * getString();
    /*
      rest of the class String
    */
};
/*End of String.h*/

/*Beginning of String.cpp*/
#include"String.h"
#include<string.h>
String::String(const char * const p)
{
    if(p==NULL)        //if default value passed...
    {
        cStr=NULL;     //...nullify
        len=0;
    }
    else               //...otherwise...
    {
        len=strlen(p);
```

```
            cStr=new char[len+1];              //…dynamically allocate a
                                               //separate memory block
            strcpy(cStr,p);                    //…and copy into it
        }
    }

    const char * String::getString()
    {
        return cStr;
    }

    /*
        definitions of the rest of the functions of class String
    */
    /*End of String.cpp*/

    /*Beginning of StringMain.cpp*/
    #include"String.h"
    #include<iostream.h>
    void main()
    {
        String s1("abc");                      //pass a string to the
                                               //parameterized constructor
        cout<<s1.getString()<<endl;            //display the string
    }
    /*End of StringMain.cpp*/
```

Output
abc

Another function called `getString()` has also been introduced to the class `String`. It will enable us to display the string itself. The function returns a `const char *` so that only a pointer to a constant can be equated to a call to this function.

```
    const char * p = s1.getString();
```

Such a pointer will effectively point at the same memory block at which the invoking object's pointer points. As a result of the above statement both 'p' and 's1.cStr' would end up pointing at the same place. Yet it will not be able to change the values contained in the memory block since it is a pointer to a constant. We must note that for securing data that is outside the object itself, extra efforts are required on the part of the library programmer.

We can reprogram the above `main()` function and verify that the newly defined constructor is capable of producing the effects depicted in Figures 4.2, 4.3, and 4.4.

4.1.3 Explicit Constructors

Note that the first statement of the `main()` function in Listing 4.8 calls the constructor of the class `String`. Now, look at the following statement.

```
    String s1 = "abc";
```

The above statement also calls the constructor of the class `String`. The above statement compiles because there is a constructor in the class `String` that takes a string as a parameter. This constructor *implicitly* converts the string "abc" into an object of the class `String`. It is as if the above statement was written as follows (note the cast):

```
    String s1 = (String)"abc";
```

But, we did not provide a cast in the statement that we wrote. Then how did the conversion take place? As mentioned earlier, it is the constructor that is carrying out the conversion for us.

However, if the constructor is declared as an explicit constructor, statements like the one above will not compile. Explicit constructors do not allow implicit conversions like the one that occurred in the above example.

Constructors are declared explicit by prefixing their declarations with the explicit keyword. Let us first look at the syntax for declaring an explicit constructor (see Listing 4.9). We will then look at a program that will illustrate the situation under which we can get the error if a constructor has been declared as an explicit constructor.

Listing 4.9   The explicit constructor

```
/*Beginning of String.h*/
class String
{
    char * cStr;
    long unsigned int len;
public:
    /*no zero-argument constructor*/
    /*
        The next statement declares an explicit constructor.
        Note the explicit keyword.
    */
    explicit String(const char * const p = NULL);
    const char * getString();
    /*
        rest of the class String
    */
};
/*End of String.h*/
```

Let us look at Listing 4.10, which illustrates the error we can get when a constructor is declared as an explicit constructor.

Listing 4.10   Error caused by the explicit constructor

```
/*Beginning of StringMain.cpp*/
#include<iostream.h>
#include"String.h"
void main()
{
    String s1("abc");              //ok: explicit constructor called
    String s2 = "def";             //error: will not compile due to
                                   //the explicit constructor
}
/*End of StringMain.cpp*/
```

Note that the error in the above program will go away if the statement is written as follows:

```
    String s2 = (String)"def";     //ok
```

It is obvious that the explicit constructor is preventing an implicit conversion of string into an object of the class String and is forcing the application programmer to do explicit conversion.

Further note that we need to mention the `explicit` keyword in the declaration of the constructor only. It is not necessary to prefix the definition of the constructor with the `explicit` keyword.

Explicit constructors can prove to be useful for the programmer if he is creating a class for which an implicit conversion by the constructor is undesirable.

4.1.4 Copy Constructor

The copy constructor is a special type of parameterized constructor. As its name implies, it copies one object to another. It is called when an object is created and equated to an existing object at the same time. The copy constructor is called for the object being created. The pre-existing object is passed as a parameter to it. The copy constructor member-wise copies the object passed as a parameter to it into the object for which it is called.

If we do not define the copy constructor for a class, the compiler defines it for us. But in either case, a call is embedded to it under the following three circumstances.

- When an object is created and simultaneously equated to another existing object, the copy constructor is called for the object being created. The object to which this object was equated is passed as a parameter to the copy constructor.

```
A A1;                           //zero-argument/default constructor called
A A2=A1;                        //copy constructor called
```

or

```
A A2(A1);                       //copy constructor called
```

or

```
A * APtr = new A(A1);           //copy constructor called
```

Here, the copy constructor is called for 'A2' and for 'Aptr' while 'A1' is passed as a parameter to the copy constructor in both cases.

- When an object is created as a non-reference formal argument of a function. The copy constructor is called for the argument object. The object passed as a parameter to the function is passed as a parameter to the copy constructor.

```
void abc(A);
A A1;                           //zero-argument/default constructor called
abc(A1);                        //copy constructor called

void abc(A A2)
{
    /*
      definition of abc()
    */
}
```

Here again the copy constructor is called for 'A2' while 'A1' is passed as a parameter to the copy constructor.

- When an object is created and simultaneously equated to a call to a function that returns an object. The copy constructor is called for the object that is equated to the function call. The object returned from the function is passed as a parameter to the constructor.

```
A abc()
{
```

```
        A A1;              //zero-argument/default constructor called
        /*
          remaining definition of abc()
        */
        return A1;
      }
      A A2=abc();    //copy constructor called
```

Once more, the copy constructor is called for 'A2' while 'A1' is passed as a parameter to the copy constructor.

The prototype and the definition of the default copy constructor defined by the compiler are as follows.

```
      class A
      {
        public:
          A(A&);       //the default copy constructor
      };

      A::A(A& AObj)    //the default copy constructor
      {
        *this=AObj;      //copies the passed object into the invoking
                         //object
      }
```

As is obvious, the default copy constructor does exactly what it is supposed to do—it copies. The statement

```
      A A2=A1;
```

is converted as follows:

```
      A A2;            //memory allocated for A2
      A2.A(A1);        //copy constructor is called for A2 and A1 is
                       //passed as a parameter to it
```

This last statement is then transformed to

```
      A(&A2,A1);       //see the section on 'this' pointer in Chapter 2
```

When the above statement executes, 'AObj' (the formal argument in the copy constructor) becomes a reference to 'A1', whereas the this pointer points at 'A2' (the invoking object). Similarly, the other statements where the object is created as a formal argument or is returned from a function can also be explained.

But why does the compiler create the formal argument of the default copy constructor as a reference object? And when the compiler does define a copy constructor in the expected way, then why should we define one on our own? Both these questions are answered now.

First, let us find out why objects are passed by reference to the copy constructor. Suppose the formal argument ('AObj') of the copy constructor is not a reference. Now, suppose the following statement executes.

```
      A A2=A1;
```

The copy constructor will be called for 'A2' and 'A1' will be passed as a parameter to it. Then the copy constructor will be called for 'AObj' and 'A1' will be passed as a parameter to it. This is because 'AObj' is a non-reference formal argument of the copy constructor. Thus, an endless chain of calls to the copy constructor will be initiated. However, if the formal argument of the copy constructor is a reference, then no constructor (not even the copy constructor) will be called for it. This is because a reference to an object is not a separate object. No separate memory is allocated for it. Therefore, a call to a constructor is not embedded for it.

Now we come to a crucial question. Why should we define our own copy constructor? After all, the default copy constructor (which is provided free of cost by the complier) does a pretty decent job. First, recollect the conditions we decided to implement for all objects of the class String. Suppose an object of the class String is created and at the same time equated to another object of the class. For example,

```
String s1("abc");
String s2=s1;   //copy constructor is called for s2 and s1
                //is passed as a parameter to it
```

Since we have not defined the copy constructor for the class String, the compiler has done it for us. What does this default copy constructor do in the above case? It simply copies the values of 's1' to 's2'! This means that the value of 's2.cStr' becomes equal to 's1.cStr'. Thus, both the pointers point at the same place! This is certainly a violation of our conditions. The behaviour of the default copy constructor is undesirable in this case. To overcome this problem of the default copy constructor, we must define our own copy constructor.

From within the copy constructor of the class String, a separate memory block must be first allocated dynamically in the heap. This memory block must be equal in length to that of the string at which the pointer of the object passed as a parameter ('s1' in this case) points. The pointer of the invoking object ('s2' in this case) must then be made to point at this newly allocated memory block. The value of 'len' variable of the invoking object should also be set appropriately. However, if the pointer in the object passed as a parameter is NULL, then the value of the pointer and 'len' variable of the invoking object must be set to NULL and zero, respectively.

Accordingly, the prototype and the definition of the copy constructor of the class String appear as shown in Listing 4.11.

Listing 4.11   A user-defined copy constructor

```
/*Beginning of String.h*/
#include<iostream.h>
class String
{
   char * cStr;
   long unsigned int len;

   public:
   String(const String&);            //our own copy constructor
   /*
      rest of the class String
   */
      explicit String(const char * const p = NULL);
const char * getString();
};
/*End of String.h*/

/*Beginning of String.cpp*/
#include"String.h"
#include<string.h>
String::String(const String& ss)   //our own copy constructor
{
   if(ss.cStr==NULL)                //if passed object's pointer is NULL…
   {
```

```
                    cStr=NULL;              //… then nullify the invoking object's
                                            //pointer too
            len=0;
        }
        else                                //otherwise…
        {
            len=ss.len;
            cStr = new char[len+1];         //…dynamically allocate a
                                            //separate memory block
            strcpy(cStr,ss.cStr);           //…and copy into it
        }
    }
    String::String(const char * const p)
    {
        if(p==NULL)                         //if default value passed…
        {
            cStr=NULL;                      //…nullify
            len=0;
        }
        else                                //…otherwise…
        {
            len=strlen(p);
            cStr=new char[len+1];           //…dynamically allocate a
                                            //separate memory block
            strcpy(cStr,p);                 //…and copy into it
        }
    }
    const char * String::getString()
    {
        return cStr;
    }
    /*End of String.cpp*/

    /*Beginning of StringMain.cpp*/
    #include"String.h"
    #include<iostream.h>
    void main()
    {
        String s1("abc");
        String s2=s1;
        cout<<s1.getString()<<endl;
        cout<<s2.getString()<<endl;
    }
    /*End of StringMain.cpp*/
```

Output

abc

abc

In the copy constructor (Listing 4.11), the formal argument is a constant. It has to be a reference in order to prevent an endless chain of calls to itself. But at the same time the library programmer would certainly want to prevent even an inadvertent change in the values of the object that gets passed to the copy constructor. He/she would like the compiler to report a compile-time error if he/she inadvertently writes statements like the following.

```
    ss.cStr=NULL;   //pointer of parameter object modified!
    ss.len++;       //len variable of the parameter object
                    //modified!
```

4.2 Destructors

The destructor gets called for each object that is about to go out of scope. It appears as a member function of each class whether we define it or not. It has the same name as that of the class but prefixed with a tilde sign. It does not take parameters. It does not return anything (not even void). The prototype of a destructor is

```
~ <class name> ();
```

The need for a function that guarantees deinitialization of member data of a class and frees up the resources acquired by the object during its lifetime will be explained soon. Destructors fulfill this need.

The compiler embeds a call to the destructor for every object when it is destroyed. Let us have one more look at the main() function of Listing 4.1.

```
void main()
{
   A A1;
} //A1 goes out of scope here
```

'A1' goes out of scope just before the main() function terminates. At this point, the compiler embeds a call to the destructor for 'A1'. It embeds the following statement.

```
A1.~A();        //destructor called … not legal C++ code
```

An explicit call to the destructor for an existing object is forbidden. The above statement is then transformed into

```
~A(&A1);                             //see chapter 2
```

The destructor will also be called for an object that has been dynamically created in the heap just before the delete operator is applied on the pointer pointing at it.

```
A * APtr;
APtr = new A;                    //object created … constructor called
. . . .
. . . .
delete APtr;                     //object destroyed … destructor called
```

The last statement is transformed into

```
APtr->~A();                      //destructor called for *APtr
delete APtr;                     //memory for *APtr released
```

First, the destructor is called for the object that is going out of scope. Thereafter, the memory occupied by the object itself is deallocated. The second last statement above is transformed into

```
~A(APtr);               //see the section on 'this' pointer in Chapter 2
```

Unlike its name, the destructor does not 'destroy' or deallocate memory that an object occupies. It is merely a member function that is called for each object just before the object goes out of scope (gets destroyed).

As can be readily observed, the compiler embeds a call to the destructor for each and every object that is going out of scope. But we did not prototype and define the destructor inside the class. Then how was the above call to the destructor resolved? The compiler prototypes and defines the destructor for us. But what statements does the definition of such a destructor have? The answer is 'nothing'. An example of a compiler-defined destructor follows.

Before

```
class A
{
    . . . .
    . . . .
    public:
        . . . .
        . . . .
        //no destructor
};
```

After

```
class A
{
    . . . .
    . . . .
    public:
        ~A();          //prototype inserted implicitly by compiler
        . . . .
        . . . .
};

A::~A()
{
    //empty definition inserted implicitly by compiler
}
```

Let us add our own destructor to the class A defined in Listing 4.2 and verify whether the destructor is actually called implicitly by the compiler or not. See Listing 4.12.

Listing 4.12   Destructor gets called for each object when the object is destroyed

```
/*Beginning of A.h*/
class A
{
    int x;
    public:
        A();
        void setx(const int=0);
        int getx();
        ~A();                        //our own destructor
};
/*End of A.h*/

/*Beginning of A.cpp*/
#include"A.h"
#include<iostream.h>
A::A()
{
    cout<<"Constructor of class A called\n";
}

A::~A()                              //our own destructor
{
    cout<<"Destructor of class A called\n";
}
/*
    definitions of the rest of the functions of class A
*/
```

```
/*End of A.cpp*/

/*Beginning of AMain.cpp*/
#include"A.h"
#include<iostream.h>
void main()
{
   A A1;
   cout<<"End of program\n";
}
/*End of AMain.cpp*/
```

Output
Constructor of class A called
End of program
Destructor of class A called

As we can see, the name of the destructor is the same as the name of the class but prefixed with a tilde sign. Moreover, the destructor does not return anything. The compiler defines the destructor in order to resolve the call to the destructor that it compulsorily places for the object going out of scope.

Destructors do not take any arguments. Therefore, they cannot be overloaded.

Why should we define our own destructor? We must remember that the destructor is also a member function. It is called for objects. Therefore, it can access the data members of the object for which it has been called.

Let us think of a relevant definition for the destructor of the class Distance. What would we like it to do for us? What should it do to the data members of the object that is going out of scope? Should it set them to zero?

```
Distance::~Distance()
{
   iFeet=0;
   fInches=0.0;
}
```

But what is the use? The object is anyway going out of scope immediately after the destructor executes.

But we must define the destructor for classes whose objects, during their lifetime, acquire resources that are outside the objects themselves. Let us take the example of the class String. We consider the following code block.

```
{
   . . . .
   . . . .
   String s1("abc");
   . . . .
   . . . .
}
```

The memory that was allocated to 's1' itself gets deallocated when this block finishes execution. But 's1.cStr' was pointing at a memory block that was dynamically allocated in the heap area. This memory block was outside the memory block occupied by 's1' itself. After 's1' gets destroyed, this memory block remains allocated as a locked up lost resource. The only pointer that was pointing at it ('s1.cStr') is no longer available. This is memory leak. It should be prevented. We should deallocate the memory block at which the pointer inside any object of the class `String` is pointing exactly when the object goes out of scope. This means that we must call the `delete` operator for the pointer inside the class `String` and place this statement inside the destructor. See Listing 4.13.

Listing 4.13   A user-defined destructor

```
/*Beginning of String.h*/
class String
{
    char * cStr;
    long unsigned int len;
  public:
    ~String();                      //our own destructor
    /*
      rest of the class String
    */
};
/*End of String.h*/

/*Beginning of String.cpp*/
#include"String.h"
#include<string.h>
String::~String()                   //our own destructor
{
  if(cStr!=NULL)                    //if memory exists
    delete[] cStr;                  //… destroy it
}

/*
  definitions of the rest of the functions of class String
*/
/*End of String.cpp*/
```

4.3   Philosophy of OOPS

Now, let us digress and appreciate the basic philosophy of OOPS. One of the aims in OOPS is to abolish the use of fundamental data types. Classes can contain huge amounts of functionality (member functions) that free the application programmer from the worry of taking precautions against bugs.

The class `String` is one such data type. By adding some more relevant functions, we can conveniently use objects of the class `String`. Consider adding the following function to the class `String`.

```
void String::addChar(char);        //function to add a character
                                   //to the string
```

As its name suggests, this function will append a character to the string at which the pointer inside the invoking object points.

```
String s1("abc");
```

As a result of this statement, the pointer inside 's1' points at a memory block of four bytes (last one containing NULL). Now, if we write

```
s1.addChar('d');                   //add a character to the string
```

the following things should happen.

- Another block of five bytes should get allocated.
- The string contained in the memory block at which 's1.cStr' is currently pointing should get copied into this new memory block.
- The character 'd' should get appended to the string.
- The null character should get further appended to the string.
- 's1.cStr' should be made to point at this new memory block.
- The memory block at which 's1.cStr' was pointing previously should be deallocated (to prevent memory leaks).

Figure 4.5 shows adding a character to a stretchable string in the object-oriented way.

Before

```
String s1("abc");
```

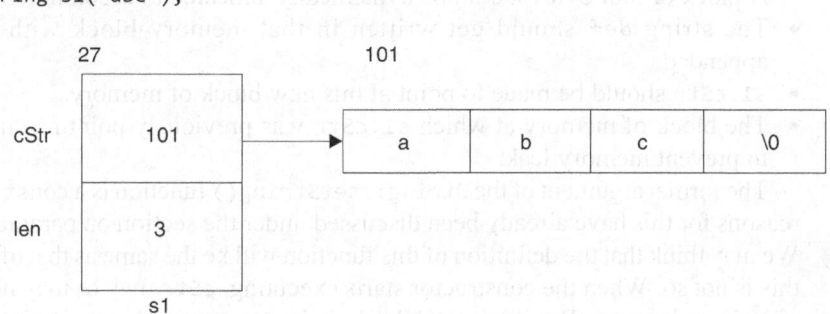

After

```
s1.addChar('d');
```

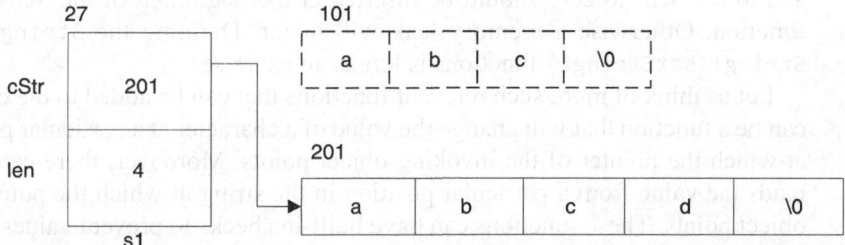

Figure 4.5   Adding a character to a stretchable string—the object-oriented way

One possible way of using this function is by using a loop to obtain a string from the user, which can be of any length. While writing the program, the application programmer need not predict the length of the string the user will enter. The following code can be used for adding a character to a stretchable string in the object-oriented way.

```
while(1)                //potentially infinite loop
{
    ch=getche();
    if(ch=='\n')                 //if user finishes entering the string
        break;                   //… break the loop
    s1.addChar(ch);             //…else append the character to it
}
```

As the user keeps adding characters to the string, the allocated memory keeps getting stretched in a manner that is transparent to the application programmer. Such an effect is simply unthinkable with character arrays.

We would also like to add a function that will replace the string associated with an object with the string that we pass to it. We let this function be

```
void String::setString(const char * const);
```

Suppose the following statements are executed.

```
String s1("abc");
s1.setString("def");                    //replace "abc" by "def"
```

Then the following events should take place when the second statement executes ('s1.cStr' is already pointing at a memory block that contains the string abc and is not NULL).

- A block of four bytes should be dynamically allocated to accommodate the string "def".
- The string def should get written in that memory block with the null character appended.
- s1.cStr should be made to point at this new block of memory.
- The block of memory at which s1.cStr was previously pointing should be deallocated to prevent memory leak.

The formal argument of the String::setString() function is a const char * const. The reasons for this have already been discussed under the section on parameterized constructor. We may think that the definition of this function will be the same as that of the constructor. But this is not so. When the constructor starts executing, cStr may or may not be NULL (it may contain junk value). But if it is not NULL, it does not mean that it is pointing at a dynamically allocated block of memory. But when the String::setString() function starts executing, if cStr is not NULL, then it is definitely pointing at a dynamically allocated block of memory. Statements to check this condition and to deallocate the memory block and to nullify cStr and to set 'len' to zero should be inserted at the beginning of the String::setString() function. Otherwise a memory leak will occur. Defining the String::addChar() and String::setString() functions is left as an exercise.

Let us think of more such relevant functions that can be added to the class String. There can be a function that will change the value of a character at a particular position in the string at which the pointer of the invoking object points. Moreover, there can be a function that reads the value from a particular position in the string at which the pointer of the invoking object points. These functions can have built-in checks to prevent values from being written to or read from bytes that are beyond the memory block allocated. Again, such a check is not built into character arrays. The application programmer has to put in extra efforts on his/her own to prevent the program from exceeding the bounds of the array.

After we have added all such functions to the class String, we will get a new data type that will be safe, efficient, and convenient to use.

Suitably defined constructors and destructors have a vital role to play in the creation of such data types. Together they ensure that

- There are no memory leaks (the destructor frees up unwanted memory).
- There are no run-time errors (no two calls to the destructor try to free up the same block of memory).
- Data is never in an invalid state and domain constraints on the values of data members are never violated.

After such data types have been defined, new data types can be created that extend the definitions of existing data types. They contain the definition of the existing data types and at the same time add more specialized features on their own. This facility of defining new data types by making use of existing data types is known as inheritance. Chapter 5 deals with this feature of OOPS and its implementation in C++.

Summary

Constructors can be used to guarantee a proper initialization of data members of a class. Domain constraints on values of data members can be implemented via constructors.

Constructors are member functions and have the same name as that of the class itself. The compiler creates a zero-argument constructor and a copy constructor if we do not define them. Constructors take parameters and, therefore, can be overloaded. They do not return anything (not even void). The compiler implicitly embeds a call to the constructor for each object that is being created. An explicit call to the constructor for an existing object is forbidden.

If necessary, destructors can be used to guarantee a proper clean up when an object goes out of scope. Destructors are member functions and have the same name as that of the class itself but with the tilde sign prefixed. The compiler creates a destructor if we do not define one. Destructors do not take parameters and, therefore, cannot be overloaded. They do not return anything (not even void). The compiler implicitly embeds a call to the destructor for each object that is going out of scope (being destroyed). An explicit call to the destructor for an existing object is forbidden.

Key Terms

constructors
- called automatically for each object that has just got created
- defined by default
- has the same name as that of the class
- does not return anything

zero-argument constructor
parameterized constructors
copy constructor
destructors

Exercises

1. What are constructors? When are they called? What is their utility?
2. Why should the formal argument of a copy constructor be a reference object?
3. What are destructors? When are they called? What is their utility?
4. Is a destructor necessary for the following class?

```
class Time
{
    int hours, minutes, seconds;
public:
    /*
        rest of the class Time … but no
        more data members
    */
};
```

5. Define a suitable parameterized constructor with default values for the class Time given in question 4.
6. Four member functions are provided by default by the compiler for each class that we define. We have studied three of them in this chapter. Name them.
7. State true or false.
   (a) Memory occupied by an object is allocated by the constructor of its class.
   (b) Constructors can be used to acquire memory outside the objects.
   (c) Constructors can be overloaded.
   (d) A constructor can have a return statement in its definition.
   (e) Memory occupied by an object is deallocated by the destructor of its class.

(f) Destructors can be used to release memory that has been acquired outside the objects.

(g) Destructors can be overloaded.

(h) A destructor can have a return statement in its definition.

8. The copy constructor has been explicitly defined for the class String so that no two objects of the class String end up sharing the same resource, that is, end up with their contained pointers pointing at the same block of dynamically allocated memory. In this case, two such blocks may contain two copies of the same data as a result of the copy constructor,

which is perfectly acceptable. However, there are situations where no two objects should share even copies of the same data. If A is a class for whose objects this restriction needs to be applied, then we should ensure that a statement like the second one below should not compile.

```
A A1;
A A2 = A1;
```

How can this objective be achieved? (*Hint:* Member functions are not always public and the copy constructor is a member function.)

5

Inheritance

This chapter discusses inheritance. Inheritance is one of the most important and useful features of the object-oriented programming system.

The chapter begins with an overview of inheritance. Basic concepts such as base class and derived class are discussed. The effects, advantages, and important points of inheritance are also discussed.

The middle portion of the chapter deals with the implications of making a base class pointer point at an object of the derived class and vice versa. Thereafter, the concept of function overriding is discussed. This is followed by a section on base class initialization in which the method of initializing base class members via constructors of the derived class is discussed.

The protected keyword is an important concept in C++. The protected keyword, along with the public and private keywords, completes the triad of access specifiers provided by C++. A separate section of this chapter elucidates this keyword and the effect of its use in inheritance.

Classes can be derived by public, private, or protected keywords. The effect caused by each of these is different. The current chapter compares this difference in a systematic manner.

Inheritance can be of various types based upon the number of classes derived from a single base class and the number of base classes for a single derived class. All of these types are dealt with in the penultimate section of the chapter.

The chapter ends with a section on the order of invocation of constructors and destructors.

5.1 Introduction

Inheritance is a very useful feature of OOPS that is supported by C++. A class may be defined in such a way that it automatically includes member data and member functions of an existing class. Additionally, member data and member functions may be defined in the new class also. This is called inheritance.

The existing class whose features are being inherited is known as the base class or parent class or super class. The new class that is being defined by inheriting from the existing class is known as its derived class or child class or sub-class. The syntax for derivation is as follows.

```
class <name of derived class> : <access specifier> <name of base class>
{
    /*
        definition of derived class
```

```
  */
};
```

Suppose a class A already exists. Then a new class B can be derived from class A as follows.

```
class B : public A
{
  /*
    new features of class B
  */
};
```

The public access specifier has been used in the foregoing example. The implications of using the other access specifiers are discussed later in this chapter.

A pointer from the derived class to the base class diagrammatically depicts derivation (see Figure 5.1).

Figure 5.1 Diagrammatic depiction of inheritance

5.1.1 Effects of Inheritance

Inheritance affects the size and behaviour of derived class objects in two ways.

- Obviously, an object of the derived class will contain all data members of the derived class. However, it will contain data members of the base class also. Thus, an object of the derived class will always be larger than an object of the base class. (The only exception to this is when neither the base class nor the derived class has data members. In that case, objects of both the base class and the derived class occupy one byte each.)
- Obviously, with respect to an object of the derived class, we can call the public member functions of the derived class in any global non-member function. However, we can call the public member functions of the base class also. (There are exceptions to this. Circumstances under which these exceptions occur are described later in this chapter.)
Listing 5.1 illustrates this.

Listing 5.1 Effects of inheritance

```
/*Beginning of A.h*/
class A
{
  int x;
  public:
  void setX(const int=0);
  int getX()const;
};
```

```
/*End of A.h*/

/*Beginning on A.cpp*/
#include"A.h"
void A::setX(const int pX)
{
    x = pX;
}
int A::getX() const
{
    return x;
}
/*End on A.cpp*/

/*Beginning of B.h*/
#include"A.h"
class B : public A          //inheriting from A
{
    int y;

    public:
    void setY(const int=0);
    int getY()const;
};
/*End of B.h*/

/*Beginning on B.cpp*/
#include"B.h"
void B::setY(const int pY)
{
    y = pY;
}
int B::getY() const
{
    return y;
}
/*End on B.cpp*/

/*Beginning of inherit.cpp*/
#include<iostream.h>
#include"B.h"
void main()
{
    cout<<sizeof(A)<<endl<<sizeof(B)<<endl;
    B B1;                           //an object of the derived class
    B1.setX(1);                     //OK: calling a base class member function
                                    //with respect to a derived class object

    B1.setY(3);
    cout<<B1.getX()<<endl;          //OK: calling a base class
                                    //member function with respect to
                                    //a derived class object

    cout<<B1.getY()<<endl;
}
/*End of inherit.cpp*/
```

Output

4
8
1
3

Defining the member functions of classes A and B is left as an exercise.

This highly simplified example (Listing 5.1) effectively illustrates the basic mechanisms of inheritance. An object of class B (the derived class) will contain two integers (one from class B and the other from class A). Therefore, its size will be 8. Also, with respect to an object of class B, we can call member functions of class B as well as those of class A.

An object of the derived class will contain the data members of the base class as well as the data members of the derived class. Thus, the size of an object of the derived class will be equal to the sum of sizes of the data members of the base class plus the sum of the sizes of the data members of the derived class.

Inheritance implements an 'is-a' relationship. A derived class is a type of the base class just like an aircraft (derived class) is a type of vehicle (base class). Contrast this to `containership` that implements a 'has-a' relationship. A class may contain an object of another class or a pointer to a data structure that contains a set of objects of another class. Such a class is known as a `container class`. For example, an aircraft has one engine or an array of engines.

Another example can be that of a `manager` class and `employee` class. A `manager` (i.e., an object of the class `manager`) is an `employee` (i.e., an object of the class `employee`). Nevertheless, it has some features that are not possessed by all employees. For example, it may have a pointer to an array of employees that report to him. Derived class object is also a base class object (as shown in the following lines of code).

```
class employee
{
    String name;
    double basic;
    Date doj;
    /*
       rest of the class employee
    */
};

class manager : public employee //manager is an employee
{
    employee * list;
    /*
       rest of the class manager
    */
};
```

A derived class contains additional data and members and is thus a specialized definition of its base class. Therefore, the process of inheritance is also known as specialization.

5.1.2 Benefits of Inheritance

This process of adding only the additional data members in the derived class has implications. The base class can have a generic common definition. The data and functions that are common to more than one class can be put together in the base class. While only the special ones can be put in each of the derived classes. Thus, inheritance is another feature of C++ that enables code reusability.

5.1.3 Inheritance in Actual Practice

In actual practice, the library programmer defines a certain class and its member functions. Another interested programmer, in order to create his/her application, then inherits from this class and adds only the special data members and the code to handle these additional data members in the derived class.

5.1.4 Base Class and Derived Class Objects

Now, many students of C++ may start believing that objects of the derived class inherit from objects of the base class. This is incorrect as an object of the derived class is not at all related to another simultaneously existing object of the base class.

An object of class A (say 'A1') will occupy four bytes containing only 'x'. Whereas an object of class B (say 'B1') will occupy a different block of eight bytes containing both 'x' and 'y', as shown in Figure 5.2. (As per the definitions of classes A and B given in Listing 5.1.)

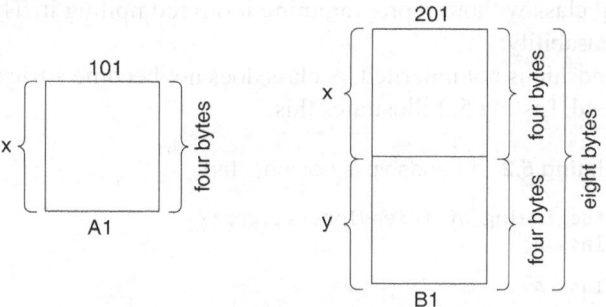

Figure 5.2   Memory layout of base class and derived class object

5.1.5 Accessing Members of the Base Class in the Derived Class

Only public members of base class can be accessed in the functions of derived class (protected members of the base class can also be accessed; we shall discuss protected members later). But, private members of the base class cannot be accessed.

Suppose in the B::setY() function we write

    x=y;

the compiler will report an error stating that private members of the base class cannot be accessed. (In this case we are trying to access 'x' in a member function of the derived class. But 'x' is a private member of the base class.)

But we can access A::setX() and A::getX() functions in the member functions of the derived class because they are public members of the base class. Private members of the base class remain private with respect to member functions of the derived class. The following lines of code demonstrate this.

```
void B::setY(const int q)
{
    y=q;
    setX(y);                            //x=y
}
```

This is as it should be. C++ prevents us from accessing private members of the base class in member functions of the derived class to fully implement data security. After all, the base class provider made some members of the base class private because he/she wanted only the member functions of the base class (which he/she has perfected) to access them. If member functions of the derived class are allowed to access private members of the base class, then one cannot identify all statements in the program that access private members of the base class by merely looking at its member and friend functions.

We may argue that the existing set of functions of the base class is sometimes not enough. We would like to create a derived class that supplements the base class by containing those member functions that we feel are *missing* in the base class. For example, suppose a function such as String::addChar (char) is not present in the class String. But in this case, the drawback is in the base class itself. It is the base class itself that should be corrected. Inheritance is not used to remove such lacuna. It is used to provide additional data and additional code to work upon the additional data in the derived class. Inheritance is used to add facilities to an existing class without reprogramming it or recompiling it. Thus, it enables us to implement code reusability.

Friendship is not inherited. A class does not become a friend to a class to which its parent is a friend. Listing 5.2 illustrates this.

Listing 5.2   Friendship is not inherited

```
/*Beginning of friendInherit.cpp*/
class B;

class A
{
   friend class B;
   int x;
};

class B
{
   void fB(A * p)
   {
      p->x=0;                      //OK: B is a friend of A
   }
};

class C : public B
{
   void fC(A * p)
   {
      p->x=0;                      //ERROR: C is not a friend of A
                                   //despite being derived from a friend
   }
};
/*End of friendInherit.cpp*/
```

5.2   Base Class and Derived Class Pointers

A base class pointer can point at an object of the derived class. However, a derived class pointer cannot point at an object of the base class. To be more precise, a base class pointer can safely point at an object of the derived class without the need for typecasting. But a derived class pointer can be made to point at an object of the base class only forcibly by typecasting. However, this can cause run-time errors.

Note: There are exceptions to the above assertion. The compiler will prevent a base class pointer from pointing at an object of the derived under certain circumstances. These circumstances are described later in this chapter.

First, let us understand why no harm can come by making a base class pointer point at an object of the derived class. To understand this, we consider the classes of Listing 5.3.

Listing 5.3 A derived class and its base class

```
/*Beginning of A.h*/
class A
{
  public:
    int x;
};
/*End of A.h*/

/*Beginning of B.h*/
#include"A.h"
class B : public A //derived from A
{
  public:
    int y;
};
/*End of B.h*/
```

These classes have only data members. There are no member functions and even these member data are public. These classes are given here to initially understand the concepts only. Explanations with classes that have private data members and public member functions are given later.

Now, let us compile the `main()` function of Listing 5.4 and see what happens.

Listing 5.4 Base class pointer pointing at a derived class object

```
/*Beginning of BasePtr01.cpp*/
#include"B.h"              //from listing 5.03
void main()
{
  A * APtr;
  B B1;
  APtr=&B1;                //line 1 - OK: base class pointer points at
                           //derived class's object
  APtr->x=10;              //line 2 - OK: accessing base class member
                           //through base class pointer
  APtr->y=20;              //line 3 - ERROR: y not found in class A
}
/*End of BasePtr01.cpp*/
```

Line 1 of Listing 5.4 will compile because line 3 will not. A base class pointer can point at an object of the derived class. Let us see why. 'APtr' is of type 'A *'. It is supposed to point at objects of the base class A. Therefore, it cannot access 'y'. There is no member of the name 'y' in class A. The fact that 'APtr' points at an object of the derived class is of no significance. Through 'APtr', it is possible to access 'x' because there is a member of the name 'x' in class A. Although 'APtr' points at 'B1', which occupies eight bytes (four for 'x' and four for 'y'), it is able to access the value contained in only the first four bytes. Thus, 'APtr' cannot access an area in the memory that has not been allocated. Therefore, a pointer of the base class type can safely point at an object of the derived class, as illustrated by Figure 5.3.

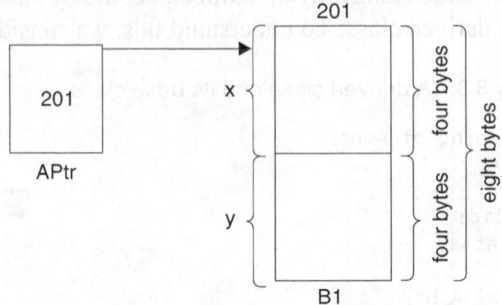

Figure 5.3   Base class pointer points at an object of the derived class

We will soon realize that making a base class pointer point at an object of the derived class is a very common requirement in C++ programming.

Now, let us find out why derived class pointers cannot be made to point at objects of the base class without explicit typecasting, and why, even that is a very unsafe thing to do. Now, let us compile the `main()` function of Listing 5.5 and see the result.

Listing 5.5   Derived class pointer pointing at a base class object

```
/*Beginning of DerivedPtr01.cpp*/
#include"B.h"              //from listing 5.03
void main()
{
    A A1;
    B * BPtr;
    BPtr=&A1;              //line 1 - ERROR. Cannot convert from B* to
                           //A*.
    BPtr->x=10;            //line 2 - OK. Derived class pointer
                           //accesses base class member.
    BPtr->y=20;            //line 3 - OK. Derived class pointer
                           //accesses derived class member.

}
/*End of DerivedPtr01.cpp*/
```

Line 1 of Listing 5.5 will not compile because line 3 will. A derived class pointer cannot point at an object of the base class. Let us see why. 'BPtr' is of type 'B *'. It is supposed to point at objects of the derived class B. Therefore, it can access 'y' also. 'BPtr' is pointing at 'A1', which occupies four bytes only. However, it is able to access the value contained in the next four bytes also. There is a member of name 'y' in class B. Thus, 'BPtr' is able to access an area in the memory that has not been allocated. Therefore, a pointer of the derived class type cannot safely point at an object of the base class, as shown in Figure 5.4.

Line 3 of Listing 5.5 would write 20 into the bytes whose addresses are from 205 to 208. But this block has not been allocated for the object at which the pointer points. But this line will compile. The problem is actually in line 1.

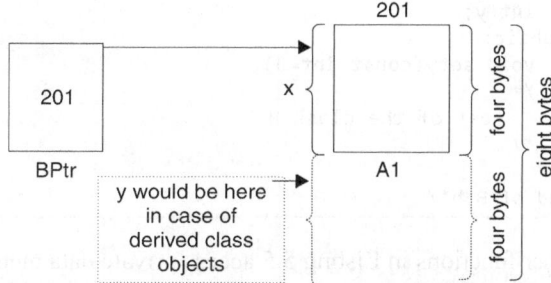

Figure 5.4   Derived class pointer pointing at an object of the base class

However, a derived class pointer *can* be forcibly made to point at an object of the derived class by explicit typecasting, as illustrated by Listing 5.6. Continuing with classes A and B given in Listing 5.3.

Listing 5.6   Forcible typecasting to make a derived class pointer point at an object of the base class

```
/*Beginning of DerivedPtrTypeCast.cpp*/
#include"B.h"                          //from listing 5.03
void main()
{
  A A1;
  B * BPtr;                            //derived class pointer
  BPtr=(B*)&A1;                        //forcible typecasting to make derived
                                       //class pointer point at base class
                                       //object

}
/*End of DerivedPtrTypeCast.cpp*/
```

But explicit address manipulation like this is obviously dangerous. Now, let us consider the realistic cases where the classes have private data members and public member functions (see Listing 5.7). The same explanations that have been given above will hold true even if the classes A and B have 'x' and 'y' as private data members, respectively.

Listing 5.7   Classes of Listing 5.3 with member functions

```
/*Beginning of A.h*/
class A
{
    int x;
  public:
    void setx(const int=0);
    /*
      rest of the class A
    */
};
/*End of A.h*/

/*Beginning of B.h*/
#include"A.h"
class B : public A
{
```

```
        int y;
    public:
      void sety(const int=0);
      /*
         rest of the class B
      */
};
/*End of B.h*/
```

The member functions in Listing 5.5 access private data members of their respective classes.

Listing 5.8   Base class pointer pointing at an object of the derived class

```
/*Beginning of BasePtr02.cpp*/
#include"B.h"                         //from listing 5.7
void main()
{
  A * APtr;
  B B1;
  APtr=&B1;                           //OK: base class pointer points at
                                      //derived class's object
  APtr->setx(10);                     //OK: accessing base class member
                                      //through base class pointer
  APtr->sety(20);                     //ERROR: sety() not a member of class A
}
/*End of BasePtr02.cpp*/
```

Listing 5.9   Derived class pointer pointing at an object of the base class

```
/*Beginning of DerivedPtr02.cpp*/
#include"B.h"                         //from listing 5.7
void main()
{
  A A1;
  B * BPtr;
  BPtr=&A1;                           //ERROR: cannot convert A* to B*
  BPtr->setx(10);                     //OK: Derived class pointer accesses
                                      //base class member.
  BPtr->sety(20);                     //OK: Derived class pointer accesses
                                      //derived class member.
}
/*End of DerivedPtr02.cpp*/
```

The fact that a base class pointer can point at an object of the derived class (see Listings 5.8 and 5.9) should not be surprising. After all, this is exactly what happens when we call a base class function with respect to an object of the derived class.

```
B1.setx(10);
```

Based upon the knowledge we have gained about the this pointer in Chapter 2, we know that the compiler will internally convert the above statement to

```
setx(&B1,10);
```

The address of 'B1' (a derived class object) is passed as a parameter to the function. But the corresponding formal argument in the A::setx() function is the this pointer of type A * const (Listing 5.10).

Listing 5.10 This pointer in a base class member function points at the derived class invoking object

```
void setx(A * const this, const int p)
{
    this->x=p;
}
```

Obviously, the `this` pointer points at 'B1', which is an object of the derived class.

5.3 Function Overriding

Member functions of the base class can be overridden in the derived class. Defining a member function in the derived class in such a manner that its name and signature match those of a base class function is known as function overriding. Function overriding results in two functions of the same name and same signature. One of them is in the base class. The other one is in the derived class. An illustrative example follows in Listing 5.11.

Listing 5.11 Function overriding

```
/*Beginning of A.h*/
class A
{
    public:
        void show()
        {
            cout<<"show() function of class A called\n";
        }
};
/*End of A.h*/

/*Beginning of B.h*/
#include"A.h"
class B : public A
{
    public:
        void show()                    //overriding A::show()
        {
            cout<<"show() function of class B called\n";
        }
};
/*End of B.h*/
```

The `show()` function of class B has overridden the `show()` function of class A. Consequently, if the `show()` function is called with respect to an object of the derived class B, the `show()` function of class B will be called instead of the `show()` function of class A. See Listing 5.12.

Listing 5.12 Calling the overriding function

```
/*Beginning of Override01.cpp*/
#include"B.h"
void main()
{
    B B1;
    B1.show();                    //B::show() called
```

```
}
/*End of Override01.cpp*/
```

Output
show( ) function of class B called

Whenever a function is called with respect to an object of a class, the compiler first searches for the function prototype in the same class. Only if this search fails, the compiler goes up the class hierarchy to look for the function prototype. In Listings 5.11 and 5.12, the show( ) function of class A was virtually hidden by the show( ) function of class B.

Of course, the overridden function of the base class will be called if it is called with respect to an object of the base class (Listing 5.13).

Listing 5.13   Calling the overridden function with respect to an object of the base class

```
/*Beginning of Override02.cpp*/
#include"B.h"
void main()
{
    A A1;
    A1.show();                    //A::show() called
}
/*End of Override02.cpp*/
```

Output
show( ) function of class A called

The overridden base class function can still be called with respect to an object of the derived class by using the scope resolution operator as illustrated in Listing 5.14.

Listing 5.14   Calling the overridden function forcibly with respect to an object of the derived class

```
/*Beginning of Override03.cpp*/
#include"B.h"
void main()
{
    B B1;
    B1.A::show();                 //A::show() called
}
/*End of Override03.cpp*/
```

Output
show( ) function of class A called

Function overriding is actually a form of function overloading. Our knowledge of the this pointer immediately makes this clear. The signatures of the overriding function and the overridden function are only apparently the same. They are actually different from each other. The actual prototype of the A::show( ) function is

```
void show(A * const);
```

On the other hand, the actual prototype of the B::show( ) function is

```
void show(B * const);
```

The overridden function can be called from the overriding function as follows.

```
void B::show()
{
   A::show();
   /*
       rest of the B::show() function
   */
}
```

The scope resolution operator is necessary to avoid infinite recursion.

But, what is the use of function overriding? Function overriding *appears* to be nothing more than a fancy language construct. Function overriding becomes significant only when the base class function being overridden is virtual. More about virtual functions and how they implement dynamic polymorphism is illustrated in Chapter 6.

5.4   Base Class Initialization

A derived class object is composed of data members of the derived class as well as those of the base class. Often we need to initialize all of these data members while creating an object of the derived class. We must remember that when an object of the derived class is created, the compiler implicitly and inevitably embeds a call to the base class constructor and then the derived class constructor with respect to the object.

Suppose A is the base class and B is its derived class. The statement

```
B B1;
```

is converted into

```
B B1;    //memory allocated for the object
B1.A(); //base class constructor called
B1.B(); //derived class constructor called
```

Destructors are called in the reverse order. As we already know, explicitly calling the constructors and destructors, with respect to an existing object, is prohibited. Now, let us look at Listing 5.15.

Listing 5.15   Unsuccessful initialization of base class members

```
/*Beginning of A.h*/
class A
{
     int x;
   public:
      A(const int=0);
      void setx(const int=0);
      int getx()const;
};
/*End of A.h*/

/*Beginning of A.cpp*/
#include"A.h"

A::A(const int p)
{
   x=p;
}
```

```cpp
void A::setx(const int p)
{
    x=p;
}

int A::getx() const
{
    return x;
}
/*End of A.cpp*/

/*Beginning of B.h*/
#include"A.h"

class B : public A
{
        int y;
    public:
        B(const int=0);
        void sety(const int=0);
        int gety()const;
};
/*End of B.h*/

/*Beginning of B.cpp*/
#include"B.h"

B::B(const int q)
{
    y=q;
}

void B::sety(const int q)
{
    y=q;
}

int B::gety() const
{
    return y;
}
/*End of B.cpp*/

/*Beginning of baseinit01.cpp*/
#include"B.h"
#include<iostream.h>

void main()
{
    B B1(20);
    cout<<B1.getx()<<endl
        <<B1.gety()<<endl;
}
/*End of baseinit01.cpp*/
```

Output

0

20

The output is explained by the simple observation that the statement

```cpp
    B B1(20);
```

gets converted to the following:

```
B B1;           //memory allocated for the object
B1.A();         //base class constructor called
B1.B(20);       //derived class constructor called
```

As we can see, base class data members of the derived class object got initialized through the base class constructor with the default value being passed to it. Thus, 'B1.y' got initialized to 20 (the value passed). But 'B1.x' got initialized to 0 (the default value). While creating an object of the derived class, we would like to pass a value explicitly to the base class constructor. Thus, in Listing 5.15, the constructor of class B should take not one but two parameters. One of these should be passed to 'y' while the other should be used to initialize 'x'. For this, the prototype and definition of the constructor of class B should be modified as shown in Listing 5.16.

Listing 5.16 Modifying the derived class constructor to ensure successful initialization of the base class members

```
/*Beginning of B.h*/
#include"A.h"

class B : public A
{
   public:
      B(const int=0, const int=0);
   /*
      rest of the class B
   */
}
/*End of B.h*/

/*Beginning of B.cpp*/
#include"B.h"

B::B(const int p,const int q):A(p)      //passing value to base
                                        //class constructor
{
   y=q;
}

/*
   Definitions of the remaining member functions of class B
*/

/*End of B.cpp*/
```

An object of class B can be declared by passing two parameters to its constructor. One of them is assigned to 'x'. The other is assigned to 'y'.

Listing 5.17 Base class initialization

```
/*Beginning of baseinit02.cpp*/
#include"B.h"
#include<iostream.h>

void main()
{
   B B1(10,20);
   cout<<B1.getx()<<endl<<B1.gety()<<endl;
```

```
}
/*End of baseinit02.cpp*/
```

Output
10
20

Again, the output of Listing 5.17 can be explained by noting that due to the modified definition of the constructor of class B, the statement

```
B B1(10,20);
```

gets converted to

```
B B1;                              //memory allocated for the object
B1.A(10);                          //base class constructor called
B1.B(20);                          //derived class constructor called
```

As per the definition of the derived class constructor in Listing 5.17, the *first* parameter passed to it was in turn passed to the base class constructor. But this is not necessary. Any of the parameters passed to the derived class constructor can be passed to the base class constructor.

5.5 Protected Access Specifier

Apart from the public and private access specifiers, there is a third access modifier in C++ known as protected. Protected members are inaccessible to non-member functions. However, they are accessible to the member functions of their own class and to member functions of the derived classes. Listing 5.18 along with its accompanying comments illustrates this.

Listing 5.18 Accessing protected members

```
/*Beginning of A.h*/
class A
{
   private:
      int x;
   protected:
      int y;
   public:
      int z;
};
/*End of A.h*/

/*Beginning of B.h*/
#include"A.h"
class B : public A                 //derived class
{
   public:
      void xyz();
};
/*End of B.h*/

/*Beginning of B.cpp*/
#include"B.h"
void B::xyz()                      //member function of derived class
```

```
{
   x=1;      //ERROR: private member of base class
   y=2;      //OK: protected member of base class
   z=3;      //OK: public member of base class
}
/*End of B.cpp*/

/*Beginning of protected.cpp*/
#include"A.h"
void main()                          //nonmember function
{
   A * Aptr;
   APtr->x=10;                       //ERROR: private member
   APtr->y=20;                       //ERROR: protected member
   APtr->z=30;                       //OK: public member
}
/*End of protected.cpp*/
```

5.6 Deriving by Different Access Specifiers

5.6.1 Deriving by the Public Access Specifier

Deriving by the public access specifier retains the access level of base class members.

Private members: Member functions of the derived class cannot access. Member functions of the subsequently derived classes cannot access them. Non-member functions cannot access them.

Protected members: Member functions of the derived class can access. Member functions of the subsequently derived classes can also access them. Non-member functions cannot access them.

Public members: Member functions of the derived class can access. Member functions of the subsequently derived classes can also access them. The non-member functions can also access them.

Errors that are encountered while compiling Listing 5.19 make this evident.

Listing 5.19 Accessing the inherited members of an object of a class derived by public access specifier

```
/*Beginning of publicInheritance.cpp*/
class A
{
   private:
      int x;
   protected:
      int y;
   public:
      int z;
};

class B : public A                  //B is a public derived class of A
{
   public:
```

```
        void f1()
        {
            x=1;            //ERROR: private member remains private
            y=2;            //OK: protected member remains protected
            z=2;            //OK: public member remains public
        }
};

class C : public B
{
    public:
        void f2()
        {
            x=1;    //ERROR: private member remains private
            y=2;    //OK: protected member remains protected
            z=2;    //OK: public member remains public
        }
};

void xyz() //non-member function
{
    B B1;           //line 1: An object of a protected derived class
    B1.z=100;       //line 2: ERROR. Cannot access public member
                    //of a base class through an object of a
                    //protected derived class.
    A * APtr;       //line 3
    APtr=&B1;       //line 4: ERROR. Cannot make a base class
                    //pointer point at an object of a protected
                    //derived class.
    APtr->z=100;    //line 5. OK. Can access public
                    //member of the base class through a base
                    //class pointer.

    /*End of publicInheritance.cpp*/
```

A base class pointer can point at an object of a derived class that has been derived by using the public access specifier. Let us redefine the xyz() function from the program in Listing 5.19 as in Listing 5.20 and see what happens if we recompile the program.

Listing 5.20 A base class pointer can point at an object of the public-derived class

```
void xyz()              //non-member function
{
    B B1;               //line 1: An object of a public derived
                        //class
    B1.z=100;           //line 2: OK. Can access public member of
                        //a base class through an object of a
                        //public derived class.
    A * APtr;           //line 3
    APtr=&B1;           //line 4: OK. Can make a base class pointer
                        //point at an object of a public derived
                        //class.
    Aptr->z=100;        //line 5. OK. Can access inherited public
                        //member of the base class through a base
                        //class pointer.

}
```

Line 4 of Listing 5.20 will compile successfully because lines 2 and 5 will. Line 2 will compile successfully because 'z' is a public member of the base class A and class B is derived from class A by using the public access specifier. In this case, the base class pointer would access the object of a public-derived class in a way (line 5 of Listing 5.20) that is anyway permitted when the object is accessed by using the name of the object itself (line 2 of Listing 5.20).

Therefore, the C++ compiler does not prevent a base class pointer from pointing at an object of the derived class if the public access specifier has been used to derive the class.

5.6.2 Deriving by the Protected Access Specifier

Deriving by the protected access specifier reduces the access level of public base class members to protected while the access level of protected and private base class members remains unchanged.

Private members: Member functions of the derived class cannot access. Member functions of the subsequently derived classes cannot access them. Non-member functions cannot access them.

Protected members: Member functions of the derived class can access. Member functions of the subsequently derived classes can also access them. Non-member functions cannot access them.

Public members: Member functions of the derived class can access. Member functions of the subsequently derived classes can also access them. Non-member functions cannot access them.

Errors encountered while compiling Listing 5.21 demonstrate this.

Listing 5.21   Accessing the inherited members of an object of a class derived by protected access specifier

```
/*Beginning of publicInheritance.cpp*/
class A
{
   private:
   int x;
   protected:
   int y;
   public:
   int z;
};
class B : public A              //B is a public derived class of A
{
   public:
   void f1()
   {
//    x=1;                       //ERROR: private member remains private
      y=2;                       //OK: protected member remains protected
      z=2;                       //OK: public member remains public
   }
};
class C : public B
{
   public:
   void f2()
   {
//    x=1;                       //ERROR: private member remains private
```

```
        y=2;                    //OK: protected member remains protected
        z=2;                    //OK: public member remains public
    }
};
void xyz()                      //non-member function
{
    B B1;                       //line 1: An object of a public derived class
    B1.z=100;                   //line 2: OK. Can access public member of
                                //a base class through an object of a
                                //public derived class.

    A * APtr;                   //line 3
    APtr=&B1;                   //line 4: OK. Can make a base class pointer
                                //point at an object of a public derived
                                //class.

    APtr->z=100;                //line 5. OK. Can access inherited public
                                //member of the base class through a base
                                //class pointer.

}
/*End of publicInheritance.cpp*/
```

A base class pointer cannot point at an object of a derived class that has been derived by using the protected access specifier. Let us redefine the xyz() function from the program in Listing 5.21 as in Listing 5.22 and see what happens if we recompile the program.

Listing 5.22 A base class pointer cannot point at an object of the protected derived class

```
void xyz()                      //non-member function
{
    B B1;                       //line 1: An object of a protected derived
                                //class
    B1.z=100;                   //line 2: ERROR. Cannot access public member of
                                //a base class through an object of a
                                //protected derived class.
    A * APtr;                   //line 3
    APtr=&B1;                   //line 4: ERROR. Cannot make a base class pointer
                                //point at an object of a protected derived
                                //class.
    Aptr->z=100;                //line 5. OK. Can access public
                                //member of the base class through a base
                                //class pointer.

}
```

Line 4 of Listing 5.22 will not compile because line 2 will not compile and line 5 will compile. Line 2 will not compile because although 'z' is a public member of the base class A, class B is derived from class A by using the protected access specifier. In this case, the base class pointer might access the object of a protected derived class in a way (line 5 of Listing 5.22) that is not permitted when the object is accessed by using the name of the object itself (line 2 of Listing 5.22).

Therefore, the C++ compiler prevents a base class pointer from pointing at an object of the derived class if the protected access specifier has been used to derive the class.

5.6.3 Deriving by the Private Access Specifier

Deriving by the private access specifier reduces the access level of public and protected base class members to private while access level of private base class members remains unchanged.

Private members: Member functions of the derived class cannot access. Member functions of the subsequently derived classes cannot access them. Non-member functions cannot access them.

Protected members: Member functions of the derived class can access. Member functions of the subsequently derived classes cannot access them. Non-member functions cannot access them.

Public members: Member functions of the derived class can access. Member functions of the subsequently derived classes cannot access them. Non-member functions cannot access them.

Errors encountered while compiling Listing 5.23 demonstrate this.

Listing 5.23 Accessing the inherited members of an object of a class derived by private access specifier

```
/*Beginning of protectedInheritance.cpp*/
class A
{
   private:
   int x;
   protected:
   int y;
   public:
   int z;
};
class B : protected A          //B is a protected derived class of A
{
   public:
   void f1()
   {
//    x=1;                      //ERROR: private member remains private
      y=2;                      //OK: protected member remains protected
      z=2;                      //OK: public member becomes protected
   }
};
class C : public B
{
   public:
   void f2()
   {
//    x=1;                      //ERROR: private member remains private
      y=2;                      //OK: protected member remains protected
      z=2;                      //OK: protected member remains protected
   }
};
void xyz()                               //non-member function
{
   B B1;           //line 1: An object of a protected derived class
   B1.z=100;       //line 2: ERROR. Cannot access public member
                   //of a base class through an object of a
                   //protected derived class.
   A * APtr;       //line 3
   APtr=&B1;       //line 4: ERROR. Cannot make a base class
                   //pointer point at an object of a protected
                   //derived class.
```

```
                  APtr->z=100;    //line 5. OK. Can access public
                                  //member of the base class through a base
                                  //class pointer.
          }
          /*End of protectedInheritance.cpp*/
```

A base class pointer cannot point at an object of a derived class that has been derived by using the private access specifier. Let us redefine the xyz() function from the above program (Listing 5.23) as in Listing 5.24 and see what happens if we recompile the program.

Listing 5.24   A base class pointer cannot point at an object of the private-derived class

```
/*Beginning of privateInheritance.cpp*/
class A
{
   private:
   int x;
   protected:
   int y;
   public:
   int z;
};
class B : private A              //B is a private derived class of A
{
   public:
   void f1()
   {
       x=1;           //ERROR: private member remains private
       y=2;           //OK: protected member becomes private in
                      //this class
       z=2;           //OK: protected member becomes private in
                      //this class
   }
};
class C : public B
{
   public:
   void f2()
   {
       x=1;           //ERROR: private member remains private
       y=2;           //ERROR: private member remains private
       z=2;           //ERROR: private member remains private
   }
};
void xyz(B * BPtr) //non-member function
{
   BPtr->x=10;    //ERROR: private member remains private
   BPtr->y=20;    //ERROR: protected member becomes private
   BPtr->z=30;    //ERROR: public member becomes private
}
/*End of privateInheritance.cpp*/
```

Line 4 of Listing 5.24 will not compile because line 2 will not compile and line 5 will compile. Line 2 will not compile because although 'z' is a public member of the base class A, class B is derived from class A by using the private access specifier. In this case, the base class pointer might access the object of a private-derived class in a way (line 5 of Listing 5.24) that is not permitted when the object is accessed by using the name of the object itself (line 2 of Listing 5.24).

Therefore, the C++ compiler prevents a base class pointer from pointing at an object of the derived class if the private access specifier has been used to derive the class.

The default access specifier for inheritance is `private`. The following declarations are equivalent:

```
class B : private A             //B is a private derived class of A
{
   /*
      definition of class B
   */
};

class B : A                     //B is still a private derived class of A
{
   /*
      definition of class B
   */
};
```

5.7 Different Kinds of Inheritance

5.7.1 Multiple Inheritance

Figure 5.5 shows that in multiple inheritance, a class derives from more than one base class.

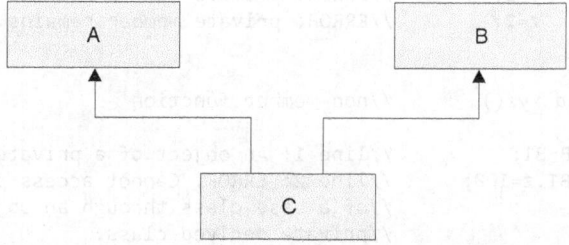

Figure 5.5 Multiple inheritance (class C derived from classes A and B)

The general syntax for multiple inheritance is as follows:

```
class <name of derived class>
: <access specifier> <name of first base class>,
  <access specifier> <name of second base class>,
  <access specifier> <name of third base class> …
{
   /*
      definition of derived class
   */
};
```

An illustrative example follows in Listing 5.25. We must note that for each of the base classes, a different access specifier can be used.

Listing 5.25   Multiple inheritance

```
/*Beginning of privateInheritance.cpp*/
class A
{
   private:
   int x;
   protected:
   int y;
   public:
   int z;
};
class B : private A              //B is a private derived class of A
{
   public:
   void f1()
   {
//    x=1;                       //ERROR: private member remains private
      y=2;                       //OK: protected member becomes private in
//this class
      z=2;                       //OK: protected member becomes private in
//this class
   }
};
class C : public B
{
   public:
   void f2()
   {
//    x=1;        //ERROR: private member remains private
//    y=2;        //ERROR: private member remains private
//    z=2;        //ERROR: private member remains private
   }
};
void xyz()        //non-member function
{
   B B1;          //line 1: An object of a private derived class
   B1.z=100;      //line 2: ERROR. Cannot access public member
                  //of a base class through an object of a
                  //private derived class.
   A * APtr;      //line 3
   APtr=&B1;      //line 4: ERROR. Cannot make a base class
                  //pointer point at an object of a private
                  //derived class.
   APtr->z=100;   //line 5. OK. Can access public
                  //member of the base class through a base
                  //class pointer.
}
/*End of privateInheritance.cpp*/
```

Output
10
20
30

An object of a class defined by multiple inheritance contains not only the data members defined in the derived class, but also the data members defined in all of the base classes. Thus, the size of such an object is equal to the sum of the sizes of the data members of all the base classes plus the sum of the sizes of the data members of all of the derived classes. Hence, the size of an object of the class C in Listing 5.25 is 12.

Moreover, with respect to such an object, it is possible to call the member functions of not only the derived class, but also the member functions of all the base classes. Therefore, in Listing 5.25, the member functions of classes A, B, and C have been called with respect to 'C1'.

5.7.2 Ambiguities in Multiple Inheritance

Multiple inheritance leads to a number of ambiguities, namely, identical members in more than one base class and diamond-shaped inheritance.

1. **Identical members in more than one base class:** The first ambiguity arises if two or more of the base classes have a member of the same name. This is illustrated in Listing 5.26.

Listing 5.26 Ambiguity due to identical member being in more than one base class

```
/*Beginning of A.h*/
class A
{
   int x;

   public:
   void setx(const int=0);
   int getx()const;
};
/*End of A.h*/

/*Beginning on A.cpp*/
#include"A.h"
void A::setx(const int pX)
{
   x = pX;
}
int A::getx() const
{
   return x;
}
/*End on A.cpp*/

/*Beginning of B.h*/
class B
{
   int y;

   public:
   void sety(const int=0);
   int gety()const;
};
/*End of B.h*/

/*Beginning on B.cpp*/
#include"B.h"
void B::sety(const int pY)
{
   y = pY;
```

```
        }
        int B::gety() const
        {
            return y;
        }
        /*End on B.cpp*/

        /*Beginning of C.h*/
        #include"A.h"
        #include"B.h"
        class C : public A, public B        //multiple inheritance
        {
            int z;

            public:
            void setz(const int=0);
            int getz()const;
        };
        /*End of C.h*/

        /*Beginning on C.cpp*/
        #include"C.h"
        void C::setz(const int pZ)
        {
            z = pZ;
        }
        int C::getz() const
        {
            return z;
        }
        /*End on C.cpp*/

        /*Beginning of multiInherit.cpp*/
        #include<iostream.h>
        #include"C.h"
        void main()
        {
          C C1;                      //declaring an object of the class that does
                                     //multiple inheritance
          C1.setx(10);              //calling member function of one base
                                     //class.
          C1.sety(20);              //calling member function of the other
                                     //base class.
          C1.setz(30);              //calling member function the derived
                                     //class.
          cout<<C1.getx()<<endl;    //calling member function of
                                     //one base class.
          cout<<C1.gety()<<endl;    //calling member function of
                                     //the other base class.
          cout<<C1.getz()<<endl;    //calling member function the
                                     //derived class.
        }
        /*End of multiInherit.cpp*/
```

In Listing 5.26, the compiler will not be able to decide which of the two show() functions it has to call. This ambiguity can be resolved by using the scope resolution operator. We can replace the main() function of Listing 5.26 with that of Listing 5.27 and see the difference.

Listing 5.27   Ambiguity resolution by using scope resolution operator

```cpp
/*Beginning of multiInheritAmbiguityResolve01.cpp*/
void<iostream.h>
Class A
{
  Public:
  Void show()
  {
    cout<<"show() function of clas A called\n";
  }
};
class B
{
  Public:
  void show()
  {
    cout<<"show() function of class B called\n";
};
class C : public A, public B
{ };
void main()
{
  C C1;
  C1.A: :show() ;              //OK: show() function of class A called
  C1.B: :show() ;              //OK: show() function of class B called
}
/*End of multiInheritAmbiguityResolve01.cpp*/
```

Output
show() function of class A called
show() function of class B called

This ambiguity can also be resolved by overriding the multiple inherited base class member as shown in Listing 5.28.

Listing 5.28   Ambiguity resolution by overriding

```cpp
/*Beginning of multiInheritAmbiguityResolve02.cpp*/
#include<iostream.h>
class A
{
  public:
    void show()
    {
      cout<<"show() function of class A called\n";
    }
};

class B
{
  public:
    void show()
```

```
        {
            cout<<"show() function of class B called\n";
        }
};

class C : public A, public B
{
    public:
        void show()        //override both of the inherited
                           //functions
        {
            cout<<"show() function of class C called\n";
        }
};

void main()
{
    C C1;
    C1.show();                            //OK: C::show() called
}
/*End of multiInheritAmbiguityResolve02.cpp*/
```

Output
show() function of class C called

We can still call the show() functions of classes A and B with respect to an object of class C by using the scope resolution operator. Let us now replace the main() function with that of Listing 5.29 and see the difference.

Listing 5.29 Calling overridden members by scope resolution operator

```
void main()
{
    C C1.A::show();
    C1.B::show();
}
```

Output
show() function of class A called
show() function of class B called

2. **Diamond-shaped inheritance:** Ambiguities can also arise if two or more base classes in turn inherit from a common base class (Figure 5.6). This is known as diamond-shaped inheritance (see Listing 5.30).

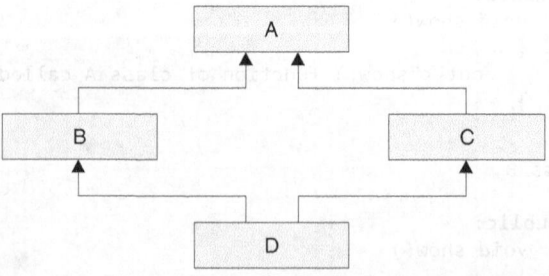

Figure 5.6 Base classes inheriting from a common base class

Listing 5.30   Diamond-shaped inheritance

```
/*Beginning of multiInheritAmbiguity02.cpp*/
class A
{
  public:
    void show();
};

class B : public A
{};

class C : public A
{};

class D : public B, public C
{};

void main()
{
  D D1;
  D1.show();                        //ERROR: ambiguous call to show()
}
/*End of multiInheritAmbiguity02.cpp*/
```

The two previous solutions—using scope resolution operator and overriding—are applicable here also. Nevertheless, a third solution is also available—that of declaring the top base class to be virtual. The ambiguity disappears if we declare class A to be a `virtual` base class of classes B and C. This is demonstrated by the following lines of code.

```
class B : virtual public A
{};
class C : virtual public A
{};
```

Now, the call to the `show()` function with respect to an object of class D is no longer ambiguous.

5.7.3 Multi-level Inheritance

When a class inherits from a derived class, it is known as multi-level inheritance. In other words, a class derives from a class that is in turn derived from another class. Figure 5.7 depicts multi-level inheritance.

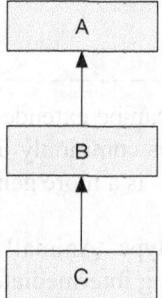

Figure 5.7   Multi-level inheritance

In Figure 5.7, class C is derived from class B, which is in turn derived from class A. The syntax for implementing this derivation is shown in Listing 5.31.

Listing 5.31   Multi-level inheritance

```cpp
/*Beginning of multiInherit.cpp*/
#include<iostream.h>

class A
{
   public:
      void fA()
      {
         cout<<"fA() called\n";
      }
};

class B : public A //B derived from A
{
   public:
      void fB()
      {
         cout<<"fB() called\n";
      }
};

class C : public B //C derived from B, B derived from A
{
   public:
      void fC()
      {
         cout<<"fC() called\n";
      }
};

void main()
{
   C C1;
   C1.fA();
   C1.fB();
   C1.fC();
}
/*End of multiInherit.cpp*/
```

Output
fA() called
fB() called
fC() called

Multi-level inheritance can be extended to any level.

Multi-level inheritance is commonly used to implement successive refinement of a data type. For instance, 'Animal' is a more generic class. 'Mammal' is a type of 'Animal'. 'Man' is a type of 'Mammal'.

In Figure 5.8, the data type 'Animal' is successively refined to 'Mammal' and then to 'Man'. The benefit of having intermediate classes, such as the class 'Mammal', is that they can then be used as a base class for some other classes also. For example, the class 'Mammal' can be used as a common base class for classes 'Whale', 'Dog', etc.

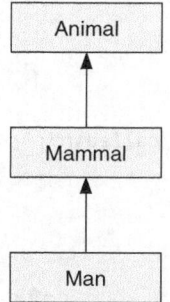

Figure 5.8   Example of using multi-level inheritance to successively refine a data type

5.7.4 Hierarchical Inheritance

In hierarchical inheritance, a single class serves as a base class for more than one derived class. Figure 5.9 illustrates this.

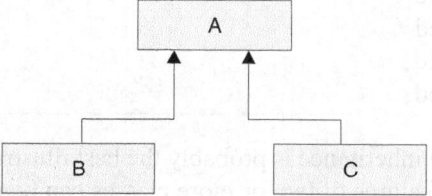

Figure 5.9   Hierarchical inheritance

In Figure 5.9, class A is the common base class for classes B and C. This is demonstrated in Listing 5.32.

Listing 5.32   Hierarchical inheritance

```
/*Beginning of hierarchicalInherit.cpp*/
#include<iostream.h>
class A
{
  public:
    void fA()
    {
      cout<<"fA() called\n";
    }
};

class B : public A              //derived from A
{
  public:
    void fB()
    {
      cout<<"fB() called\n";
    }
};
```

```
class C : public A                      //also derived from A
{
  public:
    void fC()
    {
        cout<<"fC() called\n";
    }
};
void main()
{
  B B1;
  C C1;
  B1.fA();
  B1.fB();
  C1.fA();
  C1.fC();
}
/*End of hierarchicalInherit.cpp*/
```

Output
fA() called
fB() called
fA() called
fC() called

Hierarchical inheritance is probably the best illustration of the virtues of code reusability. The common features of two or more classes can be put together in a single base class that can then be inherited by those classes. The need to duplicate the common features in more than one class is, thus, eliminated.

As an example, the class 'Mammal' can be a common base class for the classes 'Man', 'Whale', 'Dog', 'Cat', etc. The features that are common to all these derived classes can be placed in the class 'Mammal'. Only the special features may be put in the respective derived classes.

5.7.5 Hybrid Inheritance

Hybrid inheritance, as the name indicates, is simply a mixture of all the above kinds of inheritances. Figure 5.10 illustrates this.

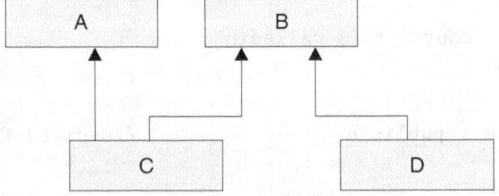

Figure 5.10   Hybrid inheritance

5.8 Order of Invocation of Constructors and Destructors

Constructors are invoked in the following order:
- Virtual base class constructors in the order of inheritance
- Non-virtual base class constructors in the order of inheritance
- Member objects' constructors in the order of declaration
- Derived class constructor

Destructors are invoked in the reverse order. Listing 5.33 illustrates this.

Listing 5.33   Order of invocation of constructors and destructors

```
/*Beginning of cd_order.cpp*/
#include<iostream.h>

class A
{
   public:
      A()
      {
         cout<<"Constructor of class A called\n";
      }
      ~A()
      {
         cout<<"Destructor of class A called\n";
      }
};

class B
{
   public:
      B()
      {
         cout<<"Constructor of class B called\n";
      }
      ~B()
      {
         cout<<"Destructor of class B called\n";
      }
};

class C : virtual public A
{
   public:
      C()
      {
         cout<<"Constructor of class C called\n";
      }
      ~C()
      {
         cout<<"Destructor of class C called\n";
      }
};

class D : virtual public A
{
   public:
      D()
      {
```

```
            cout<<"Constructor of class D called\n";
        }
        ~D()
        {
            cout<<"Destructor of class D called\n";
        }
};
class E
{
    public:
        E()
        {
            cout<<"Constructor of class E called\n";
        }
        ~E()
        {
            cout<<"Destructor of class E called\n";
        }
};
class F : public B, public C, public D
{
    private:
        E Eobj;
    public:
        F()
        {
            cout<<"Constructor of class F called\n";
        }
        ~F()
        {
            cout<<"Destructor of class F called\n";
        }
};
void main()
{
    F Fobj;
}
/*End of cd_order.cpp*/
```

Output

Constructor of class A called
Constructor of class B called
Constructor of class C called
Constructor of class D called
Constructor of class E called
Constructor of class F called
Destructor of class F called
Destructor of class E called
Destructor of class D called
Destructor of class C called
Destructor of class B called
Destructor of class A called

Summary

C++ allows a class to be defined in such a way that it automatically includes member data and member functions of an existing class. As usual, it allows additional member data and member functions to be defined in the new class also. This is called inheritance.

The existing class whose features are being inherited is known as the base class or parent class or super class. The new class that is being defined by inheriting from the base class is known as the derived class or child class or sub-class.

Objects of the derived class contain data members of the derived class as well as the base class. Objects of the base class can call member functions of the derived class as well as those of the base class.

By allowing only the common data members and common member functions in the base class, inheritance enables code reusability and eases code maintenance. Inheritance implements an 'is-a' relationship whereas containership implements a 'has-a' relationship. Friendship is not inherited.

A base class pointer can point at an object of the derived class. But a derived class pointer cannot point at an object of the base class.

Member functions of the base class can be overridden in the derived class. Defining a member function in the derived class in such a manner that its name and signature match those of a base class function is known as function overriding.

Base class members can be initialized to values that are passed to the constructor of the derived class. These values can in turn be passed to the base class constructor.

'Protected' members are inaccessible to non-member functions. But they are accessible to the member functions of their own class and to member functions of the derived classes.

Classes can be derived by the public, protected, and private keywords. Deriving by the public access specifier retains the access level of base class members. Deriving by the protected access specifier reduces the access level of public base class members to protected while the access level of protected and private base class members remains unchanged. Deriving by the private access specifier reduces the access level of public and protected base class members to private while access level of private base class members remains unchanged. The default access specifier for inheritance is 'private'.

In multiple inheritance, a class derives from more than one base class. Multiple inheritance leads to a number of ambiguities. Ambiguity arises if two or more of the base classes have a member of the same name. Ambiguity can also arise if two or more base classes in turn inherit from a common base class. This is known as diamond-shaped inheritance. These ambiguities are resolved by either of the following:

- Using the scope resolution operator and passing the name of the actual owner class to call the function
- Overriding the function of the ultimate base class in the intermediate base class
- Deriving the intermediate base classes by using the virtual keyword

When a class inherits from a derived class, it is known as multi-level inheritance. In hierarchical inheritance, a single class serves as a base class for the derived class(es). Hybrid inheritance is a mixture of all the above kinds of inheritances.

Constructors are invoked in the following order:

- Virtual base class constructors in the order of inheritance
- Non-virtual base class constructors in the order of inheritance
- Member objects' constructors in the order of declaration
- Derived class constructor

Destructors are invoked in the reverse order.

Key Terms

inheritance

base class, parent class, super class

derived class, child class, subclass

data members of base class and objects of the derived class

function members of base class and objects of the derived class

keeping common features in base class for code reusability

base class and derived class pointers

overriding of base class member functions
base class initilization
protected members
deriving by public, protected, and private specifiers
multiple inheritance

— ambiguities in multiple inheritance
multi-level inheritance
hierarchical inheritance
order of invocation of constructors and destructors

Exercises

1. What is inheritance? How does it enable code reusability?
2. How does inheritance influence the size and functionality of derived class objects?
3. How does inheritance compare with containership?
4. How does inheritance compare with nesting?
5. Create a global non-member function that has a base class pointer as its formal argument. Call member functions of the base class through the pointer from within this function. Now call the function by passing addresses of the derived class objects.
6. Override one of the base class member functions that have been called from within the function you have defined above, in the derived class. Pass the address of an object of this derived class to the function. Which function gets called—the overridden function of the base class or the overriding function of the derived class?
7. Make a derived class pointer point at an object of the base class by explicit typecasting. Now access a member of the derived class that does not exist in the base class. What happens?
8. Why is it necessary for the derived class constructor to pass values explicitly to the base class constructor for initializing base class members?
9. A base class has data members. However, a class that is derived from it does not. Does the derived class need a constructor? Why?
10. What is the effect of using the protected access specifier on the visibility of a base class member?
11. Will a function of the derived class be able to access a public member of the base class if no access specifier was used to derive the derived class? Why?
12. What are the ambiguities that arise in multiple and diamond-shaped inheritance? How can they be removed?
13. In which order are the constructors and destructors called when an object of the derived class is created?

14. State true or false
    (a) A base class object is usually smaller than an object of its derived class.
    (b) Inheritance increases the visibility of base class members.
    (c) The constructor of a virtual base class is called before the constructor of a non-virtual base class.
    (d) Inheritance implements a 'has-a' relationship.
    (e) A public member of the base class can be called with respect to an object of the derived class in a non-member function if the protected access specifier was used to derive the derived class.
15. Assume that you are building a simplified windows-based drawing program. From a menu, the user would select which type of shape—ellipse or rectangle—he/she wants to draw. After selecting, he/she would drag the mouse pointer from one point of the window to another and the selected shape would get drawn within the enclosing rectangle whose diagonally opposite points coincide with these two points.

    Create a class Shape. Derive two classes—Ellipse and Rectangle—from this class. Answer the following questions to arrive at the definitions of the classes:

    (a) Which class/classes should hold the coordinates of the enclosing rectangle as its data members—Shape, Ellipse, Rectangle or all of three?
    (b) In the chapter on virtual functions and dynamic polymorphism, you would realize that the class Shape should also have functions such as draw() and getArea(). Should these functions have only an empty definition when they are defined as members of the class Shape? Would they have empty definitions when they are defined as members of the classes Ellipse and Rectangle?

6

Virtual Functions and Dynamic Polymorphism

O
V
E
R
V
I
E
W

This chapter deals with one of the most remarkable features of C++: dynamic polymorphism and how virtual functions enable it.

Virtual functions enable the C++ programmer to create reusable code. So far, function overriding has appeared to be an unnecessary feature of C++. This chapter explains why C++ provides the feature of function overriding.

The mechanism by which C++ implements the virtual functions has also been dealt with in this chapter. Pure virtual functions, their need and usage find a prominent place in this chapter.

This chapter also discusses the use of virtual destructors and clone functions.

6.1 Need for Virtual Functions

First, let us consider Listing 6.1 and its output.

Listing 6.1 Overriding member function of base class in the derived class

```
/*Beginning of A.h*/
#ifndef _A_H_
#define _A_H_
class A
{
   public:
   void show();
};
#endif
/*End of A.h*/

/*Beginning of B.h*/
#ifndef _B_H_
#define _B_H_
#include"A.h"
class B : public A                    //class B derived from class A
{
   public:
   void show();                       //function override
};
#endif
/*End of B.h*/

/*Beginning of A.cpp*/
#include"A.h"
```

```
#include<iostream.h>
void A::show()
{
    cout<<"A\n";
}
/*End of A.cpp*/

/*Beginning of B.cpp*/
#include"B.h"
#include<iostream.h>
void B::show()
{
    A::show();                  //calling back the overridden function to
                                //logically extend the class definition
    cout<<"B\n";
}
/*End of B.cpp*/
```

Now, let us consider the client program shown in Listing 6.2.

Listing 6.2 Calling an overridden function through a pointer of base class type

```
/*Beginning of try1.cpp*/
#include"B.h"
#include<iostream.h>
void main()
{
    A A1;
    B B1;
    A * APtr;
    APtr=&A1;
    APtr->show();               //A::show() called. APtr is of type A*
    APtr=&B1;
    APtr->show();               //A::show() called. APtr is of type A*
}
/*End of try1.cpp*/
```

Output

A
A

As we will notice, the base class function is called irrespective of the type of object pointed at by the pointer. Here, the compiler decides which function is to be called by considering the type of the pointer; the type of the object pointed at by the pointer is not considered. The conclusion is that overriding in such cases is ineffective. This can be a serious problem when a client is trying to extend a class hierarchy. Why? Before we try to find an answer, let us realize that calling the function through a reference produces the same effect. See Listing 6.3.

Listing 6.3 Calling an overridden function through a reference of base class type

```
/*Beginning of try2.cpp*/
#include"B.h"                   //from listing 6.01
#include<iostream.h>
void main()
{
    A A1;
```

```
      B B1;
      A &ARef1=A1;
      ARef1.show();              //A::show() called. ARef1 is of type A&
      A &ARef2=B1;
      ARef2.show();              //A::show() called. ARef2 is of type A&
}
/*End of try2.cpp*/
```

Output

A

A

Now, let us try to understand why the ineffectiveness of overriding can be a major hindrance in the extension of a class hierarchy.

Placing the pointer and the object pointed at by the pointer in the same function as local variables does not make any sense. After all, an object can be as effectively accessed through its name itself. Instead, the pointer appears as a formal argument in function definitions and the address of the object is passed as a parameter to the function calls. Similar comments hold true for the reference variable also. Let us proceed with this piece of knowledge.

Keeping in mind the definitions of classes A and B from Listing 6.1, we have a look at the definition of function abc() of a class X in Listing 6.4.

Listing 6.4   Calling an overridden function through a pointer of base class type

```
/*Beginning of X.h*/
#ifndef _X_H_
#define _X_H_
#include"A.h"
class X
{
   public:
      void abc(A*);              //A* is the formal argument
};
#endif
/*End of X.h*/

/*Beginning of X.cpp*/
#include"X.h"
void X::abc(A * p)
{
   //some lines of (complicated) code
   p->show();
   //some more lines of (complicated) code
}
/*End of X.cpp*/

/*Beginning of try3.cpp*/
#include"X.h"
#include"B.h"
void main()
{
   X X1;
   A A1;
   B B1;
   X1.abc(&A1);                 //A::show() will be called
   X1.abc(&B1);                 //A::show() will be called
```

```
}
/*End of try3.cpp*/
```

Output

A

A

From our recent study we know that the A::show() function will be called against both of the function calls in the main() function of Listing 6.4.

Now let us take stock of the situation. The library programmer has defined the following:

- The class A
- The show() function of class A
- The class X
- The abc() function of class X

The definitions of the A::show() and X::abc() functions are final and have been put in libraries.

It is expected that a class will get derived from class A. The derived class may override the show() function of class A. The overriding function will add the extra code that is relevant to the derived class. To complete the picture, it will also call back the overridden function A::show(). In this way, the base class function will get successively refined by the overriding functions of the derived classes.

However, as Listing 6.4 shows, such an override has so far appeared ineffective. It is highly desirable that when the address of an object of the derived class B is passed to the X::abc() function, then the B::show() function should be called (see Listing 6.4). If this happens, then the *same* X::abc() function will prove useful irrespective of the type of object whose address is being passed to it. Unfortunately, such an extension of the class hierarchy has so far remained elusive.

We must realize that derived classes such as class B may be defined much after functions such as X::abc() function have been defined.

Moreover, the function X::abc() should work equally well whether the address of an object of the base class A is passed as a parameter to it or the address of an object of any of the derived classes is passed.

In the present situation, it appears necessary to redefine the X::abc() function corresponding to each derived class of class A. That is, the X::abc(A *) function should be copied and redefined with a pointer of the derived class type as a formal argument. For example, X::abc(A *), X::abc(B *), etc. This is certainly impossible because the definition of the X::abc() function will be in some library that is inaccessible to the programmer who is defining the derived classes. It is also extremely cumbersome to redefine the X::abc() function for each of the derived classes. This anyway goes against the principles of code reusability.

Thus, it proves impossible to extend an existing class hierarchy. Function overriding does not produce the desired effects. Virtual functions solve this problem.

6.2 Virtual Functions

Virtual functions provide one of the most useful and powerful features of C++ called dynamic polymorphism.

In order to appreciate the various nuances of dynamic polymorphism, let us first look at a function (shown in Listing 6.5) that returns the sum of factorials of the numbers that belong to a range whose limits are passed to it. The function may have the following definition.

Listing 6.5 Function to compute sum of factorials

```
long int factorialSum(unsigned int a, unsigned int b)
{
    int i;
    long int sum;
    for(sum=0,i=a;i<=b;i++)
        sum+=factorial(i);
    return sum;
}
```

Here, `factorial()` is a function that returns the factorial of the parameter passed to it. Similarly, the function in Listing 6.6 returns the sum of cubes of the numbers that belong to the range whose limits are passed to it.

Listing 6.6 Function to compute sum of cubes

```
long int cubeSum(unsigned int a, unsigned int b)
{
    int i;
    long int sum;
    for(sum=0,i=a;i<=b;i++)
        sum+=cube(i);
    return sum;
}
```

The `cube()` function returns the cube of the number passed as a parameter to it.

Again, the function of Listing 6.7 returns the sum of logarithms of the numbers that belong to the range whose limits are passed to it.

Listing 6.7 Function to compute sum of logarithms

```
long int logSum(unsigned int a, unsigned int b)
{
    int i;
    long int sum;
    for(sum=0,i=a;i<=b;i++)
        sum+=log(i);
    return sum;
}
```

The `log()` function returns the logarithm of the number passed as a parameter to it.

A close look at the definitions of these functions reveals that the definitions of the functions are exactly the same except for the name of the inner function they all call. Nevertheless, the similarity in their definitions is striking. It will not be entirely unreasonable on our part to expect that there must be some means of replacing all these functions by a single function. We want to make a generic function that will replace all the above functions. For this, we have to specify a function pointer as an additional formal argument in the function. See Listing 6.8.

Listing 6.8   Generic function to compute summation of series

```
//a generic sum function
long int genSum(unsigned int a, unsigned int b,
                long int (*p)())
{
    int i;
    long int sum;
    for(sum=0,i=a;i<=b;i++)
        sum+=(*p)(i);
    return sum;
}
```

Next, we can call the function by passing the function whose returned values have to be summed up as the last parameter to this generic function. The following lines of code demonstrate this.

```
x=genSum(1,5,factorial);
x=genSum(3,8,cube);
```

Now, any kind of summation can be carried out by this single generic function, provided the function whose returned values are being summed up returns a `long int` or a value of a compatible type. A very important point to be noted is that the generic sum function is capable of similarly summing up the returned values from a function that may be created well into the future! The function call,

```
(*p)(i),
```

exhibits polymorphic behaviour, because while compiling it, it is not known which function will actually be executed. This becomes known only later when the client program that calls the genSum() function is compiled.

We would like to perform a similar feat in C++ also. Let us look at the definition of X::abc() function in Listing 6.4. We would certainly like the show() function of that class to be called whose object's address is passed as its parameter. In other words, we would like to extend the class library as described in the previous section.

If the library programmer, who is defining the base class, expects and suspects overriding of a certain member function and wants to make such an override meaningful, he/she should declare the function as virtual. For declaring a function as virtual, the prototype of the function within the class should be prefixed with the virtual keyword. The virtual keyword may appear either before or after the keyword specifying the return type of the function. If the function is defined outside the class, then only the prototype should have the virtual keyword.

The syntax for declaring a virtual function as follows:

```
virtual <return type> <function name>(<formal arguments>);
```

The following lines of code illustrate how virtual functions are declared.

```
class A
{
    public:
        virtual void show();            //A::show() is virtual
};
```

or

```
class A
{
  public:
    void virtual show();          //A::show() is virtual
};
```

If we define the `A::show()` function in Listing 6.1 as a virtual function by following this syntax, then the output of Listing 6.2 will be

A

B

instead of

A

A

This means that when the base class pointer points at an object of the derived class and a call is dispatched to an overridden virtual function, then it is the overriding function of the derived class, and not the overridden function of the base class, that is called.

Now, let us take stock of the situation. The library programmer's desire to enable a logical extension of the class library is now fulfilled. Let us go back to Listing 6.4. Even if class A is derived and the `A::show()` function is overridden in the derived class much after the `X::abc()` function is defined, the correct function will be called from within the `X::abc()` function. That is, if the derived class overrides the base class function and the address of the derived class object is passed as a parameter to the `X::abc()` function, then the overriding function will be called. If no such overriding occurs, the base class function itself will be called.

The function call

```
p->show();
```

in the `X::abc()` function in Listing 6.4 exhibits polymorphic behaviour. Against this function call, the `show()` function of the base class or the overriding `show()` function of any of its derived classes will be called. However, this polymorphic behaviour is also dynamic in nature. Which function will be ultimately called is not known when the `X::abc()` function is compiled and put in a library. This is decided only when the client program that calls this function is compiled. We can therefore say that compile time for the client is run time for the library. Therefore, the polymorphic behaviour exhibited by virtual functions is also termed as *dynamic polymorphism*.

It is worthwhile to note that functions in the base class usually contain only those statements that are relevant to the base class itself. It is not always possible to provide a complete definition to them, as the base classes are sometimes abstract in nature (`start()` method in the `Vehicle` class). The overriding functions of the derived class first call back the overridden base class functions and then add the extra statements that complete the definitions with respect to the derived class itself. Having such base class functions as virtual ensures that the client is able to call both the functions in sequence as desired.

Virtual functions of the base classes reappear as virtual in the derived classes also. Again, using the virtual keyword while defining the overriding derived class function is optional. See Listing 6.9.

Listing 6.9   Virtual functions remain virtual

```
/*Beginning of autoVirtual.cpp*/
#include<iostream.h>
class A
```

```
{
  public:
    virtual void show()            //A::show() is virtual
    {
      cout<<"A\n";
    }
};
class B : public A                 //B derived from A
{
  public:
    void show()                    //B::show() is virtual
    {
      cout<<"B\n";
    }
};
class C : public B                 //C derived from B
{
  public:
    void show()                    //C::show() is virtual
    {
      cout<<"C\n";
    }
};

void main()
{
  B * BPtr;
  BPtr = new C;
  BPtr->show();
}
/*End of autoVirtual.cpp*/
```

Output
C

6.3 Mechanism of Virtual Functions

Now, let us understand the mechanism of virtual functions. For every base class that has one or more virtual functions, a table of function addresses is created during run time. This table of function addresses is called the virtual table or VTBL in short. The VTBL contains the address of each and every virtual function that has been defined in the corresponding class. Addresses of non-virtual functions do not appear in such tables.

Suppose a class A has two virtual functions—abc() and def() (Listing 6.10).

Listing 6.10 A class with two virtual functions

```
/*Beginning of A.h*/
class A
{
  public:
    virtual void abc();
    virtual void def();
};
/*End of A.h*/
```

During run time the VTBL of class A will be as shown in Figure 6.1.

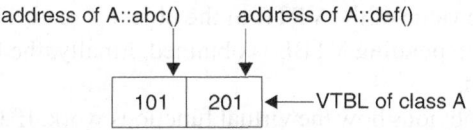

Figure 6.1   Table addresses of virtual functions of the base class

Similarly, such a table of addresses of virtual functions will be created for the derived class also. If the derived class does not redefine a certain base class member, then the table will contain the address of the inherited base class virtual function itself. But if a certain base class virtual function is redefined in the derived class, this table will contain the address of the overriding function. Finally, if the derived class defines a new virtual function, then its address will also be contained in the table. Thus, if class B is derived from class A as illustrated in Listing 6.11, then the VTBL for class B will appear as shown in Figure 6.2.

Listing 6.11   Overriding base class virtual functions and introducing new ones

```
/*Beginning of B.h*/
#include"A.h"
class B : public A
{
  public:
    void def();              //overriding the A::def() function
    virtual void ghi();      //introduces a new virtual
                             //function
};
/*End of B.h*/
```

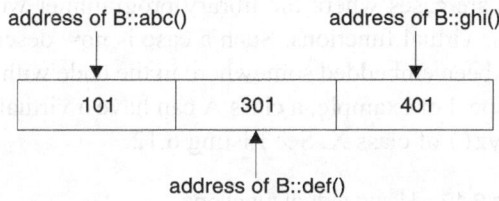

Figure 6.2   Table of addresses of virtual functions of the derived class

Notice that since the A::abc() function is not overridden in the derived class, its address reappears in the VTBL of class B. On the other hand, since the A::def() function was overridden in the derived class, therefore its address is replaced in the VTBL of class B by the address of the B::def() function. Finally, a new address appears in the VTBL of class B—the address of B::ghi() function which is a newly introduced virtual function in class B.

Finally, every object of a class that has a virtual function contains a pointer to the VTBL of the corresponding class. This pointer is also known as the virtual pointer or VPTR. For example, an object of class A, apart from all other non-static data members, will also have a pointer to the VTBL of class A. This table is depicted in Figure 6.1. Similarly, an object of class B, apart from all other non-static data members, will also have a pointer to the VTBL of class B. This table is depicted in Figure 6.2. Now, whenever a call is dispatched to a virtual function through an object or a reference to an object, or through a pointer to an object, then first of all the value of the VPTR of the object is read. Then the address of the called function from the corresponding VTBL is obtained. Finally, the function is called through the address thus obtained.

Now it is obvious how the virtual functions work. If a base class pointer points at (or a base class reference refers to) an object of the derived class and a virtual function is called with respect to it, then the derived class function will be called if it overrides the base class virtual function. If the base class virtual function is not overridden, then it itself will be called.

Note that it is the table size that varies from class to class (for each class there is only one VTBL). The size of the object does not vary. Only the size of the objects of classes with virtual functions increases uniformly by four bytes due to the presence of the additional pointer (VPTR).

We might wonder as to why C++ supports two types of binding—static and dynamic. Why does it not support dynamic binding only? In other words, why does it not declare all functions virtual by default? The reason is that virtual functions entail a run-time cost in the form of space that is wasted for creating the VTBL and embedding the VPTR in each and every object of the base/derived class. Time is also lost in searching the VTBL for the function address. If none of the member functions of a certain class will be overridden, then making them virtual will unnecessarily incur the above cost. Therefore, C++ allows the programmer to decide whether the member function has to be declared as virtual or not.

6.4 Pure Virtual Functions

From Section 6.3, we already know that it is optional to override virtual functions. A library programmer declares a member function as virtual if he/she expects overriding and wants to make the override effective.

But there are cases where the library programmer would like to enforce an override of the base class virtual functions. Such a case is now described. A call to a base class virtual function has been embedded somewhere in the code with respect to a pointer or reference of base class type. For example, a class A can have a virtual function abc() that is called from a function xyz() of class X. See Listing 6.12.

Listing 6.12 Using virtual functions

```
/* Beginning of X.xpp*/
#include"X.h"
void X::xyz(A * p)
{
    //some lines of (complicated) code
    p->abc();
    //some more lines of (complicated) code
}
/*End of X.cpp*/
```

Now, A::abc() function may satisfy either of the following descriptions.
- It has no meaningful definition with respect to the base class. For example, a function to rotate the shape cannot be defined in the class Shape itself. The algorithm to rotate the shape is not known since the shape itself is not known. See Listing 6.13.

Listing 6.13 Giving blank definition to undefinable virtual function

```
class Shape
{
  public:
    virtual void rotate();
};
void shape::rotate()
{
  //null definition!
}
```

- It has only a few lines of code, which do not really give it a complete definition. The function is such that it cannot be called in isolation. It can only be called indirectly through the derived class's overriding function that has the necessary code to complete the definition.

Obviously, C++ should provide some mechanism to the library programmer to enforce the desired override. Pure virtual functions provide this mechanism. If even one member function is declared as a pure virtual function, then the corresponding class becomes an **A**bstract **B**ase **C**lass (ABC in short). A function is declared as a pure virtual function by prefixing its prototype with the virtual keyword as before but suffixing it with an 'equal to' sign and then by a 'zero' (0).

The syntax for declaring a pure virtual function is

```
virtual <return type> <function name>(<formal
arguments>)=0;
```

Listing 6.14 illustrates this.

Listing 6.14 Defining a pure virtual function

```
/*Beginning of A.h*/
class A
{
    virtual void abc()=0;
    /*
      rest of the class A
    */
};
/*End of A.h*/
```

An abstract base class cannot be instantiated, that is, objects of an abstract base class cannot be declared. Compile-time errors defeat attempts to do so.

```
A A1;   //error
```

The derived class must override all pure virtual functions of the base class or itself get branded as an ABC by the compiler. For example, any class that derives from class A in Listing 6.14 must override the A::abc() function to become a concrete or instantiable class.

What is the utility of an ABC? The utility of an ABC lies in its use as an interface. The library programmer defines the ABC and also some generic functions that implement the general flow of a related algorithm without considering the exact data type on which they will work. An example to illustrate this point follows.

Let us consider an abstract class Shape (see Listing 6.15).

Listing 6.15   An abstract class

```
/*Beginning of Shape.h*/
class Shape
{
    int x1,y1,x2,y2;                    //coordinates of the
                                        //bounding rectangle
  public:
    void setBoundingRect(int,int,int,int);
                                        //set the bounding
                                        //rectangle for the
                                        //shape
    void move(int,int);                 //move upper left corner
                                        //of bounding rectangle
                                        //to specified
                                        //coordinates
    virtual void rotate(float)=0; //rotate by angle
                                        //specified in the
                                        //parameter
    virtual void shrink(float)=0; //shrink by percent
                                        //specified in the
                                        //parameter
    virtual void grow(float)=0;   //grow by percent
                                        //specified in the
                                        //parameter
    virtual void hflip()=0;             //flip horizontally
    virtual void vflip()=0;             //flip vertically
    virtual void draw()=0;              //draw the shape
};
/*End of Shape.h*/
```

Let us consider a client driver function that the programmer defines to operate upon an object of class Shape or any of its derived classes. This function will flash a shape in a certain sequence. While the actual object that will be flashed is not known when the function is defined, the sequence of operations for carrying out the operation has been decided. See Listing 6.16.

Listing 6.16   Client code to use the abstract class

```
/*Beginning of MyWindow.cpp*/
#include"MyWindow.h"
void MyWindow::flash(Shape * p)
{
    p->setBoundingRect(0,0,10,10);
    p->draw();
    p->rotate(90);
    for(int x=0;x<=10;x++)
        p->shrink(5);
    for(int x=0;x<=10;x++)
        p->grow(5);
    p->hlip();
    p->hflip();
    p->vflip();
    p->vflip();
}
/*
```

```
           definitions of rest of the functions of class MyWindow
    */
    /*End of MyWindow.cpp*/
```

There might be many more lines of code in the function of Listing 6.16. But the important thing to be remembered is that the class, which will be derived from the class Shape and whose object's address will be passed to this function, might be defined much later. In addition, the same function will work equally well for each such class. Moreover, there can be many such client programs. After all, what is a class library if it does not have plenty of clients! But there is absolutely no need to define such driver functions for each of the derived classes separately. However, every such class will have to define each and every pure virtual function of the class Shape. The abstract nature of the base class ensures this.

Thus, the ABC behaves just like an interface with little or no implementation of its own. The facility that the library programmer gets is that he/she is free to define generic functions without bothering about the implementation details. He/she can enforce all necessary overrides. The advantage for the application programmer is that he/she can derive any class from the ABC, provide his/her own implementations for the derived class and then use the same driver functions like MyWindow::flash() for any of these derived classes.

Abstract Base Classes are also used to build implementation in stages. We know that if a pure virtual function inherited from the base class is not defined in the derived class, it remains a pure virtual function in the derived class. Thus, the derived class also becomes an abstract class.

Let me exemplify this explanation. Suppose there is an abstract class A having a number of pure virtual functions (Listing 6.17).

Listing 6.17 An abstract base class

```cpp
class A
{
    public:
        virtual void abc()=0;
        virtual void def()=0;
        virtual void ghi()=0;
};

void main()
{
    A A1;                                //ERROR!
}
```

A class B is derived from it. This class B overrides and defines only a few of the functions of class A. Thus, class B is also an ABC. See Listing 6.18.

Listing 6.18 Not defining all base class pure virtual functions results in an abstract class

```cpp
class B : public A
{
    public:
        void abc()
        {
            //definition of B::abc() function
        }
```

```
};
void main()
{
    B B1;                                     //ERROR!
}
```

Next, a class C derives from class B. It overrides and defines the remaining pure virtual functions of class A. Thus, class C becomes a concrete class. See Listing 6.19.

Listing 6.19 Defining all the inherited pure virtual functions results in a concrete class

```
class C : public B
{
public:
    void def()
    {
        //definition of C::def() function
    }
    void ghi()
    {
        //definition of C::ghi() function
    }
};
void main()
{
    C C1;                                     //OK
}
```

We may ask why all pure virtual functions of class A were not defined in class B itself. The reason is that there is no concrete definition of the remaining functions with respect to class B. It itself serves as a base class for a number of derived classes. Each of the derived classes have a different definition of the pure virtual functions of class A that are left undefined by class B. If class B defines any of these functions, then such functions will themselves be called when a pointer of class A type points at an object of any of the derived classes of class B and calls are dispatched to the pure virtual function of class A. This is obviously undesirable. Class B will define only those pure virtual functions of class A that can have a suitable meaning with respect to it. Such definitions will be applicable to all its derived classes.

Although concrete classes must provide an implementation to all the pure virtual functions, the abstract data type may provide one as well. The derived class can invoke it by using the scope resolution operator (Listing 6.20).

Listing 6.20 Defining a pure virtual function in the abstract base class itself

```
class A                                   //An abstract base class
{
public:
    virtual void abc()=0;
};
void A::abc()                             //pure virtual function defined
{
    //definition of A::abc() function
}
```

```
class B : public A
{
    public:
        void abc();
};

void B::abc()
{
    A::abc();
    //definition of rest of the B::abc() function
}
```

The ability to provide an implementation to pure virtual methods allows data types to provide core functionality while still requiring derived classes to provide a specialized implementation. Note that the class remains abstract even if we provide an implementation for its pure virtual function.

As per requirements, a member function can be non-virtual, virtual, or pure virtual.

6.5 Virtual Destructors and Virtual Constructors

We will now study the creation and use of `virtual` constructors and destructors. We will first study `virtual` destructors. This will be followed by a study of virtual constructors.

6.5.1 Virtual Destructors

Destructors can be defined as virtual. If necessary, destructors must be defined as virtual. Why? Let us consider Listing 6.21 (A is a base class and B is a class derived from A).

Listing 6.21   Destroying a derived class object through a base class pointer

```
A * APtr;
APtr = new B;
. . . .
. . . .
delete APtr;
```

Let us consider the last line of Listing 6.21 that deletes the memory occupied by the object of class B at which 'APtr' points. Because 'APtr' is of base class type, only the base class destructor is called with respect to the object before the entire memory occupied by the object is returned to the OS. This can lead to memory leaks apart from other problems. Suppose objects of the derived class B have a pointer. It is possible that this pointer, which is contained in the object at which 'APtr' points, is assigned a dynamically allocated memory block during the lifetime of the object. Although the destructor of class B destroys that memory block to prevent memory leaks, a memory leak will still occur because the destructor of class B is not called.

On the other hand, if the destructor of class A is virtual, then against the last line of Listing 6.21, first the destructor of class B will be called, then the destructor of class A will be called. Finally, the entire memory block occupied by the object will be returned to the OS.

The conclusion is that if we expect the use of the `delete` operator on objects of a base class and the presence of pointers in the derived classes, we must declare the destructor of the base class as virtual.

An interesting point to be noted is that when a pointer of the base class points at a dynamically created object of the derived class and then deletes the memory occupied by the object, the entire block of memory is deleted. In other words, if the total size of the non-static data members of the base class is 'x' and the total size of the non-static data members of the derived class is 'y', then the total block of size 'x+y' is deleted. This is irrespective of whether the base class destructor is virtual or not.

6.5.2 Virtual Constructors

First, let us understand that constructors cannot be virtual. Declaring a constructor as virtual results in a compile-time error. Why? Consider a class A, and a class B that is derived from A. If the constructor of class A is virtual, then in the following statement

```
A * p = new B;
```

the constructor of class B alone will be called. The constructor of class A will not be called. This can lead to trouble. What will happen if class A has a pointer that the constructor correctly initializes? Since the constructor is not called, a rogue pointer will result.

However, the need to *construct virtually* arises very frequently while programming in C++. Let us consider the function in the following lines of code.

```
void abc(A * p)                //A is a class
{
    //definition of abc() function
}
```

For reasons that will be listed later, an exact copy of the object at which 'p' points is required within the 'abc()' function. This means that another object that has the same values as the object at which 'p' points needs to be created within the 'abc()' function. Calling the copy constructor seems to serve the purpose (Listing 6.22).

Listing 6.22   Trying to clone using copy constructor

```
    A * q = new A(*p);
```
or
```
    A A1(*p);
```

This will work if the designer of class A has correctly defined the copy constructor and if 'p' points at an object of class A and not at an object of a class that is derived directly or indirectly from class A. If 'p' points at an object of a class that is derived directly or indirectly from class A, the call to the copy constructor as mentioned above will merely create an object of class A. The data members of this object will have the same values as the corresponding data members of the object at which 'p' points. Nevertheless, it will not be of the same type (it will be smaller in size with less data members).

How can this problem be solved? If the designer of class A suspects and expects the need to create copies like this, he/she will define a clone function to do so. Such a function can be defined as shown in Listing 6.23.

Listing 6.23   A clone function in the base class

```
class A
{
```

```
      public:
        virtual A * clone()
        {
          return new A(*this);
        }
        /*
          definition of class A
        */
};
```

Classes that derive from class A will similarly define and override this clone function (Listing 6.24).

Listing 6.24   A clone function in the derived class

```
class B : public A
{
    public:
      virtual B * clone()
      {
        return new B(*this);
      }
      /*
        definition of class B
      */
};
```

Whenever a clone of the object is required (from within the 'abc()' function as described in Listing 6.24), the clone function is called (Listing 6.25). The clone object created is subsequently destroyed.

Listing 6.25   Using the clone function

```
void abc(A * p)
{
    . . . . .
    . . . . .
    A * q = p->clone();
    . . . . .
    . . . . .
    delete q;
}
```

Since the clone() function is virtual, its correct version is called. Thus, if 'p' points at an object of class A, then another object of class A itself is created which is an exact copy of the object at which 'p' is pointing. And, if 'p' points at an object of a class derived from A, then another object of that same class is created which is an exact copy of the object at which 'p' is pointing. Thus, the abc() function succeeds in obtaining an exact copy of the object at which 'p' is pointing while being unaware of its type.

Since the clone function constructs an object and is also virtual, we sometimes call it a *virtual constructor*! But we must remember that there is actually nothing like a *virtual constructor*.

Now let us discuss the need for the clone function. Although there are several examples that highlight this need, the following example alone should suffice.

Let us consider a function that copies and pastes a graphics object to a different place of the window. See Listing 6.26.

Listing 6.26   An example to illustrate the use of the clone function

```
void MyWindow::copyPaste(const Shape * const p,
                         unsigned int x, unsigned int y)
{
    Shape * q;
    q=p->clone();
    q->move(x,y);
    q->show();
    //code to attach the new object to the list
    //of current objects on the screen
}
```

The pointer 'p' points at the object being copied. The variables 'x' and 'y' are the coordinates of the place where the copied object is to be pasted. Although 'p' might point at an object of any of the classes that are derived from the Shape class, the entire operation of copying and pasting works in all cases. The only precondition is that the classes that are derived from the Shape class must define the clone() function, the move() function, and the show() function. This is easily ensured by declaring all these functions as pure virtual functions in the Shape class. An additional point to be noted in this specific example is that the clone object should not be destroyed. Instead, it should be added to the list of existing objects on the screen.

Summary

Generic code contained in the functions of the base class remains inextensible without the use of virtual functions. Virtual functions make expected overrides in the derived class effective. Marking a base class function as a pure virtual function forces its override in the derived class.

An abstract base class is a class that has at least one pure virtual function. An abstract base class cannot be instantiated. Virtual destructors ensure a proper cleanup operation if the 'delete' operator is applied on a base class pointer that points at a derived class object.

Although we cannot have virtual constructors, clone functions that construct virtually can be used instead. A clone function returns an exact copy of the object at which the base class pointer, with respect to which it is called, points. If the pointer points at a base class object, the clone function creates an object of the base class and returns a pointer to it. If the pointer points at a derived class object, the clone function creates an object of the derived class and returns a pointer to it.

Key Terms

virtual functions
extending class libraries by using virtual functions
pure virtual functions

abstract base class
virtual destructors
clone functions

Exercises

1. What is a virtual function? When is it needed?
2. How does the compiler resolve a call to a virtual function?
3. Suppose a member function of a class has been prototyped as virtual. The function has not been defined. Now, when we instantiate the class, the linker gives an error even if we do not call the function. Why? (*Hint:* Remember that if a non-virtual function is prototyped and then neither called nor defined, no error is generated.)
4. What is a pure virtual function? When is it needed?
5. State true or false.
   (a) Virtual functions implement static polymorphism.
   (b) We cannot have a virtual constructor.
   (c) An abstract base class cannot be instantiated.
   (d) We cannot define a pure virtual function.
6. Write a program to find out whether a virtual function can be a friend of another class.
7. Create a class Shape. It should have no data members. It should have a pure virtual function get_area().

   Derive a class Rectangle from the class Shape. It should have two data members—one for holding the width of the rectangle and the other for holding its height. Both of these data members should be of float type. Override the Shape::get_area() function inside this class. This overriding function should return the area of the rectangle. Also, write a constructor for the class.

   Derive another class Ellipse from the class Shape. It should also have two data members—one for holding the length of the major axis of the ellipse and the other for holding the length of its minor axis. Both of these data members should be of float type. Override the Shape::get_area() function inside this class. This overriding function should return the area of the ellipse. Also, write a constructor for the class.

   Create a class Canvas. It should have no data members. Its only member function, display(), will have a reference of class Shape type as a formal argument. With this reference, call the Shape::get_area() function inside Canvas::display() function.

   Finally, write a main() function to utilize these classes. Declare objects of classes Rectangle, Ellipse, and Canvas. Call the Canvas::display() function first by passing the object of class Rectangle and then by passing the object of class Ellipse to it. Observe the output and ascertain whether the base class function or the derived class function got called.

   Redefine the Shape::get_area() function as a non-virtual function and see the difference in the output.

7 Stream and File Handling

O
V
E
R
V
I
E
W

This chapter deals with handling streams. It includes a study of classes in the C++ standard library that enable a programmer to handle flow of data to and from the console and also from disk files.

Text and binary mode of handling streams and the distinction between the two forms an important part of the chapter.

The use of classes and their member functions that enable a random access to disk files is discussed. Objects can and in many cases should be made capable of outputting and loading their own data to and from disk files. This chapter tells you how.

Error handling is an important feature expected in any industrial strength software. This chapter discusses the use of error handling functions that pertain to streams.

Manipulators are a handy tool for the C++ programmer. This chapter elucidates the use of many system-defined manipulators and the method of creating user-specific ones.

7.1 Streams

Stream means flow of data. We declare variables in our C++ programs for holding the data temporarily in the memory. Streams are nothing but a flow of data to and from program variables.

Input stream is the flow of data from a file to program variables. The keyboard is also treated as source of input stream. Output stream is the flow of data to a file from program variables. The monitor is also treated as target for output stream.

7.2 Class Hierarchy for Handling Streams

C++ provides us with a library of classes that have the functionality to implement various aspects of stream handling. These classes have been arranged in a hierarchical fashion by using inheritance. The important portion of this hierarchy is depicted in Figure 7.1.

The class `ios` is the base class in this hierarchy.

The class `ostream` is derived from the class `ios` and handles the general output stream. The insertion operator (<<) is defined and overloaded in the class `ostream` to handle output streams from program variables to output files.

The class `ostream_withassign` is derived from the class `ostream`. `cout` is an object of the class `ostream_withassign` and stands for console output. As mentioned earlier, C++ treats all peripheral devices as files. It treats the monitor also as a file (for output stream). The object `cout` represents the monitor.

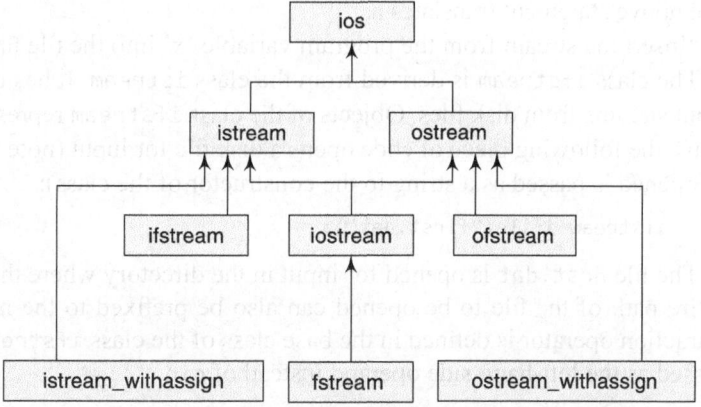

Figure 7.1   Library classes that handle streams

Thus the statement

```
cout<<x;
```

translates as:

"Insert the stream from the program variable 'x' into the file called `cout` (which is nothing but the monitor)."

The class `istream` is derived from the class `ios` and handles the general input streams. The extraction operator (>>) is defined and overloaded in the class `istream` to handle inputs streams from input files to program variables.

The class `istream_withassign` is derived from the class `istream`. `cin` is an object of the class `istream_withassign` and stands for console input. C++ treats all peripheral devices as files. It treats the keyboard also as a file (for input stream). The object `cin` represents the keyboard.

Thus the statement

```
cin>>x;
```

translates as:

"Extract the stream from the file (which is nothing but the keyboard) and place it in the program variable 'x'."

The class `iostream` is derived by multiple inheritance from the classes `istream` and `ostream`. It has the functionality to handle both input and output streams.

The class `ofstream` is derived from the class `ostream`. It has the functionality to handle output streams to disk files. Objects of the class `ofstream` represent output files on the disk. Thus, the following piece of code opens a disk file for output (note that the name of the file to be opened is passed as a string to the constructor of the class):

```
ofstream ofile("first.dat");
```

The file first.dat is opened for output in the directory where the executable will run. The entire path of the file to be opened can also be prefixed to the name of the file. Since the insertion operator is defined in the base class of the class `ofstream`, the object `ofile` can be passed as the left-hand side operand instead of `cout`.

```
ofile<<x;
```

The above statement translates as:

"Insert the stream from the program variable 'x' into the file first.dat."

The class ifstream is derived from the class istream. It has the functionality to handle input streams from disk files. Objects of the class ifstream represent input files on the disk. Thus, the following piece of code opens a disk file for input (note that the name of the file to be opened is passed as a string to the constructor of the class):

```
ifstream ifile("first.dat");
```

The file first.dat is opened for input in the directory where the executable will run. The entire path of the file to be opened can also be prefixed to the name of the file. Since the extraction operator is defined in the base class of the class ifstream, the object ifile can be passed as the left-hand side operand instead of cin.

```
ifile>>x;
```

This statement translates as:

"Extract the stream from the file first.dat and place it in the program variable 'x'."

The class fstream is derived from the class iostream. It has the functionality to handle both input and output streams from and to disk files.

The classes for handling streams to and from disk files are defined in the header file fstream.h. The classes for handling general streams are defined in the header file iostream.h. The header file iostream.h is included in the file fstream.h.

7.3 Text and Binary Input/Output

In this section, the two modes of input/output—text mode and binary mode—will be explained. The difference between them and the suitability of each mode for console I/O and disk I/O will also be explained.

7.3.1 Data Storage in Memory

During run time, the value of a character variable is stored in the memory as the binary equivalent of its ASCII equivalent. But the value of an integer, float, or double-type variable is simply stored as its binary equivalent.

For example, if the value of a character-type variable is 'A', it is stored in one byte where the bits represent the number '65', which is the ASCII equivalent of 'A', in base 2.

```
01000001
```

But if the value of an integer-type variable is '65', it is stored in four bytes where the bits represent the number '65' in base 2.

```
01000001
00000000
00000000
00000000
```

The value of a float and a double-type variable is stored in a similar fashion. Thus, the value of a numeric variable (integer, float, or double) is stored in base 2 format in the memory.

7.3.2 Input/Output of Character Data

There is no difference between text mode I/O and binary mode I/O with respect to character-type variables. In both modes, the value of the character-type data is copied from the memory into the output file as it is and copied from the input file into the memory as it is.

If a function that outputs in binary mode is called to output the value of a character variable, it will copy its value into the output file without transforming its representation in any way. A function that outputs in text mode will output the value of a character-type variable in the same way.

7.3.3 Input/Output of Numeric Data

A standard library function that outputs numeric data in text mode will reckon that the data, which is in base 2 format in the memory, needs to be output in base 10 (text) format. It will therefore read the value of the source variable from memory, *transform* the representation of the data from the existing base 2 to base 10 and only then copy it to the output file.

Whereas a standard library function that outputs numeric data in binary mode will reckon that the data, which is in base 2 format in the memory, needs to be output in base 2 (binary) format itself. It will therefore read the value of the source variable from memory, *not* transform the data from the existing base 2 to base 10 and simply copy it to the output file.

Further, a standard library function that inputs numeric data in text mode will reckon that the data, which is to be input, exists in base 10 (text) format. It will therefore read the value from the input file, *transform* the representation of the data from the existing base 10 to base 2 and only then copy it to the target variable in memory.

Whereas a standard library function that inputs numeric data in binary mode will reckon that the data, which is to be read, already exists in base 2 (binary) format. It will therefore read the value from the memory, *not* transform the data in any way and simply copy it into the target variable in memory.

Significance of the difference between binary mode and text mode I/O for numeric data

Suppose the value of an integer-type variable is '65'. The value '65' is stored, in the memory block of four bytes occupied by the variable, in binary mode.

The foregoing data will occupy four bytes with the *same* bit setting in the output disk file, if it is copied by an output function that outputs in binary mode.

If this output function is used to output to the monitor, instead of a disk file, the value 'A' followed by three blank spaces will be displayed. This is because the lowest byte of the variable contains '65', which is the ASCII equivalent of 'A' and the rest of the three bytes have all their bits set to zero. The monitor displays the ASCII equivalent of the value in each byte in the output stream that is supplied to it. But, we would like to see '65' and not 'A' followed by three blank spaces on the monitor.

However, if the same value is copied by an output function that outputs in text mode, this data will occupy two bytes with a different bit setting in the output file. The first byte will have its bits set to represent the character '6' (The ASCII equivalent of '6' will be stored in base 2 format). While the second byte will have its bits set to represent the character '5' (The ASCII equivalent of '5' will be stored in base 2 format). This is because the output function, since it works in text mode, has transformed the representation of the data from base 2 to base 10.

For the same reason, if the same output function is used to output to the monitor, instead of a disk file, the value '65' will be displayed. This is the kind of display we would desire.

An input function that inputs in binary mode will read the first four bytes from an input file if it is asked to input into an integer-type variable. It will copy the read value into the memory block of four bytes occupied by the target integer variable *without* transforming the representation of the data. This function will not transform the data because it inputs in binary mode and therefore reckons that the data existing in the input stream is already in base 2 format.

If the input is read from the keyboard instead of a disk file, the function reads the first four bytes from the keyboard and copies the read value into the memory block of four bytes occupied by an integer variable *without* transforming the representation of the data.

Further, a function that reads in text mode, reads the bytes from the input file up to the white space. It reckons that the read value is in base 10 format. It therefore determines the equivalent representation in base 2 format. This produces a value that occupies four bytes. The function then copies these four bytes into the memory block of four bytes occupied by integer variable.

If the input is read from the keyboard instead of a disk file, the function reads the bytes from the keyboard up to the white space and operates upon it in a similar fashion. For example, if the user enters the number '65', the characters '6' and '5' get stored in the keyboard buffer, which represents the input file in this case. The characters '6' and '5' that are stored in two bytes represent the number '65' in base 10 format. The input function *transforms* this representation into base 2 format and stores the resultant integer value in the four bytes occupied by the target integer variable.

A very important and interesting observation can be made here. *Text mode is suitable for console I/O* because they are in base 10 format with which we are accustomed. For reasons that will be explained shortly, *binary mode is suitable for disk I/O*.

7.3.4 Note on Opening Disk Files for I/O

In this section, that is, Section 7.3, 'Text and binary input/output', we would open files for writing through the constructor of class ofstream. If the file being opened does not exist, it would get created. If it does exist, its contents would get overwritten. For producing a different effect—appending or obtaining errors if the file does not exist—we have to apply the techniques that are explained in Sections 7.4 and 7.8. We would also open files for reading through the constructor of class ifstream. If the file being opened does not exist, a run-time error is produced. The technique of handling such errors is explained in Section 7.8.

7.4 Text Versus Binary Files

Now let us talk about text files and binary files.

In text files, binary data (numeric data that is stored in base 2 format in memory) is stored in base 10 format. In binary files, the same binary data is stored in the same format (base 2).

Before proceeding further, let us be clear that the files by themselves are neither text files nor binary files. It is the mode in which the data is written into them that defines the nature of the files.

As we have already learnt, when the value of a numeric variable (say an integer) is output in binary mode, it occupies the same number of bytes in the output file as it does in the memory, which is four. Thus, if a number of such values are output in binary mode, the size of the output file will always be a multiple of four. Obviously, we can determine the size of the file and divide it by four to easily find the number of integers (records) that are stored in the file.

We can apply this simple technique to values of other types including objects. Suppose an object consists of an integer (four bytes), a float (four bytes), and a double (eight bytes). This object occupies 16 bytes in the memory. If output in binary mode, it will occupy 16 bytes in the output file also.

The C++ standard library provides functions that input (read from files and write the read values into variables) in binary mode. These functions require the address of the variable whose data needs to be input along with its size. The code inside these functions reads the value from a point in the input file at which a temporary pointer points (more about this pointer later). The size of the block of bytes this code reads is equal to the supplied size. The code then writes the read data into the memory block whose starting address is equal to the supplied address. Functions that output in binary mode work in a similar fashion. As we can see, binary input functions treat size as the delimiter while reading data from disk files. Therefore, the binary functions that write data into the disks need not insert an artificial delimiter while the data is output.

Let us contrast this to what happens in text mode. In text mode, records stored in the output file are of variable lengths. Again, for our understanding, let us take the case of an integer-type variable. Its value is always stored in four bytes in the memory. Suppose it is output to a disk file in text mode. If its value is '1', it will occupy one byte in the output file although it occupies four bytes in the memory. If its value is '11', it will occupy two bytes in the output file although it occupies four bytes in the memory. If its value is '111', it will occupy three bytes in the output file although it occupies four bytes in the memory and so on.

Thus, in case values are output in text mode, size of the output value is not fixed. Hence, size cannot be used as the delimiter by functions that will read the output values in future. But it should be ensured that values that are output in text mode can be read correctly in future. For this, the code that calls a text mode function for output should also insert a delimiter of choice in the output file after every such call. This ensures that another piece of code is able to successfully read this output value.

Choosing a suitable delimiter is certainly an issue. There should be no chance of the delimiting character itself becoming a part of the output value anytime in the future. But this is difficult to guarantee.

There is another difficulty in outputting in text mode. The size of a file does not indicate the number of records stored in it. This is because the size of the records is not fixed.

7.5 Text Output/Input

7.5.1 Text Output

Text output is achieved in C++ by:
- The insertion operator
- The put( ) function

The insertion operator

As we have seen in the first section of this chapter, the insertion operator can be used to output values to disk files. The insertion operator outputs in text mode.

The insertion operator has been defined and overloaded in the class `ostream`. It takes an object of the class `ostream` or an object of a class that is derived from the class `ostream` as its left-hand side operand. As its right-hand side operand, it takes a value of one of the fundamental data types. It copies the value on its right into the file that is associated with the object on its left. Let us study its action on data of different types. We must keep in mind that the insertion operator has been overloaded differently for each of the data types as follows:

1. Inserting characters into output streams using the insertion operator: A character-type value occupies one byte in the memory. If output in text mode by the insertion operator, it occupies one byte in the output file too. The bit setting of both the bytes is identical. See Listing 7.1.

Listing 7.1   Outputting a character in text mode by using the insertion operator

```
/*Beginning of charFileOutput.cpp*/
#include<fstream.h>
void main()
{
    char cVar;
    ofstream ofile("first.dat");
    cVar='A';
    ofile<<cVar;
}
/*End of charFileOutput.cpp*/
```

The last statement of Listing 7.1 copies the value of `cVar` from memory to the disk file `first.dat` without transforming its representation in any way.

2. Inserting integers into output streams using the insertion operator: An integer-type value occupies four bytes in the memory. As we already know, if output in text mode by the insertion operator, the number of bytes it occupies in the output file depends upon its value. See Listing 7.2.

Listing 7.2   Outputting an integer in text mode by using the insertion operator

```
/*Beginning of intFileOutput.cpp*/
#include<fstream.h>
void main()
{
    int iVar;
    ofstream ofile("first.dat");
    iVar=111;
    ofile<<iVar;
}
/*End of intFileOutput.cpp*/
```

The last statement of Listing 7.2 copies the value of 'iVar' from memory to the disk file 'first.dat' after transforming its representation from base 2 to base 10. The value of 'iVar' will be written in text format (base 10) and will therefore occupy three bytes in the output file. If the value of 'iVar' is '11111' instead of '111', it will occupy five bytes in the output file instead of three.

3. Inserting floats and doubles into output streams using the insertion operator: A float-type value occupies four bytes in the memory. As we already know, if output in text mode by the insertion operator, the number of bytes it occupies in the output file depends upon its value. See Listing 7.3.

Listing 7.3   Outputting a float in text mode by using the insertion operator

```
/*Beginning of floatFileOutput.cpp*/
#include<fstream.h>
void main()
{
    float fVar;
    ofstream ofile("first.dat");
    fVar=1.111;
    ofile<<fVar;
}
/*End of floatFileOutput.cpp*/
```

The last statement of Listing 7.3 copies the value of 'fVar' from memory to the disk file first.dat after transforming its representation from base 2 to base 10. The value of 'fVar' will be written in text format (base 10) and will therefore occupy five bytes in the output file. If the value of 'fVar' is '11.111' instead of '1.111', it will occupy six bytes in the output file instead of five.

The insertion operator works in the same way for double-type variables.

4. Inserting strings into output streams using the insertion operator: A character array is allocated a fixed number of bytes in the memory during run time. However, the actual string contained in it usually occupies only a part of that memory. For example,

```
char cArr[20]="abcd";
```

The character array 'cArr' will be allocated 20 bytes during run time. But the string inside it will occupy only four bytes. The fifth byte will have the NULL character.

If the value of 'cArr' is output by the insertion operator, it will occupy four bytes in the output file. See Listing 7.4.

Listing 7.4   Outputting a string in text mode by using the insertion operator

```
/*Beginning of charArrFileOutput.cpp*/
#include<fstream.h>
void main()
{
    char cArr[20]="abcd";
    ofstream ofile("first.dat");
    ofile<<cArr;
}
/*End of charArrFileOutput.cpp*/
```

But if 'cArr' contains a string of length five, then five bytes will get written into the output file.

5. Inserting objects into output streams using the insertion operator: If we want to use the insertion operator for inserting objects of a particular class into the output stream, we have to overload it for that class. The concept of operator overloading, its need, and its use are elucidated in the next chapter.

The put() function

The put( ) function is a member of the ostream class. Its prototype is

```
ostream & ostream :: put(char c);
```

From the prototype, it is obvious that the function can be called with respect to an object of the ostream class or any of the classes that are derived from the ostream class. One such object is cout.

This function copies the character that is passed as a parameter to it into the output file associated with the object with respect to which the function is called. Let us consider the explanatory program given in Listing 7.5.

Listing 7.5   The put() function

```
/*Beginning of put.cpp*/
#include<fstream.h>
void main()
{
    ofstream ofile("first.dat");
    ofile.put('a');
}
/*End of put.cpp*/
```

In Listing 7.5, the put() function is called with respect to the object ofile. This object is associated with the file first.dat. Consequently, the character 'a' is written into the file.

As was mentioned earlier, the put() function can be used with the object cout also (as shown in Listing 7.6).

Listing 7.6   Using the put() function with cout object

```
/*Beginning of coutPut.cpp*/
#include<iostream.h>
void main()
{
    cout.put('a');
}
/*End of coutPut.cpp*/
```

Output

```
a
```

The call to the put() function in Listing 7.6 will display the character 'a' on the monitor.

We may wonder what is the difference between using the put() function and the insertion operator. After all we could have used the insertion operator instead of calling the put() function as follows:

```
cout<<'a';
```

The difference between the insertion operator and the put() function is that while the former modifies the format of the output with respect to the manipulators set earlier, the latter simply ignores format manipulator settings. Formatted output is dealt with in one of the later sections of this chapter.

7.5.2 Text Input

Text input is achieved in C++ by:
- The extraction operator
- The get() function
- The getline() function

The extraction operator

As we have seen earlier in this chapter, the extraction operator can be used to input values from disk files. The extraction operator inputs in text mode.

The extraction operator has been defined and overloaded in the class istream. It takes an object of the class istream or an object of a class that is derived from the class istream as its left-hand side operand. As its right-hand side operand, it takes a variable of one of the fundamental data types. It copies the value found at the current location in the file that is associated with the object on its left into the variable on its right. Let us study its action on data of different types. We must keep in mind that the extraction operator has been overloaded differently for each of the data types as follows:

1. Extracting characters from input streams using the extraction operator: If the right-hand side operand of the extraction operator is a character-type variable, it reads one byte from the input file that is attached with the object on its left and writes it into the variable (Listing 7.7).

Listing 7.7   Inputting a character in text mode by using the extraction operator

```
/*Beginning of charFileInputText.cpp*/
#include<iostream.h>
#include<fstream.h>
void main()
{
    ifstream ifile("first.dat");    //Current location is at
                                    //the beginning of the file.
                                    //Suppose first byte in the
                                    //file contains 'A'.
    char cVar;
    ifile>>cVar;
    cout<<cVar;
}
/*End of charFileInputText.cpp*/
```

Output

A

2. Extracting integers from input streams using the extraction operator: If the right-hand side operand of the extraction operator is an integer-type variable, it reads bytes from the input file that is attached with the object on its left until it finds a white space. It reckons that the read set of bytes represents an integer in base 10 format. Therefore, the extraction operator converts the read value into base 2 format. Finally, it writes the converted value into the variable.

Suppose the contents of a file first.dat are as follows:

```
11 22 33
```

We must note that there is a space after '11'. The first byte of the file has the ASCII equivalent of the character '1'. The second byte also has the ASCII equivalent of the character '1'. The third byte has the ASCII equivalent of the character ' ' (space). The fourth byte has the ASCII equivalent of the character '2' and so on.

Now let us consider Listing 7.8.

Listing 7.8   Inputting an integer in text mode by using the extraction operator

```cpp
/*Beginning of intFileInputText.cpp*/
#include<iostream.h>
#include<fstream.h>
void main()
{
    ifstream ifile("first.dat");
    int iVar;
    ifile>>iVar;
    cout<<iVar;
}
/*End of intFileInputText.cpp*/
```

Output
```
11
```

As discussed earlier, the extraction operator reads from the file until it finds a white space. Since the third byte contains a white space, it reads the first two bytes only. These two bytes represent the number eleven in base 10 format. The extraction operator converts this into base 2 format. The resultant value is in four bytes. It writes this value into the variable 'iVar'.

3. Extracting floats and doubles from input streams using the extraction operator: Values for float and double-type variables are extracted in the same as they are for integer type variables.

4. Extracting strings from input streams using the extraction operator: As in the case of integers, the extraction operator reads from the file until it finds a white space while reading value for a character array.

Suppose the contents of a file first.dat are:

```
abc def ghi
```

We must note that there is a white space after 'c'. See Listing 7.9.

Listing 7.9   Inputting a character array by using the extraction operator

```cpp
/*Beginning of charArrFileInputText.cpp*/
#include<iostream.h>
#include<fstream.h>
void main()
{
    ifstream ifile("first.dat");
```

```
    char cArr[20];
    ifile>>cArr;
    cout<<cArr;
}
/*End of charArrFileInputText.cpp*/
```

Output

abc

Obviously, the extraction operator read up to the white space and stored the read value in the character array.

5. Extracting objects from input streams using the extraction operator: If we want to use the extraction operator for extracting objects of a particular class from the input stream, we have to overload it for that class. The concept of operator overloading, its need, and its use are elucidated in a later chapter.

The get() function

The `get()` function has been defined in the class `istream`. It reads one byte from the input file and stores it in the character variable that is passed as a parameter to it (Listing 7.10).

The prototype of the `get()` function is as follows:

```
istream & istream :: get(char &);
```

Suppose the contents of a file `first.dat` are as follows:

abcd

Listing 7.10 Inputting a character by using the `get()` function

```
/*Beginning of charFileInputText.cpp*/
#include<iostream.h>
#include<fstream.h>
void main()
{
    ifstream ifile("first.dat");
    char cVar;
    ifile.get(cVar);
    cout<<cVar;
}
/*End of charFileInputText.cpp*/
```

Output

a

The getline() function

The `getline()` function reads one line from the input file. It has been defined in the class `istream`.

The prototype of the `getline()` function is

```
istream & istream :: getline(char *, int, char = '\n');
```

It takes three parameters. The first parameter is the name of the character array in which the read line will be stored. The second parameter, an integer, signifies the number of bytes that will be read from the input file. The third parameter is the delimiting character whose presence in the stream of bytes that is being read from the input file prevents the `getline()` function from reading further.

The `getline()` function reads from the file that is attached with the object with respect to which it has been called till it reads bytes whose total count is one less than the value of the second parameter or till it encounters the delimiting character specified by the third parameter, whichever occurs earlier.

Listing 7.11 shows what happens when the `getline()` function is used to read from the keyboard.

Listing 7.11   Using the `getline()` function to read from the keyboard

```
/*Beginning of getlineCin.cpp*/
#include<iostream.h>
void main()
{
    char cArr[20];
    cout<<"Enter a string: ";
    cin.getline(cArr,6,'#');
    cout<<"You entered: "<<cArr<<endl;
}
/*End of getlineCin.cpp*/
```

Output
Enter a string: **abcdefgh**⟨*enter*⟩
You entered: abcde

Output
Enter a string: **abc#defgh**⟨*enter*⟩
You entered: abc

Output
Enter a string: **aa bb cc**⟨*enter*⟩
You entered: aa bb

It can be observed that the `getline()` function reads white spaces also. It is mentioned in the prototype that the `getline()` function takes a default value, the newline character, for the third parameter. Thus, if the third parameter is not specified, it will continue to read till it encounters the newline character provided the number of bytes it has already read does not exceed the number specified by its second parameter.

The `getline()` function reads from the keyboard buffer and leaves behind the unread bytes in the buffer itself.

The `getline()` function works in a similar fashion when it reads from disk files. Suppose the contents of a file `first.dat` are

abcdefgh

Now let us consider Listing 7.12.

Listing 7.12   Using the `getline()` function to read from a disk file

```
/*Beginning of getlineFile.cpp*/
#include<iostream.h>
#include<fstream.h>
void main()
```

```
    {
        char cArr[20];
        ifstream ifile("first.dat");
        ifile.getline(cArr,6,'#');
        cout<<cArr<<endl;
    }
    /*End of getlineFile.cpp*/
```

Output

abcde

___

If the contents are

    abc#def

the output would be 'abc'.
Again, if the contents are

    aa bb cc

the output would be 'aa bb'.

7.6 Binary Output/Input

7.6.1 Binary Output—write() Function

The write() function copies the values of variables from the memory to the specified output file. It works in binary mode.

As we already know, binary mode functions are not concerned about the data type of the variable that is output. They are only interested in the address of the variable (starting point of the block whose data needs to be output) and the size of the variable (total number of bytes to be output). The prototype of the write() function makes this clear:

```
    ostream & ostream :: write(const char *, int);
```

The write() function has been defined in the class ostream. It takes two parameters. The first parameter is the address of the variable whose value needs to be outputted. The second parameter is the size of the variable. The write() function writes the value of the variable to the file that is associated with the object with respect to which it has been called.

Let us now discuss how the write() function is used to output data of various types.

1. Inserting characters into output streams using write() function: Listing 7.13 illustrates how the write() function can be used to output the value of a character-type variable to a disk file.

Listing 7.13   Using the write() function to output character-type value to a disk file

```
/*Beginning of writeCharDisk.cpp*/
#include<fstream.h>
void main()
{
    ofstream ofile("first.dat");
    char cVar;
    cVar = 'a';
    ofile.write(&cVar,sizeof(char));
}
/*Beginning of writeCharDisk.cpp*/
```

Listing 7.14 illustrates how the write() function can be used to output the value of a character-type variable to the monitor.

Listing 7.14 Using the write() function to output character-type value to the monitor

```
/*Beginning of writeCharConsole.cpp*/
#include<iostream.h>
void main()
{
    char cVar;
    cVar = 'a';
    cout.write(&cVar,sizeof(char));
}
/*End of writeCharConsole.cpp*/
```

Output

a

It is evident that there is no difference between outputting a character-type value in text mode (insertion operator, put() function) and in binary mode (write() function). There is no conversion in either case.

2. Inserting integers into output streams using write() function: Listing 7.15 illustrates how the write() function can be used to output the value of an integer-type variable to a disk file.

Listing 7.15 Using the write() function to output integer-type value to disk file

```
/*Beginning of writeIntDisk.cpp*/
#include<fstream.h>
void main()
{
    ofstream ofile("first.dat");
    int iVar;
    iVar = 65;
    ofile.write((char *)&iVar,sizeof(int));
}
/*Beginning of writeIntDisk.cpp*/
```

As we have already discussed, the value contained in the four bytes that are occupied by 'iVar' will get copied to the designated output file without any transformation.

Listing 7.16 illustrates how the write() function can be used to output the value of an integer-type variable to the monitor.

Listing 7.16 Using the write() function to output integer-type value to the monitor

```
/*Beginning of writeIntConsole.cpp*/
#include<iostream.h>
void main()
{
    int iVar;
    iVar = 65;
    cout.write((char *)&iVar,sizeof(int));
```

```
}
/*End of writeIntConsole.cpp*/
```

Output

A

___

It is interesting to understand the output of Listing 7.16. As a result of the second statement of the `main()` function, the eight bits in the first of the four bytes occupied by 'iVar' are set to represent the binary equivalent of the number '65'. The bits in the remaining three bytes are set to zero. As we know, the monitor shows the ASCII equivalent of each of the bytes that are passed to it. The ASCII equivalent of '65' is 'A'. Hence, we get this output.

It is evident that there is an important difference between outputting an integer type value in text mode (insertion operator, `put()` function) and in binary mode (`write()` function). In the former case, representation of the value that is read from the memory is transformed from base 2 to base 10 and then copied to the output file. There is no such conversion in the latter case.

3. Inserting floats and doubles into output streams using `write()` function: Float and double-type values are output in the same way in binary mode as integer-type values.

4. Inserting strings into output streams using `write()` function: Listing 7.17 illustrates how the `write()` function can be used to output the value of a character array to a disk file.

Listing 7.17   Using the `write()` function to output a string to a disk file

```
/*Beginning of writeCharArrDisk.cpp*/
#include<fstream.h>
void main()
{
    ofstream ofile("first.dat");
    char cArr[10]="abcdefgh";
    ofile.write(cArr,sizeof(cArr));
}
/*Beginning of writeCharArrDisk.cpp*/
```

The name of the array that is passed as the first parameter to the `write()` function represents its starting address. The second parameter represents the size of the memory block whose value is to be written into the output file.

The second parameter that is passed to the `write()` function in Listing 7.17 evaluates to '10' (the size of the array). For this reason, the entire set of 10 bytes is copied verbatim to the specified output file. This includes the string itself, which is of eight characters, the delimiting NULL character (a single byte with all bits set to zero) that follows the string and one byte at the end with junk value.

If '5' is passed as the second parameter, only the first five bytes of the character array are written into the file.

Listing 7.18 illustrates how the `write()` function can be used to output the value of a character array to the monitor.

Listing 7.18   Using the `write()` function to output a string to the monitor

```
/*Beginning of writeCharArrConsole.cpp*/
#include<iostream.h>
```

```
void main()
{
    char cArr[10] = "abcdefgh";
    cout.write(cArr,strlen(cArr));
}
/*End of writeCharArrConsole.cpp*/
```

Output
abcdefgh

---

5. Inserting objects into output streams using `write()` function: Listing 7.19 illustrates one of the ways of inserting a class object into output streams in binary mode. In this method, value contained in the memory block that is occupied by a class object is copied to a specified output file.

Listing 7.19   Using the `write()` function to output an object to a disk file

```
/*Beginning of writeObjectDisk.cpp*/
#include<fstream.h>
class A
{
    /*
        definition of class A
    */
};
void main()
{
    A A1;
    ofstream ofile("first.dat");
    ofile.write((char *)&A1,sizeof(A));
}
/*End of writeObjectDisk.cpp*/
```

Of course, we will notice that the value of the object is being accessed directly by a non-member function—the `main()` function. C++ does not prevent a direct access by means of such an explicit typecasting of an object's address. Statements like the following are allowed in C++.

```
char * cPtr = (char *)&A1;
```

A close look at this piece of code reveals a major drawback. Let us consider the case where an object of the class `String` is used in the above listing instead of the object of the hypothetical class A (see Listing 7.20). In such a case, the value of the pointer that is embedded within the object would get copied to the output file. However, the string that is contained in the memory and at which that pointer is pointing would not get copied.

Listing 7.20   Problem in using the `write()` function to output an object with an embedded pointer

```
/*Beginning of writeStringDisk.cpp*/
#include<fstream.h>
#include"String.h"                    //header file that contains our class
                                      //String
void main()
```

```
    {
        ofstream ofile("first.dat");
        String s1("C++ is a wonderful language");
                                //s1.cStr points at the string
        ofile.write((char *)&s1,sizeof(String));
                                //The value of s1.cStr gets stored
                                //in the file. The string itself does
                                //not get stored.
    }
    /*End of writeStringDisk.cpp*/
```

If the value that is stored in the file through the program in Listing 7.20 is later read through another program, and stored in an object of the class String declared therein, the pointer in that object would end up pointing at a place where the string itself no longer exists! The string itself would be lost in the memory and the entire purpose of storing the object would get defeated.

Client programs are not supposed to know how the actual data is managed, arranged, organized, and stored internally by the objects they are using (data abstraction). The conclusion is obvious. Objects should be responsible for outputting their own data. This conclusion becomes even more apparent if we consider the case of complex objects such as linked lists, vectors, trees, etc. where the object contains only the pointer to the first node of the data structure while the actual data structure remains outside it.

We will discuss some elementary methods of making objects capable of outputting their own data in one of the later sections of this chapter.

7.6.2 Binary Input—read() Function

The read() function copies the values from the specified input file to the memory block that is occupied by the target variable. It works in binary mode.

The logic mentioned in the introduction to the write() function holds true in this case also. We can once again conclude that the read() function accepts the address of the variable (starting point of the block into which the read data needs to be input) and the size of the variable (total number of bytes to be input). Accordingly, the prototype of the read() function is as follows:

```
    istream & istream :: read(char *, int);
```

The read() function has been defined in the class istream. It takes two parameters. The first parameter is the address of the variable into which the read value needs to be input. The second parameter is the size of the variable. The read() function reads the value for the variable from the file that is associated with the object with respect to which it has been called.

Let us now discuss how the read() function is used to input data of various types.

1. Extracting characters from input streams using read() function: Listing 7.21 illustrates how the read() function can be used to input the value for a character-type variable by making it read from a disk file.

Suppose the contents of the file first.dat are:

    xyz

Listing 7.21   Using the `read()` function to input character-type value from a disk file

```cpp
/*Beginning of readCharDisk.cpp*/
#include<iostream.h>
#include<fstream.h>
void main()
{
    ifstream ifile("first.dat");
    char cVar;
    ifile.read(&cVar,sizeof(char));
    cout<<cVar;
}
/*End of readCharDisk.cpp*/
```

Output

x

Listing 7.22 illustrates how the `read()` function can be used to input the value of a character-type variable by making it read from the keyboard.

Listing 7.22   Using the `read()` function to input character-type value from the keyboard

```cpp
/*Beginning of readCharConsole.cpp*/
#include<iostream.h>
void main()
{
    char cVar;
    cout<<"Enter a character: ";
    cin.read(&cVar,sizeof(char));
    cout<<cVar;
}
/*End of readCharConsole.cpp*/
```

Output

Enter a character: **a**<*enter*>
a

It is evident that there is no difference between inputting a character type value in text mode (extraction operator, `get()` function) and in binary mode (`read()` function). There is no conversion in either case.

2. Extracting integers from input streams using `read()` function: Listing 7.23 illustrates how the `read()` function can be used to input a value into an integer-type variable by making it read from a disk file.

Suppose the first four bytes of a disk file `first.dat` together contain the binary equivalent of number 64.

```
01000000
00000000
00000000
00000000
.  .  .  .
.  .  .  .
```

Listing 7.23   Using the `read()` function to input integer-type value from a disk file

```
/*Beginning of readIntDisk.cpp*/
#include<iostream.h>
#include<fstream.h>
void main()
{
    ifstream ifile("first.dat");
    int iVar;
    ifile.read((char *)&iVar, sizeof(int));
    cout<<iVar<<endl;
}
/*End of readIntDisk.cpp*/
```

Output

64

As expected, the `read()` function reads exactly four bytes from the input file that is associated with its invoking object. This is because the value of the second parameter that has been passed to it is four. It copies the read value into the memory block the address of whose first byte is equal to the first parameter passed to it.

Now, let us look at Listing 7.24 in which the `read()` function is used to read the value for an integer-type variable from the keyboard. As per its known characteristics, the `read()` function is expected to read four bytes from the keyboard, not convert the read bytes in any way and copy them into the four bytes that are occupied by the target integer type variable.

Listing 7.24   Using the `read()` function to input integer-type value from the keyboard

```
/*Beginning of readIntConsole.cpp*/
#include<iostream.h>
void main()
{
    int iVar;
    cout<<"Enter a number in base 2 format: ";
    cin.read((char *)&iVar, sizeof(int));
    iVar = iVar & 0x000000ff;          /*Inputting zeros in the
                                        upper 3 bytes of the four
                                        bytes of iVar*/
    cout<<iVar<<endl;
}
/*End of readIntConsole.cpp*/
```

Output

Enter a number in base 2 format: **ABCD**<*enter*>
65

The explanation of this program has been left as an exercise for the reader.

3. Extracting floats and doubles from input streams using `read()` function: Float and double-type values are input in the same way in binary mode as integer-type values.

4. Extracting strings from input streams using `read()` function: Listing 7.25 is a good example for illustrating the use of `read()` function to read character arrays from a disk file. Suppose the contents of a file first.dat are as follows:

abcdefgh

Listing 7.25 Using the read() function to input strings from disk files

```
/*Beginning of readStringDisk.cpp*/
#include<iostream.h>
#include<fstream.h>
void main()
{
    ifstream ifile("first.dat");
    char cArr[20] = "12345678";
    ifile.read(cArr,3);
    cout<<cArr<<endl;
}
/*End of readStringDisk.cpp*/
```

Output
abc45678

The number '3' has been passed as the second parameter to the read() function. It therefore reads only three characters from the file that is associated with the object that has called it.

As we know, the name of the array represents the starting address of the memory block occupied by it. Thus, the first parameter passed to the read() function in the Listing 7.25 is the address of the first byte of the memory block that the array occupies. Therefore, the read() function copies the three characters it has already read into the first three bytes of the array.

A similar method can be devised for using the read() function to read character strings from the keyboard.

5. Extracting objects from input streams using read() function: Let us consider the program of Listing 7.19 that was used to output the data of an object into a disk file. The object being output was a simple one, that is, it had no pointers as its data members. Thus, the actual data was stored in the file. Suppose the name of the file is first.dat. Listing 7.26 illustrates how the data that was stored in the disk file can be loaded back in an object.

Listing 7.26 Using the read() function to input objects from disk files

```
/*Beginning of readObj.cpp*/
#include<fstream.h>
class A
{
    /*
        definition of class A
    */
};
void main()
{
    ifstream ifile("first.dat");
    A A1;
    ifile.read((char *)&A1, sizeof(A));
}
/*End of readObj.cpp*/
```

Listing 7.26 was simple. Now, let us take the case of complex objects, that is, objects having embedded pointers.

After reading the section, 'Binary output—the write() function', it is natural to expect that the class of such complex objects will have a suitable function to output the external data structure into disk files. Thus, we can also expect the class to have a function that reads the entire data structure from disk files. Client programs should not and need not take this responsibility. We will discuss the techniques for defining such functions in one of the later sections of this chapter.

7.7 Opening and Closing Files

So far, we have output data to and input data from the same disk file by using two different programs. Data is usually output and input within the same program. For this, it is necessary to close the disk file after one operation before it is opened for another. The open() and close() functions that are provided as members of the library stream handling classes enable us to do this.

7.7.1 open() Function

So far, we have opened files through the constructors of classes ifstream and ofstream. We can do this by invoking the open() function also. This function has been provided in both of these classes.

The open() function can be called by passing the name of the disk file to be opened as the only parameter.

```
. . . .
ofstream ofile;
ofile.open("first.dat");
. . . .

. . . .
ifstream ifile;
ifile.open("first.dat");
. . . .
```

A second parameter can also be passed to this function. This parameter is known as the open mode. It is an integer-type value. There are a number of integer-type constants defined in the stream handling library. Each of these constants, when passed as the second parameter to the open() function, produces a different effect while opening the file. A list of these constants along with their use is given in Table 7.1.

Table 7.1 Table of Open Mode Bits

Constant	Meaning
ios::app	For appending to end of file
ios::ate	For going to end of file on opening
ios::binary	For opening a binary file
ios::in	For opening file for reading only
ios::nocreate	For causing open to fail if the file does not exist
ios::noreplace	For causing open to fail if the file already exists
ios::out	For opening file for writing only
ios::trunc	For deleting contents of the file if it exists

The constructor of the class ofstream and its overridden version of the open() function takes ios::out as the default value for the second parameter. Therefore, the file is opened for writing purpose only.

The constructor of the class ifstream and its overridden version of the open() function take ios::in as the default value for the second parameter. Therefore, the file is opened for reading purpose only.

These constants can be meaningfully combined together to further influence the manner in which the file is opened. Using the bitwise OR operator does this.

```
ofstream ofile;
ofile.open("first.dat", ios::app | ios::nocreate);
```

In this example, the file would be opened for appending. But if the file does not exist already, the operation would fail. The method for detecting such failures is discussed in one of the later sections of this chapter.

The difference between ios::app and ios::ate is discussed in the section on seekp() function.

7.7.2 close() Function

A currently open file may need to be closed within a program. This need arises when we want to write into a file that we have already opened for reading and vice versa. An open file can be closed by calling the close() function with respect to the object that has been used to open it.

The close() function has been defined in the istream class as well as the ostream class. The following code snippet shows how the close() function is used.

```
. . . .
ostream ofile;
ofile.open("first.dat");
. . . .
. . . .
ofile.close();
. . . .
```

7.8 Files as Objects of the fstream Class

The overloaded version of the open() function for the class fstream does not take a default value for the second parameter. We have to specify explicitly whether we want to open the file for writing or for reading. We can also specify that we want to open the file for both reading and writing.

```
. . . .
fstream iofile.
iofile.open("first.dat", ios::in | ios::out);
. . . .
```

In this example, the file will be opened for both reading and writing.

7.9 File Pointers

File pointers are created and maintained for open files during run time. There are two file pointers, the put pointer and the get pointer. The put pointer points at that byte of the open file where the next write operation will be conducted. The get pointer points at that byte of the open file where the next read operation will be conducted.

File pointers can be explicitly manipulated by the use of some functions that have been provided as members of the stream handling classes. An explanation of these functions follows.

7.9.1 `seekp()` Function

This function is used to explicitly make the `put` pointer point at a desired position in the open file. It is important to note that by default the `put` pointer points at the beginning of the file if it is newly opened for writing. In case an existing file is opened for appending, the `put` pointer points at its end by default. Also, every write operation pushes forward the `put` pointer by the number of bytes written.

The `seekp()` function has been defined in the class `ostream`. It has two versions.

```
ostream & ostream :: seekp(streampos pos);

ostream & ostream :: seekp(streamoff off,
                            ios::seek_dir dir);
```

In the first version, the `seekp()` function takes only one parameter—the absolute position with respect to the beginning of the file. The type `streampos` is type defined with `long` as the source data type. We must remember that the numbering of the position starts from zero.

In the following example, the `put` pointer is made to point at the second byte of the file:

```
ofile.seekp(1);                    //ofile is an object of class ofstream
```

In the first version, the new position of the `put` pointer can be specified with respect to the beginning of the file only. But in the second version, the `seekp()` function takes two parameters—the first parameter is the offset and the second parameter is the position in the open file with respect to which the offset is being specified. The type `streamoff` is type defined with `long` as the source data type. The type `ios::seek_dir` is an enumerated type with the following values:

ios::beg—offset will be calculated from the beginning of the file

ios::cur—offset will be calculated from the current position in the file

ios::end—offset will be calculated from the end of the file

In the following example, the `put` pointer is made to point at the last byte of the file. We must remember that the EOF character is actually the last byte of the file. Thus, in the following example, the `put` pointer will end up pointing at the last byte that was written into the file that is one byte to the left of the EOF character.

```
ofile.seekp(-1,ios::end);          //ofile is an object of class
                                   //ofstream
```

Some more examples follow:

```
ofile.seekp(0,ios::beg);           //take the put pointer to the
                                   //beginning of the file
ofile.seekp(2,ios::beg);           //take the put pointer to the
                                   //third byte from the beginning
                                   //of the file
ofile.seekp(-2,ios::cur);          //take the put pointer two
                                   //bytes to the left from the its
                                   //current position in the file
ofile.seekp(2,ios::cur);           //take the put pointer two bytes
```

```
                                       //to the right from the its
                                       //current position in the file
   ofile.seekp(0,ios::end);            //take the put pointer to the end
                                       //of the file (past the
                                       //last byte)
   ofile.seekp(-1,ios::end);           //take the put pointer to the last
                                       //byte of the file
```

Let us now understand the difference between ios::app and ios::ate flags. Both of these flags open the file for appending and make the put pointer point at the end of the opened file by default (past the last existing byte). Neither of the two overwrites an existing file. But the difference between the two is that while the flag ios::ate allows you to rewind the put pointer and modify the existing contents of the file, the flag ios::app does not allow this. In other words, if the file is opened using ios::app flag, an attempt to use the seekp() function for rewinding the put pointer will fail. The put pointer would continue to point at the end of the file. As bytes are appended to the file, the put pointer, as already mentioned, also moves forward. Thereafter, it cannot be rewound if the file was opened by using the ios::app flag. But in case of ios::ate flag, the put pointer can be rewound.

7.9.2 tellp() Function

The tellp() function returns the current position of the put pointer. It has been defined in the class ostream.

```
   streampos ostream::tellp();
```

In the following example, the current position of the put pointer is determined and stored in a program variable.

```
   long pos = ofile.tellp();            //ofile is an object of the
                                       //class ofstream
```

7.9.3 seekg() Function

This function is used to explicitly make the get pointer point at a desired position in the open file. It is important to note that by default the get pointer points at the beginning of the file that is opened for reading. Every read operation pushes forward the get pointer by the number of bytes read.

The seekg() function has been defined in the class istream. It has two versions.

```
   istream & istream :: seekg(streampos pos);

   istream & istream :: seekg(streamoff off,
                                     ios::seek_dir dir);
```

The explanation for these two versions of the seekg() function is similar to the one provided for the corresponding versions of seekp() function.

7.9.4 tellg() Function

The tellg() function, like the tellp() function, returns the current position of the get pointer. It has been defined in the class istream.

```
   streampos istream::tellg();
```

In the following example, the current position of the get pointer is determined and stored in a program variable.

```
long pos = ifile.tellg();              //ifile is an object of the
                                       //class ifstream
```

7.10 Random Access to Files

In random access, an intermediate record of a file is accessed directly without sequentially iterating through its neighbouring records. We have already studied the tools necessary for accessing a record in a disk file at random, the seekp() and seekg() functions.

Suppose we have output integer-type values into a disk file and we want to directly access the nth integer. We can do this sequentially by using a loop that starts iterating from the first record. This loop increments a counter after every read and stops when the counter indicates that the $(n-1)$th record has been read. At this point, the pointers would point at the nth record. But a more direct approach is to use either the seekp() function or the seekg() function, as the need may be, as follows:

```
iofile.seekp((n-1)*sizeof(int), ios::beg);        //iofile is an
                                                  //object of
                                                  //the class
                                                  //fstream
```

This statement causes the file pointers to point at the nth record. At this point, if the write operation is conducted, the nth record would get modified.

Note that the technique works only if the size of all the records that are stored in the file is equal. This is possible only if binary data is stored in binary mode.

The size of the file and the number of records can also be found out very easily.

```
iofile.seekp(0,ios::end);              //iofile is an object of the
                                       //class fstream
long lSize = iofile.tellp();
int iNoOfRec = lSize/sizeof(int);
```

In this example, the pointer is first forced to the end of the file. The current position of the pointer, since it points just past the last byte and the byte numbering starts from zero, denotes the size of the file in bytes. Dividing this size by the size of each record gives the number of records. Again, we must note that the technique works only if the size of all the records that are stored in the file is equal. This is possible only if binary data is stored in binary mode.

7.11 Object Input/Output Through Member Functions

We have realized that classes that have pointers that point at externally held data should also have the necessary functionality to output and input their data. Client programs of such classes should not be burdened with the responsibility of knowing how the data stored in the objects of such classes is organized.

Let us provide the String class, which has been our running example so far, with the functionality to write its data into and read its data from disk files. See Listing 7.27.

Listing 7.27 Input/output of objects through member functions

```
/*Beginning of String.h*/
#include<iostream.h>
class String
```

```cpp
{
    /*
        rest of the class String
    */
    explicit String(const char * const p = NULL);
    const char * getString();
    void diskOut(ofstream &);
    void diskIn(ifstream &);
};
/*End of String.h*/

/*Beginning of String.cpp*/
#include<fstream.h>
#include<string.h>
#include"String.h"
/*
    rest of the class String
*/
String::String(const char * const p)
{
    if(p==NULL)                         //if default value passed...
    {
        cStr=NULL;                      //...nullify
        len=0;
    }
    else                                //...otherwise...
    {
        len=strlen(p);
        cStr=new char[len+1];           //...dynamically allocate a
                                        //separate memory block
        strcpy(cStr,p);                 //...and copy into it
    }
}
const char * String::getString()
{
    return cStr;
}
void String::diskOut(ofstream & fout)
{
    fout.write((char *)&len, sizeof(int));
    for(int i = 0;i<len;i++)
    {
        fout.put(cStr[i]);
    }
}
void String::diskIn(ifstream & fin)
{
    String temp;
    fin.read((char *)&temp.len, sizeof(int));
    temp.cStr = new char[temp.len+1];
    int i;
    for(i = 0;i<temp.len;i++)
        fin.get(temp.cStr[i]);
    temp.cStr[i]='\0';
    *this = temp;
}
/*End of String.cpp*/

/*Beginning of strDiskMain.cpp*/
#include<fstream.h>
```

```
#include"String.h"
void main()
{
    String s1("abcd");
    ofstream ofile("C:\\string.dat");
    s1.diskOut(ofile);
    ofile.close();
    String s2;
    ifstream ifile("C:\\string.dat");
    s2.diskIn(ifile);
    cout<<s2.getString()<<endl;
    ifile.close();
}
/*End of strDiskMain.cpp*/
```

Output
abcd

7.12 Error Handling

Every object of the class istream, ostream or of a class that is derived from one of these two classes contains three flags that indicate state of the next byte in the associated file. These flags are:

- **eofbit**—becomes true if the end of file is encountered
- **failbit**—becomes true if the read/write operation fails (This in turn can be due to various reasons that are described shortly.)
- **badbit**—becomes true if the file being read is corrupt beyond recovery

7.12.1 eof() Function

The eof() function returns true whenever the file pointer encounters the end of file mark while reading the file that has been opened through the calling object. Whenever a stream library function, while reading from an input file, reaches the end of file mark, it sets the value of eofbit to true.

```
while(!ifile.eof())                     //read till end of file
{
    //statements to read from the file and operate upon the
    //read value
}
```

Note that the eof() function returns the result of a past read. It does not look ahead before returning the result. Therefore, the test for end of file is given at the beginning of the loop.

7.12.2 fail() Function

The fail() function returns true if the file could not be opened for any reason. Whenever the open() function fails to open a file, it sets the failbit to true.

One reason that causes the open() function to fail is the non-existence of the file that is being opened for reading or writing by using the ios::nocreate flag.

```
ifstream ifile;
ifile.open("first.dat",ios::in | ios::nocreate);
if(ifile.fail())
{
```

```
cout<<"File does not exist for reading\n";
/*
    statements to take corrective action
*/
}
```

Another reason can be that the file is being opened for writing by using the ios::noreplace flag but it already exists.

```
ofstream ofile;
ofile.open("first.dat", ios::out | ios::noreplace);
if(ofile.fail())
{
    cout<<"File already exists … overwrite (y/n)?";
    /*
        statements to record user's response and take
        appropriate action
    */
}
```

Some more reasons that cause the read/write operation to fail follow:
- The file being opened for writing is read only.
- There is no space on the disk.
- The file being opened for writing is in a disk that is write-protected.

7.12.3 bad() Function

The bad() function returns true whenever a function that is reading from a file encounters a serious I/O error. Under such circumstances, the value of the badbit flag gets set to true. It is best to abort I/O operations on the stream in this situation.

7.12.4 clear() Function

The clear() function is used to clear the bits returned by the bad() function. This is necessary under a number of circumstances. Listing 7.28 illustrates one such circumstance.

Listing 7.28   The clear() function

```
/*Beginning of clearEof.cpp*/
#include<iostream.h>
#include<fstream.h>
void main()
{
    fstream iofile("first.dat",ios::in | ios::out);
    char cArr[100];
    int i=0;
    while(!iofile.eof())
    {
        iofile.get(cArr[i++]);
    }
    iofile.clear();
    for(int j=0;j<i;j++)
        iofile.put(cArr[j]);                //append the contents of the
                                            //file to itself

}
/*End of clearEof.cpp*/
```

We must note that the use of clear() function was necessary in Listing 7.28. After the while loop ends, the eofbit flag becomes true. Any further write operation on the file will fail if the clear() function is not used.

7.13 Manipulators

Manipulators are used to format the output. C++ provides some pre-defined manipulators. The programmer can create his own application-specific manipulators too.

Manipulators can be inserted in an output stream just like values are inserted for output.

```
out << manip1 << manip2 << value1 << manip3 << value2;
```

In this example, out is an object of the class ostream or any of its derived classes. cout can also be used in place of out to format the output to the monitor.

7.13.1 Pre-defined Manipulators

C++ provides a number of handy manipulators that are pre-defined in the header file iomanip.h. Therefore, programs that use these manipulators must include this header file.

Some of the most commonly used pre-defined manipulators are listed in Table 7.2.

Table 7.2 Pre-defined Manipulators

Manipulator	Use
setw(int w)	Set the field width to w
setprecision(int d)	Set the floating point precision to d
setfill(int c)	Set the fill character to c
setiosflags(long f)	Set the format flag to f
resetiosflags(long f)	Clear the flag specified by f

The setw() manipulator

The setw() manipulator takes an integer-type variable as its only parameter. This parameter specifies the width of the column within which the next output will be output. If the value that is output after this manipulator is passed in the insertion stream occupies less number of bytes than the specified parameter, then extra space will be created in the column that will contain the output value. These extra spaces will be padded by blanks or by the character that is passed as a parameter to the setfill() function.

An example code snippet follows:

```
cout << 123 << endl;
cout << setw(3) << 10;
```

Output

```
123
 10
```

It is obvious that there is a blank space on the left of '10' in the second line of this output.

The setw() manipulator has to be used separately for each item to be displayed.

```
cout << setw(5) << 10 << setw(5) << 234 << endl;
```

No truncation of data occurs if the parameter that is passed to the setw() function is not sufficient to hold the data that is output subsequently. Instead, the padding requirement implied by the setw() function is ignored.

```
cout << 123 << endl;
cout << setw(3) << 10000;
```

Output

```
123
10000
```

The setprecision() manipulator

By default, C++ displays the values of float and double type with six digits after the decimal point. However, we can pass the number of digits we want to display after the decimal point as a parameter to the setprecision() manipulator.

```
cout << setprecision(3)
     << sqrt(3) << endl
     << 1.14159 << endl;
```

Output

```
1.732
1.142
```

We must notice how the second output got rounded off to the nearest number.

Unlike the setw() manipulator, the setprecision() manipulator retains its effect even after outputting a value.

The setfill() manipulator

By default, the setw() manipulator pads any extra spaces it finds in the column that it has created with blank spaces. However, we can also specify the padding character by passing it as a parameter to the setfill() manipulator.

```
cout << setfill('*')
     << setw(5) << 10
     << setw(5) << 234
     << endl;
```

Output
```
***10**234
```

The setiosflags() manipulator

The setiosflags() manipulator is also used to format the manner in which the output data is displayed. Two important parameters that it takes are ios::showpos and ios::showpoint.

The ios::showpos flag, when passed as a parameter to the setiosflags() manipulator, ensures that the positive sign is prefixed to numeric data when they are displayed.

```
cout << setiosflags(ios::showpos) << 10;
```

Output
```
+10
```

The ios::showpoint flag, when passed as a parameter to the setiosflags() manipulator, ensures that if the number of significant digits in the value being output is less than that specified by the setprecision() manipulator, then the extra spaces obtained thereby are filled with zeros.

```
cout << setprecision(3)
        << 2.5 <<endl
        << setiosflags(ios::showpoint)
        << 2.5 << endl;
```

Output
```
2.5
2.500
```

The second line in the output highlights the effect of the setiosflags() manipulator.

The resetiosflags() manipulator

This manipulator cancels the effect of the parameter that was passed to an earlier call to the setiosflags() manipulator. The output of the following code snippet shows how.

```
cout << setprecision(3)
        << 2.5 << endl
        << setiosflags(ios::showpoint)
        << 2.5 << endl
        << resetiosflags(ios::showpoint)
        << 2.5 << endl;
```

Output
```
2.5
2.500
2.5
```

7.13.2 User-defined Manipulators

It is possible to create requirement-specific manipulators too. A programmer can create a manipulator to satisfy his specific needs. He/she can do this by defining a function as follows:

```
ostream & <manipulator> (ostream & out)
{
    //statements
    return out;
}
```

An example of a user-defined manipulator follows:

```
ostream & currency (ostream & out)
{
    out << "$. ";
    return out;
}
```

Now if we write

```
cout << currency << 20;
```

the output would be

```
$ 20
```

User-defined manipulators enable modularity. A user-defined manipulator can be used throughout an application to format the output in a uniform manner. If a change is required, it needs to be carried out at only one place—the definition of the manipulator—and again the change occurs uniformly throughout the application.

7.14 Command Line Arguments

Command line arguments are values that are passed to executables when they are run from the command line. As we know, after we successfully compile and link a C++ program we get an executable file. These executable programs can be run from the command line of your computer's operating system.

How do we pass command line arguments to executables? Let us understand this with the help of an example.

Suppose the name of an executable that has been generated from a C++ program is 'test. exe'. We can run this executable by typing the following command on the command line and then hitting the enter key:

```
test
```

We can also run the executable by issuing the following command:

```
test.exe
```

Let us follow the first method for running the executable. (Note that the above two methods would work if the operating system on your computer is Windows. The method may change for a different operating system. Please consult the operating system's documentation or your lab instructor if the operating system on your computer is not Windows. For the purpose of this book, we will assume that the operating system on your computer is Windows.)

Suppose we want to pass the strings 'abc' and 'def' as command line arguments to the executable. We can do this by calling the executable from the command line as follows:

```
test abc def
```

Note that 'abc' and 'def' have been passed as parameters to the command for executing the executable file test.

Why are command line arguments important? Why should a C++ programmer write programs that can read the values of command line arguments? Consider a very simple program (Listing 7.29) that adds up two numbers and then displays the result.

Listing 7.29 The programmer can decide the values to be added

```
/*Beginning of add.cpp*/
/*
   A program in which two numbers are added but it is the
   programmer, and not the program's user, who decides the
   values to be added.
*/
#include <iostream.h>
void main()
{
```

```
    int x = 10, y = 20;
    int z = x + y;
    cout << z << endl;
}
/*End of add.cpp*/
```

Output

30

As can be seen, it is the programmer who declared two variables and initialized them to values of his/her choice. But, what if we need the values from the user? One way is to take inputs from the keyboard using the `cin` object. But what will happen if our executable is being run from another program? That program, when it is running, won't be able to give keyboard inputs (after all it is a program, not a human). It will obviously be much more convenient if our program accepts the values it needs, as command line arguments.

Now, we come to the most important question—how can we program our C++ programs so that they can read and process command line arguments? The `main()` function can be programmed to read command line arguments. For this, we need to define the header of the `main()` function as follows:

```
    void main(int argc, char * argv[])
```

The first argument, `argc`, gives us the number of arguments present on the command line, including the name of the executable. It is known as the argument counter. The second argument, `argv`, is an array of character pointers. Each pointer points at a separate command line argument. It is known as the argument vector.

Note that `argc` and `argv` are only the names of the `main()` function's arguments. You, while writing your own programs, can give them names of your choice. For example, you can name them 'x' and 'y'. The names `argc` and `argv` are the conventional names. And we will use them as such in our examples.

Let us again consider the previous command to execute our program.

```
    test abc def
```

In this case, two command line arguments have been passed. Therefore, the value of `argc` would be 3 (2 arguments plus the name of the executable file itself). The value of `argv[0]` would be `test`. The value of `argv[1]` would be 'abc'. The value of `argv[2]` would be `def`.

Let us look at some very simple examples that illustrate how the `main()` function reads command line arguments through its parameters (see Listing 7.30). These would be followed by programs that illustrate the possible practical ways in which command line arguments can be used.

Listing 7.30   The command line counter

```
/*Beginning of test.cpp*/
/*
   A program the displays the count of command line
   arguments.
*/
#include <iostream.h>
void main(int argc, char *argv[])
{
   cout << argc << endl;
}
/*End of test.cpp*/
```

Note that this example program displays the number of command line arguments that were passed to its executable, plus 1 (for the name of the executable itself). Suppose we run the executable file from the above program by passing no command line arguments as follows:

```
test
```

Output
1

The output is 1 because no command line arguments were passed to the executable.

Suppose we run the executable file from the above program by passing two command line arguments as follows:

```
test abc def
```

Output
3

The output is 3 because two command line arguments were passed to the executable.

Let us enhance the above program so that it not only displays the number of command line arguments, but also the arguments themselves (Listing 7.31).

Listing 7.31   The command line arguments

```
/*Beginning of test.cpp*/
/*
    A program that displays the count of command line
    arguments and the command line arguments themselves.
*/
#include <iostream.h>
void main(int argc, char *argv[])
{
    cout << argc << endl;
    for(int i = 0; i < argc; i++)
    {
        cout << argv[i] << endl;
    }
}
/*End of test.cpp*/
```

Suppose we run the above program as follows:

```
test Happy Birthday
```

The output would be as follows:

Output
3
test
Happy
Birthday

The above program first displays the count of command line arguments, which is 3. It then executes a for loop whose loop counter 'i' starts from 0 and ends at 3 (the value of argc). Therefore, the for loop displays the values of argv[0], argv[1], and argv[2]. The value of argv[0] is 'test' (the name of the executable file). The value of argv[1] is 'Happy' (the value of the first argument). The value of argv[2] is 'Birthday' (the value of the second argument).

Suppose we need to enforce a condition that the user *must* enter a certain number of command line arguments. For example, we may need that the user must enter exactly two command line arguments. If the user does not pass exactly two command line arguments, we may like to give an error message and terminate the program. Let us see how we can accomplish this. Let us continue to enhance the test program. See Listing 7.32.

Listing 7.32 Ensuring a specific number of command line arguments

```
/*Beginning of test.cpp*/
/*
A program that utilizes the command line argument counter
to ensure that the correct number of command line
arguments are passed.
*/
#include <iostream.h>
void main(int argc, char *argv[])
{
    if(argc != 3)
    {
        cout << "Incorrect number of arguments passed" << endl;
        exit();
    }
    cout << argc << endl;
    for(int i = 0; i < argc; i++)
    {
        cout << argv[i] << endl;
    }
}
/*End of test.cpp*/
```

The above main() function, at the very beginning, checks whether the value of the argument counter is 3 or not. It is actually checking whether the number of command line arguments that were passed to the executable is 2 or not (remember that the argument counter counts the executable also).

If the value of the argument counter is not 3, the main() function flashes an error message and then terminates the program by calling the exit() function. (*Note:* No arguments have been passed to the exit() function above. However, the number of arguments that the exit() function takes in your installation of the C++ library may be different. If that is the case, then consult the documentation or your lab instructor and modify the call accordingly.)

Summary

Streams are nothing but a flow of data to and from program variables. Input stream is the flow of data from a file on the permanent storage medium to program variables. The keyboard is also treated as source of input stream. Output stream is the flow of data to a file on the permanent storage medium from program variables. The monitor is also treated as target for output stream.

C++ provides us with a hierarchy of classes that have the functionality to implement various aspects of stream handling. The class ios is the base class in this hierarchy.

The class ostream is derived from the class ios and handles the general output stream. The insertion operator (<<) is defined and overloaded in the class ostream to handle output streams from program variables to output files.

The class ostream_withassign is derived from the class ostream. cout is an object of the class ostream_withassign. cout stands for console output. As mentioned earlier, C++ treats all peripheral devices as files. It treats the monitor also as a file (for output stream). The object cout represents the monitor.

The class istream is derived from ios and handles the general input streams. The extraction operator (>>) is defined and overloaded in the class istream to handle input streams from input files to program variables.

The class istream_withassign is derived from the class istream. cin is an object of the class istream_withassign. cin stands for console input. C++ treats all peripheral devices as files. It treats the keyboard also as a file (for input stream). The object cin represents the keyboard.

The class iostream is derived by multiple inheritance from the classes istream and ostream. It has the functionality to handle both input and output streams. The class ofstream is derived from the class ostream. It has the functionality to handle output streams to disk files. The class ifstream is derived from the class istream. It has the functionality to handle input streams from disk files. The class fstream is derived from the class iostream. It has the functionality to handle both input and output streams from and to disk files.

In text mode output, numeric data that exists in base 2 format in the memory variables, is first converted to base 10 format before being output. In binary mode, no such conversion occurs.

In text mode input, numeric data that is being input into a memory variable is reckoned to be in base 10 format. Therefore, it is first converted into base 2 format and then stored in the target memory variable.

The insertion operator is used to output data in text mode. The put() function is used to output a single character at a time. The extraction operator is used to input data in text mode. The get() function is used to input a single character at a time.

The write() function is used to output data in binary mode. The read() function is used to input data in binary mode.

Apart from the constructors of the library classes, the open() function can also be used to open files. The first parameter that the constructor and the open() function take is the name of the file. The second parameter specifies the open mode. Destructors of library stream classes close the files associated with them anyway. But the close() function can be used to explicitly close files.

File pointers can be manipulated by the seekp() and seekg() functions. Their current positions can be determined by the tellp() and tellg() functions. An intermediate record can be directly accessed by using the seekp() or seekg() function to make the file pointer jump to a specific byte in the file. It is mandatory to use member functions for outputting and inputting data in case of complex classes.

Every object of the class istream, ostream or of a class that is derived from either of these two classes, contains three flags that indicate state of the next byte in the associated file. These flags are:

- **eofbit**—becomes true if the end of file is encountered (The eof() function returns the state of the eofbit flag.)
- **failbit**—becomes true if the read/write operation fails (The fail() function returns the state of the failbit flag.)
- **badbit**—becomes true if the file being read is corrupt beyond recovery (The bad() function returns the state of the badbit flag.)

The clear() function is used to clear the bits described above.

Manipulators are used to format the output. C++ provides some pre-defined manipulators. The programmer can create his own application-specific manipulators too.

Command line arguments are values that are passed to executables when they are run from the command line. They enable programs to capture input values from the user and from other systems.

The main() function can be programmed to read command line arguments. We need to define the header of the main() function as follows:

```
void main(int argc, char * argv[])
```

The first argument gives us the number of arguments present on the command line, including the name of the executable. It is known as the argument counter. The second argument is an array of character pointers. Each pointer points at a separate command line argument. It is known as the argument vector.

Key Terms

streams

standard stream handling classes of C++

 - ios
 - ostream
 - ostream_withassign
 - istream
 - istream_withassign
 - iostream
 - ofstream
 - ifstream
 - fstream

text mode input/output

cout

insertion operator

put() function

cin

extraction operator

get() function

write() function

read() function

open() function

close() function

seekp() function

seekg() function

tellp() function

tellg() function

eof() function and the eofbit flag

fail() function and the failbit flag

bad() function and the badbit flag

clear() function

manipulators

Exercises

1. Briefly describe the class hierarchy provided by C++ for stream handling.
2. State true or false.
   (a) cout is an object of the class ostream_withassign.
   (b) The insertion operator (<<) is defined and overloaded in the class istream.
   (c) The header file iostream.h is included in the file fstream.h.
   (d) The insertion operator outputs in binary mode.
3. What are text mode and binary mode input/output? What are their corresponding strengths and weaknesses?
4. What is the difference between a text file and a binary file?
5. Why should read operation on a file take place in the same mode in which the write operation has occurred? Explain.

6. How are values of various types output to disk files by using the insertion operator?
7. Describe the read() and write() functions, their prototype, use, and the way they input and output data.
8. How can a file be opened for both reading and writing?
9. What is the difference between opening a file using the constructor of the stream class and the open() function.
10. Describe how the contents of a disk file can be randomly accessed in C++.
11. Describe the circumstances under which each of the flags—eofbit, failbit, and badbit—becomes true.
12. Describe the use of the following manipulators:
    setw()
    setprecision()

```
        setfill()
        setiosflags()
        resetiosflags()
```

13. How can a programmer define his/her own manipulators?

14. What are command line arguments? Why are they important?

15. How can the main() function be programmed to read command line arguments?

16. Write a program to obtain as many integers from the user as he/she wants and write them into a disk file. After the user has finished entering the integers, read them from the file and display them on the monitor.

17. Create a class whose objects would hold linked lists of integers. Apart from the regular features of linked lists, the objects would also have the necessary functionality to download their data into a specified disk file and to upload their data from specified disk files. The application would be menu-driven. The user will have the option to save the linked list and to 'save as' the linked list.

Hint:

Create two classes as follows:

```
class intNode
{
        int data;
        intNode * Next;
    public:
        //functions to set and get the data
        members
```

```
};
class intList
{
        intNode * head;
    public:
        //functions to add, delete, modify,
        save and load
};
```

18. Write a manipulator that prefixes a currency symbol to the output value. For this, the manipulator should read the symbol from a disk file.

19. Write a program that gives an error message if the number of arguments that are passed to its executable is not equal to 1 (hint: 'argc' != 2), and then terminates itself. The error message should advise the user that exactly one argument should be passed to the executable, and that it should be the name of a file.

Otherwise, if the user has passed exactly one argument to the executable, the program should open the file whose name matches the value of the argument (hint: argv[1]). It should then append the name of the executable (hint: argv[0]) into a new line in the file, along with a text that says that the executable executed successfully. For example, if the name of the executable is test, then the following line should get appended to the file:

```
test executed successfully.
```

8

Operator Overloading, Type Conversion, New Style Casts, and RTTI

Operator overloading is an extremely interesting feature of C++. It is not only interesting and exciting, but also an essential tool for the class designer. This chapter explains the following:
- the concept of operator overloading,
- the support provided by C++ for operator overloading,
- the need to overload operators,
- rules for operator overloading,
- use and misuse of operator overloading, and
- pitfalls in operator overloading.

The initial sections of the chapter give an overview of operator overloading. They contain only the skeleton code to illustrate the concepts without burdening the reader with the intricacies of the exact code. The exact code to overload various operators for various classes is dealt with in the later sections.

Type conversions from basic type to class type, from class type to basic type, and from one class type to another are also dealt with in this chapter.

C++ provides the following four new style cast operators to replace the use of the old error prone and difficult to detect C style casts:
- `dynamic_cast`
- `static_cast`
- `reinterpret_cast`
- `const_cast`

RTTI (run time type information) enables the programmer to find the type of object at which a pointer points during run time. Apart from the `dynamic_cast` operator, C++ provides the `typeid` operator for implementing RTTI.

The chapter ends with an explanation of new style cast operators and RTTI.

8.1 Operator Overloading

Let us first understand the meaning of operator overloading and how this useful feature of the C++ language is implemented.

Overloading an operator means programming an operator to work on operands of types it has not yet been designed to operate. For instance, the addition operator can work on operands of type `char`, `int`, `float`, and `double`. However, if 's1', 's2', and 's3' are objects of the class `String`, which we have defined earlier, then the following statement

```
s3 = s1 + s2
```

will not compile unless the creator of class String explicitly overloads the addition operator to work on objects of his class. The method of implementing such overloading is described next.

8.1.1 Overloading Operators—The Syntax

Operators are overloaded by writing operator-overloading functions. These functions are either member functions or friend functions of that class whose objects are intended as operands of the overloaded operator. Operator overloading functions are very similar to the member functions and friend functions we have been reading about all along. The only thing peculiar about them is their name. The names of operator-overloading functions are composed of the keyword operator followed by the symbol of the operator being overloaded.

The syntax for member functions that overload a given operator is as follows:

```
class <class_name>
{
   <return_type> operator <op> (<arg_list>); //prototype
};
<return_type> <class_name> :: operator <op> (<arg_list>)
//definition
{
   //function body
}
```

Member functions that overload operators can be private, protected, or public. The prototype of the operator-overloading function specifies a return type (as do the normal member functions). The keyword operator follows the return type. This in turn is followed by the symbol of the operator being overloaded. Finally, a pair of parentheses containing the formal arguments is specified (as do the normal member functions).

The syntax for a friend function that overloads a given operator is as follows:

```
class <class_name>
{
   friend <return_type> operator <op> (<arg_list>); //prototype
};
<return_type> operator <op> (<arg_list>) //definition
{
   //function body
}
```

We already know that a friend function takes one argument more that the member function that serves the same purpose (because the invoking object appears as an explicit parameter to the friend function whereas in member functions it is passed as an implicit parameter). The same holds true in case of operator-loading functions.

The following examples will help in clarifying this syntax.

Suppose we want to overload the addition operator (+) so that it can take objects of the class String that we defined earlier. The exact syntax for this (in case of member function) would be as shown in Listing 8.1.

Listing 8.1 Defining and using operator-overloading function as a member function

```
/*Beginning of String.h*/
class String
{
```

```
   public:
      String operator + (const String &) const; //prototype
      /*
         rest of the class String
      */
};
/*End of String.h*/

/*Beginning of String.cpp*/
#include"String.h"
String String :: operator + (const String & ss) const
                     //definition
{
   //function body
}
/*
   definitions of the rest of the functions of class String
*/
/*End of String.cpp*/

/*Beginning of SomeProgram.cpp*/
#include"String.h"
void f()                              //some function
{
   String s1,s2,s3;
   /*
      rest of the function f()
   */
   s3 = s1 + s2;
   /*
      rest of the function f()
   */
}
/*End of SomeProgram.cpp*/
```

We can notice that the function has been declared as a public member of the class. This is because the operator will usually be used in its overloaded form within the non-member functions. The reasons for the return type and signature of this function will be discussed later. Moreover, the techniques of defining such functions will be demonstrated later.

If this function were to be declared as a friend, then the syntax would be as shown in Listing 8.2.

Listing 8.2 Defining operator-overloading function as a friend function

```
/*Beginning of String.h*/
class String
{
   friend String operator + (const String &,
                             const String &);          //prototype
      /*
         rest of the class String
      */
};
/*End of String.h*/
/*Beginning of String.cpp*/
#include"String.h"
String operator + (const String & ss1, const String & ss2)
                 //definition
```

```
      {
          //function body
      }
      /*
          definitions of the rest of the functions of class String
      */
      /*End of String.cpp*/

      /*Beginning of SomeProgram.cpp*/
      #include"String.h"
      void f()                              //some function
      {
          String s1,s2,s3;
          /*
              rest of the function f()
          */
          s3 = s1 + s2;
          /*
              rest of the function f()
          */
      }
      /*End of SomeProgram.cpp*/
```

8.1.2 Compiler Interpretation of Operator-Overloading Functions

It is important to understand how the compiler interprets operator-overloading functions. The statement

```
      s3 = s1 + s2;                         //s1, s2 and s3 are objects of the class
                                            //String
```

is interpreted as

```
      s3 = s1.operator + (s2);
```

If the operator-overloading function has been declared as a member function, then this interpretation is satisfied. Otherwise, the statement is interpreted as

```
      s3 = operator + (s1, s2);
```

If the operator-overloading function has been declared as a friend function, then this interpretation is satisfied. Otherwise, the compiler reports an error to the effect that the given operator has not been overloaded for the class. It is interesting to note the compiler does not say that invalid operands have been passed to the operator!

So far, we have seen that the operators have been overloaded within the classes using member functions or friend functions. These functions are compiled and stored in the library.

We have also seen that the overloaded operators have been used within the applications using their usual syntax. As described in this section, the compiler first converts the statements where the overloaded operators are used. However, we must note that the operator-overloading functions can also be called directly from within the application programs (the way the compiler finally interprets it). Operator-overloading functions can be called directly as follows.

```
      s3 = s1.operator + (s2);             //in case of member function
```

or

```
      s3 = operator + (s1, s2);            //in case of friend function
```

The benefit of overloading the operator will not be felt if the overloaded operators are directly called in this manner. (In that case, they can be very well replaced by ordinary member functions.) Moreover, we must note that only the name of the operator-overloading function is unusual (it contains the keyword `operator`). Otherwise, the operator- overloading functions are implemented just like ordinary member, non-member, or friend functions.

Concept of overload using friend functions

We might wonder why friend functions are used to overload operators. After all, member functions seem to serve the purpose. In order to understand this, let us consider two classes A (which we have defined) and B (an existing class or an intrinsic data type). We realize that for some reason only an object of class A will be added to an object of class B to get another object of class A. This will be done as follows.

```
a2 = b1 + a1;                   //a1, a2 are objects of class A, b1 is
                                //an object of class B
```

An object of class B will not be added to an object of class A. Objects of class B will appear on the left of the addition operator and not on the right. We will soon realize that such restrictions can and do exist. Statements such as the one that follow will not be written.

```
a2 = a1 + b1;                   //a1, a2 are objects of class A, b1 is
                                //an object of class B
```

Further let us assume (rather accept) that we have no means of modifying the definition of class B. (This is a perfectly acceptable restriction. We cannot define somebody else's class definition. Class definitions are provided in read-only header files and definitions of member functions in libraries.) Now, if we define the operator-overloading function as a member function of class A as follows, the first of the two preceding statements will not compile.

```
class A
{
    public:
        A operator + (const B &);
};
```

The compiler will interpret the statement

```
a2 = b1 + a1;
```

first as

```
a2 = b1.operator + (a1);
```

and then as

```
a2 = operator + (b1,a1);
```

The prototype of the member function satisfies neither of these two interpretations. The compiler will naturally throw an error. Declaring the operator-overloading function as a friend function with an object of class B as the first formal argument solves the problem. See Listing 8.3.

Listing 8.3 Operator overloading using friend function

```
class A
{
    public:
```

```
            friend A operator + (const B &, const A &);
                            //prototype
        };
        A operator + (const B & bb, const A & aa)        //definition
        {
            //function body
        }
```

It is interesting to note that the compiler throws an ambiguity error if both member function and friend function are used to overload an operator. This is because both of them will satisfy calls to the overloaded operator. The compiler will certainly be in no position to decide with which function such a call is to be resolved.

8.1.3 Overview of Overloading Unary and Binary Operators

Member functions that overload unary operators take no operands. This is because apart from the calling object, no other parameter is passed to the operator and the calling object is passed as an implicit parameter to the object. Friend functions that overload unary operators will naturally take one parameter since the calling object will be passed as an explicit parameter to it.

Similarly, member functions that overload binary operators will take one parameter. This is because apart from the calling object, another value will be passed to the operator as an operand (binary operators take two operands). The calling object will itself be passed to the function as an implicit parameter. Again, friend functions that overload binary operators will take one operand more, that is, two operands. We can very well explain this.

8.1.4 Operator Overloading

Let us now find out the need to overload operators. After all, the operator-overloading functions can be so easily substituted by member functions or friend functions with ordinary but meaningful and relevant names. For example, the operator-overloading function to overload the addition operator (+) for objects of the class String can be easily replaced by a member function of a proper name. See Listing 8.4.

Listing 8.4 Using an ordinary member function to substitute an operator-overloading function

```
class String
{
    public:
        //String operator + (const String &);
        String add(const String &);   //prototype
};
String String :: add(const String & ss)         //definition
{
    //function body
}
void f()                                //some function
{
    String s1,s2,s3;
    /*
        rest of the function f()
```

```
*/
s3 = s1.add(s2);
/*
   rest of the function f()
*/
}
```

The definition of the `String :: add()` function can be the same as the operator- overloading function to overload the `addition` operator (+).

However, operator overloading becomes mandatory under the following circumstances:

- Objects of the class acquire resources dynamically during run time and no two objects should share the same copy of the resource.
- Objects of the class acquire some resources dynamically during run time and no two objects should share even different copies of the resource.
- Objects need to be passed as parameters in function templates and the operators being used on template class objects within the template functions should work in the same way on objects of the class.
- The default action of the dynamic memory management operators (new and `delete`) are unsuitable for the class being designed.
- Change in the implementation of the class forces an undesirable change in its interface in turn necessitating the rewriting and recompiling of the application programs.
- Overloading provides better readability of code. Although this is a somewhat weak reason, it, nevertheless, is a factor that can be considered. The statement

```
o2 = ++o1;
```

is much more readable than say a statement such as

```
o2 = o1.pre_fix_increment();
```

Let us understand these circumstances one by one. For understanding the first case, let us reconsider the class `String`. Let us try to visualize what happens at the end of the block of code given in Listing 8.5.

Listing 8.5   Undesirable default action of the assignment operator

```
String s1("abc"), s2;
s2 = s1;
```

As a result of the second statement in Listing 8.5, the scenario shown in Figure 8.1 emerges.

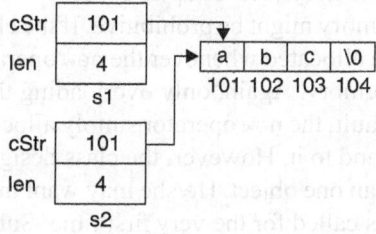

Figure 8.1   Diagram depicting the drawback in the default action of the assignment operator

As a result of the second statement in Listing 8.5, the pointers embedded in both the objects point at the same dynamically allocated memory block. The default action of the assignment operator simply copies the value of the pointer embedded in 's1' into the pointer embedded in 's2'.

The problems that arise out of such a situation have already been discussed in Chapter 4. We will notice that the same undesirable situation arose due to the initial absence of a suitable copy constructor in the class `String`. This had prompted us to define a suitable copy constructor for the class `String`. The same factors dictate that a suitable function to overload the assignment operator be defined for the class `String`. Instead of the default action of the assignment operator, execution of this function will take place when statements such as the second one in Listing 8.5 are executed.

For understanding the second circumstance where operator overloading is mandatory, let us imagine that there is a class whose objects should not share even separate copies of dynamically allocated resources. This means that statements such as the following one should not compile at all.

```
o1 = o2;      //o1, o2 are objects of the said class
```

Here the solution is quite simple. We just declare the function to overload the assignment operator in the private section of the class. Any use of the assignment operator within a non-member function will launch a call to this operator-overloading function. Since the function is private, such a call will throw a compile-time error. As desired, the use of the assignment operator will be prevented. However, what would happen if we inadvertently use the assignment operator within a member function or a friend function? The private nature of the function will not be enough to prevent such a call. However, even such calls can be prevented by not defining the function to overload the assignment operator. This trick will make the linker throw an error.

To understand the third circumstance where operator overloading is mandatory, we require the knowledge of function templates, which are discussed in the next chapter.

Now, let us understand the fourth circumstance. The new operator does a number of things by default, some, or all of which might be undesirable for the class being designed.

By default, the new operator throws an exception if it fails to allocate the amount of memory requested (exceptions are dealt with in one of the later chapters). However, this default action of the new operator may be unsuitable for the class being designed. In response to this out-of-memory condition, the class designer might instead need to call one of the member functions of the class. Only overloading the new operator can fulfill this need.

Also by default, the new operator not only allocates the amount of memory requested, it also stores the amount of memory allocated in the memory itself. This enables the `delete` operator (if it is called) to find out the size of the memory allocated so that it can then deallocate the same amount of memory (see Chapter 3). However, in memory critical applications, such expenditure of memory might be prohibitive. If the class designer knows that the same amount of memory will be allocated whenever the new operator is called, he/she can cleverly prevent this wastage of memory. Again, only overloading the new operator can do this.

Further, by default, the new operator simply allocates memory for the object whose type is passed as an operand to it. However, the class designer would not want that the class should ever have more than one object. He/she may want that an object should be created only when the new operator is called for the very first time. Subsequent calls to the new operator should not create more objects. Instead, such subsequent calls should merely return the address of the object that was created in response to the first call to the new operator.

The last circumstance that mandates operator overloading is self-explanatory.

8.1.5 Rules for Operator Overloading

The following rules must be observed while overloading operators.

1. **New operators cannot be created:** New operators (such as **) cannot be created. For example, the piece of code shown in Listing 8.6 will produce a compile-time error.

Listing 8.6 An illegal attempt to create a new operator

```
class A
{
    public:
        void operator ** ();
};
```

2. **Meaning of existing operators cannot be changed:** Any operator-overloading function (member or friend) should take at least one operand of the class of which it is a member or friend. Thus, it is not possible to change the manner in which an existing operator works on operands of fundamental types (char, int, float, double).

   In case of member functions, this condition is automatically enforced because the address of the calling object is implicitly passed as a parameter to it. However, in case of friend functions, the library programmer needs to take extra care. For example, the following piece of code (Listing 8.7) will not compile.

Listing 8.7 An illegal attempt to modify the behaviour of operators on intrinsic types

```
class A
{
    public:
        friend int operator + (int, int);        //ERROR: will not
                                                  //compile
};
```

As we can see, by ensuring that at least one operand of an operator-overloading function must be of the class type, the compiler ensures that the meanings of the existing operators cannot be changed. If the code in Listing 8.7 had compiled, the statement

```
z = x + y;                    //x, y, z are integer type
```

could have invoked the operator + () function of the class A. Of course, this is undesirable.

3. **Some of the existing operators cannot be overloaded:** The following operators cannot be overloaded:

   :: (scope resolution)

   . (member selection)

   .* (member selection through pointer to member)

   ?: (conditional operator)

   sizeof (finding the size of values and types)

   typeid (finding the type of object pointed at)

4. **Some operators can be overloaded using non-static member functions only:** The following operators can be overloaded using non-static member functions alone.

= (Assignment operator)

() (Function operator)

[] (Subscripting operator)

-> (Pointer-to-member access operator)

These operators cannot be overloaded using friend functions or `static functions`.

5. **Number of arguments that an existing operator takes cannot be changed:** Operator-overloading functions should take the same number of parameters that the operator being overloaded ordinarily takes. For example, the division operator takes two arguments. Hence, the class definition shown in Listing 8.8 causes a compile-time error 'operator / takes too few arguments' for the operator-overloading function.

Listing 8.8   An illegal attempt to modify the number of arguments that an operator takes by default

```
class A
{
   public:
      void operator / ();
};
```

6. **Overloaded operators cannot take default arguments:** The class definition shown in Listing 8.9 causes a compile-time error 'operator/cannot take default arguments' for the operator-overloading function.

Listing 8.9   An illegal attempt to assign a default value to an argument of an operator-overloading function

```
class A
{
   public:
      void operator / (int = 0);
};
```

Finally, we must note that it is highly imprudent to modify the values of the operands that are passed to the operator-overloading functions. To appreciate this point better, let us consider the function to overload the `addition` operator for the class `String`.

```
class String
{
      char * cStr;
      long int len;
   public:
      String operator + (String &);
};
```

The library programmer may mistakenly write some statements to modify the value of the implicit or the explicit parameter of the `String :: operator + ()` function (see Listing 8.10).

Listing 8.10 Modifying the left-hand side and the right-hand side operands of the addition operands in the function to overload it

```
String String :: operator + (String & ss)
{
    /*
      rest of the function String :: operator + ()
    */
    this->cStr = NULL;                  // BUG: left-hand parameter
                                        //changed!
    /*
      rest of the function String :: operator + ()
    */
    ss.cStr = NULL;                     //BUG: right-hand parameter
                                        //changed!
    /*
      rest of the function String :: operator + ()
    */
}
```

To guard against this mishap, the operator-overloading function can be declared as shown in Listing 8.11.

Listing 8.11 Making necessary use of the const keyword to prevent bugs

```
class String
{
    char * cStr;
    long int len;
  public:
    String operator + (const String &) const;
};
```

Neither of the statements given in Listing 8.10 that have bugs will compile. Let us now see how operators are actually overloaded.

8.2 Overloading Various Operators

8.2.1 Overloading Increment and Decrement Operators (Prefix and Postfix)

Let us recollect the class Distance. We can overload the increment operator for objects of the class. What would we like such a function to do? If 'd1' and 'd2' are objects of the class Distance, then the following statement

```
d2 = ++d1;
```

is interpreted by the compiler as

```
d2 = d1.operator ++ ();
```

Let us envisage that this operator-overloading function should first increment 'iFeet' portion of 'd1'. It should leave the fInches portion of 'd1' unaltered. Then it should return the resultant object. With these guidelines in mind, the prototype and definition of the operator-overloading function will be as shown in Listing 8.12.

Listing 8.12 Declaring member function to overload the increment operator

```
/*Beginning of Distance.h*/
class Distance
{
  public:
    /*
       rest of the class Distance
    */
    Distance operator ++ ();
};
/*End of Distance.h*/
/*Beginning of Distance.cpp*/
#include"Distance.h"
Distance Distance :: operator ++ ()
{
   return Distance(++iFeet, fInches);
}
/*
   definitions of the rest of the functions of class
   Distance
*/
/*End of Distance.h*/
```

The operator-overloading function should be `public` because it will mostly be called from within functions that are not members of the class `Distance`. It should not be a constant member function since it will certainly modify the value of at least one of the data members (`iFeet`) of the calling object. Although the definition of the operator-overloading function appears cryptic, it is in fact very simple (and economical). First, the increment operator works (since it is in prefix notation). Thus, the `iFeet` data member of the calling object gets incremented. Second, the explicit call to the constructor creates a nameless object of the class `Distance` by passing the incremented value of `iFeet` and the unaltered value of `fInches` as parameters. Third, the operator-overloading function returns the nameless object thus constructed. If the call to the operator-overloading function is on the right-hand side of the assignment operator, the values of the returned object will expectedly be copied to the object on the left. Thus, our purpose is served.

However, we would like a different effect to be produced if we write the statement

```
d2 = d1++;
```

In this case, we would like the initial value of 'd1' to be copied to 'd2' and, thereafter, the value of `iFeet` data member of 'd1' to get incremented. However, if the compiler interprets both the statements

```
d2 = ++d1;
```

and

```
d2 = d1++;
```

in identical ways, then we will have no way of writing the two different functions. Fortunately, this is not so. While the compiler interprets the statement

```
d2 = ++d1;
```

as

```
d2 = d1.operator ++ ();
```

it interprets the statement

```
d2 = d1++;
```

as

```
d2 = d1.operator ++ (0);
```

It implicitly passes zero as a parameter to the call to the operator-overloading function when the postfix notation is used. If it finds a prototype that matches this call exactly, it compiles without warnings or errors. However, if it finds the prototype given in Listing 8.12, it gives a warning but still compiles with the operator-overloading function Distance :: operator ++ (). The fact that the compiler first looks for a function with an integer as a formal argument provides us with a solution. We can now define an additional operator-overloading function to overload the increment operator in postfix notation. See Listing 8.13.

Listing 8.13 Overloading the increment operator in both the prefix and the postfix notation

```
/*Beginning of Distance.h*/
class Distance
{
   public:
      Distance operator ++ ();          //for prefix notation
      Distance operator ++ (int);       //for postfix notation
      /*
         rest of the class Distance
      */
};
/*End of Distance.h*/
/*Beginning of Distance.cpp*/
#include "Distance.h"
Distance "Distance :: operator ++ ()    //for prefix
                                         //notation
{
return Distance(++iFeet, fInches);      //as in listing
                                         //8.12
}
Distance Distance :: operator ++ (int) //for postfix
                                         //notation
{
   return Distance(iFeet++, fInches);
}
/*
definitions of the rest of the functions of class Distance
*/
/*End of Distance.cpp*/
```

The explanation for the definition of the function to overload the increment operator in postfix notation is as follows. The constructor gets called before the increment operator executes because the increment operator has been purposefully placed in postfix notation. Thus, a nameless object with the initial values of the calling object is created. Thereafter, the increment operator increments the value of iFeet data member of the calling object. Finally, the nameless object constructed earlier with the initial values of the calling object is returned. Since the formal parameter of the function is a dummy, therefore, its name need not be mentioned. Obviously, if the call to this operator-overloading function is on the right-hand side of the assignment operator and there is an object of the class Distance on its left, then the object on the left will get the initial values of the object on the right. The value of the object on the right will alone be incremented. These two operator-overloading functions convincingly duplicate the default action of the increment operator on intrinsic types.

Obviously, if we provide an operator-overloading function for the increment operator in prefix notation, we must provide one for the postfix notation also.

Decrement operators are overloaded in the same way as the increment operators. See Listing 8.14.

Listing 8.14 Overloading the decrement operator in both the prefix and postfix notation

```
/*Beginning of Distance.h*/
class Distance
{
    public:
        Distance operator ++ ();
        Distance operator ++ (int);
        Distance operator -- ();
        Distance operator -- (int);
        /*
            rest of the class Distance
        */
};
/*End of Distance.h*/

/*Beginning of Distance.cpp*/
#include"Distance.h"
Distance Distance :: operator -- ()
{
    return Distance(--iFeet, fInches);
}
Distance Distance :: operator -- (int)
{
    return Distance(iFeet--, fInches);
}
/*
    definitions of the rest of the functions of class Distance
*/
/*End of Distance.cpp*/
```

8.2.2 Overloading Unary Minus and Unary Plus Operator

Overloading the unary minus operator is shown in Listing 8.15.

Listing 8.15 Overloading the unary minus operator through a member function

```
/*Beginning of A.h*/
class A
{
    int x;

    public:
    A(int = 0);
    A operator - ();
};
/*End of A.h*/
```

```
/*Beginning of A.cpp*/
#include"A.h"
A::A(int p)
{
    x = p;
}
A A :: operator - ()
{
    return A(-x);
}
/*End of A.cpp*/
```

The operator can be overloaded by a friend function also (as shown in Listing 8.16).

Listing 8.16   Overloading the unary `minus` operator through a friend function

```
/*Beginning of A.h*/
class A
{
    int x;
    A(int = 0);

    public:
    friend A operator - (const A&);
};
/*End of A.h*/

/*Beginning of A.cpp*/
#include"A.h"
A::A(int p)
{
    x = p;
}
A operator - (const A& AObj)
{
    return A(-AObj.x);
}
/*End of A.cpp*/
```

Overloading the unary `plus` operator is left as an exercise for the reader.

8.2.3 Overloading Arithmetic Operators

Arithmetic operators are binary operators. Therefore, the syntax for overloading them through member functions is as illustrated in Listing 8.17.

Listing 8.17   Syntax for overloading the arithmetic operators through member functions

```
class <class_name>
{
    public:
        //prototype
        <return_type> operator<arith_op_symbol>(<param_list>);
};
//definition
<return_type> <class_name>::operator<arith_op_symbol>
                              (<param_list>)
```

```
{
    //function body
}
```

An object that will store the value of the right-hand side operand of the arithmetic operator will appear in the list of formal arguments. The left-hand side operand will be passed implicitly to the function since the operator-overloading function will be called with respect to it. The statement

```
Obj3 = Obj1 <arith_op_symbol> Obj2;
```

will be interpreted as

```
Obj3 = Obj1.operator <arith_op_symbol> (Obj2);
```

If instead a friend function overloads the arithmetic operator, the syntax will be as shown in Listing 8.18.

Listing 8.18   Syntax for overloading the arithmetic operators through friend functions

```
class <class_name>
{
   public:
     //prototype
     friend <return_type>operator<arith_op_symbol>
                            (<param_list>);
};
//definition
<return_type> operator<arith_op_symbol>(<param_list>)
{
    //function body
}
```

Objects that store the values of the left-hand side and the right-hand side operands of the arithmetic operator will appear in the list of formal arguments.
The statement

```
Obj3 = Obj1 <arith_op_symbol> Obj2;
```

will be first interpreted as

```
Obj3 = Obj1.operator <arith_op_symbol> (Obj2);
```

Since, the arithmetic operator has been overloaded through a friend function, the final interpretation will be

```
Obj3 = operator <arith_op_symbol> (Obj1,Obj2);
```

Now let us try some concrete examples. Let us find out how to overload the addition operator for the class Distance with which we are already familiar. We would like the piece of code given in Listing 8.19 to compile successfully and its output to be 10'-2'.

Listing 8.19   Using an overloaded addition operator on objects of the class Distance

```
Distance d1(5,8),d2(4,6),d3;
d3=d1+d2;
cout<<d3.getFeet()<<"'-"<<d3.getInches()<<"'"'\n";
```

For this, we must overload the `addition` operator for the class `Distance` by using either a member function or a friend function.

Let us first look at a member function to overload the `addition` operator for the class `Distance`. In this case, the statement

```
d3 = d1 + d2;
```

will be interpreted as

```
d3 = d1.operator + (d2);
```

This obviously means that the function must return an object of the class `Distance` and must accept an object of the class `Distance` as a parameter. The actual code to implement the `addition` operator so that it produces the desired effect described above is given in Listing 8.20.

Listing 8.20   Overloading the `addition` operator for the class `Distance` through member function

```
/*Beginning of Distance.h*/
class Distance
{
        int iFeet;
        float fInches;
    public:
        Distance(const int=0, const float=0.0);
        void setFeet(const int=0);
        int getFeet() const;
        void setInches(const float=0.0);
        float getInches() const;
        //prototype
        Distance operator + (const Distance) const;
};
/*End of Distance.h*/

/*Beginning of Distance.cpp*/
#include"Distance.h"
//definition
Distance Distance::operator+(const Distance dd1) const
{
    return Distance(iFeet+dd1.iFeet, fInches+dd1.fInches);
}
/*
    definitions of the rest of the functions of class Distance
*/
/*End of Distance.cpp*/
```

The code in Listing 8.20 works fine if the right-hand side operand of the `addition` operator is an object of class `Distance`. However, if it is a float-type value, then the preceding function will not work.

```
d3=d1+4.5;
```

This is because the compiler will interpret this statement as follows:

```
d3=d1.operator+(4.5);
```

The float-type value 4.5 will be passed as a parameter to the operator-overloading function. Since the formal argument of the operator-overloading function is a `Distance` type object, the compiler will throw an error. However, introducing a suitable constructor that converts from float to `Distance` solves the problem. See Listing 8.21.

Listing 8.21 Introducing a constructor in the class `Distance` to initialize its objects to float-type values

```
/*Beginning of Distance.h*/
class Distance
{
  public:
    Distance(const float);
    /*
        rest of the class Distance
    */
};
/*End of Distance.h*/

/*Beginning of Distance.cpp*/
#include"Distance.h"
Distance::Distance(const float p)
{
   iFeet=(int)p;
   fInches=(p-iFeet)*12;
}
/*
definitions of the rest of the functions of class Distance
*/
/*End of Distance.cpp*/
```

However, one condition still remains to be tackled. What if the left-hand side operand is of float type?

```
d2 = 4.75 + d1;
```

The solution is obvious. We replace the member function given in Listing 8.20 with a friend function. See Listing 8.22.

Listing 8.22 Overloading the addition operator for the class `Distance` through friend function

```
/*Beginning of Distance.h*/
class Distance
{
   int iFeet;
   float fInches;

   public:
   Distance(int, float);
   //no 'Distance operator + (const Distance) const;'
   //prototype
   friend Distance operator + (const Distance , const
                                      Distance);
   /*
   rest of the class Distance
   */
};
/*End of Distance.h*/
```

```
/*Beginning of Distance.cpp*/
#include"Distance.h"
//definition
Distance operator + (const Distance dd1, const Distance dd2)
{
    return Distance(dd1.iFeet+dd2.iFeet, dd1.fInches+dd2.fInches);
}
/*
definitions of the rest of the functions of class
Distance
*/
/*End of Distance.cpp*/
```

The friend function given in Listing 8.22 tackles all three conditions as follows:
- Both the left-hand side and the right-hand side operands are objects of class Distance:

    d3 = d1 + d2;

    The operator-overloading function is called straight away without any prior conversions.
- The right-hand side operand is a float-type value while the left-hand side operand is an object of class Distance:

    d2 = d1 + 4.75;

    The right-hand side operand is first converted into an object of the class Distance by the constructor and then the operator-overloading function is called.
- The left-hand side operand is a float-type value while the right-hand side operand is an object of class Distance:

    d2 = 4.75 + d1;

    The left-hand side operand is first converted into an object of the class Distance by the constructor and then the operator-overloading function is called.

We may wonder about the fourth possibility where both operands are float-type values. However, in that case the operator-overloading mechanism will not be invoked at all. Instead, the float-type values will simply get added to each other.
The statement

    d1 = 4.75 + 3.25;

will turn into

    d1 = 8.0;

However, there is no function in the class Distance that converts a float-type value to an object of class Distance. Surprisingly, in this case also, the constructor that takes a float-type value as a parameter and initializes the object with it will be called. This is despite the fact that the object is being created and initialized by two separate statements. Such a constructor is called an implicit constructor.

Note that in Listing 8.22, the member function to overload the addition operator is replaced by a friend function. Having both a friend function and a member function will lead to ambiguity errors.

The compiler will be able to resolve the call

```
d3 = d1 + d2;
```

by both

```
//member function
Distance Distance::operator + (const Distance);
```

and

```
//friend function
Distance operator + (const Distance, const Distance);
```

This will naturally confuse the compiler.

We have now reached the end of our discussion on overloading the addition operator. The method of overloading the remaining arithmetic operators is left as an exercise for the reader.

8.2.4 Overloading Relational Operators

Relational operators are binary operators. Therefore, the syntax for overloading them through member functions is given in Listing 8.23.

Listing 8.23   Syntax for overloading the relational operators through member functions

```
class <class_name>
{
    public:
        //prototype
        <return_type> operator <rel_op_symbol> (<param_list>);
};
//definition
<return_type> <class_name>::operator <rel_op_symbol>
                            (<param_list>)
{
    //function body
}
```

An object that will store the value of the right-hand side operand of the relational operator will appear in the list of formal arguments. The left-hand side operand will be passed implicitly to the function since the operator-overloading function will be called with respect to it. The expression

```
Obj1 <rel_op_symbol> Obj2
```

will be interpreted as

```
Obj1.operator <rel_op_symbol> (Obj2)
```

If instead, a friend function overloads the relational operator, the syntax will be as shown in Listing 8.24.

Listing 8.24   Syntax for overloading the relational operators through friend functions

```
class <class_name>
{
    public:
        //prototype
        friend <return_type> operator <rel_op_symbol>
```

```
                         (<param_list>);
};

//definition
<return_type> operator <rel_op_symbol> (<param_list>)
{
    //function body
}
```

Objects that store the values of both the left-hand side and the right-hand side operands of the relational operator will appear in the list of formal arguments.
The expression

```
Obj1 <rel_op_symbol> Obj2
```

will first be interpreted as

```
Obj1.operator <rel_op_symbol> (Obj2)
```

Since, the relational operator has been overloaded through a friend function, this interpretation will be

```
operator <rel_op_symbol> (Obj1,Obj2)
```

Now, let us find out how to overload the greater than relational operator for the class Distance. We would like the piece of code given in Listing 8.25 to compile successfully and its output to be "Greater than".

Listing 8.25   Using an overloaded greater than operator for the class Distance

```
Distance d1(5,8),d2(4,6);
if(d1>d2)
    cout<<"Greater than";
else
    cout<<"Less than";
```

For this, we must overload the 'greater than' operator for the class Distance by using either a member function or a friend function.

Let us first look at a member function to overload the greater than operator for the class Distance. In this case, the expression

```
d1>d2
```

will be interpreted as

```
d1.operator>(d2)
```

Obviously, the function must return a boolean-type value (true or false) and should accept an object of the class Distance as a parameter. The actual code to implement the greater than operator so that it produces the desired aforementioned effect is given in Listing 8.26.

Listing 8.26   Overloading the greater than operator for the class Distance through a member function

```
/*Beginning of Distance.h*/
enum bool{false, true};
class Distance
```

```
{
    int iFeet;
    float fInches;
public:
    Distance(const int=0, const float=0.0);
    bool operator > (const Distance) const;   //prototype
    /*
        rest of the class Distance
    */
};
/*End of Distance.h*/
/*Beginning of Distance.cpp*/
#include"Distance.h"
//definition
bool Distance::operator > (const Distance dd1) const
{
    if(iFeet*12+ fInches >dd1.iFeet*12 +dd1.fInches)
        return true;
    return false;
}
/*
    definitions of the rest of the functions of class Distance
*/
/*End of Distance.cpp*/
```

The code in Listing 8.26 works fine if the right-hand side operand of the greater-than operator is an object of class Distance. However, if it is a float-type value, then the expression will not compile.

```
d1>4.5
```

This is because the compiler will interpret this expression as ollows:

```
d1.operator>(4.5);
```

The float type value '4.5' will be passed as a parameter to the operator-overloading function. Since the formal argument of the operator-overloading function is a Distance type object, the compiler will throw an error. As in the case of the addition operator, introducing a suitable constructor that converts from float to Distance solves the problem (see Listing 8.21).

Nevertheless, one condition still remains to be tackled. What will happen if the left-hand side operand is of float type?

```
4.75 > d1
```

The solution is the same as in the case of the addition operator. We replace the member function given in Listing 8.26 with a friend function, as shown in Listing 8.27.

Listing 8.27 Overloading the greater-than operator for the class Distance through friend function

```
/*Beginning of Distance.h*/
class Distance
{
    int iFeet;
    float fInches;

    public:
    //no 'bool operator > (const Distance) const;'
```

```
        //prototype
        friend bool operator > (const Distance , const
                                         Distance);
        /*
        rest of the class Distance
        */
};
/*End of Distance.h*/

/*Beginning of Distance.cpp*/
#include"Distance.h"
//definition
bool operator > (const Distance dd1, const Distance dd2)
{
    if(dd1.iFeet*12+ dd1.fInches  >
    dd2.iFeet*12+dd2.fInches)
    return true;
    return false;
}
/*
    definitions of the rest of the functions of class Distance
*/
/*End of Distance.cpp*/
```

The friend function given in Listing 8.27 tackles all three conditions as follows:

- Both the left-hand side and the right-hand side operands are objects of class `Distance`:

    d1 > d2

    The operator-overloading function is called straight away without any prior conversions.

- The right-hand side operand is a float-type value while the left-hand side operand is an object of class `Distance`:

    d1 > 4.75

    The right-hand side operand is first converted into an object of the class `Distance` by the constructor and then the operator-overloading function is called.

- The left-hand side operand is a float-type value while the right-hand side operand is an object of class `Distance`:

    4.75 > d1

    The left-hand side operand is first converted into an object of the class `Distance` by the constructor and then the operator-overloading function is called.

We may again wonder about the fourth possibility where both operands are float-type values. Again, in such a case the operator-overloading mechanism will not be invoked at all. Instead, the float-type values will simply get compared to each other.

The expression

    4.75 > 3.25

will return true.

As in the case of the `addition` operator, the member function to overload the `greater than` operator is replaced by a friend function. Having both a friend function and a member function will lead to ambiguity errors.

The compiler will be able to resolve the expression

```
d1 > d2
```

by both

```
//member function
bool Distance::operator > (const Distance);
```

and

```
//friend function
bool operator > (const Distance, const Distance);
```

This will naturally confuse the compiler.

We have now reached the end of our discussion on overloading the greater than operator. The method of overloading the remaining relational operators is left as an exercise for the reader.

8.2.5 Overloading Assignment Operator

The assignment operator is a binary operator. If overloaded, it must be overloaded by a non-static member function only. Thus, the syntax for overloading the assignment operator is as shown in Listing 8.28.

Listing 8.28   Syntax for overloading the assignment operator

```
class <class_name>
{
   public:
      //prototype
      class_name & operator = (const class_name &);
};
class_name & class_name :: operator = (const class_name & rhs)   //definition
{
   //statements
}
```

We must keep in mind that, by default, the compiler generates the function to overload the assignment operator if the class designer does not provide one. This default function carries out a simple member-wise copy. See Listing 8.29.

Listing 8.29   Default assignment operator generated by the compiler

```
class A
{
   public:
      A& operator = (const A&);
};
A& A :: operator = (const A& rhs)
{
   *this = rhs;
   return *this;
}
```

In most cases, this default `assignment` operator is sufficient. However, there are cases where this default behaviour causes problems. We may recollect the section on copy constructors from Chapter 4. We discussed the ill effects of the default copy constructor for classes that acquire resources dynamically. Exactly the same problems arise due to the effect of the default assignment operator. The problems caused by the code

```
String s1, s2;
s1.setString("abcd");
s2 = s1;
```

if the `assignment` operator is not defined are the same as the problems that arise out of the code

```
String s1("abcd");
String s2 = s1;
```

if the copy constructor is not defined. As a result of the preceding `assignment` operation, the pointers of both 's1' and 's2' will end up pointing at the same memory block (see Figure 8.1). From the study of the copy constructor, we are already conversant with the havoc this situation causes. The conclusion is that the `assignment` operator must be defined for a class for whom the copy constructor has been defined. A suitable definition of the `assignment` operator for the class `String` is given in Listing 8.30.

Listing 8.30   A practical example of overloading the `assignment` operator

```
/*Beginning of String.h*/
class String
{
    char * cStr;
    unsigned int len;

    public:
    String(const String&); //the copy constructor
    String& operator = (const String&);
    /*
    rest of the class String
    */
};
/*End of String.h*/

/*Beginning of String.cpp*/
#include"String.h"
#include<string.h>
String& String :: operator = (const String& ss)
{
    if(this != &ss)
    {
        if(cStr != NULL)
        {
            delete[] cStr;
            cStr = NULL;
            len = 0;
        }
        if(ss.cStr != NULL)
        {
```

```
            len = ss.len;
            cStr = new char[len + 1];
            strcpy(cStr,ss.cStr);
        }
    }
    return *this;
}
/*
definitions of the rest of the functions of class String
*/
/*End of String.cpp*/
```

Before understanding why the outermost 'if' (if (this != &ss)) has been inserted at the top of the function and why the function returns the calling object by reference, we must appreciate that the definition of the assignment operator in Listing 8.30 convincingly handles all four possible cases as follows:

- **LHS.cStr = NULL and RHS.cStr = NULL**

  If LHS.cStr = NULL then the first inner 'if' (if (cStr != NULL)) fails and the corresponding 'if' block does not execute. If RHS.cStr = NULL then the second inner 'if' (if (ss.cStr != 0)) fails and the corresponding 'if' block does not execute. The entire function as a whole does not do anything except that it returns the calling object by reference. As expected and desired, the value of the left-hand side operand remains unchanged (as cStr = NULL and len = 0) because the corresponding values in the right-hand side object are NULL and 0, respectively.

- **LHS.cStr = NULL and RHS.cStr != NULL**

  If LHS.cStr = NULL then the first inner 'if' (if (cStr != NULL)) fails and the corresponding 'if' block does not execute. If RHS.cStr != NULL then the second inner 'if' (if (ss.cStr != 0)) succeeds and the corresponding 'if' block executes. It does the following:

  - correctly sets the value of the 'len' member of the calling object to be equal to the length of the memory block that will hold a copy of the string at which 'cStr' member of the right-hand side object is pointing,
  - allocates just enough memory to hold a copy of the string at which the **cStr** member of the right-hand side object is pointing and makes the 'cStr' member of the left-hand side object point at it, and
  - copies the string at which the 'cStr' member of the right-hand side object is pointing into the memory block at which the 'cStr' member of the left-hand side object is pointing.

- **LHS.cStr != NULL and RHS.cStr = NULL**

  If LHS.cStr != NULL then the first inner 'if' (if (cStr != NULL)) succeeds and the corresponding 'if' block executes. It deallocates the memory block at which the 'cStr' member of the left-hand side object points, sets its value to NULL and sets the value of 'len' member of the left-hand side object to 0. If RHS.cStr = NULL then the second inner 'if' (if (ss.cStr != 0)) fails and the corresponding 'if' block does not execute. As expected and desired, if it was not already so, the value of the left-hand side operand gets nullified (cStr = NULL and len = 0) because the right-hand side operand is NULL.

- **LHS.cStr != NULL and RHS.cStr != NULL**

  If LHS.cStr != NULL then the first inner 'if' (if (cStr != NULL)) succeeds and the corresponding 'if' block executes. It deallocates the memory block at which the 'cStr' member of the left-hand side object points, sets its value to NULL, and sets the value of 'len' member of the left-hand side object to 0. If `RHS.cStr != NULL` then the second inner 'if' (if (`ss.cStr != 0`)) succeeds and the corresponding 'if' block executes. It does the following:

- correctly sets the value of the 'len' member of the calling object to be equal to the length of the memory block that will hold a copy of the string at which 'cStr' member of the right-hand side object is pointing,
- allocates just enough memory to hold a copy of the string at which the 'cStr' member of the right-hand side object is pointing and makes the 'cStr' member of the left-hand side object point at it, and
- copies the string at which the 'cStr' member of the right-hand side object is pointing into the memory block at which the 'cStr' member of the left-hand side object is pointing.

Now, let us understand why the preceding function to overload the `assignment` operator accepts the argument as a const reference and also returns the calling object by reference. The function accepts the argument as a const reference to test for and guard against self-assignment. First, let us understand how this guard works. We shall then find out why this check is needed at all.

We must take note of the following two facts:

- Since the formal argument 'ss' in the above function is a reference variable, its address is the same as the address of the right-hand side object.
- The `this` pointer holds the address of the left-hand side object.

Therefore, the 'if' condition '`this == &ss`' (address of the left-hand side object == address of the right-hand side object) tests to find out whether an object is being equated with itself or not. An object may get equated with itself in a variety of ways:

```
String s1;
s1 = s1;
```

or

```
String s1;
String &s2 = s1;
s2 = s1;
```

Each of these assignments will cause an execution of the function to overload the `assignment` operator. Moreover, in each of the cases, the 'if' condition in that function will evaluate to true. For such circumstances, the main body of the operator-overloading function has been deliberately designed to remain unexecuted. Why is this necessary? The reason is simple—in case of a self-assignment, no action is necessary! This function to overload the assignment will work even if the outer 'if' condition is removed and the reference variable that appears as the formal argument is replaced by an ordinary variable. See Listing 8.31.

Listing 8.31 Bypassing the check for self-assignment in the function to overload the `assignment` operator

```
/*Beginning of String.h*/
class String
{
    char * cStr;
```

```cpp
        unsigned int len;
        public:
        String(const String&); //the copy constructor
        String operator = (const String);
        /*
        rest of the class String
        */
};
/*End of String.h*/

/*Beginning of String.cpp*/
#include"String.h"
#include<string.h>
String String :: operator = (const String ss)
{
    if(cStr != NULL)
    {
        delete[] cStr;
        cStr = NULL;
        len = 0;
    }
    if(ss.cStr != 0)
    {
        len = ss.len;
        cStr = new char[len + 1];
        strcpy(cStr,ss.cStr);
    }
    return *this;
}
/*
definitions of the rest of the functions of class String
*/
/*End of String.cpp*/
```

However, this function proves to be highly inefficient in case of a self-assignment. Suppose the statement is:

```cpp
s1 = s1;
```

This statement turns into

```cpp
s1.operator=(s1);
```

's1' is passed by value to the operator-overloading function. Therefore, the copy constructor is called with respect to the formal arguments 'ss' and 's1' is passed as a parameter to it. A properly defined copy constructor ensures that 'ss' contains a separate copy of the same string which 's1' contains. Nevertheless, the copy constructor is called. Now, when the actual function body executes, the string contained by 's1' is first deallocated by the first 'if' block and then reallocated with the same value for the string by the second 'if' block. Although the net effect is that nothing happens to the actual value of the string contained by the object, the function is nevertheless inefficient. The unnecessary deallocation and reallocation can and should be avoided. This has been done by the check for self-assignment given in Listing 8.30.

Next, let us understand why the function has been designed to return by reference. The reasons are similar to those that prompted us to pass by reference (to check for self-assignment).

The function has been designed to return by reference to prevent chaining operation from becoming inefficient, that is, to ensure an efficient execution of statements such as the following ones.

```
String s1, s2, s3;
s3 = s2 = s1;
```

This statement is interpreted as

```
s3.operator = (s2.operator = (s1));
```

Suppose the statement is written as

```
s2 = s2 = s1;
```

Notice the self-assignment embedded in the preceding statement. First, 's2' is equated with 's1'. Then the value of 's2' is returned. Suppose it is returned by value and not by reference. In this case, a copy of 's2' is created in the stack. Although the copy has a separate copy of the same string value as 's2' has, its address is nevertheless different from that of 's2'. Therefore, when the `assignment` operator executes for the second time, the reference variable 'ss' refers to this copy and not to 's2' itself. Consequently, the test for self-assignment fails and again the unnecessary deallocation and reallocation operations occur.

There is another circumstance when the library programmer would like to overload the `assignment` operator. The library programmer may not want two objects to share even different copies of the same data. In the previous example, where the `assignment` operator has been overloaded for the class `String`, objects are able to share physically separate and different copies of the same string value. To satisfy the new requirement described earlier, the `assignment` operator should be defined as a private member function (Listing 8.32).

Listing 8.32   Overloading the `assignment` operator through a private member function

```
class A
{
    A& operator = (const A&);
    public:
        /*
            rest of the class A
        */
};
```

Now, if the client programs call the `assignment` operator indirectly (**object1 = object2**) or directly (**object1.operator=(object2)**), the compiler raises an error and the assignment of one object to another is prevented. What will happen if one of the member functions or friend functions of class A calls the `assignment` operator? This compiler will certainly not complain and our safeguard will fail. For this, the library programmer can simply avoid defining the `assignment` operator. Now, if one of the member functions or friend functions of class A calls the `assignment` operator, the compiler does not complain, but the linker certainly does!

Let us understand another interesting thing about the `assignment` operator. For this, we should remember that a derived class object can be assigned to a base class object. However, the reverse is not true. See Listing 8.33. The reason is obvious. Suppose A is the base class and B is its derived class.

Listing 8.33 Assigning a derived class object to a base class object and vice versa

```
A A1;
B B1;
A1=B1;   //OK
B1=A1;   //ERROR!
```

The set of data members of the derived class is, or is reckoned to be, a proper superset of the set of data members of its base class. Thus, in the example in Listing 8.33, 'B1' will have its own copies of not only those data members that 'A1' has, but also some extra data members of its own. If the second assignment in Listing 8.33 works, then the data members of 'B1' that are common in name with those of 'A1' will get initialized. However, the data members that are exclusively in 'B1' will remain unchanged and may no longer match with rest of the data members of 'B1'. Keeping this in mind, the compiler prevents the second assignment.

However, the class designer, if he/she so desires, may provide an `assignment` operator function to the derived class so that a base class object can be assigned to a derived class object. See Listing 8.34.

Listing 8.34 Enabling a base class object to be assigned to a derived class object

```
/*Beginning of B.h*/
#include"A.h"
class B : public A
{
   public:
      B& operator=(const A&);       //to enable B1=A1;
      /*
         rest of the class B
      */
};
/*End of B.h*/
```

Statements to modify the values of the data members that are exclusive to the derived class can be provided in Listing 8.34.

Suppose there is no explicitly defined `assignment` operator-overloading function for the derived class that has a reference to the *derived* class object as a formal argument. Further, suppose there *is* an explicitly defined `assignment` operator-overloading function for the derived class that has a reference to the *base* class object as a formal argument. Even then the complier would generate an `assignment` operator that has a reference to the *derived* class object as a formal argument. For suppressing the generation of the implicit default assignment, the formal argument of the explicit operator must be of the *same* type as the class itself.

8.2.6 Overloading Insertion and Extraction Operators

The syntax for overloading the `insertion` operator is given in Listing 8.35.

Listing 8.35 Syntax for overloading the `insertion` operator

```
class A
{
```

```
public:
    //prototype
    friend ostream & operator << (ostream &, const A &);
    /*
        rest of the class A
    */
};

//definition
ostream & operator << (ostream & dout, const A & AA)
{
    /*
        rest of the function
    */
    return dout;
}
```

The statement

```
cout << A1;                        //A1 is an object of class A
```

is interpreted as

```
operator << (cout, A1);
```

The syntax for overloading the extraction operator is given in Listing 8.36.

Listing 8.36   Syntax for overloading the extraction operator

```
class A
{
    public:
        /*
            rest of the class A
        */
        //prototype
        friend istream & operator >> (istream &, A &);
};
//definition
istream & operator >> (istream & din, A & AA)
{
    /*
        rest of the function
    */
    return din;
}
```

The statement

```
cin >> A1;                         //A1 is an object of class A
```

is interpreted as

```
operator >> (cin, A1);
```

The insertion and the extraction operators are overloaded by using friend functions for reasons explained in the beginning of this chapter.

We may observe that the objects of the classes `istream` and `ostream` are passed and returned by reference in the preceding functions. Let us understand why. The copy constructor and the `assignment` operator have been declared as protected members in both the classes `istream` and `ostream`. This prevents two objects from undesirably sharing even different copies of the same stream. Thus the statements

```
ostream dout = cout;              //ERROR!
ostream dout;
dout = cout;                      //ERROR!
istream din = cin;               //ERROR!
istream din;
din = cin;                        //ERROR!
```

will throw compile-time errors. This explains why the formal arguments are reference variables.

The compulsion to return by reference is also explained similarly. If the object is returned by value, then a separate object is created in the stack. A call to the copy constructor is dispatched with respect to it and the object returned by the operator-overloading function is passed as a parameter. However, the copy constructor is a protected member! Therefore, the object must be returned by reference and not by value. But why should the object be returned at all. Can the function not return anything? Can the function not be as shown in Listing 8.37?

Listing 8.37 Overloading the `insertion` operator without returning

```
class A
{
    public:
        //prototype
        friend void operator << (ostream &, const A &);
        /*
            rest of the class A
        */
};

//definition
void operator << (ostream & dout, const A & AA)
{
    /*
        definition of the function
    */
}
```

The answer is yes. Nevertheless, how will we chain the operator?

```
cout << A1 << A2;
```

The preceding statement is interpreted as

```
operator << (operator << (cout, A1), A2);
```

If the inner nested call (whose return value becomes the first argument of the outer one) returns void instead of `ostream &`, how will the outer call execute?

The `insertion` and `extraction` operators are overloaded to achieve data abstraction—a complete independence between the interface and the implementation. The signatures and return types of member functions do not change even if the data members within the class do. Consequently, changes in the internal representation of data members of a class do not force its client programs to change. Client programs need not be aware either of the internal representation of data inside the class whose objects they are operating or of any changes therein.

Let us understand this with the help of an example. Let us consider the class `String` and the `String::getString()` function. The function returns a `char *`. This is because the string is stored in a null terminated memory block of characters. Suppose this manner of representing the data changes for some reason. Maybe the string is no longer stored as a null terminated string. Maybe the string is stored in wide characters. These changes necessitate modifications in the client programs. For example, the following statement will no longer work:

```
cout<<s1.getString()<<endl;
```

The problem with having a function return the value to be inserted is that the function must return a value and that value must have a data type—the data type of the data member that is containing the object's value. That is where the problem lies. If the data type changes, the existing clients are likely to fail.

However, if the `insertion` operator has been overloaded then the preceding statement can be rewritten as:

```
cout<<s1<<endl;
```

The responsibility of displaying the data is shifted to the object itself. The manner in which the data is stored in the object and any change therein will no longer affect the client.

Nevertheless, it seems that even if the client programs need not recompile, their object files will have to be re-linked to the new libraries, which are created out of the changed class definition, to create updated executables. However, in the actual programming world, libraries are provided as dynamic link libraries (DLLs). They do not form a part of the executables physically. They exist separately. Whenever the corresponding executable executes, they are dynamically loaded into the memory during run time and if the called functions are contained within them, they are executed. Operator overloading, together with DLLs, enables a library programmer in achieving complete data abstraction.

Can the same effect be achieved by a friend function that has the same signature as the `insertion` operator? See Listing 8.38.

Listing 8.38   A friend function as an alternative to operator overloading

```
class String
{
    public:
        friend ostream& print(ostream&, const String&);
        /*
            rest of the class String
        */
};
```

Let us output one object of the class `String` by using Listing 8.38

```
print(cout,s1);
```

In case of two objects:

```
print(print(cout,s1),s2);
```

In case of three objects:

```
print(print(print(cout,s1),s2),s3);
```

However, the statement

```
cout<<s1<<s2<<s3;
```

looks far more intuitive.

Moreover, what will happen in case of templates? Let us consider a common global template function that has calls to the `insertion` operator embedded within it. If we want to utilize such a function by passing an object of the class `String` as a parameter, the `insertion` operator would automatically get applied on the passed object. If the `insertion` operator has not been overloaded for the class `String`, compile-time error will arise. The narration and examples on function templates, from the chapter on templates (Chapter 10), clarify this point.

The `extraction` operators are overloaded for similar reasons as the `insertion` operators. The problem with `String::setString()` function is that the client needs to load the string that it wants to store in an object of the class `String` in a buffer and then pass it to a call to this function. The formal argument of this function is of the same type as the data member that is storing the string. Obviously, the buffer should also be of the same type. The problem with this function is that the buffer must be passed to the function and that array must have the same type as the data member in which the data is stored. If that type changes, the type of the buffer also needs to change. This forces the clients to change. But, if the `extraction` operator is overloaded for the class `String`, the following statement can be used instead of calls to the `String::setString()` function:

```
cin>>s1;
```

The responsibility of reading the data is shifted to the object itself. Again, the manner in which the data is stored in the object and any change therein will no longer affect the client.

The `insertion` and `extraction` operators are overloaded to achieve independence of the implementation (definitions of member functions) from the interface (prototypes of member functions).

8.2.7 Overloading new and delete Operators

The `new` and the `delete` operators can be overloaded for specific classes. The behaviour of these operators can be altered for operands of specific class types.

If these operators are overloaded for a specific class, then the functions that overload them are called when the class type is passed as a parameter to these operators. Otherwise, the global `new` and `delete` operators are called. For example, if the `new` operator has been overloaded for a class X but not for a class Y, then the statement

```
X * XPtr = new X;
```

will call the function that overloads the `new` operator of class X. But the statement

```
Y * Yptr = new Y;
```

will call the global `new` operator. It is interesting to note that the user programs may not change if the functions to overload the `new` and the `delete` operators are inserted into a class or removed from it.

The syntax for overloading the `new` operator (for allocating memory for a single object) is as shown in Listing 8.39.

Listing 8.39 Syntax for functions that overload the new operator and allocate memory for a single object

```
class <class_name>
{
  public:
    static void * operator new(size_t);      //function
                                             //prototype
    /*
       rest of the class
    */
};
void * <class_name> :: operator new ( size_t size)
                                 //function definition
{
  /*
     definition of the function
  */
}
```

The syntax for overloading the new operator (for allocating memory for an array of objects) is given in Listing 8.40.

Listing 8.40 Syntax for functions that overload the new operator and allocate memory for an array of objects

```
class <class_name>
{
  public:
    static void * operator new [](size_t);   //function
                                             //prototype
    /*
       rest of the class
    */
};
void * <class_name>::operator new [] ( size_t size)
                                 //function definition
{
  /*
     definition of the function
  */
}
```

The syntax for overloading the delete operator (for deallocating memory for a single object) is given in Listing 8.41.

Listing 8.41 Syntax for functions that overload the delete operator and deallocate memory for a single object

```
class <class_name>
{
  public:
    static void operator delete(void *,size_t);
                                 //function prototype
    /*
```

```
                    rest of the class
         */
      };
      void <class_name>::operator delete (void * p, size_t size)
                                          //function definition
      {
        /*
           definition of the function
        */
      }
```

The syntax for overloading the `delete` operator (for deallocating memory for an array of objects) is given in Listing 8.42.

Listing 8.42   Syntax for functions that overload the `delete` operator and deallocate memory for an array of objects

```
      class <class_name>
      {
        public:
           static void operator delete [] (void *, size_t );
                                           //function prototype
           /*
              rest of the class
           */
      };
      void <class_name>::operator delete [](void *, size_t size)
                                           //function definition
      {
        /*
           definition of the function
        */
      }
```

The operator new function and the operator delete function must be static. However, their prototypes may or may not be prefixed with the `static` keyword. Either way, the compiler treats these functions as static (reasons for this are explained later in this chapter).

The return type of the operator new function must be of type `void *`. The value returned by this function is the address of the memory block it captures by calling the global new operator. The operator new function should take at least one formal argument of type `size_t`. As we will discover later, the operator new function can take more than one formal argument also. The `size_t` argument holds the amount of memory to be allocated in bytes. The code in Listing 8.43 illustrates this. It also illustrates how the global new operator is used from within the member new operator function to capture memory in the heap area and how a pointer to that memory is returned.

Listing 8.43   Overloading the new operator

```
/*Beginning of A.h*/
#include<new.h>
class A
{
   int x;
   public:
```

```
    void * operator new(size_t);
    /*
    rest of the class A
    */
};
/*End of A.h*/

/*Beginning of A.cpp*/
#include<iostream.h>
#include"A.h"
void * A :: operator new(size_t size)
{
    cout << sizeof(A) << endl;
    cout << size << endl;
    void * p = :: operator new(size);
    return p;
}
/*
definitions of the rest of the functions of class A
*/
/*End of A.cpp*/

/*Beginning of Test.cpp*/
#include<iostream.h>
#include"A.h"
void main()
{
    A * APtr = new A;
}
/*End of Test.cpp*/
```

Output

4

4

It is obvious that the class designer will overload the new operator only if he/she is not satisfied with the default action of the new operator for his/her class and would therefore like to fine-tune it. For this, he/she will insert the necessary code in the function to overload the new operator. Apart from this code, statements to allocate the required amount of memory (by calling the global new operator) and then to return the address of the captured memory block are also inserted in the function to overload the new operator. Otherwise, the requested memory will never get allocated.

The return type of the operator delete function must be void as it does not return anything. Its first formal argument should be of type void *. The address of the memory block being deleted is passed to it. The second formal argument of the operator delete function is of type size_t. The size of the memory block to be deleted is passed as a parameter to it. Listing 8.44 illustrates all this. It also illustrates how the global delete operator should be used to deallocate the memory being targeted.

Listing 8.44 Overloading the delete operator

```
/*Beginning of A.h*/
#include<new.h>
class A
{
```

```
        int x;

        public:
        void operator delete(void * const, const size_t);
        /*
        rest of the class A
        */
};
/*End of A.h*/

/*Beginning of A.cpp*/
#include<iostream.h>
#include"A.h"
void A :: operator delete(void * const p, const size_t size)
{
    cout << p << endl;
    cout << sizeof(A) << endl;
    cout << size << endl;
    ::operator delete(p);
}
/*
definitions of the rest of the functions of class A
*/
/*End of A.cpp*/

/*Beginning of Test.cpp*/
#include<iostream.h>
#include"A.h"
void main()
{
    A * APtr = new A;
    cout << APtr << endl;
    delete APtr;
}
/*End of Test.cpp*/
```

Output
0xCCCCCC
0xCCCCCC
4
4

The reason for overloading the `delete` operator is similar to the reason for overloading the new operator. As in the case of the new operator, the class designer will overload the `delete` operator only if he/she is not satisfied with the default action of the `delete` operator for his/her class and would therefore like to fine-tune it. For this, he/she will insert the necessary code in the function to overload the `delete` operator. Apart from this code, a statement to deallocate the required amount of memory (by calling the global delete operator) is also inserted in the function to overload the `delete` operator. Otherwise, the requested memory will never get deallocated.

The operator new function and the operator delete functions are static by default. This means that the compiler treats them as `static functions` whether the class designer uses the `static` keyword in their declarations or not. This is because the compiler places a call to the constructor immediately after the call to the new operator and a call to the destructor immediately before the call to the `delete` operator. The statement

```
A * APtr = new A;
```

is translated by the compiler as

```
A * APtr = A::operator new(sizeof(A)); //nameless object
                                       //created
A::A(APtr); //constructor called for nameless object
```

While the statement

```
delete APtr;
```

is translated by the compiler as

```
A::~A(APtr);//destructor called for nameless object
A::operator delete(APtr, sizeof(A));   //nameless object
                                       //destroyed
```

In order to understand the implications of these translations, let us consider a class that has a pointer as one of its data members. The class designer would certainly like to initialize this pointer to some valid value (say, NULL) in the constructor of the class.

```
class String
{
       char * cStr;
    public:
       String()
       {
          cStr = NULL;
          /*
             rest of the function String::String()
          */
       }
       /*
          rest of the class String
       */
};
```

However, if access is allowed to the private data members in the new operator function, the class designer may accidentally allocate some memory dynamically in the heap and make 'cStr' point at it.

```
void * String::operator new(const size_t size)
{
    . . . .
    cStr = new char …
    . . . .
}
```

Now, when the constructor is called, a memory leak will occur because the value of 'cStr' will be straight away nullified without first deallocating the memory block at which it is pointing. We may suggest the following improvisation (Listing 8.45) in the code for the class constructor:

Listing 8.45 The new and delete operators are static

```
A::A()
{
    if(cStr != NULL)
```

```
        delete [] cStr;
    cStr = NULL;
}
```

However, there is a serious drawback in this code. It presupposes that if 'cStr' is not NULL, then it is definitely pointing at a dynamically allocated memory block that has been captured earlier by using the new operator. This is true only if the objects are created by using the new operator. However, if objects are created in the normal fashion as follows:

```
A A1;
```

then the mere fact that the code in the constructor of the class String finds that the value of 'cStr' is not NULL does not mean that 'cStr' is definitely pointing at a valid block of memory. In fact, in this case, 'cStr' is simply a rogue pointer. Using the delete operator on such a rogue pointer will naturally lead to a run-time error. For such reasons, the C++ compiler prevents access to the non-static data members of the class by treating the operator new and operator delete functions as static. It is repeated that the compiler treats these functions as static whether we mention the static keyword in its declaration or not. We cannot force access to the non-static data members in the new and delete operator functions by avoiding the static keyword in their declarations.

It will not be out of context to mention once again that the constructor does not 'construct' the object, that is, it does not actually allocate memory for the object. It is merely a function that is called immediately after the memory for the object has actually been allocated. Its job is to ensure guaranteed initialization of all data members to proper values and to acquire any resources if necessary. Similarly, the destructor does not actually destroy the object in the sense that it does not actually deallocate the memory block occupied by the object. It is merely a function that is called immediately before the memory for the object is deallocated. Its job is to ensure a proper clean-up operation and to release all resources that were acquired during the lifetime of the object. The manner in which the compiler translates calls to the new and delete operators makes all this amply clear. Moreover, we may note how the global new and delete operators are called from the class member functions that overload them.

Values are passed to the constructor in the usual way even after the new operator is overloaded (Listing 8.46).

Listing 8.46 Passing parameters to an overloaded new operator

```
A * APtr = new A(10,20);
```

is translated by the compiler as

```
A * APtr = A::operator new;
A::A(APtr,10,20);
```

We have already discussed, in brief, an overall reason for overloading the new and delete operators. The class designer overloads these operators if he/she considers their default action inappropriate or inefficient for his/her class. Now, we will learn about the specific cases where overloading these operators becomes beneficial.

First, let us see how the new operator works. In order to deallocate the correct amount of memory, the delete operator must know how much memory the new operator has allocated. The compilers solve this problem by prefixing the memory block allocated by the new operator with the amount of memory allocated. Therefore, as a result of the statement

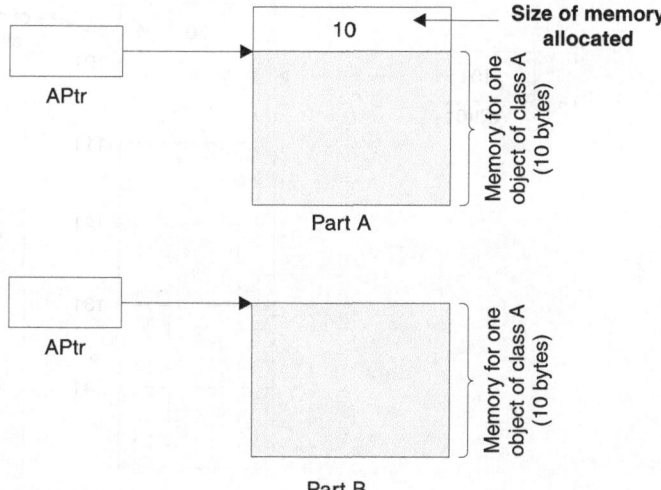

Figure 8.2   Wastage of memory due to the default action of the new operator

```
A * APtr = new A;
```

we get Part A and not Part B of Figure 8.2 (suppose objects of class A occupy 10 bytes)

This means that every time the new operator is called for the class A, a separate block to store the amount of memory allocated will also be allocated. This consumption of memory can be a real bottleneck in applications where memory is critical.

Before we come to a solution to this problem, we should know that even if the 'new' operator allocates an array of objects, only one memory slice will be prefixed to the allocated memory block in order to hold its size. Therefore, the amount of extra memory allocated remains the same whether one object is created in the heap or an array of objects is created in the heap. The class designer can take advantage of this fact.

The class designer can ensure that when the new operator is called for the first time, a memory to hold a large number of objects gets allocated and the address of the memory block gets returned. The address returned will obviously be the address of the first object in the pool. Thereafter, every call to the new operator will return the address of the next available block from the pool.

This solution is explained in Figures 8.3 and 8.4. Suppose A is a class whose objects occupy 10 bytes. The class designer reckons that the pool will hold five objects at a time. Therefore, the pool size will be equal to 50 bytes. Let us consider the piece of code given in Listing 8.47.

Listing 8.47   Calling an overloaded new operator

```
. . . . .
. . . . .
A * APtr01 = new A;                    //line 1
A * APtr02 = new A;                    //line 2
A * APtr03 = new A;                    //line 3
A * APtr04 = new A;                    //line 4
A * APtr05 = new A;                    //line 5
A * APtr06 = new A;                    //line 6
. . . . .
. . . . .
```

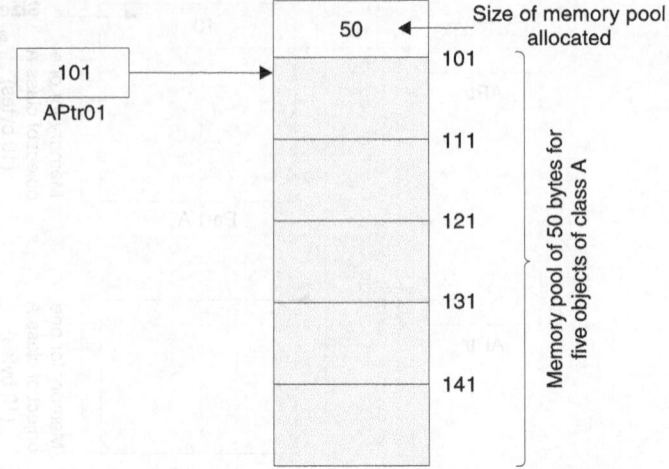

Figure 8.3   Saving memory by overloading the new operator and modifying its behaviour

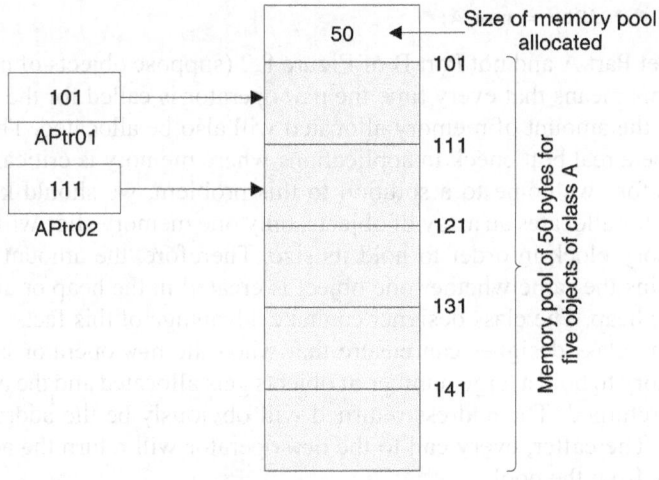

Figure 8.4   Accessing the memory pool allocated by the overloaded new operator

A memory pool of 50 bytes (10 bytes for each of the five objects) will be created when line 1 executes (because the new operator is being called for the first time). When lines 2 to 5 execute, addresses of adjacent blocks are returned sequentially from this pool. After the first line executes, the following scenario emerges.

The address of the allocated memory block is '101' (say). Therefore, the value of 'APtr01' becomes '101'. The address block from '101' to '150' has been allocated as a result of the first line. As we can see, the size of the memory block (50) has been prefixed to the memory block itself. The second line will not cause another memory block to be allocated. Instead, the address of the next segment from the memory pool having address '111' will be returned. Therefore, the value of 'APtr02' will become '111'. The following scenario will emerge.

This process will continue until the sixth line is reached. After the fifth line finishes execution, the memory pool will get exhausted. At this point of time, another memory pool of the same size (50 bytes—10 bytes for five objects each) will get allocated and the process will repeat itself. All this is the effect of the code the class designer has written in the function that overloads the new operator.

The actual code is given in Listing 8.48.

Listing 8.48   Overloading the new operator to improve efficiency

```
/*Beginning of NewDeleteForMemorySave.h*/
#include<new.h>
class ClassNewDelete
{
   union
   {
      int x;
      ClassNewDelete * next;
   }v;
   static int NO_OF_OBJECTS;
   static ClassNewDelete * head;

   public:
   void setx(const int = 0);
   int getx() const;
   static void * operator new(const size_t);
};
/*End of NewDeleteForMemorySave.h*/

/*Beginning of NewDeleteForMemorySave.cpp*/
#include"NewDeleteForMemorySave.h"
int ClassNewDelete::NO_OF_OBJECTS = 5;
ClassNewDelete * ClassNewDelete::head;
int ClassNewDelete::getx() const
{
   return v.x;
}
void ClassNewDelete::setx(const int p)
{
   v.x=p;
}
void * ClassNewDelete::operator new(const size_t size)
{
   ClassNewDelete * temp,*p;
   temp = head;
   if(!temp)
   {
      temp = (ClassNewDelete *)::operator new(sizeof(class ClassNewDelete)*NO_
                                                                 OF_OBJECTS);
      for(p=temp;p!=&temp[NO_OF_OBJECTS-1];p++)
         p->v.next=p+1;
      p->v.next=0;
   }
   head=temp->v.next;
   return temp;
}
/*End of NewDeleteForMemorySave.cpp*/

/*Beginning of NewDeleteForMemorySaveMain.cpp*/
#include<iostream.h>
#include"NewDeleteForMemorySave.h"
void main()
```

```
{
    ClassNewDelete * ClassNewDeletePtr01 = new ClassNewDelete;
    ClassNewDeletePtr01->setx(10);
    cout<<ClassNewDeletePtr01->getx()<<endl;
    ClassNewDelete * ClassNewDeletePtr02 = new ClassNewDelete;
    ClassNewDeletePtr02->setx(20);
    cout<<ClassNewDeletePtr02->getx()<<endl;
    ClassNewDelete * ClassNewDeletePtr03 = new ClassNewDelete;
    ClassNewDeletePtr03->setx(30);
    cout<<ClassNewDeletePtr03->getx()<<endl;
    ClassNewDelete * ClassNewDeletePtr04 = new ClassNewDelete;
    ClassNewDeletePtr04->setx(40);
    cout<<ClassNewDeletePtr04->getx()<<endl;
    ClassNewDelete * ClassNewDeletePtr05 = new ClassNewDelete;
    ClassNewDeletePtr05->setx(50);
    cout<<ClassNewDeletePtr05->getx()<<endl;
    ClassNewDelete * ClassNewDeletePtr06 = new ClassNewDelete;
    ClassNewDeletePtr06->setx(60);
    cout<<ClassNewDeletePtr06->getx()<<endl;
}
/*End of NewDeleteForMemorySaveMain.cpp*/
```

Output
```
10
20
30
40
50
60
```

When this program runs, first memory for the static data members of class ClassNew gets allocated. The static data member NO_OF_OBJECTS stores how many blocks (objects) will coexist in each pool. This data member should be static because it contains information for the set of objects and is therefore not particular to any specific object. The value of this data member should be chosen with care. A value that is too large will waste memory and thereby prove counterproductive. Large portions of the pool may remain unutilized for long periods or for the entire lifetime of the program. A very small value will necessitate a frequent allocation of more pools, thereby slowing down the program. If it is felt that large number of objects will exist simultaneously at any given point of time, the value of this variable should be kept large, otherwise this value should be small. In our case, we have initialized NO_OF_OBJECTS to '5'.

Next, memory for another static data member head is allocated. This pointer points at the next available block from the pool. This data member should also be static because it will function for the entire set of objects and will, therefore, not be a part of any particular object. Every call to the new operator returns the current value of this pointer and increments its value so that it then points at the next available block in the pool. This pointer has been initialized to NULL for reasons that will soon become apparent.

Now the main function begins execution. Memory for ClassNewPtr01 (four bytes since it is a pointer) is allocated. Currently, it has junk value. Next, the new operator function for class ClassNew is called. Two pointers, temp (for holding the current value of head so that head can move to the next block) and 'p' (for traversing through the pool) are created. The pointer temp is initialized to the current value of head. Now, the current value of the head pointer is evaluated. During the first call to the new operator, its value will be NULL. We will soon see that its value will be NULL under a slightly different circumstance also. The test expression in the if construct succeeds. Therefore, the if block executes. Sufficient memory for holding NO_OF_OBJECTS number of objects is allocated by calling the global new operator. The address of this pool (in other words the address of the first object or block in this pool) is then stored in the temp pointer. After this, the for loop makes the value of the next pointer of each object (except the last object) in the newly created pool equal to the address of the next object. After the loop terminates, the last statement of the if block makes the next pointer of the last object NULL. With this, the if block terminates. The second last statement of the function makes the head pointer point at the second object of the pool. The value of temp, that is, the address of the first object of the pool is then returned by the operator new function. Thus, ClassNewPtr01 now points at the first object of the pool. ClassNewPtr01 pointer now operates on the first object of the pool by calling the member functions of the class ClassNew.

Now let us look at the fourth statement of the main function in Listing 8.48. The operator new function of class ClassNew will be called for a second time. Again, temp pointer will be initialized to the current value of head which is not NULL (head is pointing at the second object of the pool). The if block will therefore be skipped. Only the last two statements execute. The head pointer is again incremented to point at the next object (in this case the third object) and the address of the object (in this case the second object) at which temp is currently pointing is returned.

This process will continue till the operator new function of the class ClassNew is called for the fifth time (ClassNew * ClassNewPtr05 = new ClassNew). Although this time also the test expression of the if block will fail, the value of the head pointer will become NULL while the address of the fifth and last block in the pool will be returned. Now, when the operator new function is called for the sixth time, the test expression of the if block succeeds. A fresh pool is allocated and the process repeats itself.

In order to make the operator new function succeed, it is necessary to thread the memory by using the for loop. This necessitates the presence of the next pointer in each object of the pool. Wastage of memory because of this next pointer, which would otherwise defeat the very purpose for which the new operator was overloaded, is elegantly prevented by the use of a union.

Now let us see how we can overload the delete operator for the class ClassNew. The delete operator will be overloaded in a manner that will not actually deallocate the memory. Instead, the block at which the pointer, on whom the delete operator is being applied points, will be put back in the free list. When the new operator is called for the next time, the address of that block will be returned. Before looking at the actual code, let us see its effects.

Let us consider the case where the new operator is called once only. This solitary call is followed by a call to the delete operator (Listing 8.49).

Listing 8.49 Calling an overloaded delete operator

```
/*Beginning of NewDeleteForMemorySaveMain.cpp*/
#include<iostream.h>
#include"NewDeleteForMemorySave.h"
void main()
{
    ClassNewDelete * ClassNewDeletePtr01 = new ClassNewDelete;
    ClassNewDeletePtr01->setx(10);
```

```
        cout<<ClassNewDeletePtr01->getx()<<endl;
        delete ClassNewDeletePtr01;
    }
    /*End of NewDeleteForMemorySaveMain.cpp*/
```

After the execution of the first statement, the scenario shown in Figure 8.5 emerges.

Memory for five objects gets allocated in a pool. The addresses of the blocks in the pool are displayed on the right, while the values of the next pointers embedded in each object is shown within the rectangles that represent the objects. The amount of memory allocated (20 bytes for five objects @ 4 bytes per object) has been prefixed to the pool. After the second statement executes, the following scenario shown in Figure 8.6 emerges.

The value of the member 'x' of the first block is modified to '10'. The third statement does not alter the pool in any way. Now let us consider the fourth statement. The delete operator is being applied on the pointer ClassNewPtr01. It is pointing at the block with address '101'. The operator delete function will copy the current value of the head pointer to the next pointer of this block. Thus, the next pointer of the block will point at the head of the free list. Thereafter, the address of this block will be copied to the head pointer. As a result, the scenario shown in Figure 8.7 will emerge.

Now, if the 'new' operator is called, the address of the first block (101) will be returned by the operator new function.

Question: For the following two circumstances, try to explain this action of the operator delete function.

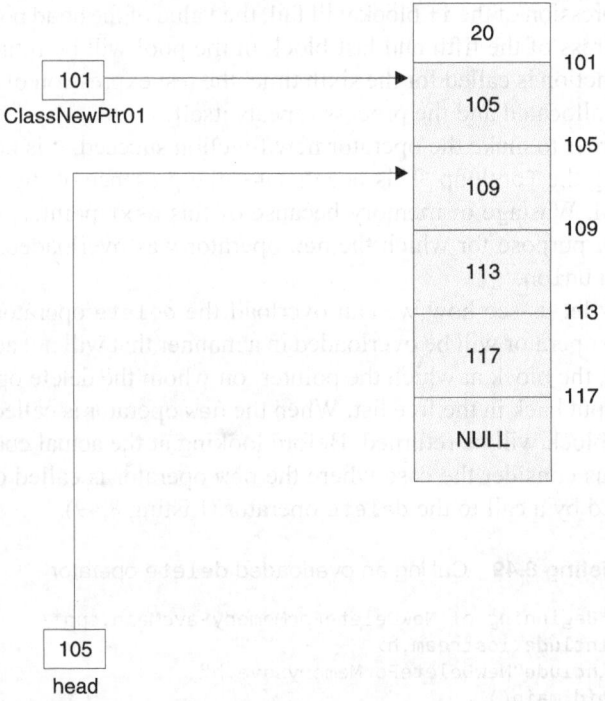

Figure 8.5   Effect of the overloaded delete operator

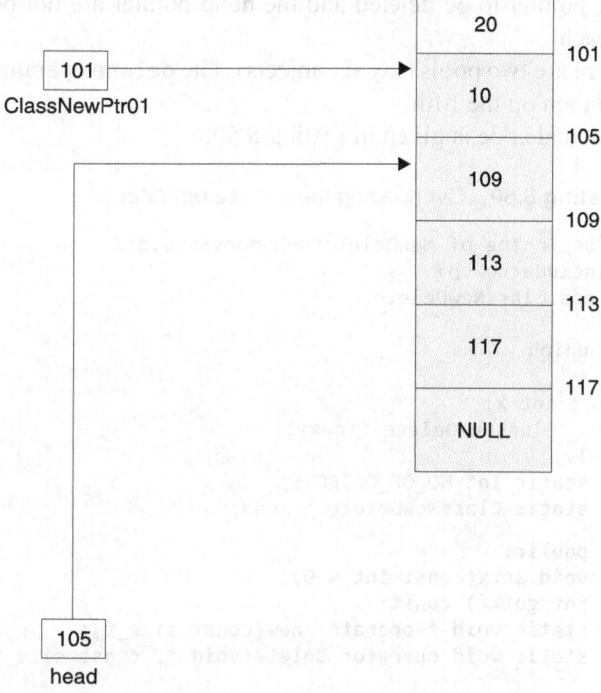

Figure 8.6   Effect of the overloaded `delete` operator

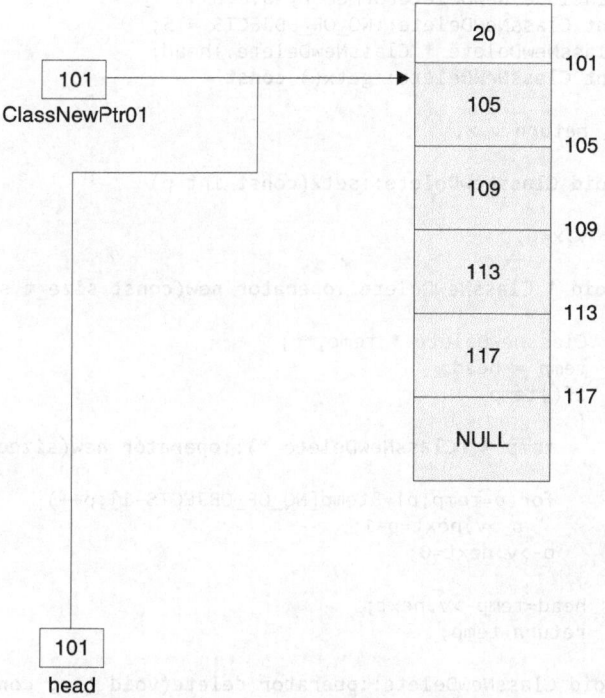

Figure 8.7   Effect of the overloaded `delete` operator

- The pointer to be deleted and the `head` pointer are not pointing to blocks that are next to each.
- There are two pools (say six objects). The `delete` operator is applied on the sixth pointer and then on the fifth.

The actual code is given in Listing 8.50.

Listing 8.50 Overloading the delete operator

```
/*Beginning of NewDeleteForMemorySave.h*/
#include<new.h>
class ClassNewDelete
{
   union
   {
      int x;
      ClassNewDelete * next;
   }v;
   static int NO_OF_OBJECTS;
   static ClassNewDelete * head;

   public:
   void setx(const int = 0);
   int getx() const;
   static void * operator new(const size_t);
   static void operator delete(void *, const size_t);
};
/*End of NewDeleteForMemorySave.h*/

/*Beginning of NewDeleteForMemorySave.cpp*/
#include"NewDeleteForMemorySave.h"
int ClassNewDelete::NO_OF_OBJECTS = 5;
ClassNewDelete * ClassNewDelete::head;
int ClassNewDelete::getx() const
{
   return v.x;
}
void ClassNewDelete::setx(const int p)
{
   v.x=p;
}
void * ClassNewDelete::operator new(const size_t size)
{
   ClassNewDelete * temp,*p;
   temp = head;
   if(!temp)
   {
      temp = (ClassNewDelete *)::operator new(sizeof(class ClassNewDelete)*
                                                      NO_OF_OBJECTS);

      for(p=temp;p!=&temp[NO_OF_OBJECTS-1];p++)
         p->v.next=p+1;
      p->v.next=0;
   }
   head=temp->v.next;
   return temp;
}
void ClassNewDelete::operator delete(void * p, const size_t size)
{
   ClassNewDelete * temp = (ClassNewDelete *)p;
```

```
   temp->v.next = head;
   head = temp;
}
/*End of NewDeleteForMemorySave.cpp*/

/*Beginning of NewDeleteForMemorySaveMain.cpp*/
#include<iostream.h>
#include"NewDeleteForMemorySave.h"
void main()
{
   ClassNewDelete * ClassNewDeletePtr01 = new ClassNewDelete;
   ClassNewDeletePtr01->setx(10);
   cout<<ClassNewDeletePtr01->getx()<<endl;
   delete ClassNewDeletePtr01;
}
/*End of NewDeleteForMemorySaveMain.cpp*/
```

Let us end this discussion with a word of caution. Operator new and operator delete functions get inherited. This gives rise to bugs. We will soon see why this is so. However, first let us prove that this inheritance does occur. See Listing 8.51.

Listing 8.51 Operator new and delete functions get inherited

```
/*Beginning of A.h*/
#include<new.h>
class A
{
   int x;

   public:
   void setx(const int = 0);
   int getx() const;
   static void * operator new(const size_t);
   static void operator delete(void * const, const size_t);
};
/*End of A.h*/

/*Beginning of A.cpp*/
#include"A.h"
#include<iostream.h>
void A::setx(const int p)
{
   x=p;
}
int A::getx() const
{
   return x;
}
void * A::operator new(const size_t size)
{
   cout<<"operator new of class A called\n";
}
void A::operator delete(void * const p, const size_t size)
{
   cout<<"operator delete of class A called\n";
}
/*End of A.cpp*/

/*Beginning of B.h*/
```

```
#include"A.h"
class B : public A
{
    int y;

    public:
    void sety(const int = 0);
    int gety() const;
};
/*End of B.h*/

/*Beginning of B.cpp*/
#include"B.h"
void B::sety(const int q)
{
    y=q;
}
int B::gety() const
{
    return y;
}
/*End of B.cpp*/

/*Beginning of Main.cpp*/
#include<iostream.h>
#include"B.h"
void main()
{
    B * BPtr01 = new B;
    delete BPtr01;
}
/*End of Main.cpp*/
```

Output

operator new of class A called
operator delete of class A called

Thus, when the new and delete operators are called by passing the derived class type as parameter, it is seen that the new and delete operator functions of the base class are called. How can this be a problem?

The problem this inheritance causes is due to the fact that when the new operator is called, the head pointer points at the wrong place. Let us consider the overloaded new operator in Listing 8.48. Suppose the new operator is overloaded for class A in Listing 8.51 in the same way it is overloaded for class ClassNew in Listing 8.48. After the new operator executes for the first time, the head pointer points four bytes away from the first byte of the pool even if the derived class type is passed as a parameter to the new operator. Thus, when the new operator is called for the second time, the address of the fifth byte is returned and not the ninth byte. The address of the ninth object is desired because an object of the class B will occupy eight bytes—four for 'x' and four for 'y'. The problem that arises because of this can be clearly understood from Listing 8.52.

Listing 8.52   Undesirable effect of operator new and delete functions getting inherited

```
/*Beginning of Main.cpp*/
#include"B.h"
```

```
void main()
{
    B * BPtr01 = new B;
    B * BPtr02 = new B;
    BPtr02->setx(20);
    cout<<BPtr02->getx()<<endl;
    BPtr01->sety(10)<<endl;
    cout<<BPtr02->getx()<<endl;
}
/*End of Main.cpp*/
```

Output
20
10

After the first two statements in Listing 8.52 execute, 'BPtr01' will point at the first byte of the memory pool and 'BPtr02' will point at the fifth. The third statement writes 20 into the block of bytes from the fifth byte to the eighth byte. However, the fifth statement writes '10' into the same memory block!

In order to neutralize this effect of inheritance, the size of memory block being targeted for allocation or deallocation should be compared with the size of the class for which the operator is being overloaded. If these two do not match, then the global new or the global delete operator should be called (see Listing 8.53).

Listing 8.53   Preventing the ill effects of the new and delete operators getting inherited

```
void * A::operator new(const size_t size)
{
    if(size != sizeof(class A))        //true if derived class type
                                       //passed as parameter
        return ::operator new(size);
    //rest of the code
}

void A::operator delete(void * const p, const size_t size)
{
    if(size != sizeof(class A))        //true if derived class type
                                       //passed as parameter
    {
        ::operator delete(p);
        return;
    }
    //rest of the code
}
```

8.2.8 Overloading Subscript Operator

The syntax for overloading the subscript operator is shown in Listing 8.54.

Listing 8.54   Syntax for overloading the subscript operator

```
class <class_name>
{
```

```
    public:
        <return_type> operator[](<param_list>);   //prototype
};
//definition
<return_type> <class_name> :: operator[](<param_list>)
{
    //statements
}
```

The function that overloads the subscript operator must be a non-static member of the class.

Let us overload the subscript operator for the class String. We will define the operator so that it returns the character stored in the position that is passed as a parameter to it. See Listing 8.55.

Listing 8.55 Overloading the subscript operator for the class String

```
/*Beginning of String.h*/
class String
{
    public:
        char& operator[](const int);
        /*
            rest of the class String
        */
};
/*End of String.h*/
/*Beginning of String.cpp*/
#include"String.h"
char& String :: operator[] (const int p)
{
    if(p<0 || p>len-1)
        throw "Invalid Subscript";
    return cStr[p];
}
/*
    definitions of the rest of the functions of class String
*/
/*End of String.cpp*/
/*Beginning of StringMain.cpp*/
#include"String.h"
#include<iostream.h>
void main()
{
    String s("abcd");
    cout<<s.getString()<<endl;
    cout<<s[0]<<endl;
    s[1]='x';
    cout<<s.getString()<<endl;
}
/*Beginning of StringMain.cpp*/
```

Output

abcd

a

abxd

For the time being, we must ignore the `throw` statement (explained in Chapter 11) within the `String :: operator[]()` function. The definition of the `String :: operator[]()` function is quite simple. It finds out whether the subscript passed is within the acceptable limits or not. If not, it throws an exception. As we will learn in Chapter 11, throwing exceptions is a very effective and efficient way of error handling. If the subscript passed is within acceptable limits, the function returns the corresponding element by reference. Why is the element returned by reference? This is because the subscript operator might be used on the left-hand side of the `assignment` operator also. Under such circumstances, returning by reference causes the returned element to be assigned to the value passed on the right-hand side of the `assignment` operator.

```
s[1]='x';                    //assign 'x' to the second character in the
                             //string held by s.
```

However, the definition of the `String :: operator[]()` function has a flaw. Suppose there is a constant object.

```
const String s("abcd");
```

Now, if we call the `subscript` operator with respect to the constant object, the compiler correctly throws a compile-time error.

```
cout << s[1] << endl;                //ERROR!
```

This is because the `String :: operator[]()` function is not a constant function and therefore cannot be called with respect to the constant object. Let us therefore introduce another constant function that overloads the `subscript` operator in the same way as the non-constant function. See Listing 8.56.

Listing 8.56 Overloading the `subscript` operators for constant objects

```
/*Beginning of String.h*/
class String
{
   public:
      char& operator[](const int);          //for non-constant
                                             //objects
      char& operator[](const int) const;     //for constant
                                             //objects

      /*
         rest of the class String
      */
};
/*End of String.h*/
/*Beginning of String.cpp*/
#include"String.h"
char& String :: operator[] (const int p)      //for non-constant
                                              //objects
{
   if(p<0 || p>len-1)
      throw "Invalid Subscript";
   return cStr[p];
}
char& String :: operator[] (const int p) const//for
                                              //constant objects
{
   if(p<0 || p>len-1)
```

```
        throw "Invalid Subscript";
        return cStr[p];
    }
    /*
        definitions of the rest of the functions of class String
    */
    /*End of String.cpp*/
```

Now, there are separate functions to overload the subscript operator for constant and non-constant objects. However, the constant function given in Listing 8.56 is still imperfect. Let us consider the following piece of code.

```
const String s("abcd");
s[1]='x';                    //unacceptable, but the compiler doesn't
                             //complain!
```

The second statement in the code calls the constant function with respect to the constant object. The function returns the selected element by reference and the value of the selected element gets set to 'x'. Although the compiler will compile, our perception of a constant tells us that the second statement above should not compile. In order to ensure this, we must make the constant String :: operator[]() function return the value as a constant reference and not as a non-constant reference. See Listing 8.57.

Listing 8.57 Returning a constant value for constant objects

```
/*Beginning of String.h*/
class String
{
    public:
        char& operator[](const int);   //for non-constant
                                       //objects
        const char& operator[](const int) const;        //for constant
                                                        //objects

        /*
           rest of the class String
        */
};
/*End of String.h*/
/*Beginning of String.cpp*/
#include"String.h"
char& String :: operator[] (const int p)        //for non-constant
                                                //objects

{
    if(p<0 || p>len-1)
        throw "Invalid Subscript";
    return cStr[p];
}
const char& String :: operator[] (const int p) const
                                          //for constant
                                          //objects

{
    if(p<0 || p>len-1)
        throw "Invalid Subscript";
    return cStr[p];
}
/*
```

```
         definitions of the rest of the functions of class String
      */
      /*End of String.cpp*/
```

As desired, statements such as

```
    s[1]='x';
```

will no longer compile if the calling object 's' is a constant.

We conclude this section on overloading the subscript operator with one last piece of information. The formal argument of the function that overloads the subscript operator can be of any type. In the example given in Listing 8.57, the formal argument was of type const int. However, it can be of any type, such as char, float, double. See Listing 8.58.

Listing 8.58   Formal argument of the function that overloads the subscript operator can be of any type

```
/*Beginning of String.h*/
class String
{
   public:
      int operator[](const char);              //for non-constant
                                                //objects
      int operator[](const char) const;        //for constant
                                                //objects
      /*
          rest of the class String
      */
};
/*End of String.h*/
```

8.2.9 Overloading Pointer-to-member (->) Operator (Smart Pointer)

Overloading the pointer-to-member (->) operator is slightly complicated. First, let us understand that it is a postfix unary operator. If it is overloaded as follows:

```
class A
{
   public:
      B * operator->();
      /*
         rest of the class A
      */
};
```

then the second statement that follows

```
    A p;
    p->abc();
```

translates to

```
    (p.operator->())->abc();
```

Obviously, 'abc()' must be a member of class B.

The pointer-to-member (->) operator can be overloaded to create smart pointers.

Smart pointers, unlike the ordinary unsmart pointers, can be designed to inevitably point at valid objects. In contrast, the ordinary unsmart pointers have to be explicitly initialized by the client. Consequently, they have to be tested for validity before every use. Smart pointers are class objects. Let us create a class whose objects will behave like pointers to the class String. See Listing 8.59.

Listing 8.59 A class of smart pointers

```
/*Beginning of StrPtr.h*/
#include"String.h"
class StrPtr
{
    String * p;
  public:
    StrPtr(String&);              //the one and only one constructor
};
/*End of StrPtr.h*/
/*Beginning of StrPtr.cpp*/
#include"StrPtr.h"
StrPtr::StrPtr(String& ss)
{
    p=&ss;
}
/*End of StrPtr.cpp*/
```

We must notice how a zero-argument constructor has been deliberately left out from the class definition in Listing 8.59. This forces clients to invariably pass an object of the class String as a parameter whenever they create objects of the class StrPtr. Therefore, the embedded pointer of the class StrPtr always points at an object of the class String. The client can create an object of the class in Listing 8.59 as follows:

```
String s1("abc");
StrPtr p(s1);
```

To mimic a pointer completely, objects of the class StrPtr should be capable of being used as follows:

```
p->setString("def");
```

For this, the pointer-to-member operator (->) needs to be overloaded for the class StrPtr. This can be done as shown in Listing 8.60.

Listing 8.60 Overloading the pointer-to-member operator for smart pointers

```
/*Beginning of StrPtr.h*/
#include"String.h"
class StrPtr
{
    String * p;
  public:
    StrPtr(String&);              //the one and only one constructor
    String * operator->();        //the overloaded operator
};
/*End of StrPtr.h*/
/*Beginning of StrPtr.cpp*/
#include"StrPtr.h"
```

```
StrPtr::StrPtr(String& ss)
{
    p=&ss;
}
String * StrPtr::operator->()
{
    return p;
}
/*End of StrPtr.cpp*/
```

Contrast objects of the class StrPtr with ordinary pointers that point at objects of the class String. In case of ordinary pointers, there is no guarantee that the pointer being used is pointing at a valid block of memory.

```
void f1(String * p)
{
    p->setString("abc");              //No way to check the validity of p
}
```

On the other hand, an attempt to similarly initialize an object of the class StrPtr results in a compile-time error.

```
StrPtr p;                             //ERROR: no zero-argument constructor
```

Therefore, in case of smart pointers, there is a guarantee that the pointer being used is pointing at a valid block of memory.

```
void f1(StrPtr p)
{
    p->setString("abc");              //p is definitely valid
}
```

8.3 Type Conversion

In this section, we shall be dealing with techniques for converting variables from one type to another. Conversion of one type to another is achieved by the use of constructors and type-conversion functions.

8.3.1 Basic Type to Class Type

Conversion for basic type to class type is achieved by introducing a suitable constructor in the class. Suppose it is desired that the following statement should make d1.iFeet equal to '1' and d1.fInches equal to '9'.

```
Distance d1 = 1.75;                   //OR Distance d1(1.75);
```

A value ('1.75') which is of a basic type (float) needs to be converted into an object of the class Distance. A suitable constructor in the class Distance can carry out this conversion (Listing 8.61).

Listing 8.61   Using constructors for converting a value of basic type to class type

```
/*Beginning of Distance.h*/
class Distance
{
```

```
          int iFeet;
          float fInches;
        public:
          Distance(const float);
          /*
             rest of the class Distance
          */
      };
      /*End of Distance.h*/

      /*Beginning of Distance.cpp*/
      #include"Distance.h"
      Distance::Distance(const float p)
      {
         iFeet=(int)p;
         fInches=(p-iFeet)*12;
      }
      /*
         definitions of the rest of the functions of class Distance
      */
      /*End of Distance.cpp*/
```

An ambiguity arises when two classes convert from the same type. Let us consider the two classes shown in Listing 8.62.

Listing 8.62 Ambiguity due to conversion from the same type

```
/*Beginning of ambiguity.cpp*/
class A
{
   public:
   A(int);
};

class B
{
   public:
   B(int);
};

void f(A);
void f(B);//function f() is overloaded

void g()
{
   f(1); //ERROR: ambiguous call - f(X(1)) or f(Y(1))?
}
/*End of ambiguity.cpp*/
```

The ambiguity in Listing 8.62 can be resolved by an explicit-type conversion:

```
f(X(1));                          //OK
f(Y(1));                          //OK
```

8.3.2 Class Type to Basic Type

Type-conversion operators achieve the conversion of class type to basic type. The syntax for the type-conversion functions is shown in Listing 8.63.

Listing 8.63   Syntax for converting values from class type to basic type

```
class <class_name>
{
    public:
        operator <type_name> ();         //prototype
        /*
            rest of the class
        */
};
<class_name> :: operator <type_name> ()         //definition
{
    /*
        definition of the function
    */
}
```

We must notice that the return type is not mentioned. Type-conversion operators resemble constructors in this respect. Let us introduce a function in the class `Distance` for converting its objects into float type variables. In particular, we would like the value of the variable 'x' in the following piece of code to become '1.75'.

```
Distance d1(1,9);
float x=d1;
```

The code to achieve this transformation is as given in Listing 8.64.

Listing 8.64   Converting from class type to basic type

```
/*Beginning of Distance.h*/
class Distance
{
    int iFeet;
    float fInches;
    public:
        operator float();
        /*
            rest of the class Distance
        */
};
/*End of Distance.h*/
/*Beginning of Distance.cpp*/
#include"Distance.h"
Distance::operator float()
{
    return (iFeet+(fInches/12));
}
/*
    definitions of the rest of the functions of class Distance
*/
/*End of Distance.cpp*/
```

8.3.3 Class Type to Class Type

Conversion of one class-type value to another can be achieved by both a constructor and a type-conversion operator. Which of these two techniques will be used depends upon the class that is being provided the capability to convert the value.

If it is desired that the object on the left side of the assignment should have the ability, then a suitable constructor should be introduced in that object's class. If it is desired that the object on the right side of the assignment should have the ability, then a suitable conversion operator should be introduced in that object's class. See Listing 8.65.

Listing 8.65   Assigning an object of one class to another

```
/*Beginning of ClassToClass01.cpp*/
class A {};
class B {};
void f()
{
   A A1;
   B B1;
   A1=B1; //either class A should have a constructor or
      //class B should have a type conversion operator
}
/*End of ClassToClass01.cpp*/
```

The constructor can be introduced in class A as shown in Listing 8.66.

Listing 8.66   Using a constructor for converting from one class type to another

```
/*Beginning of ClassToClass02.cpp*/
class A
{
   public:
   A(const B&); //prototype
};
A::A(const B& b) //definition
{
   /*
      definition of the function
   */
}
/*End of ClassToClass02.cpp*/
```

The type conversion operator can be introduced in class B as shown in Listing 8.67.

Listing 8.67   Using a type conversion operator for converting from one class type to another

```
/*Beginning of ClassToClass03.cpp*/
class B
{
   public:
   operator A(); //prototype
};
B::operator A() //definition
{
   /*
   definition of the function
   */
}
/*End of ClassToClass03.cpp*/
```

Care should be taken to ensure that only one of these two techniques is used on the pair of classes. If both are used together, the compiler throws an ambiguity error when the objects of the two classes are equated. This is because both the techniques can carry out the conversion and the compiler is not in a position to choose between the two.

8.4　New Style Casts and the `typeid` Operator

C++ provides a new set of operators for `typecasting`. These operators can be used instead of the highly error-prone method of `typecasting` provided by the C language. An example of the traditional method of typecasting was mentioned in the section titled 'Explicit address manipulation' in Chapter 2.

The new style casts are safe to use and can be easily located in source codes by using the search facility of the editor in which the source code has been opened. The latter benefit is especially useful in large source codes.

Ideally, a program should not need casts at all. However, there are various programming patterns where they are necessary. In order to meet this need, new style casts should be used instead of the old traditional style.

There are four new style cast operators.

- `dynamic_cast`
- `static_cast`
- `reinterpret_cast`
- `const_cast`

Each of the these operators converts the object, which is passed to it as an operand, in a pre-defined way and returns the converted object. The general syntax of these operators is:

```
operator <type>(value whose type is to be converted)
```

The `typeid` operator is similar to the `dynamic_cast` operator.

8.4.1　`dynamic_cast` Operator

Run time type information (RTTI) enables us to find the type of a value and to compare the types of two values. C++ provides `dynamic_cast` operator and the `typeid` operator for implementing RTTI.

The `dynamic_cast` operator is used to determine whether a particular base class pointer points at an object of the base class or an object of one of the derived classes at run time. It is also used to determine whether a base class reference refers to an object of the base class or an object of one of the derived classes at run time.

We know from Chapter 5 that a base class pointer can point at an object of the derived class while a derived class pointer cannot point at an object of the base class.

Let A be a base class and B be its derived class.

```
A A1, * APtr;
B B1, * BPtr;
APtr=&B1;            //line 1: OK: Can convert from B* to A*
BPtr=&A1;            //line 2: ERROR: Cannot convert from A* to B*
BPtr=APtr;           //line 3: ERROR: Cannot convert from A* to B*
```

However, in the first line of this piece of code, 'APtr' (a base class pointer) points at 'B1' (an object of the derived class). In this particular case, there should be no harm in assigning the value of the base class pointer to the derived class pointer (see the third line). After all, the base class pointer contains the address of a derived class object and a derived class pointer can certainly point at an object of the derived class.

However, a statement that assigns the value of a base class pointer to a derived class pointer (line 3) will not compile. The compiler has no way of knowing the type of the object whose address would get assigned to the base class pointer at run time.

As we already know, a pointer usually appears as function argument. Usually, it is not a local variable. The library programmer puts the prototypes of his/her functions, including the ones that have pointers as formal arguments, in header files and their compiled definitions in libraries. These functions are called from functions that are defined in application codes or in other library codes. In case the particular library function being called has a pointer as a formal argument, the application source code passes a suitable address to it. This address can be the address of a base class object or a derived class object. However, within the definition of the library function, there is no way of determining the exact type of the object whose address will be passed to it. Therefore, a line within the library function such as the third line in the foregoing code snippet will not compile.

However, the library programmer may need to assign the value of a base class pointer to a derived class pointer if the base class pointer points at an object of the same derived class. The dynamic_cast operator enables us to know the type of the object whose address gets assigned to a base class pointer during run time.

Please refer to the general syntax of the new style cast operators given at the beginning of this section. If 'type' is a derived class pointer type and the value to be converted is the address of an object of the same derived class, then the dynamic_cast operator returns a pointer to the object. Else, it returns NULL. Remember that for the dynamic_cast operator to operate, the base class should be polymorphic in nature, that is, it should have at least one virtual function. Listing 8.68 shows an illustrative program follows.

Listing 8.68 Using the dynamic_cast operator with pointers

```
/*Beginning of dynamicCast01.cpp*/
#include<iostream.h>
class A
{
    public:
    virtual void f1()
    {
        cout<<"A::f1() called\n";
    }
};
class B : public A
{
    public:
    void f2()
    {
        cout<<"B::f2() called\n";
    }
};
class C : public A
{
    public:
```

```
    void f3()
    {
        cout<<"C::f3() called\n";
    }
};
void main()
{
    A * APtr;
    B B1, * BPtr;
    C C1;
    APtr=&B1;                        //APtr points at an object of class B.
    BPtr=dynamic_cast<B*>(APtr);     //APtr is actually of
                                     //type B* and type is
                                     //also B*. Hence, cast
                                     //returns address of B1.
    if(BPtr!=NULL)                   //BPtr is not NULL. It contains the
                                     //address of B1.
        BPtr->f2();
    else
        cout<<"Invalid cast\n";
    APtr=&C1;                        //APtr points at an object of class C.
    BPtr=dynamic_cast<B*>(APtr);     //APtr is actually of
                                     //type C* and type is
                                     //B*. Hence, cast
                                     //returns NULL.
    if(BPtr!=NULL)                   //BPtr is NULL.
        BPtr->f2();
    else
        cout<<"Invalid cast\n";
}
/*End of dynamicCast01.cpp*/
```

Output
B::f(2) called
Invalid cast

The process implemented in Listing 8.68 for safely casting a pointer of base class type to a pointer of derived class type is known as safe downcasting. This process enables us to access those features of the derived class that are not present in the base class.

If the `dynamic_cast` operator is used with references, it throws an exception of type Bad_ cast where it would have otherwise returned NULL, had pointers been used. Understanding this requires preliminary knowledge of exception handling. Therefore, Listing 8.69 can be read after reading Chapter 11 on exception handling.

Listing 8.69   Using the `dynamic_cast` operator with references

```
/*Beginning of dynamicCast02.cpp*/
#include<iostream.h>
#include<typeinfo.h>
class A
{
    public:
    virtual void f1()
    {
        cout<<"A::f1() called\n";
    }
```

```
    };
    class B : public A
    {
      public:
      void f2()
      {
        cout<<"B::f2() called\n";
      }
    };
    class C : public A
    {
      public:
      void f3()
      {
        cout<<"C::f3() called\n";
      }
    };
    void main()
    {
      B BObj;
      C CObj;
      A & ARef1=BObj;              //ARef1 is a reference to an object of
                                   //class B
      try
      {
        B & BRef1=dynamic_cast<B &>(ARef1);
                                   //ARef1 is actually of type B& and
                                   //type is also B&. Hence, cast
                                   //returns reference to BObj.
        BRef1.f2();
      }
      catch(bad_cast)
      {
        cout<<"Invalid cast\n";
      }
      A & ARef2=CObj;              //ARef2 is a reference to an object of
                                   //class C
      try
      {
        B & BRef2=dynamic_cast<B &>(ARef2);
                                   //ARef2 is actually of type C& and
                                   //type is B&. Hence, cast
                                   //throws an exception of type
                                   //bad_cast.
        BRef2.f2();
      }
      catch(bad_cast)
      {
        cout<<"Invalid cast\n";
      }
    }
    /*End of dynamicCast02.cpp*/
```

Output

B::f2() called

Invalid cast

8.4.2 `static_cast` Operator

The only difference between the `static_cast` operator and the `dynamic_cast` operator is that while the `dynamic_cast` operator carries out a run-time check to ensure a valid conversion (it returns NULL or throws an exception of type `Bad_cast`), the `static_cast` operator caries out no such check. See Listing 8.70.

Listing 8.70   The `static_cast` operator

```
/*Beginning of typeid.cpp*/
#include<iostream.h>
#include<typeinfo.h>
void main()
{
    char c;
    int i;
    float f;
    double d;
    cout<<typeid(c).name()<<endl;
    cout<<typeid(i).name()<<endl;
    cout<<typeid(f).name()<<endl;
    cout<<typeid(d).name()<<endl;
    if(typeid(i)==typeid(1.1))                  //comparing int with float
        cout<<"i is of the same type as 1.1";
    else
        cout<<"i is not of the same type as 1.1";
}
/*End of typeid.cpp*/
```

Output
B::setx() called
1
B::setx() called
2

The first conversion by the `static_cast` operator in Listing 8.70 is correct. 'BPtr' (of type 'B*') points at 'B1' (of type B).

However, the second conversion by the `static_cast` operator is incorrect. 'BPtr' (of type 'B*') points at 'C1' (of type C). Since 'BPtr' is of type 'B*', the member functions of class B alone can be called with respect to it.

It is interesting to note what happens when 'BPtr' points at 'C1' and the `B::setx()` function is called for it. The statement

```
x=p;
```

in `B::setx()` function simply stores the value '2' in the first four bytes of the object at which 'BPtr' points. This is because 'B::x' is an integer-type value and is the only data member of class B. However, these four bytes are occupied by 'C1.y'! Therefore, the output of the last statement in Listing 8.70 is '2'. The error-prone nature of the `static_cast` operator is quite evident from this.

However, this does not mean that the old style cast ('B*') is as good as the `static_cast` operator. The `static_cast` operator is still a better choice because it can be easily located in the source codes by searching for the string `static_cast`. Bugs suspected due to an invalid-type conversion can thus be easily found out.

8.4.3 `reinterpret_cast` Operator

Just like the old style cast, the `reinterpret_cast` operator allows us to cast one type to another.

Suppose 'cPtr' is a character pointer and 'vPtr' is a void pointer. If the value of 'vPtr' is to be assigned to 'cPtr', it needs to be typecast first.

```
cPtr=(char *)vPtr;
```

However, the preceding statement can be rewritten as

```
cPtr=reinterpret_cast<char *>(vPtr);
```

The compiler generates errors or warnings if casts are absent from conversion statements where a value of one type is being converted to an incompatible type. These errors and warnings can be switched off by inserting cast operators. Inserting a cast operator is a way of expressing our awareness and acceptance of the potential consequences to the compiler and the reader.

As in the case of `static_cast`, the `reinterpret_cast` operator seems to be an unnecessary substitute of the old style cast. Again, as in the case of `static_cast`, the visibility of the new style cast is considerably greater than the old style cast, which makes tracking down a rogue old style cast much easier.

8.4.4 `const_cast` Operator

The `const_cast` operator serves the same purpose as the `mutable` keyword that has been explained in Chapter 2. The `const_cast` operator is used to cast away the constness of a pointer.

We may recall the following listing on mutable data members from Chapter 2 (Listing 2.21).

```
/*Beginning of mutable.h*/
class A
{
    int x;                    //non-mutable data member
    mutable int y;            //mutable data member
  public:
    void abc() const          //a constant member function
    {
       x++;          //ERROR: cannot modify a non-mutable data
                     //member in a constant member function
       y++;          //OK: can modify a mutable data member in a
                     //constant member function
    }
    void def()                //a non-constant member function
    {
       x++;          //OK: can modify a non-mutable data member
                     //in a non-constant member function
       y++;          //OK: can modify a mutable data member in a
                     //non-constant member function
    }
```

```
};
/*End of mutable.h*/
```

Listing 2.21 can be rewritten by using the const_cast operator instead of declaring the desired data member as mutable as shown in Listing 8.71.

Listing 8.71   The const_cast operator

```
/*Beginning of const_cast.h*/
class A
{
      int x;                        //non-mutable data member
      int y;                        //non-mutable data member
   public:
      void abc() const              //a constant member function
      {
         x++;                       //ERROR: cannot modify a non-constant data
                                    //member in a constant member function
         const_cast<A*>(this)->y++;
                                    //OK: can modify a non-mutable data member
                                    //in a constant member function by casting
                                    //away the constness of the this pointer

      }
      void def()                    //a non-constant member function
      {
         x++;           //OK: can modify a non-mutable data member
                        //in a non-constant member function
         y++;           //OK: can modify a mutable data member in a
                        //non-constant member function

      }
};
/*End of const_cast.h*/
```

The compiler treats the this pointer as a constant pointer inside non-constant functions. However, it treats the this pointer as a constant pointer to a constant inside constant functions. In the A::abc() function in Listing 8.71, the constness of the this pointer is cast away. This enables us to modify a non-mutable data member in a constant function.

We may note that by passing 'A*' to the const_cast operator in the A::abc() function in Listing 8.71, the this pointer was made an ordinary pointer that is neither a constant nor supposed to point at a constant object. We could have very well passed 'A * const' instead and still ensured a successful compilation of the statement. This is because passing 'A * const' to the const_cast operator would have rendered the this pointer a constant pointer that points at a non-const object.

The motive for using the const_cast operator is the same as the motive for using the mutable keyword.

As in the case of the other new style cast operators, using the const_cast operator indicates the programmer's awareness and acceptance of the possible negative consequences of its use.

8.4.5 typeid Operator

Apart from the dynamic_cast operator, C++ provides the typeid operator for implementing RTTI (typeid is a keyword in C++). The typeid operator takes a value as its only parameter.

It returns the type of the passed value as a reference to an object of class `type_info`. The class `type_info` is defined in the header file `typeinfo.h`.

Two objects of the class `type_info` can be compared by using the 'equality' operator. The name of the type of value passed to the `typeid` operator can also be determined by using the `type_info::name()` function.

Values of fundamental data types, pointers to values of fundamental data types, and references to values of fundamental data types can be passed to the `typeid` operator. See Listing 8.72.

Listing 8.72   The typeid operator

```
/*Beginning of typeid.cpp*/
#include<typeinfo.h>
void main()
{
    char c;
    int i;
    float f;
    double d;

    cout<<typeid(c).name()<<endl;
    cout<<typeid(i).name()<<endl;
    cout<<typeid(f).name()<<endl;
    cout<<typeid(d).name()<<endl;

if(typeid(i)==typeid(1.1))            //comparing int with float
        cout<<"i is of the same type as 1.1";
    else
        cout<<"i is not of the same type as 1.1";
}
/*End of typeid.cpp*/
```

Output
char
int
float
double
i is not of the same type as 1.1

Class objects, pointers to class objects, or references to class objects can also be passed to the `typeid` operator. However, for the `typeid` operator to work correctly, the class whose object, pointer, or reference is passed to it should be polymorphic in nature. Otherwise, either of the following will happen depending upon the compiler and its settings:
- The compiler would issue a compile-time warning against the statement in which the `typeid` operator has been called. The OS would throw a run-time error.
- If a dereferenced base class pointer that points at a derived class object is passed as a parameter to the `typeid` operator, the `typeid` operator would not be able to determine the type of the object pointed at by the pointer. It would instead return the base class type as the type of the object pointed at by the base class pointer, which of course is undesirable.

```
class A {};                                    //no virtual function
class B : public A {};
B B1;
A * APtr=&B1;
cout<<typeid(*APtr).name()<<endl;             //prints: class A
```

Had the base class A in the preceding code contained at least one virtual function, the last cout statement would have printed class B as desired.

Given that class A does have a virtual function, what would the following tests evaluate to?

```
typeid(APtr) == typeid(A*)                     //comparing pointers
typeid(*APtr) == typeid(A)                     //comparing objects pointed
                                               //at
```

The first of these test expressions would return true while the second one would return false. In the first case, the types of the pointers, and not the types of the objects being pointed at, are being compared. Since 'APtr' is of type 'A*', the first statement returns true. In the second case, the types of the objects being pointed at, and not the types of the pointers, are being compared. Since '*APtr' is of type B, the second statement returns false.

Summary

In C++, the library programmer can provide existing operators with additional capabilities to operate upon objects of his/her class. This is known as operator overloading.

Operators can be overloaded by functions having their names composed of the keyword operator and the symbol of the operator being overloaded. These functions may be member functions or friend functions. Friend functions are used when the objects of the class for which the operator is being overloaded invariably appear on the right-hand side of the operator.

Operators are overloaded to

- Neutralize the effect of the functions that are generated by default (the assignment' operator).
- To make the operation of the operators more efficient (the new and delete operators).
- To provide capabilities to the class so that its objects can be used in predefined templates.

The rules for operator overloading are as follows:

- New operators cannot be created.
- Meaning of existing operators cannot be changed.
- The following operators cannot be overloaded:
  :: (scope resolution)

. (member selection)
.* (member selection through pointer to member)
?: (conditional operator)
sizeof (finding the size of values and types)
typeid (finding the type of object pointed at)

- The following operators can be overloaded using member functions alone:
  = (Assignment operator)
  () (Function operator)
  [] (Subscripting operator)
  -> (Pointer-to-member access operator)

- Number of arguments that an existing operator takes cannot be changed.

The following type conversions can be carried out:

- basic type to class type (by using a constructor),
- class type to basic type (by using a type conversion operator), and
- class type to class type (by using either a constructor or a type conversion operator).

The C++ language provides a new set of operators for typecasting. These operators can be used instead of the highly error-prone method of typecasting provided by the C language.

The new style casts are safe to use and can be easily located in source codes by using the search facility of the editor in which the source code has been opened. The latter benefit is especially useful in large source codes.

There are four new style cast operators.

- dynamic_cast
- static_cast
- reinterpret_cast
- const_cast

Each of the new style cast operators converts the object that is passed to it as an operand in its own way and returns the converted object. The general syntax of these operators is:

operator <type>(value whose type is to be converted)

The dynamic_cast operator is used to determine whether a particular base class pointer points at an object of the base class or an object of one of the derived classes at run time. It is also used to determine whether a base class reference refers to an object of the base class or an object of one of the derived classes at run time.

In the general syntax, if type is a derived class pointer type and the value to be converted is the address of an object of the same derived class, then the dynamic_cast operator returns a pointer to the object. Else, it returns NULL. For the dynamic_cast operator to operate, the base class should be polymorphic in nature, that is, it should have at least one virtual function.

The dynamic_cast operator enables us to access those features of the derived class that are not present in the base class.

If the dynamic_cast operator is used with references, it throws an exception of type Bad_cast where it would have otherwise returned NULL had pointers been used.

While the dynamic_cast operator carries out a run-time check to ensure a valid conversion, the static_cast operator caries out no such check.

The reinterpret_cast operator allows us to cast one type to another.

New style casts are definitely a better choice than the old C-style casts. Visibility of the new style cast is considerably greater than the old style cast, which makes tracking down a rogue old style cast much easier.

The const_cast operator serves the same purpose as the mutable keyword. The const_cast operator is used to cast away the constness of a pointer.

Apart from the dynamic_cast operator, C++ provides the typeid operator for implementing RTTI (typeid is a keyword in C++). The typeid operator takes a value as its only parameter. It returns the type of the passed value as a reference to an object of class type_info. The class type_info is defined in the header file typeinfo.h.

Two objects of the class type_info can be compared by using the equality operator. The name of the type of value passed to the typeid operator can also be determined by using the type_info::name() function.

Class objects, pointers to class objects, or references to class objects can be passed to the typeid operator. However, for the typeid operator to work correctly, the class whose object, pointer, or reference is passed to it should be polymorphic in nature.

Key Terms

operator overloading
syntax for operator overloading
using friend functions for operator overloading
need for operator overloading
type conversions
 – basic type of class type
 – class type of basic type

 – class type of class type
dynamic_cast operator
static_cast operator
reinterpret_cast operator
const_cast operator
typeid operator

Exercises

1. What is operator overloading?
2. How are operators overloaded?
3. How does the compiler interpret the operator-overloading functions?
4. Why are operators overloaded?
5. Under what circumstances does overloading using friend functions become necessary?
6. What is the difference between the functions that overload the increment operator in prefix and in postfix formats?
7. Why does the function to overload the assignment operator receive and return by reference?
8. Explain why the function to overload the assignment operator for the class String returns *this and not the passed parameter.
9. Why is the assignment operator function not inherited? Explain. Why does the compiler generate the assignment operator for a class, for which the class designer has not defined one, and even if its base class already has the assignment operator function implicitly or explicitly defined?
10. Why are objects of the classes istream and ostream passed and returned by reference in the functions to overload the insertion and extraction operators?
11. How is data abstraction achieved by overloading the insertion and extraction operators?
12. Why does the function to overload the subscript operator return by reference?
13. What special precautions should be taken while overloading the subscript operator for constant objects?
14. What are smart pointers? How are they created?
15. How are values of fundamental data types converted to class objects?
16. What ambiguity can arise in the following code? How can it be resolved?

```
class A
{
  public:
    A(int);
};
class B
{
  public:
    B(int);
};
void f(A);
void f(B);//function f() is overloaded
void g()
{
  f(1);
}
```

17. How can a class object be converted to a value of fundamental data type?
18. What are the two ways of converting an object of one class to an object of another? Describe the ambiguity that can arise if both methods are applied.
19. What is the advantage of using the new style casts over the old C-style casts?
20. Name the four new style casts provided by C++.
21. What is RTTI? What are its practical uses?
22. What is the difference between the static_cast and dynamic_cast operators?
23. What does the const_cast operator do? Which keyword of C++ can it be used instead of?
24. How can the typeid operator be used to find the type of a particular object?
25. State true or false.
    (a) New operators can be created by operator overloading.
    (b) The sizeof operator cannot be overloaded.
    (c) Number of arguments that an existing operator takes cannot be changed by operator overloading.
    (d) Functions to overload the new and delete operators are always static.
    (e) The dynamic_cast operator throws an error if the type of the pointer that is passed to it does not match the type that is passed to it.
26. Modify the code given under the section on overloading the new operator to save memory when a large number of objects are created. Instead of having a union with the next pointer as a member, put another static data member that will count how many objects from the pool have had their addresses returned. When this counter becomes equal to the number of objects, another pool can be allocated. Compare the two codes for efficiency in memory usage.
27. Overload the equality operator (==) for the class Distance.
28. Overload the insertion and extraction operators for the class String.
29. Overload the subscript operator for the class String so that it takes a character as a parameter and returns the position of its first occurrence. The output of the following code should be two.

```
String s1("abcd");
cout << s1['c'] << endl;
```

30. Overload the addition operator for the class String so that it adds two strings and returns the result.

The output of the following piece of code should be 'abcxyz'.

```
String s1("abc"),s2("xyz"),s3;
s3 = s1 + s2;
cout << s3 << endl;
```

31. Overload the addition operator for the class String so that the output of the following code is 'c'. Introduce suitable checks for array bounds.

```
String s1("abcd");
cout << s1 + 2 << endl;
```

Moreover, the output of the following piece of code should be 'abxd'.

```
String s1("abcd");
s1 + 2 = 'x';
cout << s1 << endl;
```

32. Overload the bitwise exclusive OR operator (^) for the class Distance. The overloading function should return true if the value of either of the two objects that are passed to the operator is not equal to zero. For the rest of the cases, the function should return false.

33. Refer to the section on overloading the pointer-to-member operator. The operator has been overloaded so that objects of the class StrPtr can mimic the behaviour of pointers. In order to complete the picture, overload the dereferencing operator so that

the following statements become equivalent ('p' is an object of the class StrPtr).

```
p->setString("abcd");
*p.setString("abcd");
```

34. Define two classes Polar and Rectangle to represent points in the polar and rectangle systems. Introduce a conversion operator function in class Polar to convert its objects into objects of class Rectangle and a conversion operator function in class Rectangle to convert its objects into objects of class Polar.

35. Consider the following class hierarchy:

```
class A
{
  public:
      virtual void f1() {}
};
class B : public A {};
class C : public B {}
```

In which of the following would the dynamic_cast operator return zero?

(a) A * APtr = new C;
    C * CPtr = dynamic_cast<C *>(APtr);

(b) A * APtr = new B;
    C * CPtr = dynamic_cast<C *>(APtr);

(c) A * APtr = new C;
    B * BPtr = dynamic_cast<B *>(APtr);

9

Data Structures

This data structures are very useful in the world of programming. They are nothing but special ways in which various pieces of data are arranged and related to each other during run time. We are already familiar with one data structure—arrays. However, arrays have various limitations.

You can create various data structures like lists, trees, etc. Lists are a superior substitute for arrays. Data structures are used to solve a number of programming problems. They can be created using various programming languages, including C++. This chapter explains and illustrates the most important data structures—linked lists and trees. It also includes full fledged programs that can be used to create various data structures.

9.1 Introduction

As mentioned in the overview, data structures are special ways in which pieces of data are arranged and related to each other during run-time. These pieces of data can be integers, character constants, strings, etc. Each such piece of data is embedded in a node that contains the piece of data itself along with one or more pointers that either point at other similar nodes or have null values.

We will soon learn to create such nodes ourselves. Let us first look at the following figure that clearly illustrates two such nodes. Each node contains an integer and a pointer. The value of the integer in the first node is 10, while the value of the integer in the second node is 20. The pointer in the first node points at the second node. Let us assume that the address of the second node is 1296. Therefore, the value of the pointer in the first node will be 1296. The pointer in the second node has NULL value. This means that the pointer in the second node is not pointing at any other node. This also means that the second node is the last node in the list (Figure 9.1).

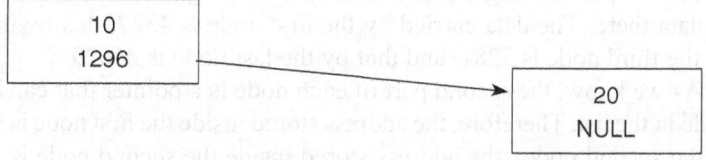

Figure 9.1 Nodes of a data structure

We are already familiar with one data structure—arrays. However, arrays have the limitation that their size cannot be modified during run time. Whatever size the programmer specifies for the array while writing the program remains fixed during run time. But, during run time, the user of the program may find that the size of the array is not enough to hold the number of elements that he/she needs to create.

Conversely, if the programmer specifies a very large value for the size of the array, the user may not use all of the elements of the array during run time. But the array, when it gets created during run time, occupies the space for all of its elements even if they are not in use. This will lead to wastage of space especially if each element is a large object. Also, we cannot easily insert a new element at the beginning or in the middle of the array.

Linked lists (a type of data structure) are a good substitute for arrays. They do not have the above limitations of arrays. But, in order to use them and other data structures, you need to either write special programs to create and then use them or use libraries that can create them for your use.

Arrays have one more limitation. They have a linear structure. One element of the array is followed by only one element. But our programming need may require us to link one element to two or more elements. Trees (another type of data structure) enable us to fulfill this programming need. Again, just like linked lists, you need to either write special programs to create and then use trees or use libraries that can create them for your use.

Data structures can be used to solve a number of programming problems like creating database software, engineering problems, etc. They can be created using various programming languages, including C++. We can create various data structures by utilizing classes, functions, pointers, the new and the delete operators, etc.

9.2 Linked Lists

Linked lists are linear data structures. They consist of nodes that are linked to each other in a linear fashion. Each node in a linked list is an object that is made up of two parts. The first part is the data carried by the node. The second part of each node is a pointer that carries the address of the next node in the list. This is how a node is linked to the next node.

Each node in a single linked list is linked to exactly one more node (Note that we are talking about single linked lists here. We also have double linked lists where one node is connected to two nodes—the next node in the list and the previous node in the list.). Figure 9.2 illustrates a sample structure of a single linked list.

This figure shows an example of a single linked list of four nodes. In order to understand the figure, keep in mind that each of the four boxes represents a node and the address of each node has been mentioned above the box that represents it. The address of the first node is 6327, that of the second node is 9243, that of the third node is 743, and that of the last node is 8138. Let us ignore the box labelled head for the time being.

In this specific case, each node carries an integer as the data. But, we can embed any type of data there. The data carried by the first node is 4327, that by the second node is 55, that by the third node is 3281, and that by the last node is 21629.

As we know, the second part of each node is a pointer that carries the address of the next node in the list. Therefore, the address stored inside the first node is 9243 (which is the address of the second node), the address stored inside the second node is 743 (which is the address of the third node), and the address stored inside the third node is 8138 (which is the address of the fourth node). The address stored inside the fourth node is NULL (which indicates that it is not connected to any other node and is therefore the last node).

We also need to store the address of the first node. This is where the head pointer comes into play. It stores the address of the first node (6327 in this case).

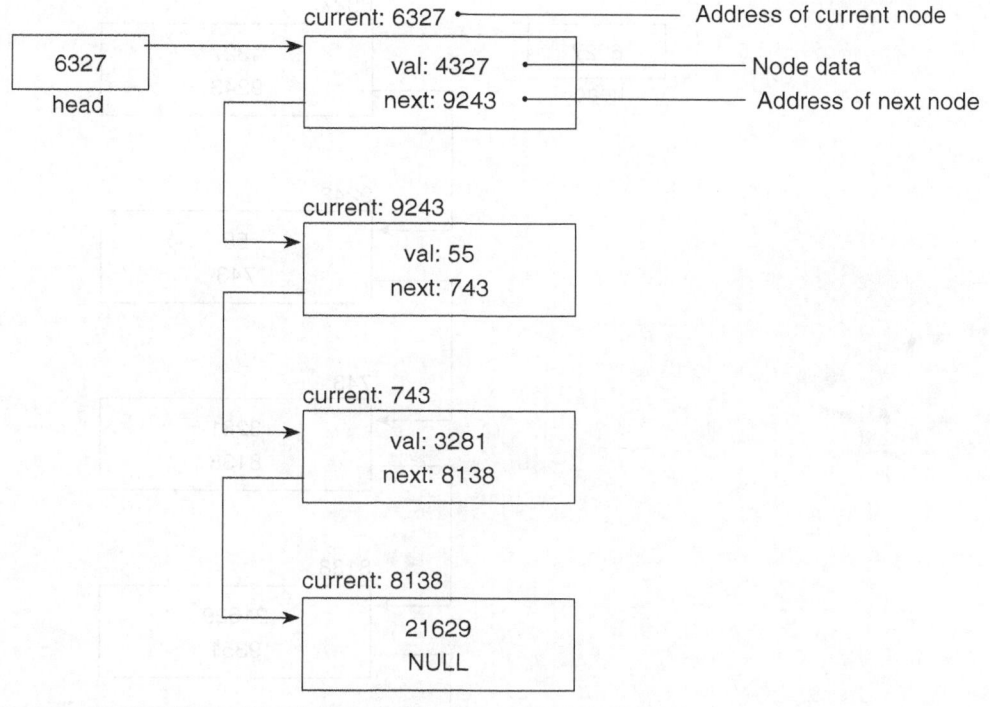

Figure 9.2   A sample linked list

We will soon learn how to create single linked lists of our own. Let us first view some figures that depict the process of appending nodes to single linked lists. Let us see how a node is appended to the list we have seen above. After that we will see how the first node gets appended to an empty list.

Let us assume that a node with value 41 has been appended to the list shown in Figure 9.2. Figure 9.3 shows how the list will look now. As you can see, the address of this new node is 9351, and this node now stores the address NULL. That is, it now becomes the last node in the list.

Figure 9.4 shows a linked list with no nodes.

The head pointer contains NULL value because there are no nodes in the list (remember that the head pointer is supposed to point at the first node). Let us see how the linked list will look like when a node is added to this empty list. Let us assume that a node with value 5287 has been appended to the list above. Figure 9.5 shows how the list will look now.

You must be very eager to look at the code that can enable you to create linked lists. Let us look at the code now.

We will study two classes:

- A node class whose objects will be the actual nodes of the single linked list.
- A single linked list class each object of which will represent a separate linked list of nodes.

Please keep in mind that you will have to study a number of building blocks before you are able to write an executable program that creates linked lists. Have patience!

We will first look at a header file that contains the declaration of the node class. Like the other class declarations, this class declaration will also include the declarations of the data

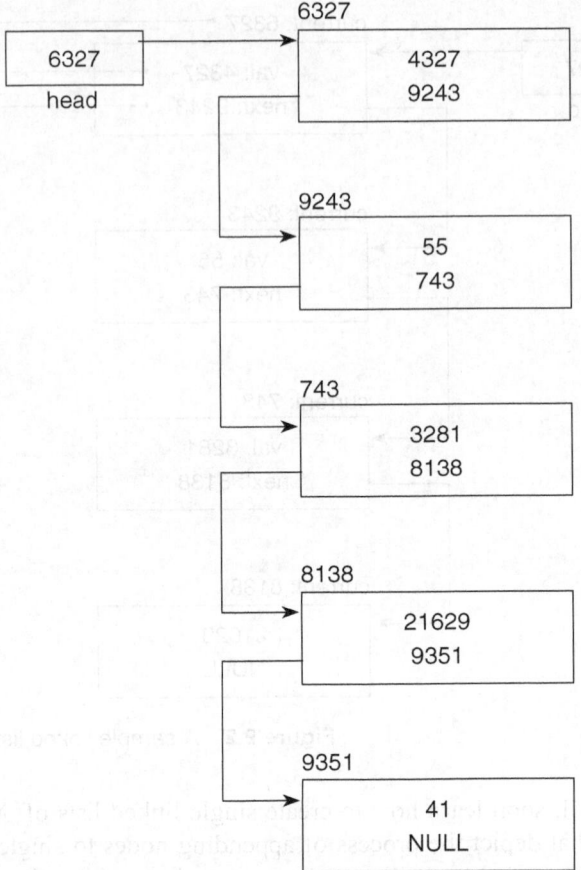

Figure 9.3   Addition of a node to a linked list

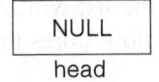

Figure 9.4   An empty linked list

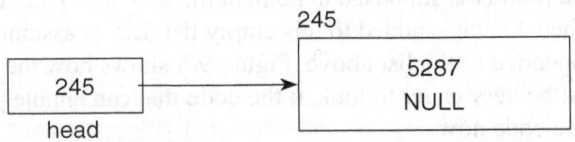

Figure 9.5   A node added to an empty list

members and member functions of the class. Thereafter, we will look at the implementation file that contains the definitions of the member functions of the node class.

We will next look at a header file that contains the declaration of the single linked list class. Like the other class declarations, this class declaration will also include the declarations of the data members and member functions of the class. Thereafter, we will look at the implementation file that contains the definitions of the member functions of the single linked list class.

You will find a lot of comments in the program listings. Please ensure that you read them. Reading these comments will make it much easier to understand the code.

Let us start with studying the header file that contains a declaration of the node class (Listing 9.1).

Listing 9.1 Header file containing declaration of single linked list node class

```
/*
    Beginning of SingleLinkedListNode.h
*/
#ifndef _SINGLE_LINKED_LIST_NODE_H
#define _SINGLE_LINKED_LIST_NODE_H
/*
    The node class.
    Each instance of this class willbe a node in the single
    linked list.
*/
class SingleLinkedListNode
{
    private:
    /*
        The data part of the nodes.
    */
    int val;
    /*
        The next pointer will exist in each node and will
        point at the next node (or be NULL)
    */
    SingleLinkedListNode * next;

    public:
    /*
        The constructor of the node class. It will nullify
        the next pointer by default.
    */
    SingleLinkedListNode();
    /*
        This function sets the value of the data part.
    */
    void setVal(int);
    /*
        This function returns the data part.
    */
    int getVal();
    /*
        This function sets the value of the next pointer.
    */
    void setNext(SingleLinkedListNode *);
    /*
        This function returns the value of the next pointer.
    */
    SingleLinkedListNode * getNext();
    /*
        The destructor of the class.
    */
```

```
        ~SingleLinkedListNode();
    };

    #endif
    /*
       End of SingleLinkedListNode.h
    */
```

The header file begins with a comment that specifies the name of the header file and also announces the beginning of the file. This is followed by pre-processor directives that prevent multiple inclusion of the header file in other source codes (you must have studied this in your C language course). This is followed by the declaration of the node class. The second last line of the header file contains the end of the pre-process block and the last line contains a comment that marks the end of the header file.

Each object of the `SingleLinkedListNode` class will be a node in the linked list. This class has an integer data member, `val`, which is supposed to contain the value of the node. In this example, each node has this integer-type variable as the data member. However, the data part can be of any type, including class objects.

The other data member of the node class is `next`. It is a pointer. It is obvious from its definition that `next` is supposed to point at another node, i.e. another object of the same class. In our program, it will either be made to point at the next node in the linked list or will be assigned the NULL value (to indicate that the current node is the last node).

Let us look at the implementation file (Listing 9.2) that contains the definitions of the member functions of the node class. It is important to clearly understand these functions because they serve as the building blocks for the functions of the single linked list class.

Listing 9.2   Implementation file of the linked list node class

```
/*
    Beginning of SingleLinkedListNode.cpp
*/
#include "SingleLinkedListNode.h"

/*
    The constructor of the node class. It will nullify the
    next pointer by default.
*/
SingleLinkedListNode::SingleLinkedListNode()
{
    /*Set the data part to zero.*/
    val = 0;
    /*Set the next pointer to NULL.*/
    next = NULL;
}

/*
    This function sets the value of the data part.
*/
void SingleLinkedListNode::setVal(int pVal)
{
    /*
        Set the value of the data part to the value of the
        passed parameter.
    */
    val = pVal;
}
```

```
/*
    This function returns the data part.
*/
int SingleLinkedListNode::getVal()
{
    /*
        Return the value of the data part.
    */
    return val;
}

/*
    This function sets the value of the next pointer.
*/
void SingleLinkedListNode::setNext(SingleLinkedListNode * pNext)
{
    /*
        Set the value of the next pointer to the value of the
        passed parameter.
    */
    next = pNext;
}

/*
    This function returns the value of the next pointer.
*/
SingleLinkedListNode * SingleLinkedListNode::getNext()
{
    /*
        Return the value of the next pointer.
    */
    return next;
}

/*
    The destructor of the class.
*/
SingleLinkedListNode::~SingleLinkedListNode()
{
    /*
        Right now the destructor has empty definition.
        But we may like to insert some statements here later.
    */
}
/*
    End of SingleLinkedListNode.cpp
*/
```

The implementation file begins with a comment that specifies the name of the implementation file and also announces the beginning of the file. This is followed by an include directive that includes the header file, which contains the declaration of the node class. This is followed by the definitions of the member functions of the node class. The last line contains a comment that marks the end of the implementation file.

To understand the implementation, let us start with the constructor of the node class.

```
/*
    The constructor of the node class. It will nullify the
    next pointer by default.
*/
```

```
SingleLinkedListNode::SingleLinkedListNode()
{
    /*
       Set the data part to zero.
    */
    val = 0;
    /*
       Set the next pointer to NULL.
    */
    next = NULL;
}
```

As a result of the constructor, whenever an object of the `SingleLinkedListNode` class is created, the value of its `val` data member will be set to zero and the value of its `next` data member will be set to NULL.

Nullifying the `next` pointer will make it easier for us to define the rest of the functions because we can be sure that the value of the `next` pointer will be NULL for any new object of the node class. Let us understand the constructor with the help of (Listing 9.3). Suppose a new object of the node class is created as follows.

Listing 9.3   Executing the constructor of the single linked list node class

```
/*
   Beginning of NodeConstructor.cpp
*/
#include <iostream.h>
#include "SingleLinkedListNode.h"

void main()
{
    SingleLinkedListNode * temp = new SingleLinkedListNode();
}
/*
   End of NodeConstructor.cpp
*/
```

The result can be diagrammatically represented as shown in Figure 9.6.

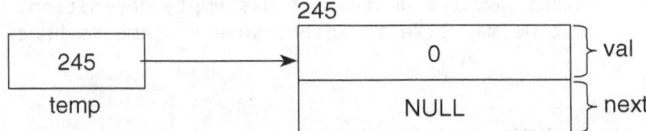

Figure 9.6   Effect of the node class constructor

The box on the right represents the newly created object of the node class. Its data members—val and next—have been labelled. As can be seen, their values are 0 and NULL respectively. They have been separated by a line in the box. Let us assume that the address of this node is 245. The value of the temp pointer will therefore be 245.

It is very important to note that since the new operator was used in the above statement to create the object, the created object will occupy memory in the heap area. This block of memory will continue to be allocated even after the block of code that contains the above statement ends.

Let us now look at the setVal() function.

```
/*
    This function sets the value of the data part.
*/
void SingleLinkedListNode::setVal(int pVal)
{
    /*
        Set the value of the data part to the value of the
        passed parameter.
    */
    val = pVal;
}
```

This is a very simple function. It assigns the value of the parameter that is passed to it to the val data member. Continuing with our previous example, it may be called as follows (Listing 9.4).

Listing 9.4   Executing the setVal() function of the single linked list node class

```
/*
    Beginning of SetVal.cpp
*/
#include <iostream.h>
#include "SingleLinkedListNode.h"

void main()
{
    SingleLinkedListNode * temp = new SingleLinkedListNode();
    temp -> setVal(10);
}
/*
    End of SetVal.cpp
*/
```

A diagrammatic representation of the effects of the above statement is shown in Figure 9.7.

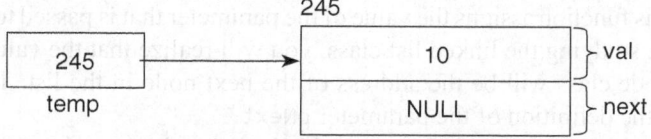

Figure 9.7   Effect of setVal() function

The next function we need to look at is the getVal() function (Listing 9.5).

```
/*
    This function returns the data part.
*/
int SingleLinkedListNode::getVal()
{
    /*
        Return the value of the data part.
    */
    return val;
}
```

Again, this is a simple function. It simply returns the value of the val data member. Still continuing with our previous example, suppose we call it as follows.

Listing 9.5   Executing the getVal() function

```
/*
   Beginning of GetVal.cpp
*/
#include <iostream.h>
#include "SingleLinkedListNode.h"

void main()
{
   SingleLinkedListNode * temp = new SingleLinkedListNode();
   temp -> setVal(10);
   int x = temp -> getVal();
   cout << x << endl;
}
/*
   End of GetVal.cpp
*/
```

Output

10

Next is the setNext() function.

```
/*
   This function sets the value of the next pointer.
*/
void SingleLinkedListNode::setNext(SingleLinkedListNode * pNext)
{
   /*
      Set the value of the next pointer to the value of the
      passed parameter.
   */
   next = pNext;
}
```

This function assigns the value of the parameter that is passed to it to the next data member. While studying the linked list class, you will realize that the value passed to this function of the node class will be the address of the next node in the list. This should also be obvious from the definition of the parameter pNext.

Let us understand this function with the help of an actual program (Listing 9.6) and figures that illustrate the effects of its statements.

Listing 9.6   Executing the setNext() function

```
/*
   Beginning of SetNext.cpp
*/
#include <iostream.h>
#include "SingleLinkedListNode.h"

void main()
{
   /*
      Create a fresh node and assign its address to a
      pointer.
   */
   SingleLinkedListNode * temp = new SingleLinkedListNode();
```

```
    /*
        Set the value of val data member in the new node.
    */
    temp -> setVal(10);
    /*
        Create another fresh node and assign its address to
        another pointer.
    */
    SingleLinkedListNode * temp1 = new
                                SingleLinkedListNode();
    /*
        Set the value of val data member in the new node.
    */
    temp1 -> setVal(20);
    /*
        Make the next pointer of the existing node point at the
        freshly created node.
    */
    temp -> setNext(temp1);
}
/*
    End of SetNext.cpp
*/
```

Let us look at the statements one-by-one.

```
/*
    Create a fresh node and assign its address to a pointer.
*/
SingleLinkedListNode * temp = new SingleLinkedListNode();
```

This statement will create a new node and make the pointer `temp` point to it. Figure 9.8 represents the result diagrammatically.

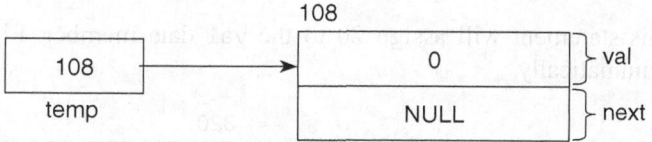

Figure 9.8   Creating a temporary node

The box on the right represents the newly created object of the node class. Its data members—`val` and `next`—have been labelled. As can be seen, their values have been set to 0 and NULL respectively (by the constructor). They have been separated by a line in the box. Let us assume that the address of this node is 108. The value of the `temp` pointer will therefore be 108.

```
/*
    Set the value of val data member in the new node.
*/
temp -> setVal(10);
```

This statement will assign 10 to the `val` data member. Figure 9.9 shows the result diagrammatically.

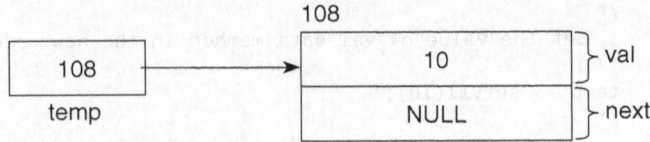

Figure 9.9   Effect of setVal() function

```
/*
    Create another fresh node and assign its address to
    another pointer.
*/
SingleLinkedListNode * temp1 = new SingleLinkedListNode();
```

This statement will create a new node and make the pointer temp1 point to it. Figure 9.10 shows the result diagrammatically.

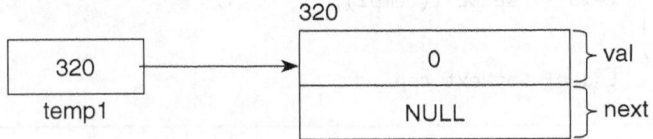

Figure 9.10   Creating a temporary node

No explanation is needed for the above figure because a similar statement has already been explained above.

```
/*
    Set the value of val data member in the new node.
*/
temp1 -> setVal(20);
```

This statement will assign 20 to the val data member. Figure 9.11 shows the result diagrammatically.

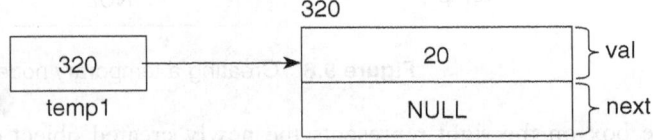

Figure 9.11   Effect of setVal() function

```
/*
    Make the next pointer of the existing node point at the
    freshly created node.
*/
temp -> setNext(temp1);
```

Figure 9.12 shows the result diagrammatically.

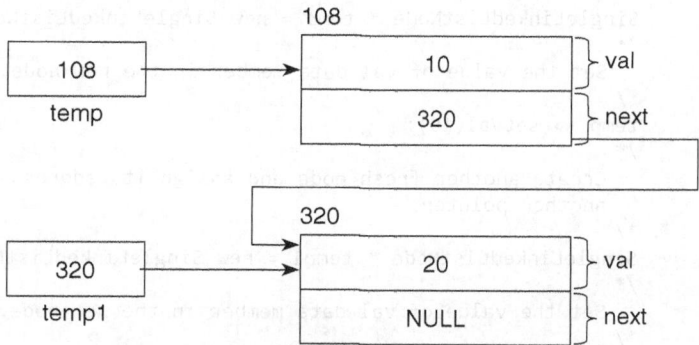

Figure 9.12 Effect of `setNext()` function

We can see from its definition that the `setNext()` function assigns the value of its parameter to the next data member of the object for which it has been called. In the above case, the function has been called for the object at which `temp` points. The value passed to it as parameter is the value of `temp1`, which is 320. As a result, the value of the `next` pointer of the object at which `temp` points is set to 320 and it now points at the freshly created node. You can already see a linked list getting created!

Now for the `getNext()` function.

```
/*
    This function returns the value of the next pointer.
*/
SingleLinkedListNode * SingleLinkedListNode::getNext()
{
    /*
        Return the value of the next pointer.
    */
    return next;
}
```

Again, this is a simple function. It simply returns the value of the `next` data member. Still continuing with our previous example, let us understand what happens when it is called (see Listing 9.7).

Listing 9.7 Executing the `getNext()` function

```
/*
    Beginning of GetNext.cpp
*/
#include <iostream.h>
#include "SingleLinkedListNode.h"

void main()
{
    /*
        Create a fresh node and assign its address to a
        pointer.
    */
```

```
SingleLinkedListNode * temp = new SingleLinkedListNode();
/*
   Set the value of val data member in the new node.
*/
temp -> setVal(10);
/*
   Create another fresh node and assign its address to
   another pointer.
*/
SingleLinkedListNode * temp1 = new SingleLinkedListNode();
/*
   Set the value of val data member in the new node.
*/
temp1 -> setVal(20);
/*
   Make the next pointer of the existing node point at the
   freshly created node.
*/
temp -> setNext(temp1);
/*
   Reset temp1 so that it points at the first node.
*/
temp1 = temp;
/*
   Display the value in the node that temp1 points at.
*/
cout << temp1->getVal() << endl;
/*
   Increment the temp1 pointer so that it points at the
   second node.
*/
temp1 = temp1 -> getNext();
/*
   Display the value in the node that temp1 points at.
*/
cout << temp1->getVal() << endl;
}
/*
   End of GetNext.cpp
*/
```

Output
```
10
20
```

We know that at the end of the statement

```
temp -> setNext(temp1);
```

the linked list looks like Figure 9.13.

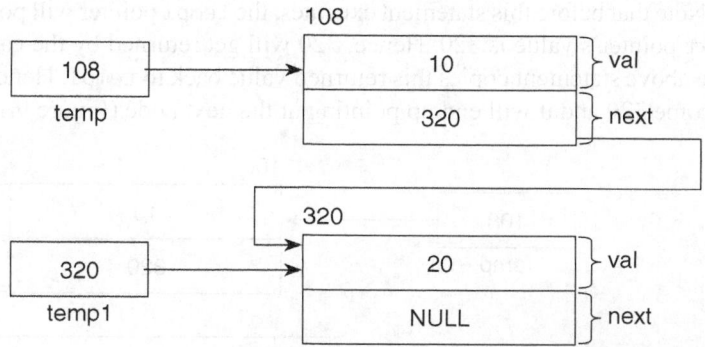

Figure 9.13   Effect of the setNext() function

Let us look at the rest of the statements.

```
/*
    Reset temp1 so that it points at the first node.
*/
temp1 = temp;
```

The above statement will copy the value of temp to temp1. This will cause temp1 to point at the same node as temp, which is the first node (Figure 9.14).

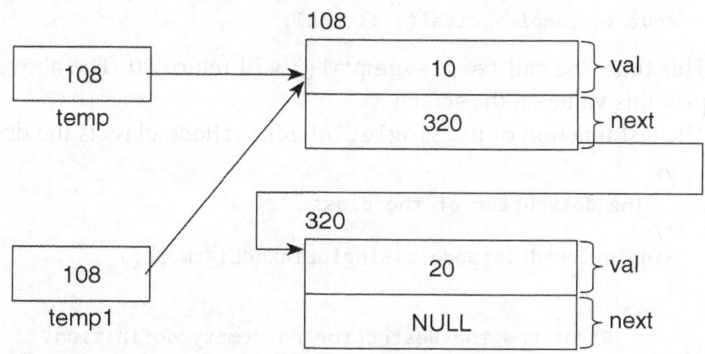

Figure 9.14   Copying the value of one temporary pointer to another.

After this, we have

```
/*
    Display the value in the node that temp1 points at.
*/
cout << temp1->getVal() << endl;
```

This time, the call temp1->getVal() will return 10. The above statement will therefore display this value on the screen.

Now, we get to look at a call to the getNext() function, which is the topic of our current discussion.

```
/*
    Increment the temp1 pointer so that it points at the
    second node.
*/
temp1 = temp1 -> getNext();
```

Note that before this statement executes, the `temp1` pointer will point at the first node, whose next pointer's value is 320. Hence, 320 will get returned by the call `temp1 -> getNext()`. The above statement copies this returned value back to `temp1`. Hence, the value of `temp1` will become 320 and it will end up pointing at the next node (Figure 9.15).

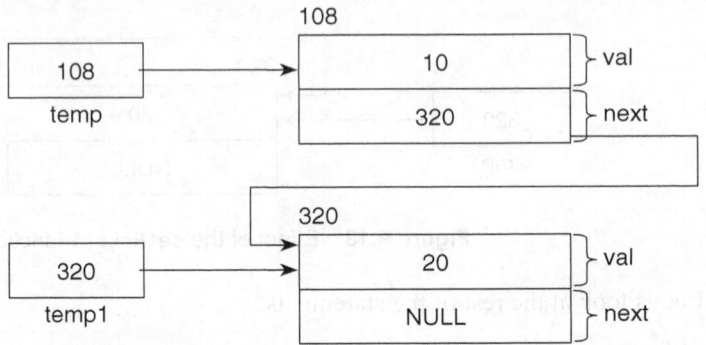

Figure 9.15   Incrementing the value of the temporary pointer

```
/*
    Display the value in the node that temp1 points at.
*/
cout << temp1->getVal() << endl;
```

This time, the call `temp1->getVal()` will return 20. The above statement will therefore display this value on the screen.

The last function of the `SingleLinkedListNode` class is the destructor.

```
/*
    The destructor of the class.
*/
SingleLinkedListNode::~SingleLinkedListNode()
{
    /*
        Right now the destructor has empty definition.
        But we may like to insert some statements here later.
    */
}
```

Like all destructors, this destructor gets called whenever the `delete` operator is called on a pointer that is defined to point at objects of the `SingleLinkedListNode` class. It gets called for the object at which such a pointer points. The block of heap memory occupied by the object at which the pointer points also gets deallocated.

Let us see what happens when the `delete` operator is called for the `temp` pointer, thereby triggering a call to the destructor for the object at which `temp` points (see Listing 9.8).

Listing 9.8   Executing the destructor of the single linked list node class

```
/*
    Beginning of NodeDestructor.cpp
*/
#include <iostream.h>
#include "SingleLinkedListNode.h"
```

```
void main()
{
    /*
        Create a fresh node and assign its address to a
        pointer.
    */
    SingleLinkedListNode * temp = new SingleLinkedListNode();
    /*
        Delete the memory occupied by the new node.
    */
    delete temp;
}
/*
    End of NodeDestructor.cpp
*/
```

Two things happen as a result of the last statement in the above program. One, the destructor is called for the object at which `temp` points. Second, the memory block occupied by the object at which `temp` points gets deallocated (is returned to the system for use). Since the destructor has a blank definition, no code gets executed.

Let us now study the linked list class. Let us start by looking at the header file of the linked list class (Listing 9.9).

Listing 9.9 Header file having declaration of single linked list class

```
/*
    Beginning of SingleLinkedList.h
*/
#ifndef _SINGLE_LINKED_LIST_H
#define _SINGLE_LINKED_LIST_H

#include "SingleLinkedListNode.h"

/*
    The single linked list class.
    Each instance of this class will represent a single
    linked list.
*/
class SingleLinkedList
{
    private:
        /*
            The head pointer. It will point at the first node of
            the list.
            It will be NULL when the list id empty.
        */
        SingleLinkedListNode * head;

    public:
        /*
            The constructor of the single linked list class. It
            will nullify the head pointer.
        */
        SingleLinkedList();
        /*
            Function to add a node at the bottom of the list.
        */
```

```
        void appendNode(int);
        /*
            Function to insert a node at the beginning of the
            list.
        */
        void prependNode(int);
        /*
            Function to find whether a node with a particular value
            exists or not.
        */
        bool find(int);
        /*
            Function to delete the first node.
        */
        void delBeg();
        /*
            Function to delete the last node.
        */
        void delEnd();
        /*
            Function to display the nodes in the list.
        */
        void display();
        /*
            The destructor of the class. It will delete the memory
            occupied by all nodes of the list.
        */
        ~SingleLinkedList();
    };

    #endif
    /*
        End of SingleLinkedList.h
    */
```

Just like the header file for the node class, this header file also begins with a comment that specifies the name of the header file and announces the beginning of the file. This is followed by pre-processor directives that prevent multiple inclusion of the header file in other source codes. This is followed by the declaration of the linked list class. The second last line of the header file contains the end of the pre-process block and the last line contains a comment that marks the end of the header file.

Each object of the SingleLinkedList class will be a linked list. This class has a data member, head, which is a pointer. It is obvious from its definition that head is supposed to point at the first node of the linked list. In our program, it will either be made to point at the first node in the linked list or will be assigned the NULL value (to indicate that the current list is empty).

Let us look at the implementation file (Listing 9.10) that contains the definitions of the member functions of the single linked list class.

Listing 9.10   Implementation file of single linked list

```
    /*
        Beginning of SingleLinkedList.cpp
    */
    #include <iostream.h>
```

```cpp
#include "SingleLinkedList.h"

/*
   The constructor of the single linked list class. It will
   nullify the head pointer.
*/
SingleLinkedList::SingleLinkedList()
{
   /*
      Nullify the head pointer by default.
   */
   head = NULL;
}

/*
   Function to add a node at the bottom of the list.
*/
void SingleLinkedList::appendNode(int pVal)
{
   /*
      Create a temporary node that we will append to the
      list.
      The constructor of SingleLinkedListNode class will
      nullify the next pointer of this node.
   */
   SingleLinkedListNode * temp = new SingleLinkedListNode();
   /*
      Copy the parameter value passed to the function, to the
      new node.
   */
   temp->setVal(pVal);
   /*
      If the head pointer is NULL (list is empty) ...
   */
   if(head == NULL)
   {
      /*
         ... make the head pointer point at the temporary node
         ...
      */
      head = temp;
   }
   /*
      ... otherwise ...
   */
   else
   {
      /*
         ... make a temporary pointer, ...
      */
      SingleLinkedListNode * iter;
      /*
         ... make it point at the first node, traverse to the
         end of the list and ...
      */
      for(iter = head; iter->getNext() != NULL;
                                    iter = iter->getNext());
      /*
```

```
        ... make the next pointer of the last node point at
        the temporary node.
    */
    iter->setNext(temp);
  }
}

/*
  Function to insert a node at the beginning of the list.
*/
void SingleLinkedList::prependNode(int pVal)
{
  /*
    Create a temporary node that we will prepend to the
    list.
    The constructor of SingleLinkedListNode class will
    nullify the next pointer of this node.
  */
  SingleLinkedListNode * temp = new SingleLinkedListNode();
  /*
    Copy the parameter value passed to the function, to the
    new node.
  */
  temp->setVal(pVal);
  /*
    If the head pointer is NULL (list is empty) ...
  */
  if(head == NULL)
  {
    /*
      ... make the head pointer point at the temporary node
      ...
    */
    head = temp;
  }
  /*
    ... otherwise ...
  */
  else
  {
    /*
      ... make the next pointer of the temporary node point
      at the first node and ...
    */
    temp->setNext(head);
    /*
      ... make the head pointer point at the temporary
      node.
    */
    head=temp;
  }
}

/*
  Function to display the nodes in the list.
*/
void SingleLinkedList::display()
{
```

```
    /*
        If the head pointer is NULL (list is empty) ...
    */
    if(head == NULL)
    {
        /*
            ... display error message ...
        */
        cout << "No nodes in list\n";
    }
    /*
        ... otherwise ...
    */
    else
    {
        /*
            ... make a temporary pointer point at the first node,
            iterate over the list and ...
        */
        for(SingleLinkedListNode * iter = head;iter != NULL;
                                    iter = iter->getNext())
        {
            /*
                ... display the value in the node being pointed
                at.
            */
            cout << iter->getVal() << endl;
        }
    }
}

/*
    Function to find whether a node with a particular value
    exists or not.
*/
bool SingleLinkedList::find(int pTarget)
{
    /*
        Initialize a flag to false, ...
    */
    bool found = false;
    /*
        ... make a temporary pointer point at the first node,
        iterate over the list and ...
    */
    for(SingleLinkedListNode * iter = head;iter != NULL;
        iter = iter->getNext())
    {
        /*
            ... if the value matches ...
        */
        if(iter->getVal() == pTarget)
        {
            /*
                ... set the flag to true and ...
            */
            found = true;
            /*
```

```
                    ... break the loop and ...
            */
            break;
        }
    }
    /*... return the value of the flag.*/
    return found;
}

/*
    Function to delete the first node.
*/
void SingleLinkedList::delBeg()
{
    /*
        Delete only if the list is empty.
    */
    if(head != NULL)
    {
        /*
            Make a temporary pointer point at the first node.
        */
        SingleLinkedListNode * temp = head;
        /*
            Make the head pointer point at the second node.
        */
        head = head -> getNext();        //head becomes NULL if only
                                         //one node in the list.
        /*
            Delete the first node.
        */
        delete temp;
    }
    /*
        Don't do anything if list is empty (no else).
    */
}

/*
    Function to delete the last node.
*/
void SingleLinkedList::delEnd()
{
    /*
        Delete only if the list is empty.
    */
    if(head != NULL)
    {
        /*
            If there is only one node ...
        */
        if(head -> getNext() == NULL)
        {
            /*
                ... delete it and ...
            */
            delete head;
            /*
```

```
            ... nullify the head pointer.
    */
    head = NULL;
}
/*
    ... otherwise ...
*/
else
{
    /*
        ... declare a temporary pointer, ...
    */
    SingleLinkedListNode * iter;
    /*
        ... iterate the list to point at the second last
            node, ...
    */
    for(iter = head;
        iter -> getNext() -> getNext() != NULL;
        iter = iter -> getNext());
    /*
        ... delete the last node and ...
    */
    delete iter -> getNext();
    /*
        ... nullify the next pointer of the second last
            node ...
    */
    iter -> setNext(NULL);
}
}
/*
    Don't do anything if list is empty (no else).
*/
}

/*
    The destructor of the class. It will delete the memory
    occupied by all nodes of the list.
*/
SingleLinkedList::~SingleLinkedList()
{
    /*
        Delete only if no nodes in the list.
    */
    if(head != NULL)
    {
        /*
            As long as the head pointer does not get a NULL value
            ...
        */
        while(head != NULL)
        {
            /*
                ... keep calling the delEnd() function to keep
                deleting the last node.
            */
            delEnd();
```

```
        }
    }
    /*
        Don't do anything if list is empty (no else).
    */
}
/*
    End of SingleLinkedList.cpp
*/
```

The implementation file begins with a comment that specifies the name of the implementation file and also announces the beginning of the file. This is followed by an include directive that includes the header file, which contains the declaration of the linked list class. This is followed by the definitions of the member functions of the linked list class. The last line contains a comment that marks the end of the implementation file.

Let us start with the constructor of the linked list class. After this we will study the appendNode() function. This will be followed by a study of the display() function. The rest of the functions will follow thereafter.

```
/*
    The constructor of the single linked list class. It will
    nullify the head pointer.
*/
SingleLinkedList::SingleLinkedList()
{
    /*
        Nullify the head pointer by default.
    */
    head = NULL;
}
```

As a result of the constructor, whenever an object of the SingleLinkedList class is created, the value of its head data member will be set to NULL. Nullifying the pointer will make it easier for us to define the rest of the functions because we can be sure that the value of the head pointer will be NULL for any new object of the linked list class. Let us understand the constructor with the help of an example. Suppose a new object of the linked list class is created as shown in Listing 9.11.

Listing 9.11 Executing the constructor of the single linked list class

```
/*
    Beginning of ListConstructor.cpp
*/
#include "SingleLinkedList.h"

void main()
{
    /*Create a list object*/
    SingleLinkedList list1;
}
/*
    End of ListConstructor.cpp
*/
```

The result can be diagrammatically represented as shown in Figure 9.16.

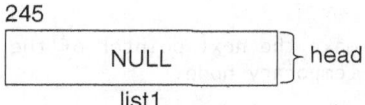

Figure 9.16   Effects of the list class constructor

list1 is an object of the SingleLinkedList class. The box depicts the memory block occupied by list1. It is evident from the definition of the SingleLinkedList class that an object of the class will have only one data member. The name of this data member is head. The constructor of the class will fire at the time the object is created. It will set the value of the head pointer to NULL.

Let us look at the next function appendNode().

```
/*
    Function to add a node at the bottom of the list.
*/
void SingleLinkedList::appendNode(int pVal)
{
    /*
        Create a temporary node that we will append to the
        list.
        The constructor of SingleLinkedListNode class will
        nullify the next pointer of this node.
    */
    SingleLinkedListNode * temp = new SingleLinkedListNode();
    /*
        Copy the parameter value passed to the function, to the
        new node.
    */
    temp->setVal(pVal);
    /*
        If the head pointer is NULL (list is empty) ...
    */
    if(head == NULL)
    {
        /*
            ... make the head pointer point at the temporary node
            ...
        */
        head = temp;
    }
    /*
        ... otherwise ...
    */
    else
    {
        /*
            ... make a temporary pointer, ...
        */
        SingleLinkedListNode * iter;
        /*
            ... make it point at the first node, traverse to the
            end of the list and ...
        */
        for(iter = head; iter->getNext() != NULL;
            iter = iter->getNext());
```

```
        /*
           ... make the next pointer of the last node point at
           the temporary node.
        */
        iter->setNext(temp);
    }
}
```

The above function is designed to add a node to the linked list. Let us first understand what we will like the above function to do. Then, by studying the definition of the function (Listing 9.12), we will decide whether it actually does what we want it to do or not.

Listing 9.12 Executing the appendNode() function

```
/*
   Beginning of AppendNode01.cpp
*/
#include "SingleLinkedList.h"

void main()
{
    /*
       Create a list object
    */
    SingleLinkedList list1;
    /*
       Call the appendNode() function on the list1 object.
    */
    list1.appendNode(5287);
}
/*
   End of AppendNode01.cpp
*/
```

After the first statement in the above program, because of the constructor of the SingleLinkedList class, the value of the head pointer inside the object will be set to NULL. This can be depicted by Figure 9.17.

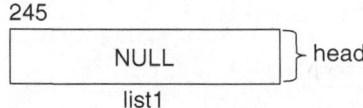

Figure 9.17 Effects of the list class constructor

The above box depicts the object named list1 (labelled at the bottom of the box). Since it is an object of the SingleLinkedList class, it has only one data member—head (labelled on the right of the box). The constructor of the class sets the head data member to NULL.

Let us look at the call to the appendNode() function on the list1 object.

```
list1.appendNode(5287);
```

If the function has been defined correctly, then, at the end of its execution, the linked list should look like Figure 9.18.

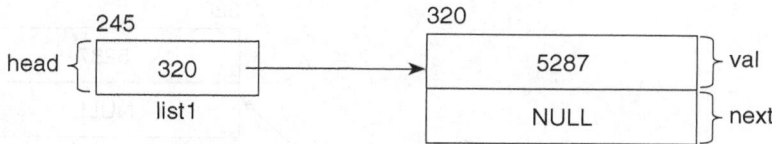

Figure 9.18   Expected effect of the appendNode() function

Let us see whether the function performs as expected or not. Before the function executes, the value of the head pointer is NULL. When the function starts executing, the value of the function's parameter pVal gets set to 5287 because that is the value that has been passed to the function. After this, a temporary node gets created by the new operator and the temporary pointer temp is made to point at it (Figure 9.19).

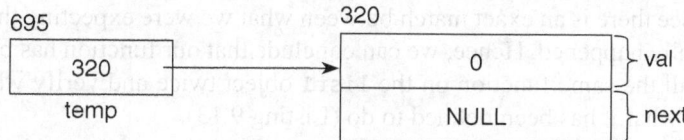

Figure 9.19   The creation of a temporary node that will be added to the list by the appendNode() function

The next statement is:

```
temp->setVal(pVal);
```

This will copy the value of pVal, which is 5287, to the val data member of the node. After this, the if statement will check whether the value of the head pointer is NULL or not. This test will return true at this time because the list is empty. The if block will execute and the value of temp will be copied to head. This will cause the head pointer to also point at the temporary node that has been created earlier. Figure 9.20 illustrates this.

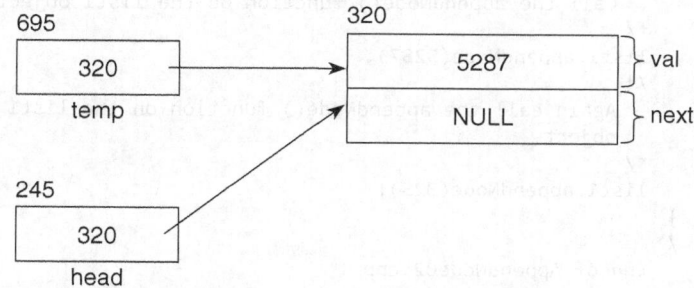

Figure 9.20   Value of the temp pointer copied to the head pointer

The else block will not execute and the function will come to an end. Since temp is a local variable, it goes out of scope and what we will be left with is a linked list that looks like Figure 9.21.

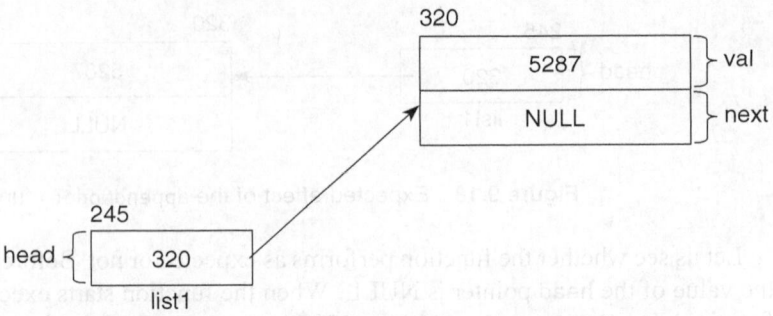

Figure 9.21 Observed effect of the appendNode() function

Compare Figure 9.21 with Figure 9.18, which depicts what we were expecting. As you can see there is an exact match between what we were expecting the function to do and what actually happened. Hence, we can conclude that our function has been defined correctly. Let us call the same function on the list1 object twice and verify whether or not the function does what it has been defined to do (Listing 9.13).

Listing 9.13   Executing the appendNode() function

```
/*
   Beginning of AppendNode02.cpp
*/
#include "SingleLinkedList.h"

void main()
{
   /*
      Create a list object
   */
   SingleLinkedList list1;
   /*
      Call the appendNode() function on the list1 object.
   */
   list1.appendNode(5287);
   /*
      Again call the appendNode() function on the list1
      object.
   */
   list1.appendNode(325);
}
/*
   End of AppendNode02.cpp
*/
```

At the end of the execution of the above program, we will expect the linked list to look like Figure 9.22.

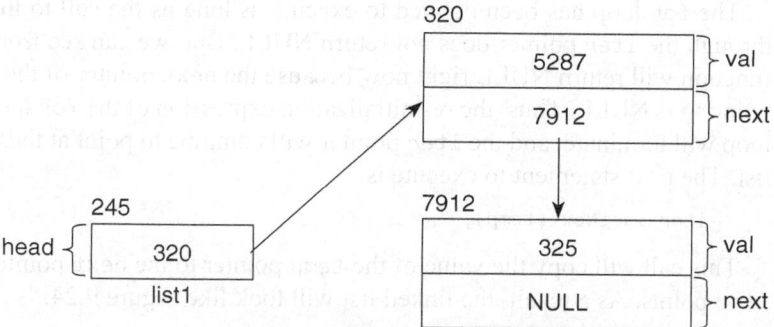

Figure 9.22   Expected effect of the appendNode() function

Let us trace the function once more and see whether it does what we want it to do or not. Let us start from the second call to the function because we have already seen the effects of the previous portion of the program.

Keep in mind that the head pointer is NOT NULL when the function is called for a second time. The execution is the same as the previous one till the point where the if statement checks whether the value of the head pointer is NULL or not. This test will return false this time because the list is not empty. The if block will not execute. Instead, the else block will execute. The first statement of the else block declares a pointer called iter that is supposed to point at objects of the class SingleLinkedListNode. Note that the for loop does not have a body. At the start of the loop, the value of the head pointer is copied to the pointer iter. Thus, iter ends up pointing at the first node of the list. The resulting situation is depicted by Figure 9.23.

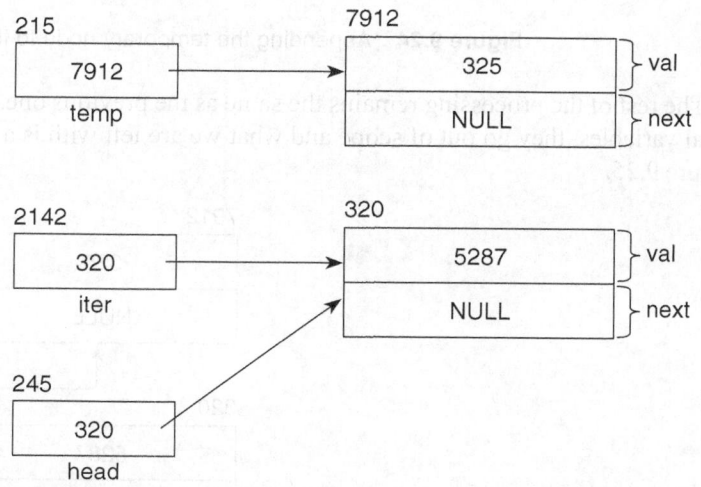

Figure 9.23   The temporary node and the iterator iterating over the list

The statements before the if statement will create a node and make a temporary pointer, called temp, to point at the node. This is depicted by the upper half of the above figure. The head pointer will already be pointing at the one and only node in the list that was created by the previous call to the appendNode() function. Now, the value of the head pointer has been copied to the pointer called iter. Hence, iter will also point at the first node of the list.

The for loop has been defined to execute as long as the call to the getNext() function through the iter pointer does not return NULL. But, we can see from Figure 9.23 that this function will return NULL right now because the next pointer of the node at which iter is pointing is NULL. Thus, the re-initialization expression of the for loop will not execute, the loop will terminate, and the iter pointer will continue to point at the first node of the linked list. The next statement to execute is:

```
iter->setNext(temp);
```

This call will copy the value of the temp pointer to the next pointer of the node at which iter points. As a result, the linked list will look like Figure 9.24.

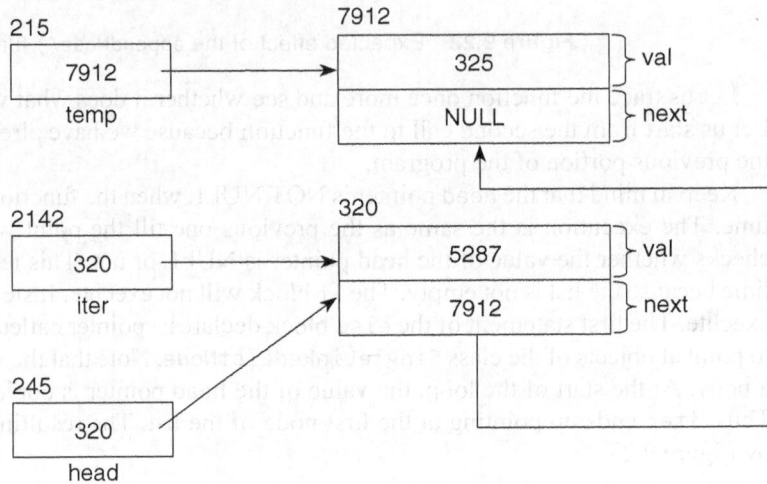

Figure 9.24 Appending the temporary node to the list

The rest of the processing remains the same as the previous one. Since temp and iter are local variables, they go out of scope and what we are left with is a linked list that looks like Figure 9.25.

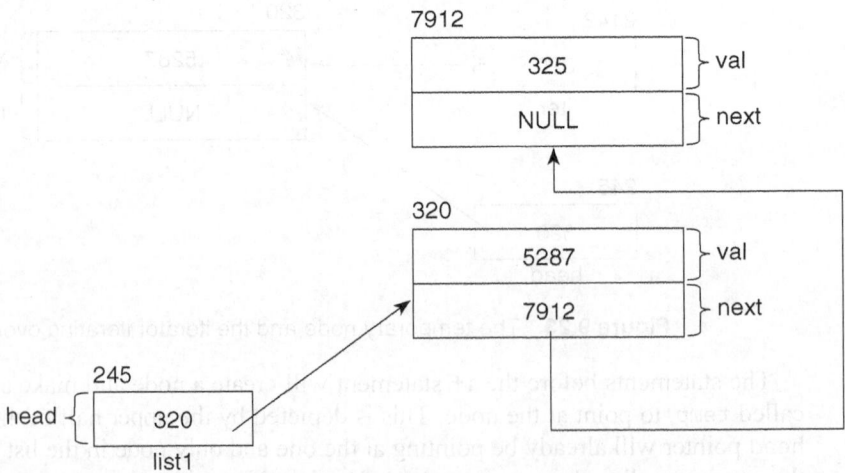

Figure 9.25 Observed effect of the appendNode() function

Compare Figure 9.25 with Figure 9.22, which depicts what we were expecting. As you can see there is an exact match between what we were expecting the function to do and what actually happened. Hence, we can again conclude that our function has been defined correctly.

Now, go ahead and verify that the function has been defined correctly by finding out what will happen if the function is called for yet another time on the same object.

Let us now try to understand the `display()` function.

```
/*
    Function to display the nodes in the list.
*/
void SingleLinkedList::display()
{
    /*
        If the head pointer is NULL (list is empty) ...
    */
    if(head == NULL)
    {
        /*
            ... display error message ...
        */
        cout << "No nodes in list\n";
    }
    /*
        ... otherwise ...
    */
    else
    {
        /*
            ... make a temporary pointer point at the first node,
            iterate over the list and ...
        */
        for(SingleLinkedListNode * iter = head;iter != NULL;
            iter = iter->getNext())
        {
            /*
                ... display the value in the node being pointed at.
            */
            cout << iter->getVal() << endl;
        }
    }
}
```

As before, let us start with a new object of the linked list class, which will create an empty list, and then call the `display()` function on the new object (Listing 9.14). We will thereafter compare the actual execution with the expected execution.

Listing 9.14 Executing the `display()` function

```
/*
    Beginning of ListDisplay01.cpp
*/
#include "SingleLinkedList.h"

void main()
{
    /*
        Create a list object.
```

```
    */
    SingleLinkedList list1;
    /*
        Display the contents.
    */
    list1.display();
}
/*
    End of ListDisplay01.cpp
*/
```

Output

No nodes in list

Since the list is empty, we will expect the function to display a message that says that the list is empty. Let us see whether this happens or not.

Note that the value of the head pointer inside the list1 object will get set to NULL at the time of creation because of the constructor. Hence, it will be NULL at the time the display() function gets called.

Now, when the function begins executing, the if block compares the value of the head pointer with NULL. Since the value of the head pointer is NULL, the test expression in the if statement returns true. Therefore, the if block executes. This causes the string 'No nodes in list' to get displayed on the monitor. Naturally, the else block does not execute and the function comes to an end. And this is what we were expecting.

Let us take the other case where the list is not empty (Listing 9.15).

Listing 9.15 Executing the display() function

```
/*
    Beginning of ListDisplay02.cpp
*/
#include "SingleLinkedList.h"

void main()
{
    /*
        Create a list object.
    */
    SingleLinkedList list1;
    /*
        Add a node to the list.
    */
    list1.appendNode(5287);
    /*
        Add another node.
    */
    list1.appendNode(325);
    /*
        Display the contents.
    */
    list1.display();
}
/*
    End of ListDisplay02.cpp
*/
```

Output
5287
325

We now know that after the second call to the appendNode() function above, the linked list will look like Figure 9.26.

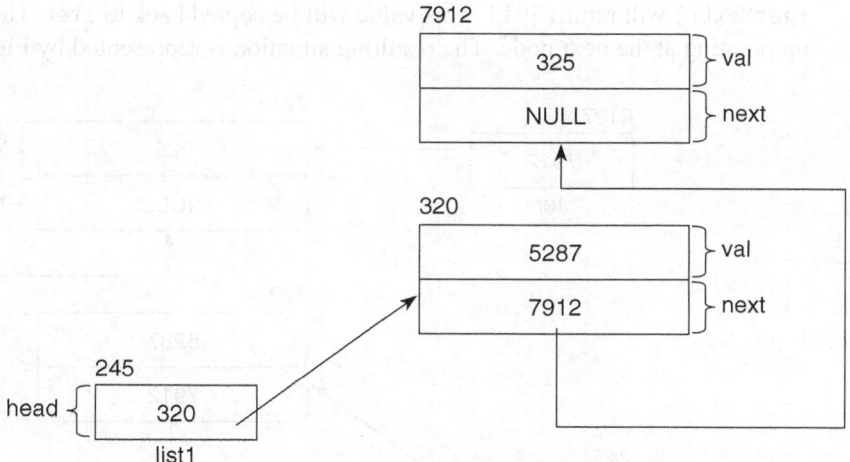

Figure 9.26   The list as it looks before the display() function executes

As a result of the call to the display() function, we will expect the values in the nodes 5287 and 325 to get displayed on the monitor. Let us see whether this happens or not.

Note that the head pointer is not NULL in this case. Therefore, the if block in the function will not execute. Instead, the else block will execute. This will cause the for loop to start. The value of the head pointer will get copied to the temporary pointer called iter. The resulting situation is represented by Figure 9.27.

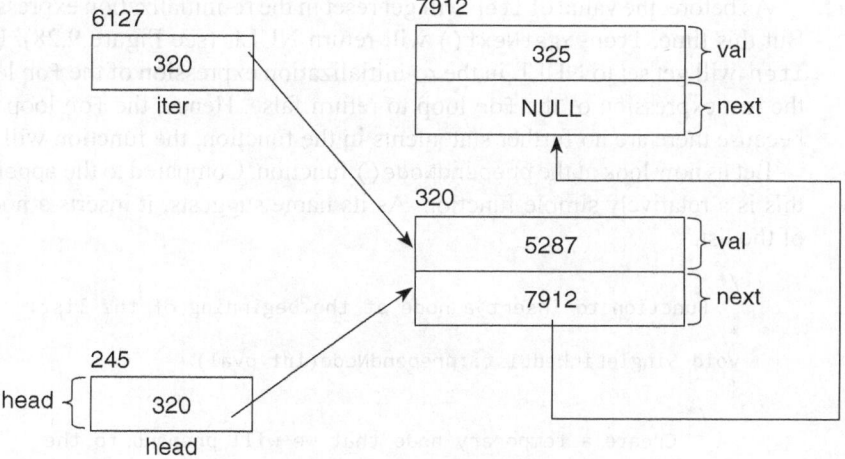

Figure 9.27   Iterator iterating over the list

We can see that the value of iter is not NULL. Hence, the test expression of the for loop will return true. This will cause the body of the loop to execute. The statement in the loop's body is:

```
cout << iter->getVal() << endl;
```

iter->getVal() will return 5287. Hence, the above statement will display 5287 on the monitor. Thereafter, the re-initialization expression of the for loop will execute. iter->getNext() will return 7912. This value will be copied back to iter. Hence, iter will end up pointing at the next node. The resulting situation is represented by Figure 9.28.

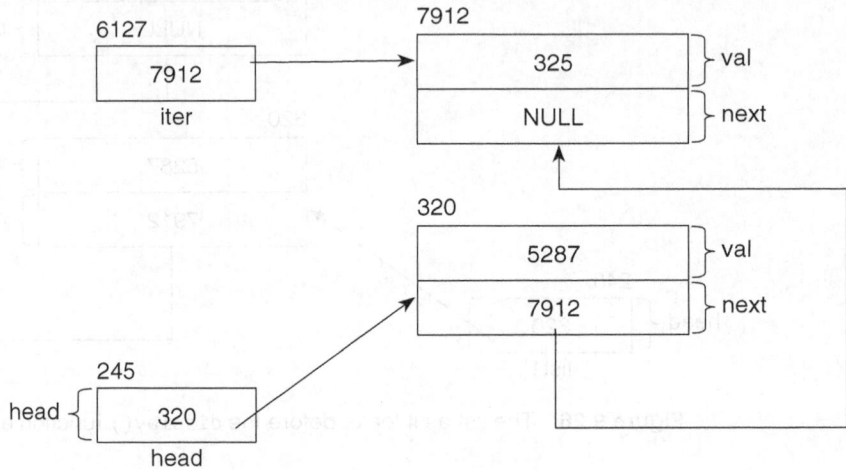

Figure 9.28   Iterator iterating over the list

Next, the test expression of the for loop will execute once more. Since iter is still not NULL, the test expression will again return true. This will cause the loop to execute once more. But this time, iter->getVal() will return 325. Hence, 325 will be displayed on the computer's monitor.

As before, the value of iter will get reset in the re-initialization expression of the for loop. But this time, iter->getNext() will return NULL (see Figure 9.28). Hence, the value of iter will get set to NULL in the re-initialization expression of the for loop. This will cause the test expression of the for loop to return false. Hence, the for loop will terminate and, because there are no further statements in the function, the function will also terminate.

Let us now look at the prependNode() function. Compared to the appendNode() function, this is a relatively simple function. As its name suggests, it inserts a node at the beginning of the list.

```
/*
   Function to insert a node at the beginning of the list.
*/
void SingleLinkedList::prependNode(int pVal)
{
   /*
      Create a temporary node that we will prepend to the
      list.
      The constructor of SingleLinkedListNode class will
      nullify the next pointer of this node.
```

```
    */
    SingleLinkedListNode * temp = new SingleLinkedListNode();
    /*
        Copy the parameter value passed to the function, to the
        new node.
    */
    temp->setVal(pVal);
    /*
        If the head pointer is NULL (list is empty) ...
    */
    if(head == NULL)
    {
        /*
            ... make the head pointer point at the temporary node
            ...
        */
        head = temp;
    }
    /*
        ... otherwise ...
    */
    else
    {
        /*
            ... make the next pointer of the temporary node point
            at the first node and ...
        */
        temp->setNext(head);
        /*
            ... make the head pointer point at the temporary
            node.
        */
        head=temp;
    }
}
```

As before, let us first understand what we would like the above function to do (Listing 9.16). Then, by studying the definition of the function, we will decide whether it actually does what we want it to do or not.

Listing 9.16 Executing the prependNode() function

```
/*
    Beginning of PrependNode01.cpp
*/
#include "SingleLinkedList.h"

void main()
{
    /*Create a list object*/
    SingleLinkedList list1;
    /*
        Call the prependNode() function on the list1 object.
    */
    list1.prependNode(5287);
```

```
    }
    /*
        End of PrependNode01.cpp
    */
```

After the first statement in the above program, because of the constructor of the `SingleLinkedList` class, the value of the `head` pointer inside the object will be set to NULL. This is depicted by Figure 9.29.

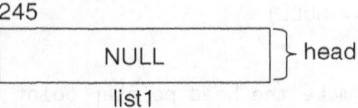

245

NULL   — head

list1

Figure 9.29   Empty list prior to the call to the `prependNode()` function

The box shown in the figure depicts the object named `list1` (labelled at the bottom of the box). Since it is an object of the `SingleLinkedList` class, it has only one data member—head (labelled on the right of the box). The constructor of the class sets the `head` data member to NULL.

Let us look at the call to the `prependNode()` function on the `list1` object.

```
    list1.prependNode(5287);
```

If the function has been defined correctly, then, at the end of its execution, the linked list should look like Figure 9.30.

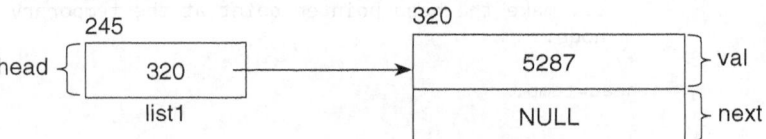

Figure 9.30   Expected effect of the `prependNode()` function

Let us see whether the function performs as expected or not. Before the function executes, the value of the `head` pointer is NULL. When the function starts executing, the value of the function's parameter `pVal` gets set to 5287 because that is the value that has been passed to the function. After this, a temporary node gets created by the new operator and the temporary pointer `temp` is made to point at it (Figure 9.31).

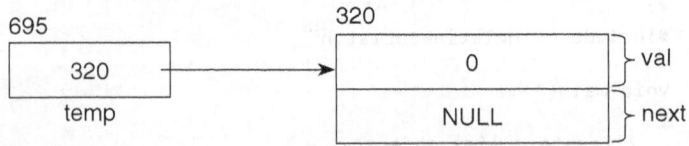

Figure 9.31   Creation of a temporary blank node

The next statement is:

```
    temp->setVal(pVal);
```

This will copy the value of pVal, which is 5287, to the data member of the node. After this, the test expression in the if statement will check whether the value of the head pointer is NULL or not. This test will return true at this time because the list is empty. The if block will execute and the value of temp will be copied to head. This will cause the head pointer to also point at the temporary node that has been created earlier. Figure 9.32 illustrates this.

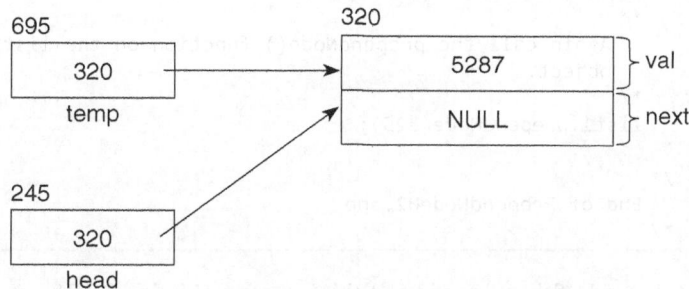

Figure 9.32   Initialization of the temporary node and making the head pointer point at it

The else block will not execute and the function will come to an end. Since temp is a local variable, it goes out of scope and what we will be left with is a linked list that looks like Figure 9.33.

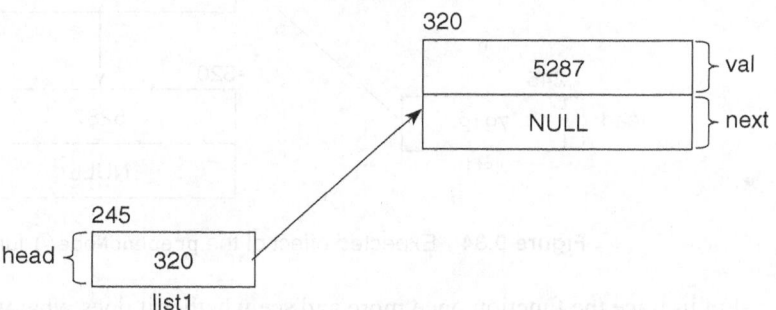

Figure 9.33   Observed effect of the prependNode() function

Compare Figure 9.33 with Figure 9.30, which depicts what we were expecting. As you can see there is an exact match between what we were expecting the function to do and what actually happened.

Let us call the same function on the list1 object twice (Listing 9.17) and verify whether or not the function does what it has been defined to do.

Listing 9.17   Executing the prependNode() function

```
/*
    Beginning of PrependNode02.cpp
*/
#include "SingleLinkedList.h"

void main()
{
    /*
```

```
        Create a list object
    */
    SingleLinkedList list1;
    /*
        Call the prependNode() function on the list1 object.
    */
    list1.prependNode(5287);
    /*
        Again call the prependNode() function on the list1
        object.
    */
    list1.prependNode(325);
}
/*
    End of PrependNode02.cpp
*/
```

At the end of the execution of this program (Listing 9.17), we will expect the linked list to look like Figure 9.34.

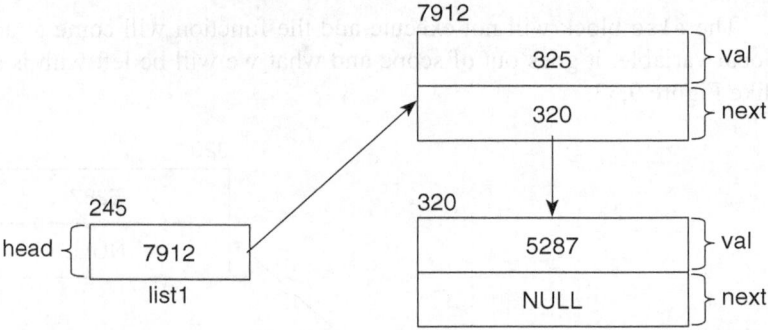

Figure 9.34 Expected effect of the prependNode() function

Let us trace the function once more and see whether it does what we want it to do or not. Let us start from the second call to the function because we have already seen the effects of the previous portion of the program. At this point, the linked list looks like this.

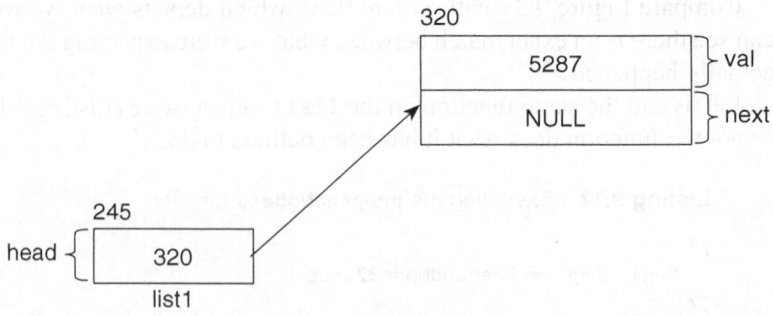

Figure 9.35 Addition of the first node by the prependNode() function

At this point, the function is called for the second time. Notice that the head pointer is *not* NULL at this time (its value is 320, which is the address of the first node at which it points).

The execution is the same as the previous one till the point where the test expression in the if statement checks whether the value of the head pointer is NULL or not. This test will return false this time because the list is not empty. The if block will not execute. Instead, the else block will execute. The first statement of the else block copies the value of the head pointer to the next pointer of the temporary node created at the beginning of the function. The resulting situation can be depicted by Figure 9.36.

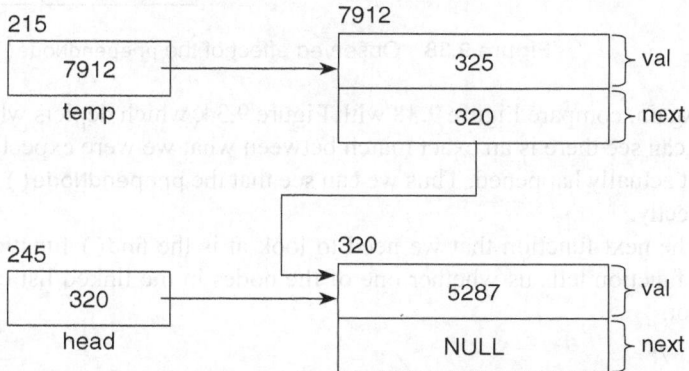

Figure 9.36 Linking of the new node to the old node

The next statement copies the value of the temp pointer to the head pointer. Thus, the head pointer ends up pointing at the temporary node. Figure 9.37 depicts this situation.

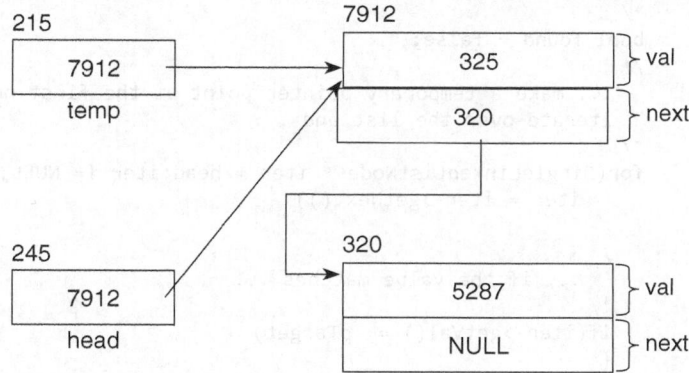

Figure 9.37 Making the head pointer point at the new temporary node

Since temp is a local variable, it goes out of scope and what we will be left with is a linked list that looks like Figure 9.38.

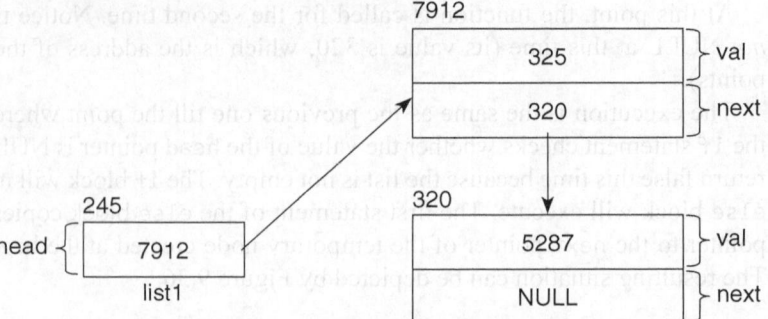

Figure 9.38 Observed effect of the `prependNode()` function

Again, compare Figure 9.38 with Figure 9.34, which depicts what we were expecting. As you can see there is an exact match between what we were expecting the function to do and what actually happened. Thus we can see that the `prependNode()` function has been defined correctly.

The next function that we need to look at is the find() function. As its name suggests, this function tells us whether one of the nodes in the linked list contains a particular value or not.

```
/*
    Function to find whether a node with a particular value
    exists or not.
*/
bool SingleLinkedList::find(int pTarget)
{
    /*
        Initialize a flag to false, ...
    */
    bool found = false;
    /*
        ... make a temporary pointer point at the first node,
        iterate over the list and ...
    */
    for(SingleLinkedListNode * iter = head;iter != NULL;
        iter = iter->getNext())
    {
        /*
            ... if the value matches ...
        */
        if(iter->getVal() == pTarget)
        {
            /*
                                            ... set the flag to true and ...
            */
            found = true;
            /*
                                            ... break the loop and ...
            */
            break;
        }
    }
    /*
```

```
    ... return the value of the flag.
    */
    return found;
}
```

Let us look at a program that calls this function and the expected output (Listing 9.18). We will then analyse the function's definition and verify whether it can give the expected output or not.

Listing 9.18   Executing the find() function (Note: On the computer used to execute this function, 1 gets displayed instead of true and 0 gets displayed instead of false.)

```cpp
/*
    Beginning of ListNodeFind.cpp
*/
#include "SingleLinkedList.h"

void main()
{
    /*
        Create a list object
    */
    SingleLinkedList list1;
    /*
        Declare a Boolean variable to store the result of our
        search.
    */
    bool result;
    /*
        Call the prependNode() function on the list1 object.
    */
    list1.prependNode(5287);
    /*
        Call the find() function on the list1 object.
    */
    result = list1.find(5287);
    /*
        Display the result.
    */
    cout << result << endl;
    /*
        Again call the find() function on the list1 object.
    */
    result = list1.find(325);
    /*
        Display the result.
    */
    cout << result << endl;
}
    /*
        End of ListNodeFind.cpp
    */
```

Output

1
0

We will expect the first call to the find() function to return true because the value that has been passed to it (5287) should exist in the list as a result of the call to the prependNode() function in the previous statement. Because 325 has not been inserted to the list, we will also expect the second call to the find() function to return false.

Let us now look at the function and see whether it is capable of giving us the results we are expecting.

We know that when the find() function is called for the first time, the linked list looks like Figure 9.39 (because of the previous call to the prependNode() function).

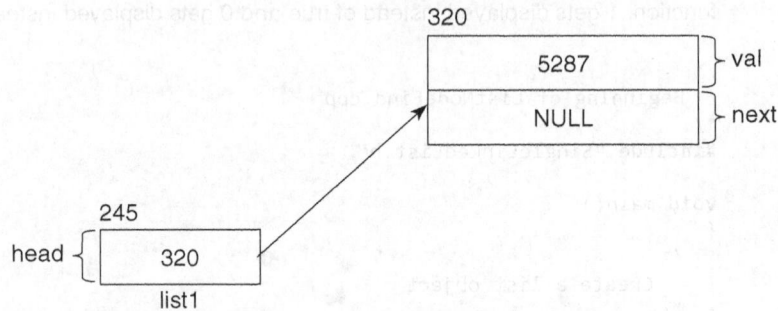

Figure 9.39 What the linked list looks like before the call to the find() function

The value passed to the function, 5287, gets copied to the parameter pTarget. Next, a local variable, found, gets created and initialized to false. After this, the for loop starts. The temporary pointer iter gets created and the value of the head pointer gets copied to it. Hence, it ends up pointing at the first node. The resulting scenario is depicted by Figure 9.40.

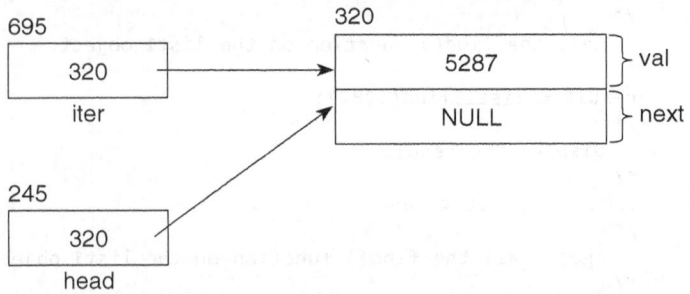

Figure 9.40 Iterator iterating over the list

The test expression of the for loop will return true because the value of iter is not NULL (its value is 320). The test expression of the if block will get evaluated. The expression 'iter->getVal() will return 5287. Because the value of pTarget is also 5287, the test expression will return true. The first statement in the if block will set the value of the variable found to true. The second statement will cause the loop to break. The only remaining statement in the function will return the value of found, which is true.

When the find() function is called for the second time, the value of pTarget will be 325. The processing will be the same as the previous execution of the function till the point where the for loop executes for the first time. The local variable, found, will get created and initialized to false. After this, the for loop will start. The temporary pointer iter will get created and the value of the head pointer will get copied to it. Hence, it will end up pointing at the first node. The resulting scenario will be the same as before (Figure 9.41).

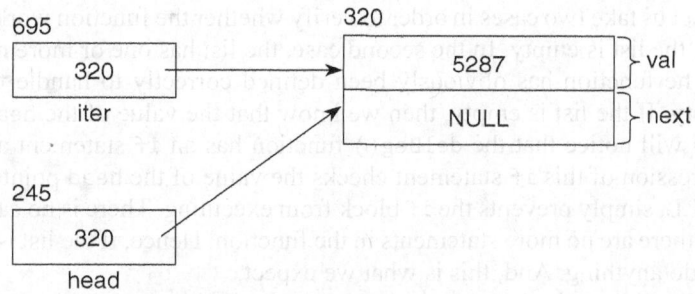

Figure 9.41 Iterator iterating over the list

The test expression of the for loop will return true because the value of iter is not NULL (its value is 320). The test expression of the if block will get evaluated. The expression iter->getVal() will return 5287. Because the value of pTarget is also 325, the test expression will return false. Therefore, the if block will not execute. And there is no else block. The re-initialization expression of the loop will execute. The expression iter->getNext() will return NULL. Therefore, the value of iter will become NULL.

Now, when the loop executes again, its test expression returns false because the value of iter is now NULL. The loop terminates and the function returns the value of the variable found, which has remained false. Thus, we can see that the find() function has been defined in the way we expect it.

The next function to be studied is delBeg(). As the name indicates, this function will delete the first node from the list, if it exists.

```
/*
    Function to delete the first node.
*/
void SingleLinkedList::delBeg()
{
    /*
        Delete only if the list is empty.
    */
    if(head != NULL)
    {
        /*
            Make a temporary pointer point at the first node.
        */
        SingleLinkedListNode * temp = head;
        /*
            Make the head pointer point at the second node.
        */
        head = head -> getNext();      //head becomes NULL if only
                                       //one node in the list.
        /*
            Delete the first node.
        */
        delete temp;
    }
}
```

```
    /*
        Don't do anything if list is empty (no else).
    */
}
```

Let us take two cases in order to verify whether the function works correctly or not. In case one, the list is empty. In the second case, the list has one or more nodes.

The function has obviously been defined correctly to handle the case where the list is empty. If the list is empty, then we know that the value of the head pointer will be NULL. You will notice that the delBeg() function has an if statement at the beginning. The test expression of this if statement checks the value of the head pointer and, if it finds that it is NULL, simply prevents the if block from executing. There is no else block for the if block and there are no more statements in the function. Hence, if the list is empty, the function does not do anything. And, this is what we expect.

Now, let us take the other case where the list is not empty. Let us look at a sample execution of the function and see whether the function executes as expected or not. Consider Listing 9.19.

Listing 9.19   Executing the delBeg() function

```
/*
    Beginning of DelBeg.cpp
*/
#include "SingleLinkedList.h"

void main()
{
    /*
        Create a list object
    */
    SingleLinkedList list1;
    /*
        Call the prependNode() function on the list1 object.
    */
    list1.prependNode(5287);
    /*
        Again call the prependNode() function on the list1
        object.
    */
    list1.prependNode(325);
    /*
        Delete the first node
    */
    list1.delBeg();
    /*
        Display the values in the list.
    */
    list1.display();
}
/*
    End of DelBeg.cpp
*/
```

Output

5287

We know that after the second call to the prependNode() function, the list will look like Figure 9.42.

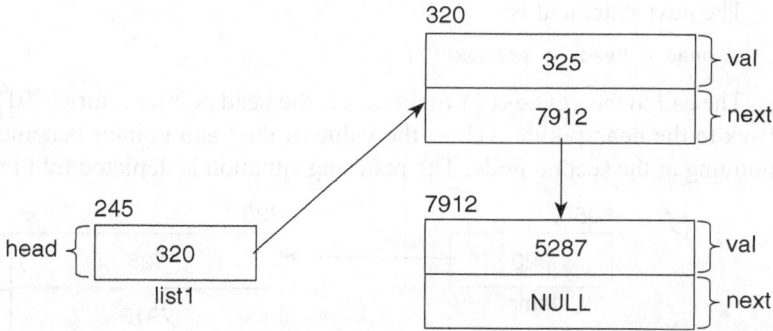

Figure 9.42   The structure of the list prior to the call to the delBeg() function

The delBeg() function has been called at this point in the program. At the end of its execution, we will expect the list to look like Figure 9.43.

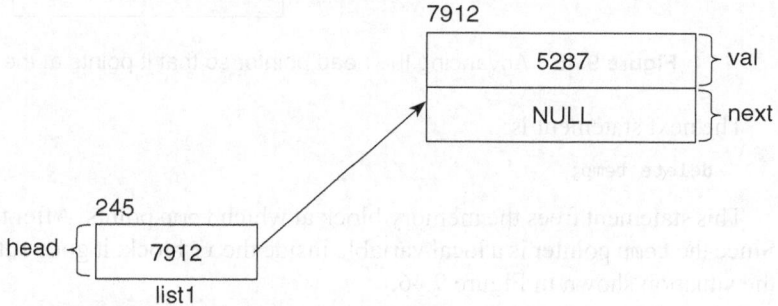

Figure 9.43   Expected effect of the delBeg() function

Let us review the function and see whether it has been defined correctly or not. When the delBeg() function starts, the test expression of the if statement gets evaluated. It checks whether the value of the head pointer is NULL or not. At this point, the value of the head pointer is 320 (it points at the first of two nodes that are currently in the list). Therefore, the test expression returns true and the if block executes.

The first statement in the if block declares a temporary pointer and copies the value of the head pointer to it. Figure 9.44 depicts the resulting situation.

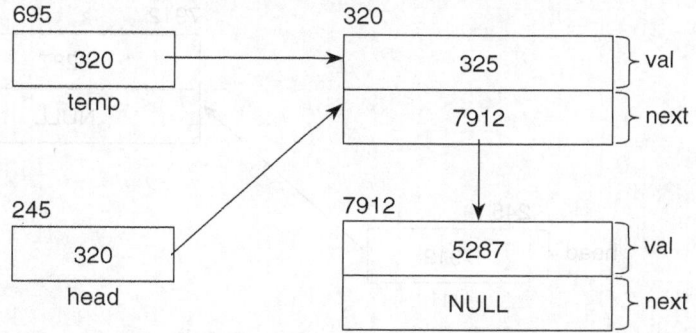

Figure 9.44   Making a temporary pointer point at the node to be deleted

The next statement is:

```
head = head -> getNext();
```

The call to the getNext() function via the head pointer returns 7912. This value is copied back to the head pointer. Thus, the value of the head pointer becomes 7912 and it ends up pointing at the second node. The resulting situation is depicted by Figure 9.45.

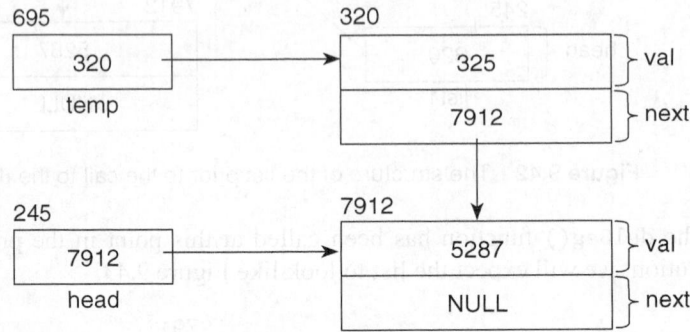

Figure 9.45   Advancing the head pointer so that it points at the second node

The next statement is:

```
delete temp;
```

This statement frees the memory block at which temp points. After this, the if block ends. Since the temp pointer is a local variable inside the if block, it goes out of scope and we have the situation shown in Figure 9.46.

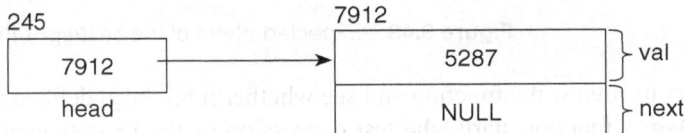

Figure 9.46   The linked list after the temporary pointer has deleted the first node and has itself gone out of scope

The delBeg() has no more statements after the if block. Hence, it comes to an end and we have the scenario shown in Figure 9.47.

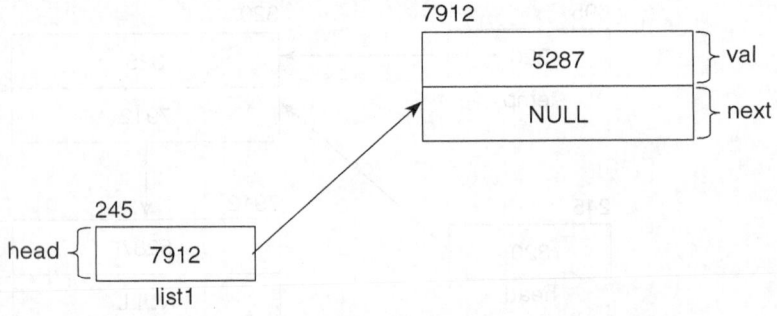

Figure 9.47   Observed effect of the delBeg() function

Compare Figure 9.47 with Figure 9.43. You can see that the delBeg() function did what we were expecting it to do.

Let us now study the delEnd() function. As the name suggests, this function deletes the last node from the list. Compared to the delBeg() function, this a slightly complicated function.

```
/*
   Function to delete the last node.
*/
void SingleLinkedList::delEnd()
{
    /*
       Delete only if the list is empty.
    */
    if(head != NULL)
    {
        /*
           If there is only one node ...
        */
        if(head -> getNext() == NULL)
        {
            /*
               ... delete it and ...
            */
            delete head;
            /*
               ... nullify the head pointer.
            */
            head = NULL;
        }
        /*
           ... otherwise ...
        */
        else
        {
            /*
               ... declare a temporary pointer, ...
            */
            SingleLinkedListNode * iter;
            /*
               ... iterate the list to point at the second last
               node, ...
            */
            for(iter = head; iter -> getNext() -> getNext() !=
                NULL; iter = iter -> getNext());
            /*
               ... delete the last node and ...
            */
            delete iter -> getNext();
            /*
               ... nullify the next pointer of the second last
               node ...
            */
            iter -> setNext(NULL);
        }
    }
    /*
       Don't do anything if list is empty (no else).
    */
}
```

The function is supposed to ideally delete the last node under three different circumstances—list is empty, list has exactly one node, and list has more than one node.

The case where the list is empty is handled in exactly the same way as it was handled by the delBeg() function. No further explanation is needed.

Let us take the case where there is exactly one node in the list. Consider Listing 9.20.

Listing 9.20 Executing the delEnd() function

```
/*
   Beginning of DelEnd01.cpp
*/
#include "SingleLinkedList.h"

void main()
{
   /*
      Create a list object
   */
   SingleLinkedList list1;
   /*
      Call the prependNode() function on the list1 object.
   */
   list1.prependNode(5287);
   /*
      Delete the last node
   */
   list1.delEnd();
   /*
      Display the values in the list.
   */
   list1.display();
}
/*
   End of DelEnd01.cpp
*/
```

Output
No nodes in list

We will expect the structure of the linked list after the call to the delEnd() function to be like Figure 9.48.

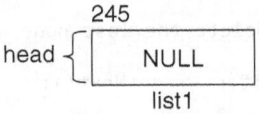

Figure 9.48   Expected effect of the delEnd() function

Let us see whether this happens or not. We know that the structure of the linked list after the call to the prependNode() function will look like Figure 9.49.

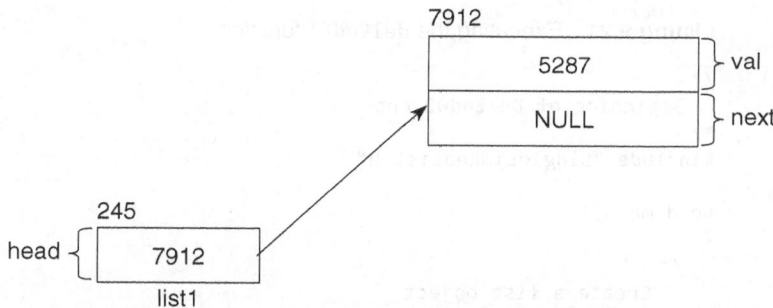

Figure 9.49   The structure of the linked list before the delEnd() function is called.

This is followed by a call to the delEnd() function. The test expression of the first if block in the function checks whether the value of head is NULL or not. The check returns true because head is not NULL (its value is 7912 because it points at the first node, whose address is 7912).

This causes the test expression of the embedded if block to get tested. This test also returns true. This is because the call to the getNext() function via the head pointer will return NULL. This in turn is because the head pointer points at the first node and, in this case, the next pointer of this first node is NULL.

The nested if block executes. The first statement calls the delete operator and passes the head pointer as parameter. This causes the memory block at which the head pointer points to be returned to the operating system. The next statement assigns NULL to the head pointer. The resulting scenario is depicted by Figure 9.50.

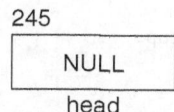

Figure 9.50   Structure of the linked list after the first and only node has been deleted through the head pointer and the head pointer has been nullified

The else block does not execute (because the if block has executed). There are no further statements in the function and the function comes to an end. We get the structure shown in Figure 9.51.

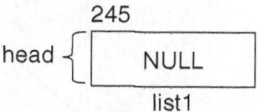

Figure 9.51   Observed effect of the delEnd() function

Compare Figure 9.51 with Figure 9.48. As you can see, the effect of the function is exactly the same as what we had expected. Hence, the call to the display() function displays 'No nodes in list'.

Finally, let us take the case where the list has more than one node. Consider Listing 9.21.

Listing 9.21   Executing the delEnd() function

```
/*
   Beginning of DelEnd02.cpp
*/
#include "SingleLinkedList.h"

void main()
{
   /*
      Create a list object
   */
   SingleLinkedList list1;
   /*
      Call the prependNode() function on the list1 object.
   */
   list1.prependNode(5287);
   /*
      Call the prependNode() function on the list1 object.
   */
   list1.prependNode(325);
   /*
      Delete the last node
   */
   list1.delEnd();
   /*
      Display the values in the list.
   */
   list1.display();
}
/*
   End of DelEnd02.cpp
*/
```

Output
325

We will expect the structure of the linked list after the call to the delEnd() function to be like Figure 9.52.

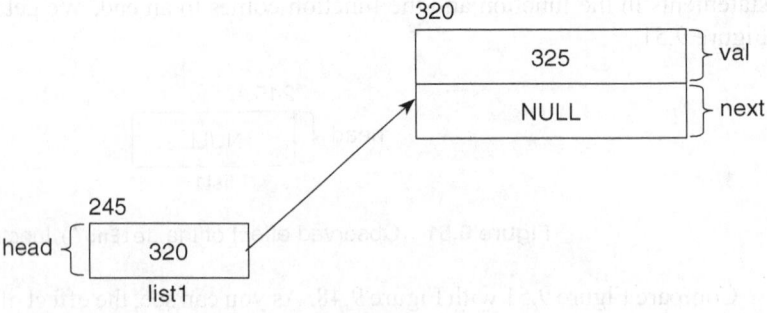

Figure 9.52   Expected effect of the delEnd() function

Let us see whether this happens or not. We know that the structure of the linked list after the second call to the prependNode() function will look like Figure 9.53.

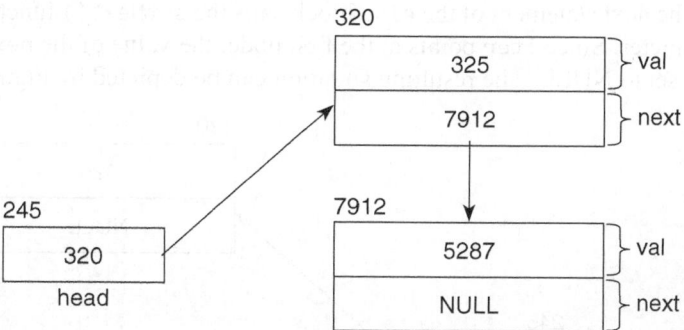

Figure 9.53   Structure of the linked list before the call to the delEnd() function

The delEnd() function has been called after the second call to the prependNode() function. We already know that the test expression in the outer if block inside the delEnd() function will return true. However, the test expression in the inner if block, which calls the getNext() function via the head pointer, will return false. This is because the next pointer of the node at which the head pointer points is not NULL. Its value is 7912. It points at the second node. Therefore, the else block will execute.

The first statement in the else block declares a temporary pointer called iter. The second statement calls a for loop that does not have a body (there is a semicolon at the end of the statement). The initialization statement of the for loop copies the value of the head pointer to iter (Figure 9.54).

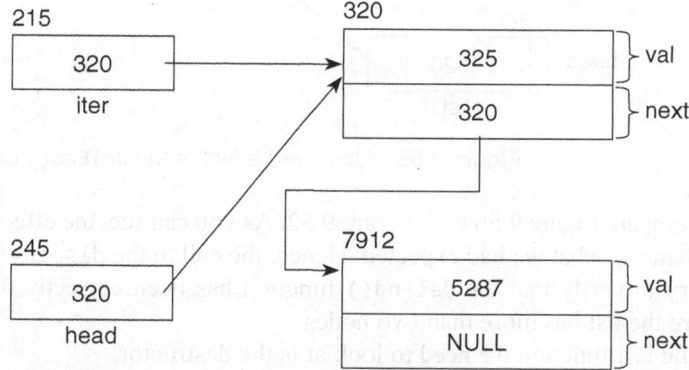

Figure 9.54   A temporary iterator pointing at the first node

Now, look carefully at the test expression of the for loop. The call iter -> getNext() returns a pointer to the second node. The chained call to the getNext() function returns the value of the second node's next pointer. As can be seen from Figure 9.54, this value is NULL. The test expression therefore returns false and the loop breaks.

The next statement calls the getNext() function via iter. It passes the value returned by this call, as a parameter to the delete operator. However, this call to the getNext() function returns a pointer to the second node. Therefore, the delete operator gets called on the second node. This causes the memory occupied by the second node to get returned to the operating system.

The next statement of the else block calls the setNext() function and passes NULL as a parameter. Since iter points at the first node, the value of the next pointer in the first node gets set to NULL. The resulting situation can be depicted by Figure 9.55.

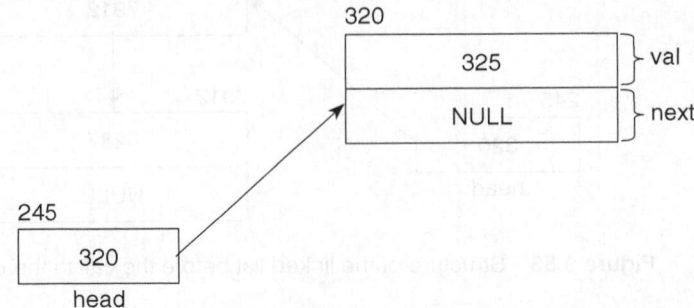

Figure 9.55 Structure of the linked list after the second (and last) node has been deleted

Since there are no more statements in the else block and in the function itself, the call to the function comes to an end. We are left with a linked list that looks like Figure 9.56.

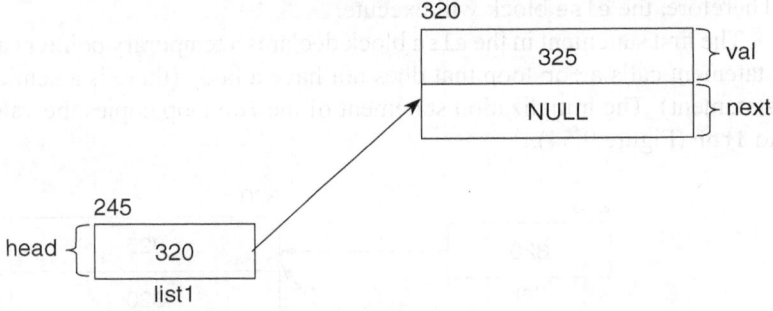

Figure 9.56 Observed effect of the delEnd() function

Compare Figure 9.56 with Figure 9.52. As you can see, the effect of the function is exactly the same as what we had expected. Hence, the call to the display() function displays 325.

Try to verify that the delEnd() function has been correctly defined to handle the case where the list has more than two nodes.

The last function we need to look at is the destructor.

```
/*
    The destructor of the class. It will delete the memory
    occupied by all nodes of the list.
*/
SingleLinkedList::~SingleLinkedList()
{
    /*
        Delete only if no nodes in the list.
    */
    if(head != NULL)
    {
        /*
            As long as the head pointer does not get a NULL value
            ...
```

```
    */
    while(head != NULL)
    {
        /*
            ... keep calling the delEnd() function to keep
            deleting the last node.
        */
        delEnd();
    }
}
/*
    Don't do anything if list is empty (no else).
*/
}
```

The destructor will be called whenever an object of the linked list class will go out of scope. It has been designed to return the memory occupied by the nodes of the linked list back to the operating system. The function itself is simple. If the list is empty, it does not do anything. Otherwise, it simply keeps calling the delEnd() function as long as the list does not become empty.

When the delEnd() function is called repeatedly, it keeps deleting the nodes from the end of the list. However, remember that the delEnd() function makes the head pointer NULL when it is called to delete a linked list that has only one node. Therefore, when the delEnd() function is called when the list has only one node left, it will make the list empty and also make the head pointer NULL. At this point, the test expression of the while loop will return false, and the loop will break.

Also, remember that one function of a class (in this case, the destructor) can call another function of the same class [in this case, the delEnd() function].

One point about the significance of the destructor—suppose an object of the linked list class has been created in the main() function. When the main() function ends, the program also terminates. The memory occupied by the nodes in the linked list will anyway get returned to the operating system. You may think that the destructor is superfluous. However, objects of the linked list class may not always get created in the main() function. Consider Listing 9.22.

Listing 9.22   Illustrating the importance of the destructor

```
/*
    Beginning of ListDestructor.cpp
*/
#include "SingleLinkedList.h"

void f1()
{
    /*
        Create a list object
    */
    SingleLinkedList list1;
    /*
        Call the prependNode() function on the list1 object.
    */
    list1.prependNode(5287);
    /*
        Call the prependNode() function on the list1 object.
    */
```

```
        list1.prependNode(325);
        /*
           Display the values in the list.
        */
        list1.display();
    }

    void main()
    {
        f1();
        /*
           More statements and function calls….
        */
    }
    /*
       End of ListDestructor.cpp
    */
```

Output

325
5287

The linked list has been created from within the f1() function. The f1() function has been called from within the main() function. Suppose, after the call to the f1() function, there are several statements and function calls in the main() function. If the destructor has not been defined, then the memory occupied by the nodes in the linked list will continue to occupy memory. The destructor ensures that when the f1() function terminates (and the list1 object goes out of scope), the memory occupied by the nodes in the linked list is returned to the operating system.

9.3 Stacks

Stacks are also data structures. They are very similar to the linked lists we have just studied. Just like linked lists, stacks also consist of nodes, where each node is linked to exactly one other node (with the exception of the last node, which is not connected to any other node).

We have learnt that we can add a node to the beginning as well as the end of a linked list. However, in a stack, we can add a node only to the beginning. This operation is called *push operation*.

We have also learnt that we can delete a node from the beginning as well as the end of a linked list. However, in a stack, we can delete a node only from the beginning. This operation is called *pop operation*.

Thus, stacks are said to have a LIFO (last-in-first-out) operation. The last node to get in is the first to get out.

Let us look at the definitions of the stack class and its functions. Let us start with the header file (Listing 9.23).

Listing 9.23   Header file of the stack class

```
/*
   Beginning of Stack.h
*/
#ifndef _STACK_H_
```

```
#define _STACK_H_

#include "SingleLinkedList.h"
/*
    The stack class.
    Each instance of this class will represent a stack.
*/
class Stack : private SingleLinkedList
{
    public:
    /*
        Function to push a value to the top of the stack.
    */
    void push(int);
    /*
        Function to display the values in the nodes of the
        stack.
    */
    void display();
    /*
        Function to pop a value from the top of the stack.
    */
    void pop();
};

#endif
/*
    End of Stack.h
*/
```

The header file of Listing 9.23 contains the definition of the stack class. As we can see, the Stack class gets private inheritance from the SingleLinkedList class. We will soon understand the reason for inheriting privately. The class does not have any data members. It has a set of public member functions.

Let us first understand why the Stack class has been defined to inherit from the SingleLinkedList class. We will then understand why it has been defined to inherit *privately* from the SingleLinkedList class.

We know that stacks share two functionalities with linked lists. One of these functionalities is the addition of nodes to the beginning and the other one is the deletion of nodes from the beginning. Another shared functionality is displaying the values in the nodes.

We have already defined functions that implement these functionalities in the SingleLinkedList class. The prependNode() function inserts a node at the beginning. The delBeg() function deletes a node from the beginning. It makes sense to inherit from the SingleLinkedList class instead of redefining them in the Stack class. We know that, due to inheritance, we will be able to call these functions with respect to objects of the Stack class.

For example, suppose stack1 is an object of the Stack class. We will like to call the prependNode() function with respect to it.

```
    stack1.prependNode(10);
```

Let us now understand why we have inherited privately. As we know, we are supposed to add nodes only at the beginning of stack objects. However, the base class has a function that adds nodes to the end of the list also [the appendNode() function]. While we will like to call some functions of the SingleLinkedList class with respect to objects of the Stack class, there are some function calls that we will like to be disallowed. For example, a user program of the Stack class may call the appendNode() function as follows (stack1 is an object of the Stack class):

```
stack1.appendNode(10);
```

We will not like the above statement to compile. This is because the above call will add a node at the end of the stack, which we do not want to allow. Inheriting privately makes all public functions of the base class private in the derived class and therefore causes statements like the one above to throw compile-time errors.

As we can see, inheriting privately solves one problem for us. But, it leads to another. While it prevents calls to unwanted functions of the base class, it prevents calls to the wanted functions too! How can this problem be solved? The problem can be solved by defining functions in the derived class that internally call the wanted functions of the base class. The implementation file of the Stack class (Listing 9.24) shows how this can be done. So, let us have a look at it.

Listing 9.24   Implementation file of the Stack class

```
/*
    Beginning of Stack.cpp
*/
#include "Stack.h"

/*
    Function to push a value to the top of the stack.
*/
void Stack::push(int pVal)
{
    /*
        Call the base class function.
    */
    prependNode(pVal);
}

/*
    Function to display the values in the nodes of the stack.
*/
void Stack::display()
{
    /*
        Call the base class function.
    */
    SingleLinkedList::display();
}
/*
    Function to pop a value from the top of the stack.
*/
void Stack::pop()
{
    /*
        Call the base class function.
    */
    delBeg();
}
/*End of Stack.cpp*/
```

Let us start with the push() function. This function simply calls the prependNode() function of the base class and passes the value that was passed to it to the called function. This causes a node to get added to the beginning of the stack.

Although the prependNode() function becomes a private member of the Stack class, the push() function has full rights to call it because it is a member function of the Stack class (remember that member functions of a class have access to private members of the class).

The next function is the display() function. All this function needs to do is to call the display() function of the base class. However, doing so without the class name qualifier will lead to infinite recursion. Hence, the call to the base class's display() function has been qualified with the base class name.

The last function is the pop() function. Like the push() function, it calls the relevant function of the base class, which is the delBeg() function in this case. This causes the first node of the stack to get deleted.

Again, the pop() function has full rights to call the delBeg() function for reasons explained earlier.

Let us look at Listing 9.25, which puts this all of this together.

Listing 9.25   An example user program of the Stack class

```
/*
    Beginning of StackUser.cpp
*/
#include <iostream.h>
#include "Stack.h"
void main()
{
    Stack stack1;
    cout << "Displaying a new stack:" << endl;
    stack1.display();
    cout << endl;

    stack1.push(30);
    cout << "Displaying after pushing 30:" << endl;
    stack1.display();
    cout << endl;

    stack1.push(20);
    cout << "Displaying after pushing 20:" << endl;
    stack1.display();
    cout << endl;

    stack1.push(10);
    cout << "Displaying after pushing 10:" << endl;
    stack1.display();
    cout << endl;

    stack1.pop();
    cout << "Displaying after popping:" << endl;
    stack1.display();
    cout << endl;

    stack1.pop();
    cout << "Displaying after popping:" << endl;
    stack1.display();
    cout << endl;

    stack1.pop();
```

```
cout << "Displaying after popping:" << endl;
stack1.display();
cout << endl;
}
/*
   End of StackUser.cpp
*/
```

Output

Displaying a new stack:

No nodes in list

Displaying after pushing 30:

30

Displaying after pushing 20:

20

30

Displaying after pushing 10:

10

20

30

Displaying after popping:

20

30

Displaying after popping:

30

Displaying after popping:

No nodes in list

9.4 Queues

Queues are data structures too. They are very similar to stacks. The only difference between the two is in their push operations. In a stack, the push operation causes the new node to get added to the beginning. But, in a queue, the push operation causes the new node to get added to the end.

Thus, queues are said to have a FIFO (first-in-first-out) operation. The first node to get in is the first to get out.

Let us look at the definitions of the queue class and its functions. Let us start with the header file (Listing 9.26).

Listing 9.26   Header file of the queue class

```
/*
   Beginning of Queue.h
*/

#ifndef _QUEUE_H_
#define _QUEUE_H_

#include "SingleLinkedList.h"

/*
```

```
   The queue class.
   Each instance of this class will represent a queue.
*/
class Queue : private SingleLinkedList
{
  public:
  /*
     Function to push a value to the end of the queue.
  */
  void push(int);
  /*
     Function to display the values in the nodes of the
     queue.
  */
  void display();
  /*
     Function to pop a value from the top of the queue.
  */
  void pop();
};

#endif
/*
   End of Queue.h
*/
```

The above header file contains the definition of the queue class. As we can see, the Queue class does private inheritance from the SingleLinkedList class. We already know the reason for inheriting from the SingleLinkedList class. We also know the reason for inheriting privately.

Let us have a look at the implementation file of the Queue class (Listing 9.27).

Listing 9.27   Implementation file of the Queue class

```
/*
   Beginning of Queue.cpp
*/
#include "Queue.h"

/*
   Function to push a value to the end of the queue.
*/
void Queue::push(int pVal)
{
  /*
     Call the base class function.
  */
  appendNode(pVal);
}
/*
   Function to display the values in the nodes of the queue.
*/
void Queue::display()
{
  /*
     Call the base class function.
  */
```

```
        SingleLinkedList::display();
}
/*
    Function to pop a value from the top of the queue.
*/
void Queue::pop()
{
    /*
        Call the base class function.
    */
    delBeg();
}
/*End of Queue.cpp*/
```

As we can see, all functions of the Queue class are identical to those of the Stack class, except the push() function. This function calls the appendNode() function of the base class instead of the prependNode() function. This causes a node to get added to the end of the stack instead of the beginning.

Let us look at Listing 9.28, which puts this all of this together.

Listing 9.28   An example user program of the Queue class

```
/*
    Beginning of QueueUser.cpp
*/
#include <iostream.h>
#include «Queue.h»
void main()
{
    Queue queue1;
    cout << "Displaying a new queue:" << endl;
    queue1.display();
    cout << endl;

    queue1.push(30);
    cout << "Displaying after pushing 30:" << endl;
    queue1.display();
    cout << endl;

    queue1.push(20);
    cout << "Displaying after pushing 20:" << endl;
    queue1.display();
    cout << endl;

    queue1.push(10);
    cout << "Displaying after pushing 10:" << endl;
    queue1.display();
    cout << endl;

    queue1.pop();
    cout << "Displaying after popping:" << endl;
    queue1.display();
    cout << endl;

    queue1.pop();
    cout << "Displaying after popping:" << endl;
    queue1.display();
    cout << endl;
```

```
        queue1.pop();
        cout << "Displaying after popping:" << endl;
        queue1.display();
        cout << endl;

}
/*
    End of QueueUser.cpp
*/
```

Output
Displaying a new queue:
No nodes in list
Displaying after pushing 30:
30
Displaying after pushing 20:
30
20
Displaying after pushing 10:
30
20
10
Displaying after popping:
20
10
Displaying after popping:
10
Displaying after popping:
No nodes in list

9.5 Trees

Trees, unlike linked lists, stacks, and queues, do not have a linear structure. In the lists we have studied so far in this chapter, each node was connected to a maximum of one other node. But, in a tree, each of the nodes may be connected to more than one node.

We encounter tree-like structures in our everyday life. Such a real example of a tree can be that of a directory structure in a computer. Figure 9.57 shows a possible directory structure (each box represents a directory):

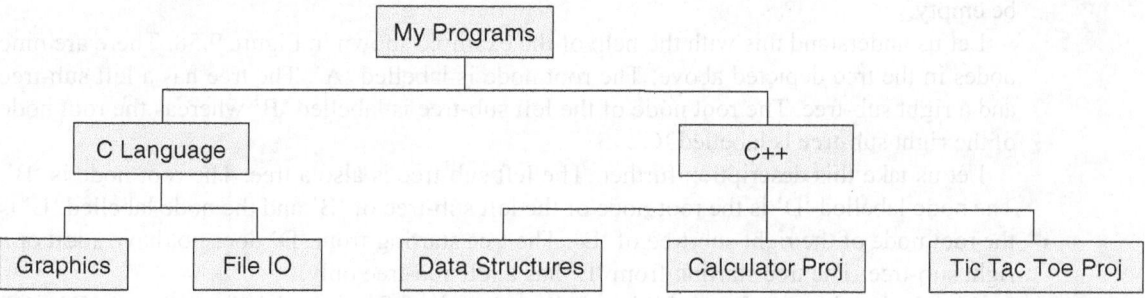

Figure 9.57 Directory structure looks like a tree

The 'My Programs' folder has two folders beneath it—'C Language' and 'C++'. But the 'C++' folder has three folders beneath it—'Data Structures', 'Calculator Proj', and 'Tic Tac Toe Proj'.

Suppose this folder structure is represented by a data structure, in which each folder is represented by a node. It is obvious that each such node will contain, apart from the name of the folder, one or more pointers to other similar nodes. Such a data structure is called a tree. Trees can be created in C++ in order to model these real-world tree-like structures.

9.5.1 Binary Trees

A binary tree is a tree in which each node is linked to a maximum of two nodes. Let us look at a simplified figure of a binary tree (Figure 9.58). In this figure, the nodes have been represented by circles. Each node has been labelled with a different alphabet. The links between nodes have been represented with straight lines.

The tree has been drawn in a top-down fashion. This means that A is the root node. The figure will be described in greater detail shortly.

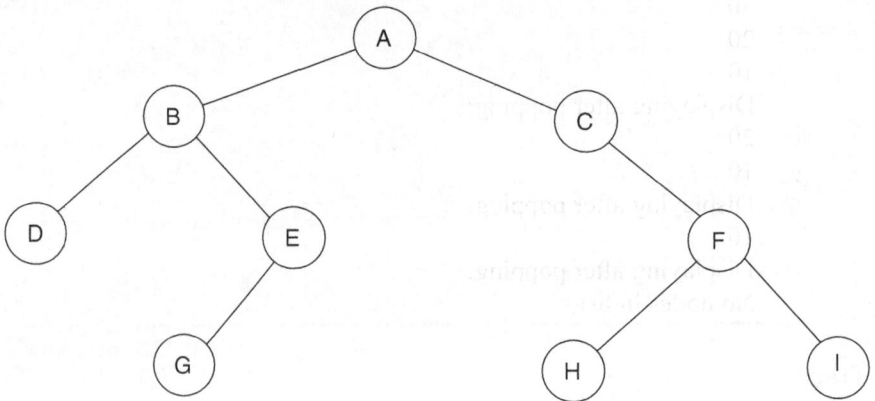

Figure 9.58   A binary tree

A binary tree is a finite set of elements. It is either empty or is partitioned into three disjoint subsets. The first subset contains only one element, which is the root of the tree. The other subsets are themselves binary trees. One of them is considered to be the left sub-tree and the other one is considered to be the right sub-tree. Either or both of the sub-trees can be empty.

Let us understand this with the help of the example shown in Figure 9.58. There are nine nodes in the tree depicted above. The root node is labelled 'A'. The tree has a left sub-tree and a right sub-tree. The root node of the left sub-tree is labelled 'B' whereas the root node of the right sub-tree is labelled 'C'.

Let us take this description further. The left sub-tree is also a tree. The root node is 'B'. The node labelled 'D' is the root node of the left sub-tree of 'B' and the node labelled 'E' is the root node of the right sub-tree of 'B'. The tree starting from 'D' does not have a left or a right sub-tree. The tree starting from 'E' has a left sub-tree only.

A node that does not have children is known as leaf. Thus, in the above figure, 'D', 'G', 'H', and 'I' are leaves.

As per the definition of a tree, these three sets should be disjointed—the root, the set of nodes in the left sub-tree, and the set of nodes in the right sub-tree. Accordingly, the structures shown in Figure 9.59 are not trees.

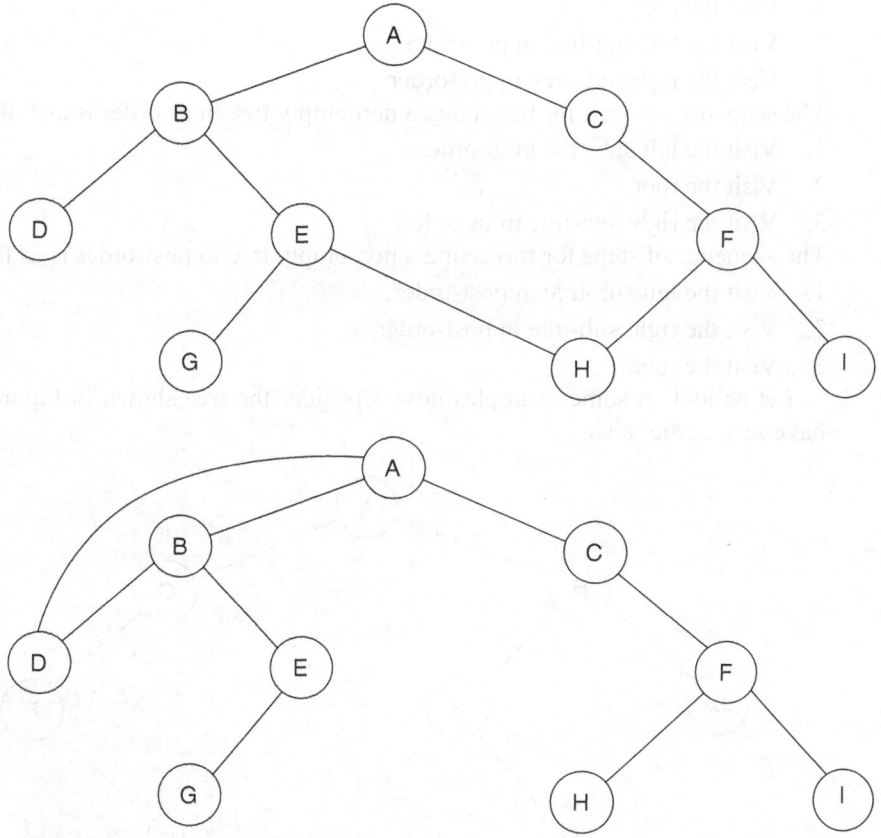

Figure 9.59   Structures that are not binary trees

Natural trees usually grow upwards, with their roots in the ground and the branches and leaves growing in an upward direction. But, in data structures, trees are depicted to grow downwards, with their root at the top and the branches and leaves growing downwards.

Recursive Nature of Binary Trees

If you look closely, you will observe that binary trees have recursive structures. The entire tree has a root, a left sub-tree, and a right sub-tree. Both of the sub-trees are trees themselves. Both of them in turn have roots and sub-trees.

While programming functions that model operations on trees, we can exploit this recursive nature of trees and make them recursive too. This will make the functions shorter and reduce our programming effort. You will understand this while studying these functions.

Traversal of a Binary Tree

Traversing a linked list is simple because it has a linear structure. We simply visit the nodes from the first to the last. However, trees do not have a linear structure. How can we traverse a tree? There are three ways of doing it—pre-order, in-order, and post-order. Keep in mind that we stop as soon as we encounter an empty tree.

The sequence of steps for traversing a non-empty tree in pre-order is as follows:
1. Visit the root.
2. Visit the left sub-tree in pre-order.
3. Visit the right sub-tree in pre-order.

The sequence of steps for traversing a non-empty tree in in-order is as follows:
1. Visit the left sub-tree in in-order.
2. Visit the root.
3. Visit the right sub-tree in in-order.

The sequence of steps for traversing a non-empty tree in post-order is as follows:
1. Visit the left sub-tree in post-order.
2. Visit the right sub-tree in post-order.
3. Visit the root.

Let us look at some examples now. Consider the tree shown in Figure 9.60, which we have seen earlier also.

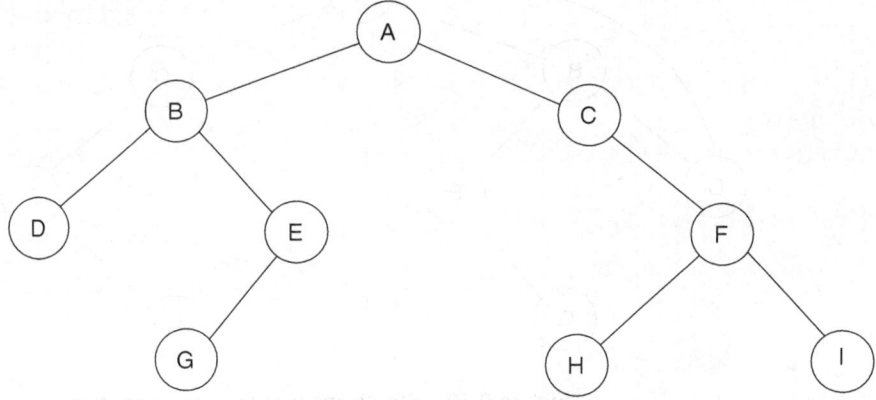

Figure 9.60 A binary tree

Let us see the sequence in which we visit the nodes when we follow each of the traversal methods. Let us start with pre-order traversal.

In pre-order traversal, we visit the root first. Hence, we get 'A'. Then we visit the left sub-tree of 'A' in pre-order (visiting the right sub-tree of 'A' is pending at this time). We visit the root first. Hence, we get 'B'. Then, we visit the left sub-tree of 'B' in pre-order (visiting the right sub-tree of 'B' is pending at this time). We visit the root first. Hence, we get 'D'. Then, we visit the left sub-tree of 'D' in pre-order (visiting the right sub-tree of 'D' is pending at this time). There is no left sub-tree for 'D'. So, we visit the right sub-tree of 'D' in pre-order, which was pending. There is no left sub-tree for 'D'. Hence, we go one step back. We visit the right sub-tree of 'B' in pre-order, which was pending. If you continue like this after 'A', 'B', and 'D', you will get 'E', 'G', 'C', 'F', 'H', 'I'.

To conclude, the result of a pre-order traversal of the above tree will be 'ABDEGCFHI'.

Similarly, the result of an in-order traversal will be 'DBGEACHFI'. And the result of a post-order traversal will be 'DGEBHIFCA'.

9.5.2 Binary Search Trees

A binary search tree is a special form of binary tree. In a binary search tree, for any given node, the value contained in its left child is less than the value contained in the node and the value contained in the node is less than the value contained in its right child. For example, the tree shown in Figure 9.61 is a binary search tree.

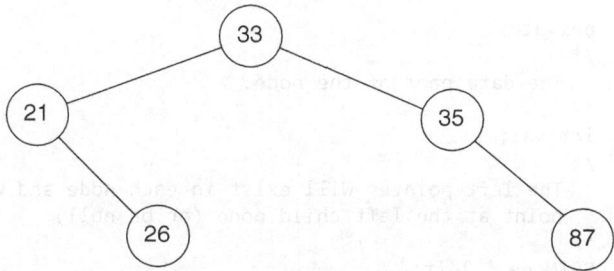

Figure 9.61   A binary search tree

But the binary tree shown in Figure 9.62 is not a binary search tree. This is because 81 is larger than 49 and cannot be the value of the left child of the node that has 49.

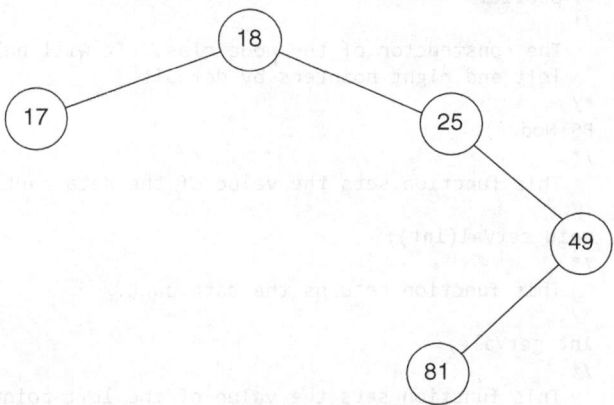

Figure 9.62   A structure that is not a binary search tree

If you traverse a binary search tree in in-order (left, root, right), and display the value of each node as you visit, then you will end up printing the values in ascending order. Try to draw a binary search tree and see whether this happens or not.

Let us now look at the code that can be used to generate binary search trees (BSTs). Broadly, we will be studying two classes—BSTNode and BST. The first class will help us in creating the nodes of BSTs whereas the second class will help us in creating the BSTs themselves.

Let us start with the first class. See Listing 9.29.

Listing 9.29   The BSTNode class

```
/*Beginning of BSTNode.h*/
#ifndef _BSTNODE_H_
```

```cpp
#define _BSTNODE_H_

/*
   The node class.
   Each instance of this class will be a node in the binary
   search tree.
*/
class BSTNode
{
  private:
  /*
     The data part of the node.
  */
  int val;
  /*
     The left pointer will exist in each node and will
     point at the left child node (or be null)
  */
  BSTNode * left;
  /*
     The right pointer will exist in each node and will
     point at the right child node (or be null)
  */
  BSTNode * right;

    public:
  /*
     The constructor of the node class. It will nullify the
     left and right pointers by default.
  */
  BSTNode();
  /*
     This function sets the value of the data part.
  */
  void setVal(int);
  /*
     This function returns the data part.
  */
  int getVal();
  /*
     This function sets the value of the left pointer.
  */
  void setLeft(BSTNode *);
  /*
     This function returns a reference to the left pointer.
  */
  BSTNode *& getLeft();
  /*
     This function sets the value of the right pointer.
  */
  void setRight(BSTNode *);
  /*
     This function returns a reference to the right pointer.
  */
  BSTNode *& getRight();
  /*
     The destructor of the class.
  */
  ~BSTNode();
```

```
};

#endif
/*End of BSTNode.h*/
```

Each object of the above class will be a node in the BST. Each node will have three data members—val, left, and right. The data of each node will be stored in the first member, val. This is an integer-type variable, which means that the nodes will contain integer type values. The remaining data members are left and right. Each of these is a pointer to another node. As we know, each node of a BST has either a left child or a right child or both or neither. If a node has a left child node, then the left data member will point at that node. Otherwise, it will be NULL. The same holds true for the right data member.

Figures 9.63 and 9.64 show some nodes.

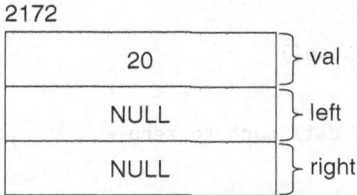

Figure 9.63   A BST node (object of the BSTNode class) with no children.

Figure 9.63 depicts an object of the BSTNode class. This particular object represents a node of the binary search tree that has no child nodes. Hence, both the left and the right data members are NULL. Moreover, the value of the val data member is 20. Finally, the address of the node itself is 2172.

Let us see what happens if a node, having a value of 10, gets added to the above node (Figure 9.64). It will get added as the left child of the existing node because 10 is smaller than 20.

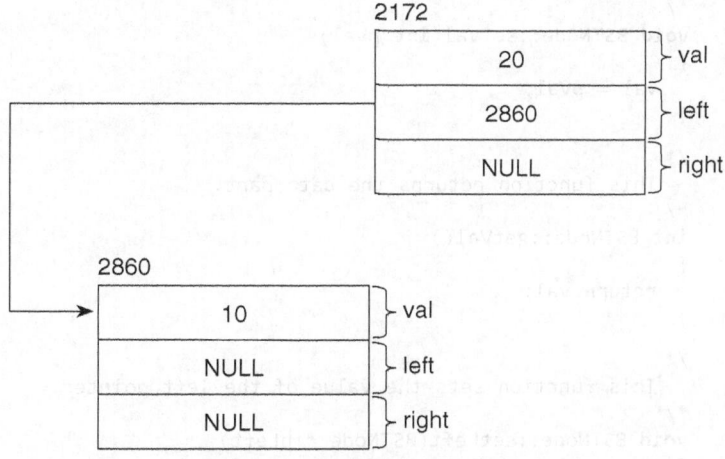

Figure 9.64   A node with only a left child

Now that we have had a glimpse of the data members of the node class, let us have a brief look at the declaration of its member functions. All of the declarations are self-evident. The only declarations we need to study separately are those of the functions that return references to the `left` and the `right` pointers [the `getLeft()` and `getRight()` functions respectively]. You will understand why they return by reference (and not by value) when you study the `insert()` function of the BST class.

Let us look at the definitions of the member functions of the BSTNode class (Listing 9.30).

Listing 9.30 Implementation file for the BSTNode class

```cpp
/*Beginning of BSTNode.cpp*/
#include "BSTNode.h"

/*
    The constructor of the node class. It will nullify the
    left and right pointers by default.
*/

BSTNode::BSTNode()
{
    /*
        Set the data part to zero.
    */
    val = 0;
    /*
        Set the left pointer to null.
    */
    left = NULL;
    /*
        Set the right pointer to null.
    */
    right = NULL;
}
/*
    This function sets the value of the data part.
*/
void BSTNode::setVal(int pVal)
{
    val = pVal;
}

/*
    This function returns the data part.
*/
int BSTNode::getVal()
{
    return val;
}

/*
    This function sets the value of the left pointer.
*/
void BSTNode::setLeft(BSTNode * pLeft)
{
    left = pLeft;
}
/*
    This function returns a reference to the left pointer.
```

```
*/
BSTNode *& BSTNode::getLeft()
{
    return left;
}

/*
   This function sets the value of the right pointer.
*/
void BSTNode::setRight(BSTNode * pRight)
{
    right = pRight;
}

/*
   This function returns a reference to the right pointer.
*/
BSTNode *& BSTNode::getRight()
{
    return right;
}

/*
   The destructor of the class.
*/
BSTNode::~BSTNode()
{
}
/*End of BSTNode.cpp*/
```

Let us have a closer look at the getLeft() and getRight() functions. As you can see, each of these functions returns a reference to either the left or the right pointer respectively. It is important to understand the implications of this if we later want to understand the insert() function of the BST class, which, as the name indicates, inserts a node in the BST. Let us take the getLeft() function. Suppose, node1 is an instance of the BSTNode class and contains the value 20, as shown in Figure 9.65.

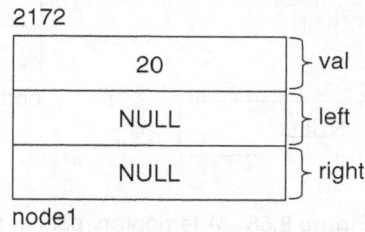

Figure 9.65   A BST node

Before going any further, you need to understand that the address of the left pointer is 2176. Why is the address of the left pointer 2176? This is because the address of the node is 2172. The first data member in the node is val, which is an integer-type variable. Since integer-type variables occupy 4 bytes, the first 4 bytes of node1 will be occupied by val. The left pointer is the second data member. Hence its address will be 2176 (2172 + 4). Can you calculate the address of the right pointer?

Now, consider Listing 9.31.

Listing 9.31 Testing the BSTNode class

```
/*
   Beginning of BSTNodeTest01.cpp
*/
#include "BSTNode.h"
void main()
{
  BSTNode node1;
  node1.setVal(20);
  BSTNode * & temp = node1.getLeft();
  temp = new BSTNode();
  temp -> setVal(10);
  cout << node1.getLeft()->getVal() << endl;
}
/*
   End of BSTNodeTest01.cpp
*/
```

Output

10

The first statement of the above program declares an object of the BSTNode class and the second statement sets the value of the node to 20. Let us analyse Listing 9.31 from the third statement onwards.

```
BSTNode * & temp = node1.getLeft();
```

Since the call to the getLeft() function returns a reference to the left pointer of the node1 object and because the temp pointer is a reference variable, therefore the temp pointer ends up being a reference for the left pointer of the node1 object, as shown in Figure 9.66.

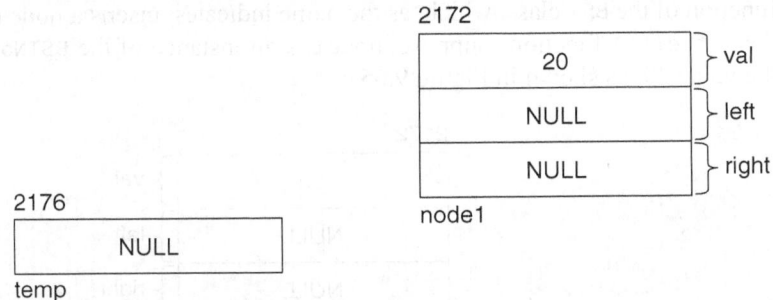

Figure 9.66 A temporary pointer pointing at a BST node

Since temp is a reference to the left pointer, its address will be the same as that of the left pointer, which is 2176. And, from our knowledge of reference variables, we know that any change to the value of temp will cause the same change to the value of the left pointer (because they are essentially two names for the same memory block). Thus, if the following statement executes now, it will change the value of the left pointer.

The next statement in the program is:

```
temp = new BSTNode();
```

The above statement will create a new object of the BSTNode class and assign its address to the temp pointer. Consequently, the value of the left pointer in the node1 object will also become equal to the address of the newly created object, as shown in Figure 9.67.

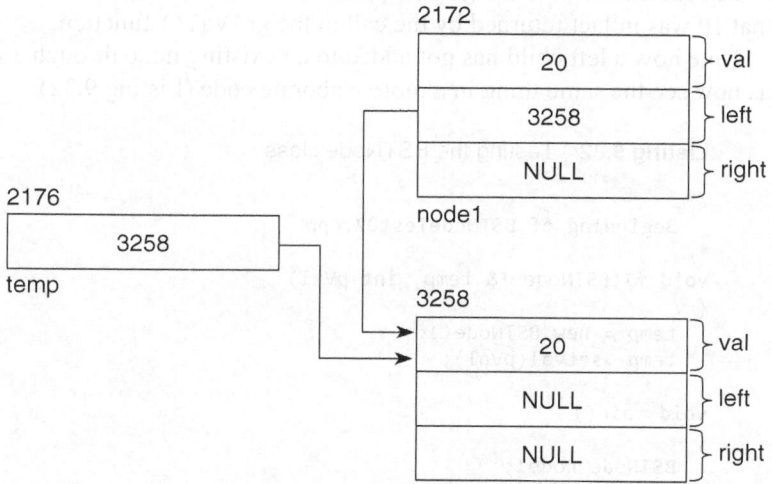

Figure 9.67   Temporary pointer and left pointer of existing node pointing at a newly created node

In this situation, the address of the newly created node is 3258. Therefore, the values of temp and the left pointer of the existing node have become 3258. The next statement is:

```
temp -> setVal(10);
```

This will assign 10 to the node at which temp points, as shown in Figure 9.68.

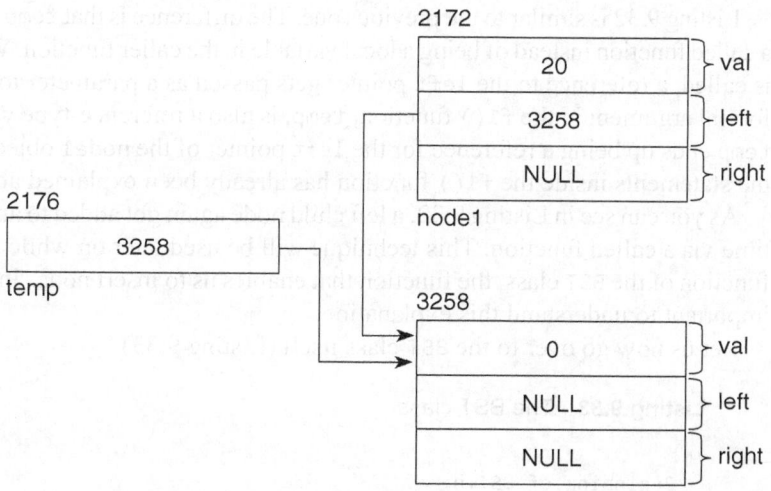

Figure 9.68   Newly created node populated by a value

The next statement is:

```
cout << node1.getLeft()->getVal() << endl;
```

The above statement tells us whether `temp` and the `left` pointer really point at the same node or not. If `temp` and the `left` pointer really point at the same node, then the call to the `getLeft()` function in the above statement should return a pointer to the newly created node. In that case, the call to the `getVal()` function should return 10. We can see from the output that 10 was in fact returned by the call to the `getVal()` function.

Note how a left child has got added to an existing node through a temporary pointer. Let us now see the same thing in a more elaborate code (Listing 9.32).

Listing 9.32   Testing the BSTNode class

```
/*
   Beginning of BSTNodeTest02.cpp
*/
void f1(BSTNode *& temp, int pVal)
{
   temp = new BSTNode();
   temp->setVal(pVal);
}
void main()
{
   BSTNode node1;
   node1.setVal(20);
   f1(node1.getLeft(), 10);
   cout << node1.getLeft() -> getVal() << endl;
}
/*
   End of BSTNodeTest02.cpp
*/
```

Output
10

Listing 9.32 is similar to the previous one. The difference is that `temp` is a formal argument in a called function instead of being a local variable in the caller function. When the `f1()` function is called, a reference to the `left` pointer gets passed as a parameter to it. The corresponding formal argument in the `f1()` function, `temp`, is also a reference-type variable. Consequently, `temp` ends up being a reference for the `left` pointer of the `node1` object. The consequence of the statements inside the `f1()` function has already been explained above.

As you can see in Listing 9.32, a left child node again got added to an existing node, but this time via a called function. This technique will be used later on while defining the `insert()` function of the BST class, the function that enables us to insert nodes in the BST. It is therefore important to understand this explanation.

Let us now go over to the BST class itself (Listing 9.33).

Listing 9.33   The BST class

```
/*
   Beginning of BST.h
*/
#ifndef _BST_H_
#define _BST_H_

#include "BSTNode.h"
```

```
/*
    The binary search tree class. Each object of this class
    will represent a BST.
*/
class BST
{
    private:
    /*
        The root pointer of the BST. It will either point at
        the root node or be NULL.
    */
    BSTNode * root;
    /*
        Private function to insert the node. Will be called
        from the public function.
    */
    void insert(BSTNode *&, int);
    /*
        Private function to do pre-order traversal. Will be
        called from the public function.
    */
    void preorder(BSTNode *);
    /*
        Private function to do in-order traversal. Will be
        called from the public function.
    */
    void inorder(BSTNode *);
    /*
        Private function to do post-order traversal. Will be
        called from the public function.
    */
    void postorder(BSTNode *);

    public:
    /*
        The constructor of the BST class. It will nullify the
        root pointer by default.
    */
    BST();
    /*
        Function to insert a node at the correct place in the
        BST.
    */
    void insert(int);
    /*
        Function to do pre-order traversal.
    */
    void preorder();
    /*
        Function to do in-order traversal.
    */
    void inorder();
    /*
        Function to do post-order traversal.
    */
    void postorder();
    /*
        The destructor of the class.
    */
```

```
        ~BST();
};

#endif
/*End of BST.h*/
```

This class has only one data member—root—which is private. Consequently, root will be the only data member in all objects of the BST class, and the constructor of the BST class will ensure that it gets nullified in each newly created object.

As the definition suggests, root will point at an object of the node class BSTNode. As the name suggests, it will point at the first node of the BST.

Let us look at the implementation of the member functions now (Listing 9.34).

Listing 9.34   Implementation file of BST class

```
/*Beginning of BST.cpp*/
#include <iostream.h>
#include "BST.h"

/*
   Private function to insert the node. Will be called from
   the public function.
*/
void BST::insert(BSTNode * &nodePtr, int pValue)
{
   /*
      Reference to a pointer is passed as one parameter.
   */
   /*
      If the pointer is NULL ...
   */
   if(nodePtr == NULL)
   {
      /*
         ... create a node and make the pointer point at it
         and ...
      */
      nodePtr = new BSTNode();
      /*
         ... copy the value passed to the function to the new
         node and ...
      */
      nodePtr -> setVal(pValue);
      /*
         ... return.
      */
      return;
   }
   /*
      If the value in the current node is larger than the
      value passed ...
   */
   if(nodePtr -> getVal() > pValue)
   {
      /*
         ... call the function recursively starting with the
         left child.
```

```
        */
        insert(nodePtr -> getLeft(), pValue);
    }

    /*
        If the value in the current node is smaller than the
        value passed ...
    */
    if(nodePtr -> getVal() < pValue)
    {
        /*
            ... call the function recursively starting with the
            right child.
        */
        insert(nodePtr -> getRight(), pValue);
    }
}

/*
    Private function to do pre-order traversal. Will be
    called from the public function.
*/
void BST::preorder(BSTNode * nodePtr)
{
    /*
        As long as the passed pointer is not NULL ...
    */
    if(nodePtr != NULL)
    {
        /*
            ... display the value of the current node first ...
        */
        cout << nodePtr -> getVal() << endl;
        /*
            ... then call the function recursively for the left
            child ...
        */
        preorder(nodePtr -> getLeft());
        /*
            ... and then call the function recursively for the
            right child.
        */
        preorder(nodePtr -> getRight());
    }
}
/*
    Private function to do in-order traversal. Will be called
    from the public function.
*/
void BST::inorder(BSTNode * nodePtr)
{
    /*
        As long as the passed pointer is not NULL ...
    */
    if(nodePtr != NULL)
    {
        /*
            ... call the function recursively for the left child
            first...
```

```
        */
        inorder(nodePtr -> getLeft());
        /*
            ... then display the value of the current node ...
        */
        cout << nodePtr -> getVal() << endl;
        /*
            ... and then call the function recursively for the
            right child.
        */
        inorder(nodePtr -> getRight());
    }
}
/*
    Private function to do post-order traversal. Will be
    called from the public function.
*/
void BST::postorder(BSTNode * nodePtr)
{
    /*
        As long as the passed pointer is not NULL ...
    */
    if(nodePtr != NULL)
    {
        /*
            ... call the function recursively for the left child
            first...
        */
        postorder(nodePtr -> getLeft());
        /*
            ... then call the function recursively for the right
            child ...
        */
        postorder(nodePtr -> getRight());
        /*
            ... and then display the value of the current node.
        */
        cout << nodePtr -> getVal() << endl;
    }
}
/*
    The constructor of the BST class. It will nullify the
    root pointer by default.
*/
BST::BST()
{
    /*
        Nullify the root pointer.
    */
    root = NULL;
}

/*
    Function to insert a node at the correct place in the
    BST.
*/
void BST::insert(int pValue)
```

```
{
    /*
        Call the private function to insert the node at the
        correct place in the BST.
    */
    insert(root, pValue);
}
/*
    Function to do pre-order traversal.
*/
void BST::preorder()
{
    /*
        Call the corresponding private function.
    */
    preorder(root);
}

/*
    Function to do in-order traversal.
*/
void BST::inorder()
{
    /*
        Call the corresponding private function.
    */
    inorder(root);
}
/*
    Function to do post-order traversal.
*/
void BST::postorder()
{
    /*
        Call the corresponding private function.
    */
    postorder(root);
}

/*
    The destructor of the class.
*/
BST::~BST()
{
}
/*End of BST.cpp*/
```

The BST class has a few private member functions. We will return to them later on. Let us start looking at the public member functions.

The definition of the constructor is obvious. It simply nullifies the root pointer for each newly created object of the BST class.

The next public function is insert(). This function has been designed to create a new node and insert it at the appropriate place in the BST. It accepts the value to be inserted as a parameter. It in turn calls an overloaded private member function. It transfers its parameter to the called function. It also passes the root pointer to the called function.

Let us come back to the definition of the `insert()` function after understanding the calling pattern that we observe here. Please keep in mind that the functions of the BST class that carry out the actual task are recursive and therefore need the `root` pointer to be passed as an initial parameter to them. But, at the same time, we cannot expect the programs that use the BST class to pass the value of the `root` pointer when they call its functions (they have no way of knowing the value of the `root` pointer anyway).

So, what is the way out? The problem can be solved by creating a public function that does not expect the `root` pointer to be passed to it, but in turn calls a private function, which does the actual work, and passes the `root` pointer to it. Thus, we are able to ensure that the functions that do the actual work get the `root` pointer as a parameter, without expecting the calling program to pass it for us.

For example, if `tree1` is an instance of the BST class (created in one of the user programs of the BST class) and we need to insert the value 20 into the tree, then the public `insert()` function will be called as follows:

```
tree1.insert(20);
```

The definition of the public `insert()` function is as follows:

```
/*
    Function to insert a node at the correct place in the
    BST.
*/
void BST::insert(int pValue)
{
    /*
        Call the private function to insert the node at the
        correct place in the BST.
    */
    insert(root, pValue);
}
```

As can be seen, the public function in turn calls the private function. It transfers the data value that was passed to it to the private function. It also passes the value of the `root` pointer to the private function.

Let us look at the definition of the private version of this function, which does the actual work for us.

```
/*
    Private function to insert the node. Will be called from
    the public function.
*/
void BST::insert(BSTNode * &nodePtr, int pValue)
{
    /*
        Reference to a pointer is passed as one parameter.
    */
    /*
        If the pointer is NULL ...
    */
    if(nodePtr == NULL)
    {
        /*
            ... create a node and make the pointer point at it
            and ...
        */
```

```
        nodePtr = new BSTNode();
        /*
            ... copy the value passed to the function to the new
            node and ...
        */
        nodePtr -> setVal(pValue);
        /*
            ... return.
        */
        return;
    }
    /*
        If the value in the current node is larger than the
        value passed ...
    */
    if(nodePtr -> getVal() > pValue)
    {
        /*
            ... call the function recursively starting with the
            left child.
        */
        insert(nodePtr -> getLeft(), pValue);
    }
    /*
        If the value in the current node is smaller than the
        value passed ...
    */
    if(nodePtr -> getVal() < pValue)
    {
        /*
            ... call the function recursively starting with the
            right child.
        */
        insert(nodePtr -> getRight(), pValue);
    }
}
```

This complicated looking function is actually very simple. Let us start by considering the case where the tree is empty (Listing 9.35).

Listing 9.35 Testing the insert() function

```
/*Beginning of BSTInsert01.cpp*/
#include "BST.h"
void main()
{
    BST tree1;
    tree1.insert(20);
}
/*End of BSTInsert01.cpp*/
```

The first statement in the above program will create an object of the BST class called tree1. Figure 9.69 depicts tree1 after it has got created in the memory.

tree1

Figure 9.69   An object of the BST class

As per the definition of the BST class, tree1 has only one data member, called root. The address of the object is 2172. Since root is the only data member of the object, its address is also 2172. Keep in mind that when the tree is empty, the root pointer's value will be NULL.

The second statement in the above program calls the public insert() function as follows:

```
tree1.insert(20);
```

This in turn will call the private function as follows:

```
insert(root, 20);
```

Note that nodePtr, which is the first formal argument of the private function, is a reference-type variable. Thus, as a result of the above call, nodePtr will end up being a reference to the root pointer. Thus, any change in the value of nodePtr will cause the same change to the value of the root pointer. This is a very important point and must be kept in mind. Also, the value of pValue, which is the second formal argument, will get set to 20. The resulting situation is depicted in Figure 9.70.

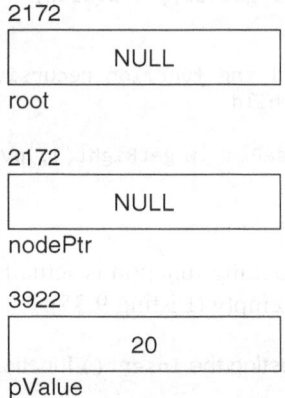

Figure 9.70   Situation resulting out of a call to the insert() function

As can be seen, root and nodePtr have the same address, which is 2172. This is because nodePtr is a reference to root. Naturally, they have the same values too. pValue is a separate integer type variable. Its value is 20.

Now, the function will start executing. The value of nodePtr will be tested for NULL value in the test expression of the first if block. The test will return true because the value of the root pointer is NULL and the value of nodePtr is the same as the value of the root pointer.

The if block will execute. A new node will get created and the value of its address will get copied to nodePtr. This will cause the value of the root pointer to become equal to the address of the newly created node because nodePtr is a reference to root as shown in Figure 9.71. Suppose, the address of the newly created node is 6221, then the value of both root and nodePtr will become 6221. This is the importance of declaring nodePtr as a reference variable.

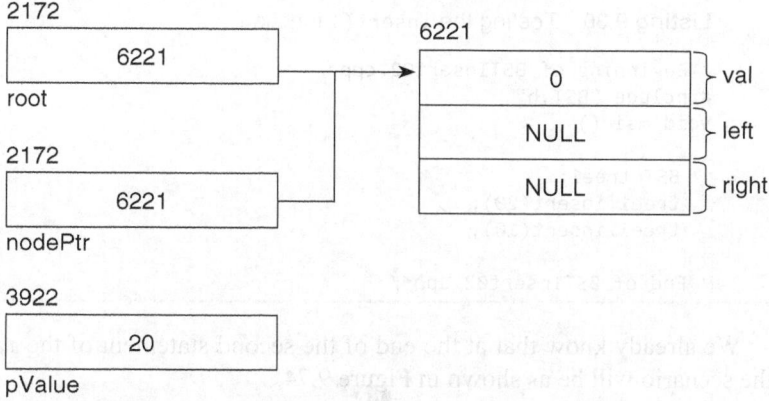

Figure 9.71   A newly created node added to the root pointer

The next statement in the if block will copy the value of pValue to the data part of the newly created node giving rise to the situation shown in Figure 9.72.

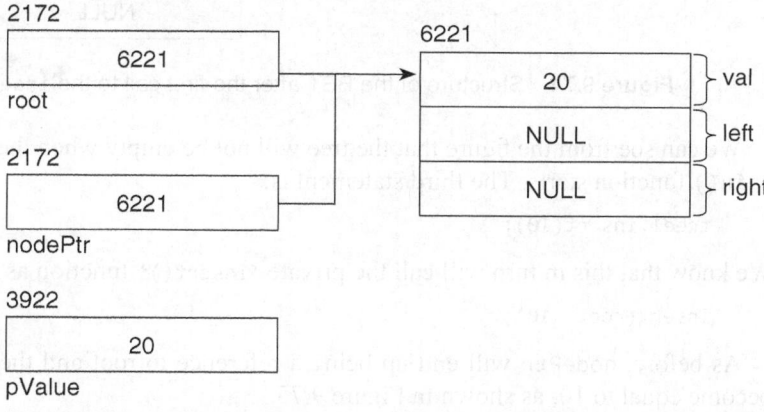

Figure 9.72   Populating the newly created node with data

Finally, the last statement of the if block will cause the function to return and the remaining part of the function will not execute. The local variables nodePtr and pValue will go out of scope. We will be left with the root pointer and the newly created node. Thus, a new node, with value 20, will get added to the tree. Figure 9.73 shows what the tree will look like.

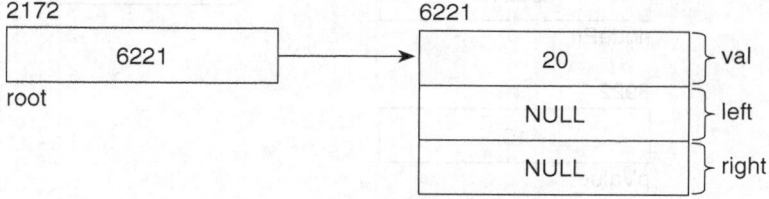

Figure 9.73   Situation at the end of the insert() function

Thus, it is clear that the `insert()` function will work correctly when the tree is empty. Let us now consider the case where the tree is not empty (Listing 9.36).

Listing 9.36   Testing the `insert()` function

```
/*Beginning of BSTInsert02.cpp*/
#include "BST.h"
void main()
{
    BST tree1;
    tree1.insert(20);
    tree1.insert(10);
}
/*End of BSTInsert02.cpp*/
```

We already know that at the end of the second statement of the `main()` function above, the scenario will be as shown in Figure 9.74.

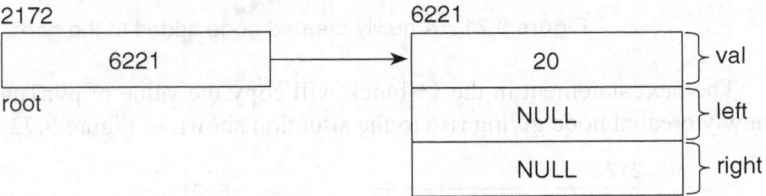

Figure 9.74   Structure of the BST after the first call to the `insert()` function

We can see from the figure that the tree will not be empty when the third statement in the `main()` function starts. The third statement is:

```
tree1.insert(10);
```

We know that this in turn will call the private 'insert()' function as follows:

```
insert(root, 10);
```

As before, `nodePtr` will end up being a reference to root and the value of `pValue` will become equal to 10, as shown in Figure 9.75.

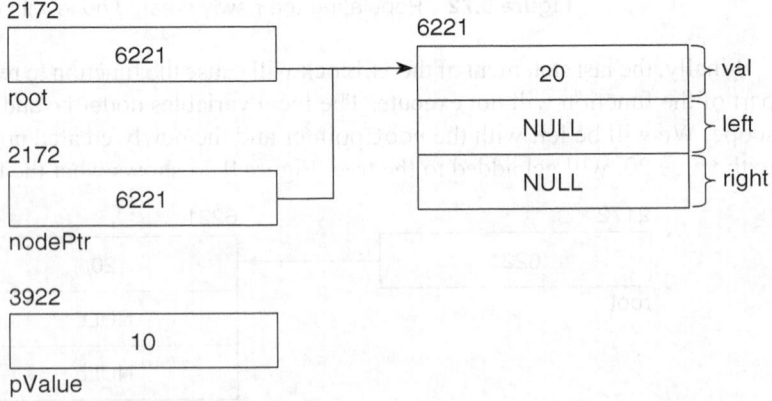

Figure 9.75   First generation of the call to the `insert()` function

As before, the test expression inside the `if` statement will be tested. However, this time, the test will fail. Therefore, the first `if` block will be bypassed. The test expression in the next `if` statement will get tested. This will return true because the value in the node at which `nodePtr` points is 20 and is greater than the value of `pValue`, which is 10.

Now comes the tricky part. The second `if` block will execute. The `insert()` function will be called recursively and the second generation of the function will start executing. Look closely at the first value that is being passed to the recursive call to the `insert()` function. It is as follows:

```
nodePtr -> getLeft()
```

We know that this function call will return a reference to the `left` pointer of the node at which `nodePtr` points currently (and we know that `nodePtr` currently points at the first node). Thus, when the second generation of the function gets called, `nodePtr`, which is one of the formal arguments, ends up being a reference to the `left` pointer of the first node. Since the address of the first node is 6221, the address of its `left` pointer will be 6225 (we already know why). Therefore, the address of `nodePtr` will also be 6225. Its value will also be NULL because the value of the `left` pointer of the first node is NULL.

The other formal argument, `pValue`, gets created as a local variable in the second generation, and its value becomes 10. Let us assume that its address is 6720. Figure 9.76 explains what is happening.

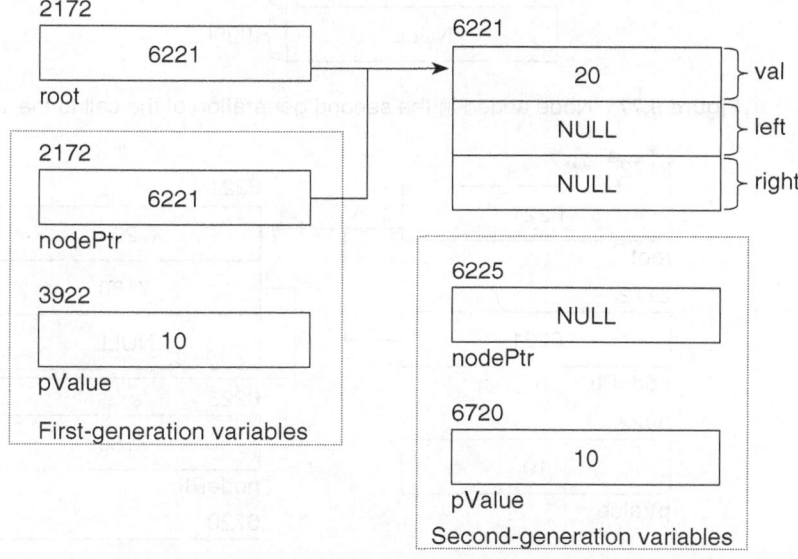

Figure 9.76 First and second generations of the call to the `insert()` function

In the above figure, `nodePtr` and `pValue` on the left are from the first generation while those on the right are from the second generation of the function call.

Now, the body of the second generation of the function call will start executing. The test expression of the first `if` statement will return true because the value of `nodePtr` is null. A new node will get created and its address will get copied to `nodePtr`. Since `nodePtr` is a reference to the `left` pointer of the first node, the value of the `left` pointer of the first node will also become equal to the address of the newly created node. Let us look at Figure 9.77, which depicts this scenario.

After this, the value of `pValue` will get copied to the `val` data member of the new node giving rise to the structure shown in Figure 9.78.

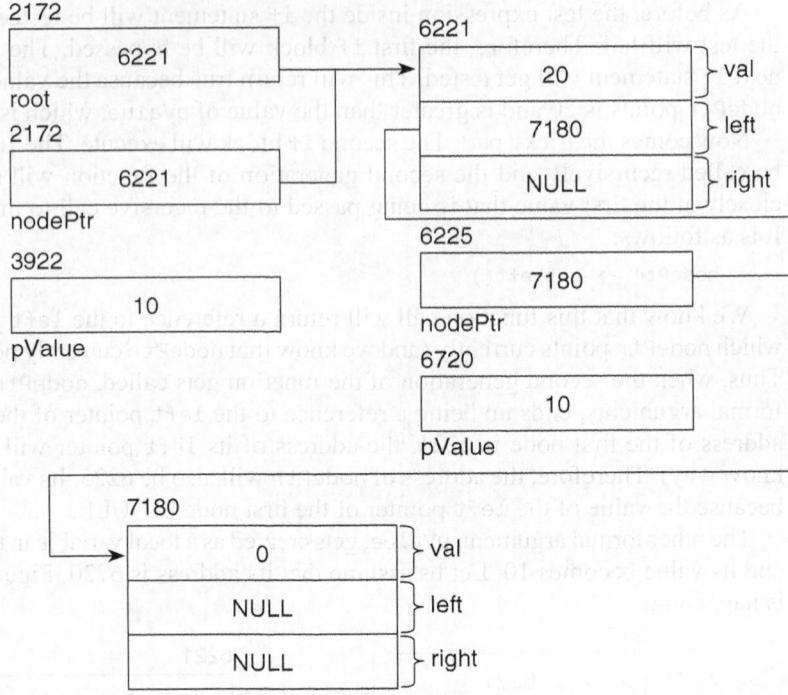

Figure 9.77   Node added in the second generation of the call to the insert() function

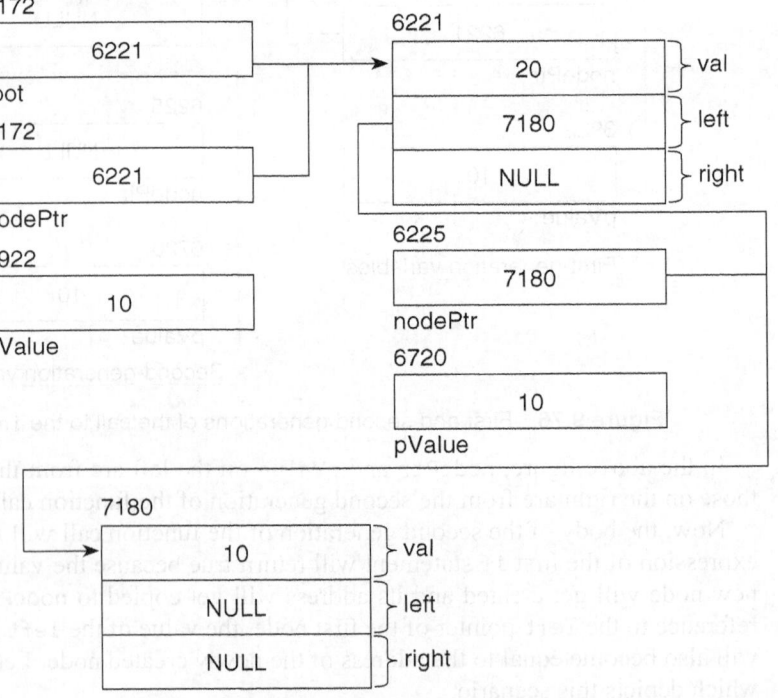

Figure 9.78   Newly created node populated with value

After this, the return statement of the second generation call will execute and the second generation will terminate. The local variables of the second generation—nodePtr and pValue—will cease to exist. We will then be left with the structure shown in Figure 9.79.

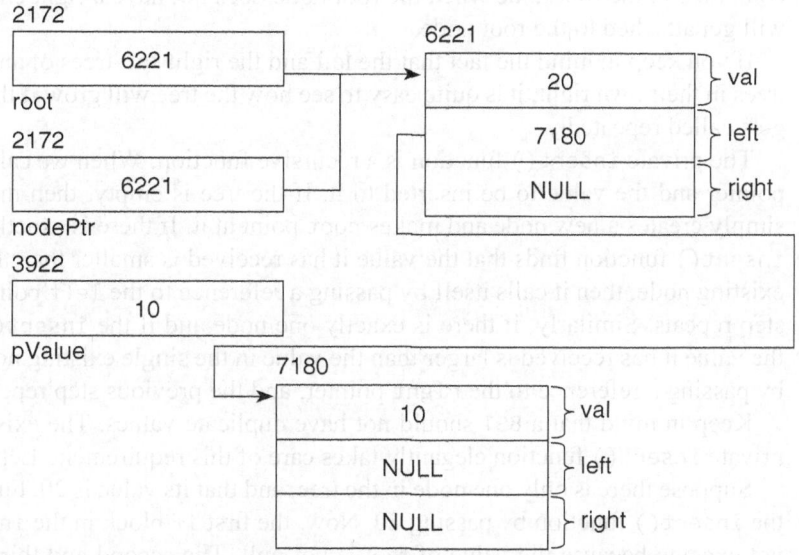

Figure 9.79 Situation after the second generation of the call to the insert() function ends

This will bring the second if block of the first generation to an end. The third if block will not execute because its test expression will return false. Thus, the first generation will terminate. The local variables of the first generation—nodePtr and pValue—will cease to exist. We will then be left with the structure shown in Figure 9.80.

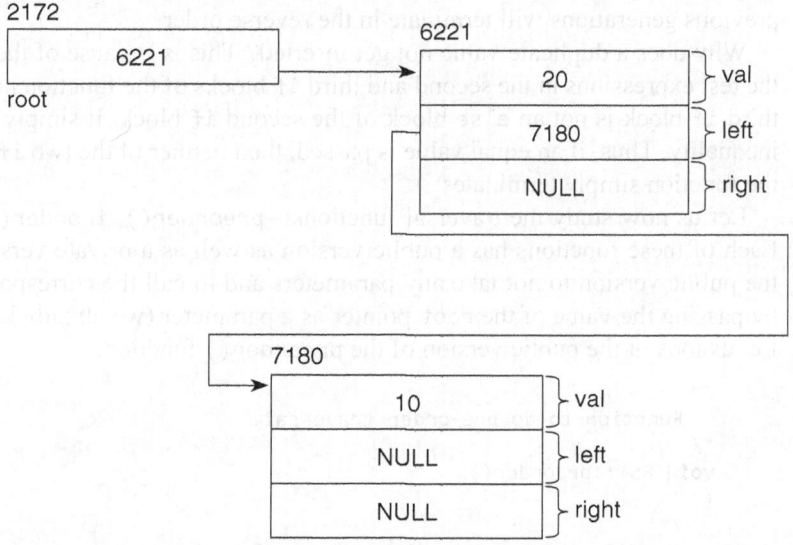

Figure 9.80 Situation after the first generation of the call to the insert() function ends

We can see that a new node has got attached to the left of the first node. This is what we were expecting. It is clear that the insert() function will work correctly if the tree is not empty.

Similarly, if we call the insert() function by passing a value that is larger than the value contained in the root node when the root node does not have a right child, then a right child will get attached to the root node.

If you keep in mind the fact that the left and the right sub-trees of any node in the tree are trees in their own right, it is quite easy to see how the tree will grow if the insert() function gets called repeatedly.

The private insert() function is a recursive function. When we call it, we pass the root pointer and the value to be inserted to it. If the tree is empty, then the insert() function simply creates a new node and makes root point at it. If there is exactly one node and if the insert() function finds that the value it has received is smaller than the value in the single existing node, then it calls itself by passing a reference to the left pointer, and the previous step repeats. Similarly, if there is exactly one node and if the insert() function finds that the value it has received is larger than the value in the single existing node, then it calls itself by passing a reference to the right pointer, and the previous step repeats.

Keep in mind that a BST should not have duplicate values. The existing definition of the private insert() function elegantly takes care of this requirement. Let us understand how.

Suppose there is only one node in the tree, and that its value is 20. Further suppose we call the insert() function by passing 20. Now, the first if block in the insert() function will not execute because the value of root is not null. The second and third if blocks will also not execute because the value passed to the function is neither smaller than nor greater than 20 (it is equal to 20). The function will terminate without doing anything.

By extrapolation, it is easy to understand that if we pass a value that is the duplicate of a value that is several levels down in the tree, then also the value will not get inserted. When the function keeps getting called recursively till the point the node that contains the duplicate value is reached, the same thing happens as has been described in the previous paragraph. The current generation of the function call will terminate without doing anything. And the previous generations will terminate in the reverse order.

Why does a duplicate value not get inserted? This is because of the clever way in which the test expressions in the second and third if blocks of the function have been defined. The third if block is not an else block of the second if block. It simply tests for the opposite inequality. Thus, if an equal value is passed, then neither of the two if blocks executes, and the function simply terminates.

Let us now study the traversal functions—preorder(), inorder(), and postorder(). Each of these functions has a public version as well as a private version. We have defined the public version to not take any parameters and to call the corresponding private version by passing the value of the root pointer as a parameter (we already know why we do this). Let us look at the public version of the preorder() function.

```
/*
    Function to do pre-order traversal.
*/
void BST::preorder()
{
    /*
        Call the corresponding private function.
    */
    preorder(root);
```

```
    }
```

As we can see, the public version of the function calls its private version and passes the `root` pointer to it. Let us look at the private function of the function.

```
/*
    Private function to do pre-order traversal. Will be
    called from the public function.
*/
void BST::preorder(BSTNode * nodePtr)
{
    /*
        As long as the passed pointer is not NULL ...
    */
    if(nodePtr != NULL)
    {
        /*
            ... display the value of the current node first ...
        */
        cout << nodePtr -> getVal() << endl;
        /*
            ... then call the function recursively for the left
            child ...
        */
        preorder(nodePtr -> getLeft());
        /*
            ... and then call the function recursively for the
            right child.
        */
        preorder(nodePtr -> getRight());
    }
}
```

This function is actually very simple. When this function is called for the first time, the value of `root` gets copied to `nodePtr`. If `nodePtr` is NULL, then the function terminates without doing anything. Otherwise, it displays the value of the first node. It then traverses the left sub-tree by passing the value of the `left` pointer of the node, at which `nodePtr` points, to the recursive call to the function. Thereafter, it traverses the left–right sub-tree by passing the value of the `right` pointer of the node at which `nodePtr` points to the recursive call to the function. Keep in mind that as long as the first recursive call to the function is executing, the second recursive call will not start. Also, in every new generation of the function, `nodePtr` will point at the `root` node of the lower sub-tree.

The `inorder()` and `postorder()` functions can be explained in the same way.

Summary

Data structures are special ways in which pieces of data are arranged and related to each other during run time. Each such piece of data is embedded in a node that contains the piece of data itself along with one or more pointers that either point at other similar nodes or have null values.

Linked lists are linear data structures. They consist of nodes that are linked to each other in a linear fashion.

Each node in a single linked list is an object that is made up of two parts. The first part is the data carried by the node. The second part of each node is a pointer that carries the address of the next node in the list. This is how a node is linked to the next node.

There are two classes that enable us to create linked lists:

- A node class whose objects will be the actual nodes of the single linked list. The class that we have created is called `SingleLinkedListNode`.
- A single linked list class, each object of which will represent a separate linked list of nodes. The class that we have created is called `SingleLinkedList`.

Each object of the `SingleLinkedListNode` class will be a node in the linked list. This class has an integer data member, `val`, which is supposed to contain the value of the node.

Each object of the `SingleLinkedList` class will be a linked list. This class has a data member, `head`, which is a pointer. This pointer is defined to point at the first node of the linked list. In our program, it will either be made to point at the first node in the linked list or will be assigned the NULL value (to indicate that the current list is empty).

Stacks are also data structures. Just like linked lists, stacks also consist of nodes where each node is linked to exactly one other node (with the exception of the last node, which is not connected to any other node). In a stack, we can add a node only to the beginning. This operation is called push. In a stack, we can delete a node only from the beginning. This operation is called pop. Thus, stacks are said to have a LIFO (last-in-first-out) operation. The last node to get in is the first to get out.

Queues are data structures too. They are very similar to stacks. The only difference between the two is in their push operations. In a stack, the push operation causes the new node to get added to the beginning. But, in a queue, the push operation causes the new node to get added to the end. Thus, queues are said to have a FIFO (first-in-first-out) operation. The first node to get in is the first to get out.

Trees, unlike linked lists, stacks and queues, do not have a linear structure. In a tree, each of the nodes may be connected to more than one node.

A binary tree is a tree in which each node is linked to a maximum of two nodes. A binary tree is a finite set of elements. It is either empty or is partitioned into three disjoint subsets. The first subset contains only one element, which is the root of the tree. The other subsets are themselves binary trees. One of them is considered to be the left sub-tree and the other one is considered to be the right sub-tree. Either or both of the sub-trees can be empty.

Binary trees have recursive structures. The entire tree has a root, a left sub-tree, and a right sub-tree. Both of the sub-trees are trees themselves. Both of them in turn have roots and sub-trees.

While programming functions that model operations on trees, we can exploit this recursive nature of trees and make them recursive too. This will make the functions shorter and reduce our programming effort.

There are three ways of traversing a tree—in pre-order, in-order, and post-order.

A binary search tree is a special form of binary tree. In a binary search tree, for any given node, the value contained in its left child is less than the value contained in the node and the value contained in the node is less than the value contained in its right child.

If you traverse a binary search tree in in-order (left, root, right), and display the value of each node as you visit, then you will end up printing the values in ascending order.

In order to create trees, we have defined two classes – 'BSTNode' and 'BST'. The first class helped us in creating the nodes of BSTs whereas the second class helped us in creating the BSTs themselves.

Key Terms

data structures

arrays have limitations—fixed size, difficulty in inserting values

linked lists

linked list node—value part and next pointer

`SingleLinkedListNode` class

`SingleLinkedList` class

head pointer

append nodes to single linked lists

prefix nodes to single linked lists

find nodes in single linked lists

delete nodes from single linked lists

display nodes of single linked lists

stacks

push operation

pop operation

LIFO in stacks

queues

FIFO in queues

trees

non-linear structure of trees
binary trees
three disjoint sets of binary trees—root, left sub-tree, and right sub-tree
binary trees are recursive
traversal of binary trees—pre-order, in-order, and post-order

binary search trees
BSTNode class
BST class
data part of tree node
left pointer of tree node
right pointer of tree node
root pointer of the tree class

Exercises

1. What are the limitations of arrays?
2. Describe the parts of each of the nodes of a single linked list.
3. Explain the function that appends nodes to single linked lists.
4. Explain the function that finds nodes in single linked lists that have a specific value.
5. Explain the function that deletes nodes from the beginning of single linked lists.
6. Explain the three orders of traversing a binary tree with the aid of figures of small binary trees.
7. Explain why the 'getLeft()' and 'getRight()' functions have been defined to return by reference.
8. Write a function to iterate forwards in a linked list using recursion.
9. Add a pointer as a new data member to the SingleLinkedList class. This pointer should point at the last node of the list (or have NULL value in case the list is empty). Update the member functions of the SingleLinkedList class in order to ensure this. Also, simplify the functions by taking advantage of the presence of this pointer. Do we still need to ensure that the next pointer of the last node is always NULL?
10. Introduce function to the SingleLinkedList class that would return the count of nodes in the linked list.
11. Can the above function be called with respect to an object of the stack class? If not, then what is the solution?

12. Define a function to search for a specified value in binary search trees. The function should return true if the specified value is found and false otherwise.
13. State true or false
    (a) In a single linked list, the next pointer of the last node is always NULL.
    (b) Linked lists are non-linear data structures.
    (c) Each node of a single linked list can contain only integer-type values in its data part.
    (d) In a stack, you can add a node only at the beginning.
    (e) Queues implement FIFO operation.
    (f) A binary tree is a finite set of elements, which is either empty or is partitioned into two disjoint subsets.
14. Fill in the blanks
    (a) The maximum number of nodes a node of a single linked list is attached to is ....
    (b) The number of parts each node of a single linked list is ....
    (c) Adding a node to a stack or a queue is known as ....
    (d) Deleting a node from a stack or a queue is known as ....
    (e) The number of parts each node of a binary tree is ....
    (f) The three orders of traversing a binary tree are ...., ..., and ....

10

Templates

This chapter explains the concept of generic programming using templates. Function templates along with their use and benefits are included. Class templates, their use, and benefits are also included.

The Standard Template Library provides a number of useful class templates that can be used to meet various common programming needs. Important class templates of this library are also described in this chapter.

10.1 Introduction

We frequently come across functions that work in exactly the same way for different data types. Each of these functions has been designed to handle a specific data type. For different types of variables, only the keyword used to declare the variables upon which they work changes. The algorithm that these functions implement remains the same and therefore the structure of the function remains the same. One such function that immediately comes to mind is the one used to swap two values (Listing 10.1).

Listing 10.1 A function to swap two integers

```
void swap(int & a,int & b)
{
    int temp;
    temp=a;
    a=b;
    b=temp;
}
```

The preceding swap function swaps the values of two integers. A swap function that swaps two floats will have the definition shown in Listing 10.2.

Listing 10.2 A function to swap two float-type numbers

```
void swap(float & a,float & b)
{
    float temp;
    temp=a;
    a=b;
    b=temp;
}
```

We can notice that the two `swap` functions are exactly alike except for the data type of the variables upon whom they work. It would be quite reasonable to expect that the C++ language provides us with a facility to write a common function that is independent of a data type but which embodies the common algorithm and that the C++ language on its own creates the actual function as and when the need arises. Having code at a common place has obvious advantages, namely ease in code development and ease in code maintenance.

This facility is provided in the form of templates. The programmer can create a template with some or all variables therein having unspecified data types. Whenever the template is invoked by passing arguments of a certain type, the C++ language on its own replaces the unspecified type with the type of the arguments passed. Such templates can be created for individual functions as well as entire classes.

10.2   Function Templates

The syntax for creating a template for a generic function is given in Listing 10.3.

Listing 10.3   Syntax for a function template

```
template <class T, …>
return_type function_name(T arg1, …)
{
    //statements
}
```

The template definition begins with the `template` keyword. This is followed by a list of generic data types in angular brackets. Each generic type is prefixed with the `class` keyword and, if the template function works on more than one generic type, commas separate them. Thereafter, the function template is defined just like an ordinary function. The return type comes first. This is followed by the name of the function, which in turn is followed by a pair of parentheses enclosing the list of formal arguments the function takes. However, there should be at least one formal argument of each one of the generic types mentioned within the angular brackets.

For example, the template for the function `swap` can be as given in Listing 10.4.

Listing 10.4   Template for the function swap

```
/*Beginning of swap.h*/
template <class T>
void swap(T & a, T & b)
{
    T temp;
    temp=a;
    a=b;
    b=temp;
}
/*End of swap.h*/
```

Now, suppose the function `swap` is called by passing two integers. The compiler generates an actual definition for the function by replacing each occurrence of T by the keyword `int`. See Listing 10.5.

Listing 10.5   Calling the template for the function swap by passing integers

```
/*Beginning of swap01.cpp*/
#include<iostream.h>
#include"swap.h"
void main()
{
    int x,y;
    x=10;
    y=20;
    cout<<"Before swapping\n";
    cout<<"x="<<x<<" y="<<y<<endl;
    swap(x,y);                      //compiler generates swap(int&, int&); and
                                    //resolves the call
    cout<<"After swapping\n";
    cout<<"x="<<x<<" y="<<y<<endl;
}
/*End of swap01.cpp*/
```

Output
Before swapping
x=10 y=20
After swapping
x=20 y=10

Similarly, if the function swap is called by passing two floats, the compiler generates an actual definition for the function by replacing each occurrence of T by the keyword float and so on. See Listing 10.6.

Listing 10.6   Calling the template for the function swap by passing floats

```
/*Beginning of swap02.cpp*/
#include<iostream.h>
#include"swap.h"
void main()
{
    float x,y;
    x=1.1;
    y=2.2;
    cout<<"Before swapping\n";
    cout<<"x="<<x<<" y="<<y<<endl;
    swap(x,y);                      //compiler generates swap(float&, float&);
                                    //and resolves the call
    cout<<"After swapping\n";
    cout<<"x="<<x<<" y="<<y<<endl;
}
/*End of swap02.cpp*/
```

Output
Before swapping
x=1.1 y=2.2
After swapping
x=2.2 y=1.1

Objects of classes can also be passed to the function swap. The compiler will generate an actual definition by replacing each occurrence of T by the name of the corresponding class. See Listing 10.7.

Listing 10.7 Calling the template for the function swap by passing objects of the class Distance

```
/*Beginning of swap03.cpp*/
#include<iostream.h>
#include"swap.h"
#include"Distance.h"
void main()
{
    Distance d1(1,1.1),d2(2,2.2);
    cout<<"Before swapping\n";
    cout<<"d1="<<d1.getFeet()<<"'-"<<d1.getInches()<<"'"'\n";
    cout<<"d2="<<d2.getFeet()<<"'-"<<d2.getInches()<<"'"'\n";
    swap(d1,d2);                      //compiler generates swap(Distance&,
                                      //Distance&); and resolves the call
    cout<<"After swapping\n";
    cout<<"d1="<<d1.getFeet()<<"'-"<<d1.getInches()<<"'"'\n";
    cout<<"d2="<<d2.getFeet()<<"'-"<<d2.getInches()<<"'"'\n";
}
/*End of swap03.cpp*/
```

Output
Before swapping
d1=1'-1.1"
d2=2'-2.2"
After swapping
d1=2'-2.2"
d2=1'-1.1"

We must note the amount of effort saved in code development. Only one definition suffices for all possible types! Templates are a very handy tool provided by C++ for implementing code reusability.

Further, the compiler generates an actual function from a template only once for a given data type. For example, if the function swap is called by passing integers for the first time, the compiler will generate a function definition from its template. Subsequent calls with the same data type will not generate the definition again. This is for the simple reason that the compiler first looks for an exact match to resolve a function call before looking for a template (the next paragraph explains this with the help of an example). If it finds exact match, it does not look for a template. Since the first function call itself generates the function definition, subsequent calls do not do so.

Evidently, the entire definition of the function must appear in the header file. Otherwise, the compiler would not be able to generate the correct definition while compiling a user program in which the function template has been called.

The library programmer may like to put the definition of the template function in a library while keeping only the prototype in the header file. There is a keyword called export that is supposed to fulfill this need. However, not all compilers support this keyword.

It is sometimes necessary to override the function template by an actual function. In order to understand this, let us consider the template for a function to return the larger of the two arguments that are passed to it (Listing 10.8).

Listing 10.8 Template for the larger function

```
template <class T>
T& larger(const T& a, const T& b)
{
    return a>b? a:b;
}
```

This function works correctly if variables of ordinary data types such as int and float are passed to it. However, it does not work correctly if strings are passed to it. See Listing 10.9.

Listing 10.9 Calling the larger function by passing strings

```
char * s1="abcd", * s2="efgh";
char * s3=larger(s1,s2);          //compiler generates larger(const
                                  //char *&, const char *&); and
                                  //resolves the call
```

We notice that, during execution, the larger(char *&, char *&) function in Listing 10.9 compares only the addresses of the two strings and not their contents! This is certainly not wanted. For this special case, we would like a special version of the function larger for the character strings to execute. It is precisely a special version of the function larger that we would define along with the template. See Listing 10.10.

Listing 10.10 Overriding the template for the function larger

```
char * larger(char * a, char * b)
{
    return strcmp(a,b) > 0 ? a : b;
}
```

Now, if the function larger is called by passing two strings, the function in Listing 10.9 will be called while the template will be ignored. Function templates can be overloaded. See Listing 10.11.

Listing 10.11 Overloading a function template

```
#include<iostream.h>
template <class T>
void display(const T & a)
{
    cout << a << endl;
}

template <class T>
void display(const T & a, const int n) //overloaded version
                                       //of display()
```

```
{
    int ctr;
    for(ctr=0;ctr<n;ctr++)
        cout << a << endl;
}

void main()
{
    char c = 'a';
    int i = 10;
    display(c);
    cout<<endl;
    display(c,3);
    cout<<endl;
    display(i);
    cout<<endl;
    display(i,5);
    cout<<endl;
}
```

Output

```
a

a
a
a

10

10
10
10
10
10
```

More than one generic type can also be mentioned in the template definition. See Listing 10.12.

Listing 10.12 More than one generic type in a function template

```
template <class T, class U>
void f1(const T & a, const U & b)
{
    //statements
}
```

Here we should go back to Chapter 8 on Operator Overloading. It was mentioned that the need to make objects of a class capable of being used in function templates necessitates the overloading of operators for the class. We may look at the template for the function `larger`. The `greater than` operator is embedded within its definition. When objects of a certain class are passed as parameters to it, the `greater than` operator will attempt to compare them. If this operator has not been overloaded for the class, the compiler will immediately report an error. Thus, in order to take advantage of the template, the greater than operator should be overloaded for the class.

10.3　Class Templates

The need for class templates is similar to the need for function templates. The need for generic classes (Queue, Stack, Array, etc.) that handle data of different types is felt frequently. Let us consider the set of three classes in Listing 10.13 whose member functions have similar definitions, the mere difference being the type of the private data members upon whom they operate.

Listing 10.13　Classes with similar definition

```cpp
class X_for_int
{
     int val;
   public:
     void f1(const int &);
     void f2(const int &);
     /*
        rest of the class X_for_int
     */
};

class X_for_char
{
     char val;
   public:
     void f1(const char &);
     void f2(const char &);
     /*
        rest of the class X_for_char
     */
};

class X_for_string
{
     string val;
   public:
     void f1(const string &);
     void f2(const string &);
     /*
        rest of the class X_for_string
     */
};
```

The classes X_for_int, X_for_char, and X_for_string defined in Listing 10.13 are similar in every respect except for the type of their data members. As expected, the presence of three different classes that are different only in the data type of the data members upon whom their member functions work creates huge difficulties in code maintenance. Any change in one of the classes will have to be replicated in all of the others. This situation certainly demands the creation of a template class. Such a template class can be created as illustrated by Listing 10.14.

Listing 10.14   A class template

```
template<class T>
class X
{
      T val;
   public:
      void f1(const T &);
      void f2(const T &);
      /*
         rest of the class X
      */
};
```

The definition of the template class begins with the keyword `template`. This is followed by the list of type and non-type template arguments enclosed in angular brackets. `Type` template arguments are those that represent a data type. An actual built-in or user-defined type replaces them when an object is declared. Each type template argument is preceded by the keyword `class`. Non-type template arguments are variables of built-in or user-defined type. Actual constant values are passed for these non-type template arguments. The data type precedes each non-type template argument. Thereafter, the class is defined using the usual syntax.

Member functions of class templates are defined as in Listing 10.15.

Listing 10.15   Defining the member function of a class template

```
template<class T>
void X<T> :: f1(const T & p)
{
   /*
      definition of the function
   */
}
```

Member functions of a template class are defined in the same way as the template class itself. The definition begins with the `template` keyword. This is followed by the list of type and non-type template arguments enclosed in angular brackets. Each type template argument is preceded by the keyword `class`; each non-type template argument is preceded by its data type. Thereafter, the function is defined using the usual syntax except for one important difference. The class name given before the scope resolution operator is followed by the names of all template arguments enclosed in angular brackets.

Objects of this template class can be declared as follows:

```
X<int> intObj;
```

While declaring the object, the class name is followed by the type and non-type template parameter(s) enclosed in angular brackets. This is followed as usual by the name of the object itself. When the compiler sees the declaration of the object, it replaces each occurrence of the template argument by the template parameter in the definition of the class template and generates a separate class. In the preceding case, each occurrence of the token T in the class X will be replaced by the keyword int.

Objects of template classes, once declared, can be used just like any other object.

```
X<int> intObj01,intObj02;
intObj01.f1(intObj02);
```

The compiler generates the exact definition of a class from a given class template once only for each data type. For example, if two objects of the template class X are declared with the data type int, the compiler will generate the exact definition for the first object only.

```
X<int> intObj01;                    //definition generated and used
X<int> intObj02;                    //no definition generated
```

As in the case of non-member function templates, member functions of class templates are also defined in the header files themselves.

The section on Standard Template Library, which follows this section, has many instructive and practical examples of built-in class templates that are provided by all standard C++ compilers. Before moving on to that section, let us have a look at some fine points on class templates.

- A template class can take more than one template type argument. Listing 10.16 illustrates this.

Listing 10.16 More than one template-type argument in a class template

```
template<class T, class U>
class X
{
    T val1;
    U val2;
    /*
      rest of the class X
    */
};
```

- A template class can take a non-type template argument. Listing 10.17 illustrates this.

Listing 10.17 A non-type template argument in a class template

```
template<class T, int v>
class X
{
    T val1;
    /*
      rest of the class X
    */
};
```

While declaring an object of such a class, a data type will be passed as a parameter for the template-type argument. However, an actual value will be passed for the non-type template argument.

```
X<int,5> intObj;
```

- The name of the template argument cannot be used more than once in the template class's list of template arguments. Listing 10.18 illustrates this.

Listing 10.18 Error due to identical names of more than one type template arguments

```
template<class T, class T>           //ERROR: duplicate name in
                                     //parameter list!
class X
{
    /*
       definition of class X
    */
};
```

- The same name for a template argument can be used in the list of template arguments of two different template classes. Listing 10.19 illustrates this.

Listing 10.19 Same name can be used for a type template argument in more than one class template

```
template<class T>
class X
{
    /*
       definition of class X
    */
};

template<class T>                    //OK: Same name T used in two different
                                     //classes
class Y
{
    /*
       definition of class Y
    */
};
```

- The name of a template argument need not be the same in the declaration and the definition of the template class. Listing 10.20 illustrates this.

Listing 10.20 Name of a type template argument can be different in a template class declaration and its definition

```
template<class T>
class X;                             //declaration

template<class U>                    //OK: different name for the template
                                     //argument in the
class X                              //definition
{
    /*
       definition of class X
    */
};
```

- Formal arguments of template functions can be objects of a template class. Listing 10.21 illustrates this.

Listing 10.21 Formal argument of a template function can be the object of a template class

```
template<class T>
class X
{
    /*
        definition of class X
    */
};

template<class U>
void f1(X<U> v)
{
    /*
        definition of the function
    */
}
```

10.3.1 Nested Class Templates

Nested classes can be created for template classes in the same way as they are created for non-template classes. Listing 10.22 illustrates this.

Listing 10.22 A nested template class

```
template<class T>
class A
{
    class B
    {
        T x;            //enclosing template type can be used in the
                        //nested class
        /*
            rest of the class B
        */
    };
    /*
        definition of the class A
    */
};
```

10.4 Standard Template Library

Would it not be of use if C++ provided class templates for meeting common programming requirements? For example, it would be highly convenient to have a class template that enables us to create a linked list of objects of any type of our choice.

The standard implementation of C++ does provide a set of header files where a large number of useful class templates have been defined. These files contain definitions of the class templates, their member functions, and a number of global associated functions. The global associated functions implement commonly used algorithms. This library of class templates and their helper global functions is known as the Standard Template Library (STL).

A complete study of all of these templates is beyond the scope of this book. However, we will study the more important class templates in the next section. The commonly used member functions and the associated global functions are explained with the help of examples.

10.4.1 list Class

The list class is used to create sequential containers. Elements of the list are single objects.
Objects of the list class are declared as follows:

```
list<char> clist;              //creating a list of characters
list<float> flist;             //creating a list of floats
list<int> ilist;               //creating a list of integers
```

For using the list template class, the header file list needs to be included in the source code.

```
#include<list>
```

The elements of a list occupy a non-contiguous memory. They are doubly linked through a pair of pointers. One of the pointers points at the next element and the other points at the previous element of the list. This allows both forward and backward traversal.

The number of elements a list object would have can be specified at the time of declaration.

```
list<int> ilist(3);            //list of integers with three initial
                               //elements.
```

A default value can be specified for these elements.

```
list<int> ilist(3, -1);        //list of integers with three
                               //initial elements each having -1.
```

A list can be created from an existing array. We can do this by passing a pointer that points at the first element of the array and a second pointer that points 1 past the last element of the array to be copied.

```
int iArr[6] = {0,1,2,3,4,5};   //an array with six elements
list<int> ilist(iArr, iArr+6); //list also has six
                               //elements with the same
                               //values
```

Let us have a look at the important member functions of this class.

The list<>::push_front() *Function*

This function is used to insert elements at the beginning of the list.

```
list<int> ilist;
ilist.push_front(1);           //inserts 1 at the beginning of
                               //the list
ilist.push_front(2);           //inserts 2 at the beginning of
                               //the list … list becomes 2,1.
```

The list<>::push_back() *Function*

This function is used to insert elements at the end of the list.

```
list<int> ilist;
ilist.push_back(1);                    //inserts 1 at the end of the list
ilist.push_back(2);                    //inserts 2 at the end of the list …
                                       //list becomes 1,2.
```

The list<>::pop_front() *Function*

This function is used to delete the first element of the list.

```
list<int> ilist;
ilist.push_back(1);                    //inserts 1 at the end of the list
ilist.push_back(2);                    //inserts 2 at the end of the list …
                                       //list becomes 1,2.
ilist.push_back(3);                    //inserts 3 at the end of the list …
                                       //list becomes 1,2,3.
ilist.pop_front();                     //deletes the first element … list
                                       //becomes 2,3.
```

The list<>::pop_back() *Function*

This function is used to delete the last element of the list.

```
list<int> ilist;
ilist.push_back(1);                    //inserts 1 at the end of the list
ilist.push_back(2);                    //inserts 2 at the end of the list …
                                       //list becomes 1,2.
ilist.push_back(3);                    //inserts 3 at the end of the list …
                                       //list becomes 1,2,3.
ilist.pop_back();                      //deletes the last element … list
                                       //becomes 1,2.
```

Traversing a List using the Iterator

An iterator enables us to traverse the list elements in sequence. The following lines of code illustrate the syntax used for its declaration and its use.

```
list<int> ilist;
ilist.push_back(1);
ilist.push_back(2);
ilist.push_back(3);
list<int>::iterator iter=ilist.begin();       //iter points
                                              //at the first
                                              //element of
                                              //the list
for(;iter!=ilist.end();++iter)
    cout<<*iter<<endl;                        //an iterator can be dereferenced
                                              //just like a pointer
```

The list::begin() function returns an iterator that points at the first element of the list. The list::end() function returns an iterator that points 1 past the last element of the list. The increment operator advances the iterator to point at the next element of the list. The indirection operator (*) returns the value of the element pointed at by the iterator.

The list<>::insert() *Function*

This function enables a random insertion into a list.

```
list<int> ilist;
ilist.push_back(1);                       //inserts 1 at the end of the list
ilist.push_back(2);                       //inserts 2 at the end of the list …
                                          //list becomes 1,2.
ilist.insert(ilist.begin(),-20);         //inserts -20 at the
                                          //beginning of the list
                                          //… list becomes
                                          //-20,1,2.
```

The list<>::insert() function is used with the find() function for random insertion into a list.

The find() *Function*

This global function searches specified values in lists. If the searched value is found in an element of the list, it returns an iterator to the element. Else, it returns the value of the list::end() function.

The following program searches for the value '10' from the beginning of the list to the end. It inserts the value '–1' before '10' in the list, if the value is found. Else, it appends '–1' at the end of the list.

```
list<int>::iterator iter;
iter=find(ilist.begin(),ilist.end(),10);          //searching
                                          //from the first element to
                                          //the last element of the
                                          //list for the value 10
ilist.insert(iter,-1);
```

The list<>::size() *Function*

This function enables us to determine the number of elements currently in this list.

```
list<int> ilist;
ilist.push_back(1);                       //inserts 1 at the end of the list
ilist.push_back(2);                       //inserts 2 at the end of the list …
                                          //list becomes 1,2.
cout<<ilist.size()<<endl;                 //outputs 2
```

The list<>::erase() *Function*

This function enables random deletion from the list. The iterator to the position of the element to be deleted is passed to the list::erase() function.

Suppose we want to delete the element with value '19' from a list. We can use the find() function to obtain the iterator to the element and pass it to the list::erase() function.

```
iter=find(ilist.begin(),ilist.end(),19);          //obtaining an
                                          //iterator to the element
                                          //with value 19
if(iter!=ilist.end())                     //checking whether element
                                          //with value 19 exists or not
ilist.erase(iter);                        //removing the element if
                                          //found
```

The list<>::clear() *Function*

This function erases all elements in a list.

```
list<int> ilist;
ilist.push_back(1);
ilist.push_back(2);
ilist.push_back(3);
cout<<ilist.size()<<endl;        //outputs 3
ilist.clear();                   //removes all elements of the
                                 //list

cout<<ilist.size()<<endl;        //outputs 0
```

The list<>::empty() Function

This function is used to test whether a list is empty or not.

```
if(ilist.empty())
    //do something
else
    //do something else
```

Insertion into and deletion from an intermediate position in a list is efficient. This is because for such operations only the pointers of the affected element need to be reassigned.

On the other hand, random access to a particular element is inefficient. For traversing to the element that has our desired value, value of the pointer in each of the preceding elements has to be read starting from the first element since the elements are not in contiguous blocks of memory.

10.4.2 vector Class

The vector class is used to create sequential containers. Elements of the list are single objects.

The names of member functions of the vector class are the same as those of the list class. Global functions, such as the find() function that works on objects of the list class, have been overloaded to work upon objects of the vector class too.

However, the layout of elements in a vector is completely different from that in a list. In a vector, unlike a list, elements are stored in contiguous blocks (just like an array).

For using the vector template class, the header file vector needs to be included in the source code.

```
#include<vector>
```

A vector does not actually regrow itself with each individual insertion. The amount of memory a vector captures is larger than the number of elements it actually stores. When this storage becomes full, it again regrows itself by a certain amount to accommodate the latest insertion. The amount by which a vector regrows differs from compiler to compiler.

This brings us to two important concepts about vectors, namely capacity and size.

Capacity is the total size of the block currently captured by a vector. Obviously, it is directly proportional to the total number of elements that can be inserted into the vector before it needs to regrow.

Size, on the other hand, is the number of elements actually stored in the memory block that has been captured by the vector. Obviously, size of a vector is always less than or equal to its capacity.

The vector class has two functions that enable us to find the capacity and the size of the vector. These are vector::size() and vector::capacity().

Insertion into and deletion from an intermediate position in a vector is inefficient. This is because for such operations all elements starting from the insertion point need to be pushed up or pushed down as the case may be.

On the other hand, random access to a particular element is efficient. For traversing to the element that has our desired value, only the internal iterator has to be incremented since the elements are in contiguous blocks of memory.

10.4.3 pair Class

Objects of the pair class represent a pair of values that may or may not be of the same type.

```
pair<string, int> player("Kasparov",1795);
```

The object player in this statement may represent the number of games in our database that have been played by the player with name 'Kasparov' (the string class is discussed later in this chapter). Obviously, we would like to create more variables of the same type later in the program. Using the keyword typedef allows us to do so.

```
typedef pair<string, int> Player;
Player kasparov("Kasparov",1795);
Player fischer("Fischer",2162);
Player karpov("Karpov",1525);
```

For using the pair template class, the header file utility needs to be included in the source code.

```
#include<utility>
```

The two elements of the objects of the pair class can be accessed as first and second. For this, the member access operator can be used as follows:

```
cout<<"Number of games of "<<kasparov.first
    <<" are "<<kasparov.second;
```

10.4.4 map Class

The map class is used to create associative containers. Elements of the list are key/value pairs. The map class does not allow duplicates.

For using the map template class, the header file map needs to be included in the source code.

```
#include<map>
```

Each record in the map class is an object of the pair class. Listing 10.23 illustrates all the important functionalities of the map class.

Listing 10.23 The map class

```
/*Beginning of map.cpp*/
#include<iostream.h>
#include<map>
#include<utility>
void main()
```

```
            {
                map<string, int> chessbase;
                typedef pair<string, int> Player;    //should be of the
                                                     //same type as map
                Player kasparov("Kasparov",1795);
                Player fischer("Fischer",2162);
                Player karpov("Karpov",1525);

                chessbase.insert(kasparov);      //inserting a record
                chessbase.insert(fischer);       //inserting another record
                chessbase.insert(karpov);        //inserting another record

                //The first member of each record is treated as the key.
                //The corresponding second member is the value and can be
                //retrieved as follows:
                cout<<"Number of games of Kasparov is: "
                    <<chessbase["Kasparov"]<<endl;
                cout<<"Number of occurrences of Kasparov is: "
                    <<chessbase.count("Kasparov")<<endl;

                //Using the subscript operator to query the value for a
                //key as above inserts it in the map!
                cout<<"Number of occurrences of Anand is: "
                    <<chessbase.count("Anand")<<endl;        //returns zero
                cout<<"Number of games of Anand is: "
                    <<chessbase["Anand"]<<endl;       //returns zero … but a
                                                      //record got added with
                                                      //key as "Anand" and
                                                      //value as zero because
                                                      //value is of integer
                                                      //type and zero is taken
                                                      //as default value for
                                                      //integers.
                cout<<"Number of occurrences of Anand is: "
                    <<chessbase.count("Anand")<<endl;        //return 1!!

                //An iterator can also be used. The iterator points at a
                //pair rather than a single value. The pair is returned
                //by the find function.
                map<string, int>::iterator iter;
                iter=chessbase.find("Tendulkar");
                cout<<"Number of occurrences of Tendulkar is: "
                    <<chessbase.count("Tendulkar")<<endl; //return 0
                if(iter!=chessbase.end())
                   cout<<"Number of games of "<<iter->first<<" is: "
                       <<iter->second<<endl;
                else
                   cout<<iter->first<<" not found\n";
                cout<<"Number of occurrences of Tendulkar is: "
                    <<chessbase.count("Tendulkar")<<endl; //return 0 …
                                                          //no new
                                                          //record
                                                          //inserted
            }
/*End of map.cpp*/
```

Output

Number of games of Kasparov is: 1795
Number of occurrences of Kasparov is: 1

Number of occurrences of Anand is: 0
Number of games of Anand is: 0
Number of occurrences of Anand is: 1
Number of occurrences of Tendulkar is: 0
Tendulkar not found
Number of occurrences of Tendulkar is: 0

10.4.5 set Class

The set class is used to create sequential containers. Elements of the list are single objects. A set stores a collection of keys in a sorted manner. The data itself serves as the keys to the set. The set contains the elements in a sorted fashion and duplicates are discarded during insertion.

For using the set template class, the header file set needs to be included in the source code.

```
#include<set>
```

An illustrative program follows in Listing 10.24.

Listing 10.24 The set class

```
/*Beginning of set.cpp*/
#include<set>
#include<string>
#include<iostream.h>
void main()
{
    set<char> set1;                   //a set of characters

    string s1("I am indeed a cat. This is indeed a hat");
    cout<<s1<<endl;

//Putting all the characters of the string s1 in the
//set. Characters get automatically sorted while
//duplicates get automatically rejected
set1.insert(s1.begin(),s1.end());

set<char>::iterator iter;
for(iter = set1.begin(); iter!=set1.end(); iter++)
    {
        cout << *iter;                //outputting the set
    }
}
/*End of set.cpp*/
```

Output
I am indeed a cat. This is indeed a hat
.Itacdehimnst

10.4.6 multimap Class

The only difference between the map and the multimap class is that while the map class does not allow duplicate key values (it overrides the old value associated with a key), the multimap class does allow duplicate key values. Therefore, the `multimap` class does not support the `subscript` operator.

For using the `multimap` template class, the header file `map` needs to be included in the source code.

```
#include<map>
```

10.4.7 multiset Class

The only difference between the `set` and the `multiset` class is that while the `set` class does not allow duplicate key values (it overrides the old key value), the `multiset` class does allow duplicate key values.

For using the `multiset` template class, the header file `set` needs to be included in the source code.

```
#include<set>
```

Summary

Templates enable generic programming. Templates are created for functions and classes that are similar to each other in every respect except for the type of data they work upon.

The compiler generates an actual function or a class from a template once and only once for a given data type.

The syntax for creating a template for a generic function is as follows:

```
template <class T, …>
return_type function_name(T arg1, …)
{
    //statements
}
```

The compiler generates an actual function definition from a function template when the function is called. The types of the template arguments in the function template are replaced by the data type of the parameters passed.

```
int x,y;
function_name(x,y);  //definition function_
                       name(int arg1,
//int arg2) generated
```

The syntax for creating a template for a generic class is as follows:

```
template <class T, …>
```

```
class class_name
{
    T data_member_names;
    . . . .
    . . . .
  public:
    return_type function_name(parameter_
    names);
    . . . .
    . . . .
};
```

The syntax for defining member functions of template class is as follows:

```
template<class T, …>
return_type  class_name<T,…>::function_
name(parameter_names)
{
    . . . .
    . . . .
}
```

The compiler generates an actual class definition from a class template when an object of the class is created. The types of the template arguments in the class template are replaced by the data type of the parameters passed to the object.

```
class_name<int> obj; //actual definition
```

```
              of class
              //class_name generated
              by
              //replacing    every
              occurrence of T
              //by int.
```

A template class can take more than one template-type argument.

A template class can take a non-type template argument.

The name of the template argument cannot be used more than once in the template class's list of template arguments.

The same name for a template argument can be used in the list of template arguments of two different template classes.

The name of a template argument need not be the same in the declaration and the definition of the template class.

Formal arguments of template functions can be objects of template class.

Nested classes can be created for template classes in the same way as they are created for non-template classes.

The standard implementation of C++ provides a set of header files where a large number of useful class templates have been defined. These files contain definitions of the class templates, their member functions, and a number of global associated functions. The global associated functions implement commonly used algorithms. This library of class templates and their helper global functions is known as the Standard Template Library or STL.

The `list` class is used to create sequential containers. Elements of the list are single objects.

For using the `list` template class, the header file `list` needs to be included in the source code.

#include`<list>`

The elements of a list occupy a non-contiguous memory. They are doubly linked through a pair of pointers. One of the pointers points at the next element and the other points at the previous element of the list. This allows both forward and backward traversal.

The `vector` class is used to create sequential containers. Elements of the list are single objects.

In a vector, unlike a list, elements are stored in contiguous blocks (just like an array).

For using the `vector` template class, the header file `vector` needs to be included in the source code.

#include`<vector`

Objects of the `pair` class represent a pair of values that may or may not be of the same type.

For using the `pair` template class, the header file `utility` needs to be included in the source code.

#include`<utility>`

The `map` class is used to create associative containers. Elements of the list are key/value pairs. The `map` class does not allow duplicates.

For using the `map` template class, the header file `map` needs to be included in the source code.

#include`<map>`

Each record in a `map` class is an object of the `pair` class.

The `set` class is used to create sequential containers. Elements of the list are single objects. A set stores a collection of keys in a sorted manner. The data itself serves as the keys to the set. The set contains the elements in a sorted fashion and duplicates are discarded during insertion.

For using the `set` template class, the header file `set` needs to be included in the source code.

#include`<set>`

The only difference between the `map` and the `multimap` class is that while the `map` class does not allow duplicate key values (it overrides the old value associated with a key), the `multimap` class does allow duplicate key values.

For using the `multimap` template class, the header file `map` needs to be included in the source code.

#include`<map>`

The only difference between a `set` and a `multiset` class is that while the `set` class does not allow duplicate key values (it overrides the old key value), the `multiset` class does allow duplicate key values.

For using the `multiset` template class, the header file `set` needs to be included in the source code.

#include`<set>`

Key Terms

function templates
class templates
STL
– list class
– vector class

– pair class
– map class
– set class
– multimap class
– multiset class

Exercises

1. What are function templates? What is the need for function templates? How are they created?
2. When and how does the C++ compiler generate an actual function definition from its template?
3. How is a function template overridden for a specific data type?
4. What are class templates? What is the need for class templates? How are they created?
5. When and how does the C++ compiler generate an actual class definition from its template?
6. State true or false.
   (a) The compiler generates an actual function definition from a function template only once for the same type of parameters.
   (b) Function templates cannot be overloaded.
   (c) A template class cannot take a non-type template argument.
   (d) The name of a template argument need not be the same in the declaration and the definition of the template class.
7. What is the Standard Template Library? Name some of the template classes that are available in the STL.
8. Create a template for the bubble sort function.
9. Create a template for the Array class.
10. Write a program that will show the following menu to the user:
    (a) Insert an integer at the end of the list
    (b) Insert an integer at the beginning of the list
    (c) Insert an integer before a specified integer in the list
    (d) Delete the first integer from the list
    (e) Delete the last integer from the list
    (f) Delete a specified integer from the list
    (g) Display the list of integers
    (h) Save the list of integers
    (i) Quit
    Implement the above menu by using the list class of the STL.

11. Assume that the user has used the program in Exercise 10 to save a list of integers (with plenty of duplicates) in a file. Declare a vector that would contain all positions of a given integer in the file. Suppose the contents of the file are:

    21
    19
    3254
    937
    19
    19
    4253
    335
    19
    9825
    19

    The vector for the integer 19 would contain the elements 2, 5, 6, 9, and 11. Write a code to populate the vector.
12. Create a pair class that has the integer whose positions are to be stored as its first member and the vector that contains these positions as its second member. Rewrite the program in Exercises 10 and 11 to create such a pair object and assign 19 to its first member and a vector of its position as the second member.
13. Create a map of two integers. The first member of the map would represent a number that has been found in the file. The second member would represent the last position of the integer in the file. Write code to populate this map by the integers and their last positions in the file.
14. Declare a set of integers at the beginning of the program that you have written for Exercise 10. Keep updating the set as the integers are inserted into or deleted from the list.

11

Exception Handling

This chapter deals with exception handling. The benefits of exception handling and the much-needed protocol it establishes between the library and its applications are discussed. The chapter begins with a critical study of the C-style solution to the problem of exception handling. It then elucidates the use and mechanism of exception handling (the try-throw-catch mechanism). The need to throw class objects, the method of accessing members of thrown objects, and the use of nested exception classes are also discussed. The chapter concludes with a study of the limitations of exception handling.

11.1 Introduction

Let us begin by assuming the role of a library programmer. While defining non-member or member functions, we face situations where the function may or may not be able to execute further. For example, we write a statement to divide one double-type variable with another. Before this statement executes, we want to ensure that the denominator is not zero. We want to prevent the function from executing further if denominator is zero. This is only one of the conditions under which we want to prevent the further execution of the function. More such conditions exist (the function tries to open an unavailable file or requests more memory than is available). We know fully well the conditions under which the function should be aborted. However, we cannot decide the appropriate handling strategy. *While the library function can easily detect error conditions, it cannot decide upon an appropriate handling strategy.*

Now, let us assume the role of the application programmer. While calling a function, we should not be burdened with the task of detecting each error in the parameters that we pass to the functions we call. On the other hand, only we can decide what action should be taken whenever a particular error condition is met by the function being called. *While the user of the library function cannot detect error conditions, it can decide upon an appropriate handling strategy.*

Exception handling allows the library to sense and dispatch error conditions, and the client to handle them. It is usual for the library to know how to detect errors without knowing the appropriate handling strategy. It is just as usual for the client programs to understand how to deal with errors without being able to detect them.

We may wonder why a library function does not simply terminate the program when it detects invalid data input. Why does the library function not return an error value? All these questions will be answered in this chapter. Superiority of exception handling mechanism of C++ over the C-style error handling will also be discussed.

11.2 C-Style Handling of Error-generating Code

Let us study a function hmean() that takes two float-type numbers as parameters and computes their harmonic mean. See Listing 11.1.

Listing 11.1 Function to compute harmonic mean

```
float hmean(const float a, const float b)
{
    return 2.0*a*b/(a+b);
}
```

Clearly 'a' and 'b' should not be the negative of each other, else it would result in division by zero. Every effort should be put in to prevent the evaluation of the return expression and the consequent run-time error if 'a' and 'b' are the negative of each other.

There are three traditional C-style solutions to this problem.

- Terminate the program
- Check the parameters before function call
- Return a value representing an error

These methods are discussed below.

11.2.1 Terminate the Program

Let us look at this solution (Listing 11.2).

Listing 11.2 Terminating the program when an error condition is met

```
/*Beginning of hmean.h*/
float hmean(const float, const float);
/*End of hmean.h*/

/*Beginning of hmean.cpp*/
#include"hmean.h"
#include<stdlib.h> // for abort()
float hmean(const float a, const float b)
{
    if(a==-b)
        abort();
    return 2.0*a*b/(a+b);
}
/*End of hmean.cpp*/

/*Beginning of hmeanmain.cpp*/
#include<iostream.h>
#include"hmean.h"
void main()
{
    float x,y,z;
    cout<<"Enter a number: ";
    cin>>x;
    cout<<"Enter another number: ";
    cin>>y;
    z=hmean(x,y);
```

```
    cout<<"Harmonic mean = "<<z<<endl ;
}
/*End of hmeanmain.cpp*/
```

Output

Enter a number: **10**<*enter*>
Enter another number: **-10**<*enter*>
Abnormal program termination

This solution of terminating the program (as in Listing 11.2) is too extreme and drastic. The library function simply terminates the program on detecting an invalid input. Even if we do not provide the abort() function, the OS anyway throws a similar or same error (depending upon the implementation) and terminates the program. This solution does not achieve anything tangible. The library user does not get a chance to take a corrective action of its choice. The library can and should do better.

11.2.2 Check the Parameters before Function Call

A program to prevalidate the function parameters is given in Listing 11.3.

Listing 11.3 Prevalidating function parameters to avoid error condition

```
/*Beginning of hmean.h*/
float hmean(const float, const float);
/*End of hmean.h*/

/*Beginning of hmean.cpp*/
#include"hmean.h"
float hmean(const float a, const float b)
{
    return 2.0*a*b/(a+b);
}
/*End of hmean.cpp*/
/*Beginning of hmeanmain.cpp*/
#include<iostream.h>
#include"hmean.h"
void main()
{
    float x,y,z;
    while(1)
    {
        cout<<"Enter a number: " ;
        cin>>x;
        cout<<"Enter another number: " ;
        cin >>y ;
        if(x!=-y)
            break;
        cout<<"Invalid entry - enter again\n";
    }
    z=hmean(x,y) ;
    cout<<"Harmonic mean = "<<z<<endl ;
}
```

Output

Enter a number: **3**<*enter*>
Enter another number: **-3**<*enter*>
Invalid entry – enter again
Enter a number: **2**<*enter*>
Enter another number: **6**<*enter*>
Harmonic mean = 3

This method relies upon the application programmer to prevalidate the data before passing them as parameters to the function call. However, it is not safe to rely upon the application programmer to know (or care) enough to perform such a check. A properly designed library function need not and should not burden the user with the task of checking the parameters for all invalid conditions.

11.2.3 Return a Value Representing an Error

Another approach is to use the function's return value to indicate a problem. Let us use a pointer argument or a reference argument to get a value back to the calling program and use the function's return value to indicate success or failure. By informing the calling function of the success or failure, we give the program the option of taking a suitable action of its choice. Listing 11.4 shows an example of this approach. It redefines hmean() function as an int function whose return value indicates success or failure. It adds a third argument for obtaining the answer.

Listing 11.4   Returning an error condition from the library function

```
/*Beginning of hmean.h*/
int hmean(const float, const float, float const *);
/*End of hmean.h*/

/*Beginning of hmean.cpp*/
#include"hmean.h"
int hmean(const double a, const double b,double const * c)
{
   if(a==-b)
   {
     *c = 0;
     return 0; //return failure
   }
   else
   {
     *c=2.0*a*b/(a+b) ;
     return 1; //return success
   }
}
/*End of hmean.cpp*/

/*Beginning of hmeanmain.cpp*/
#include<iostream.h>
#include"hmean.h"
void main()
{
   float x,y,z;
   int r;
```

```
      while(1)
      {
         cout<<"Enter a number: " ;
         cin >>x;
         cout<<"Enter another number:  " ;
         cin >>y;
         r=hmean(x,y,&z);
         if(r==1) //if success
            break;
         cout<<"Invalid entry - enter again\n" ;
      }
      cout<<"Harmonic mean = "<<z<<endl ;
}
/*End of hmeanmain.cpp*/
```

Output

Enter a number: **2**<*enter*>
Enter another number: **-2**<*enter*>
Invalid entry – enter again
Enter a number: **2**<*enter*>
Enter another number: **6**<*enter*>
Harmonic mean = 3

The definition of the `hmean` function as in Listing 11.4 does not burden the application program with the responsibility of prevalidating the parameters. It also allows the application program to take corrective action if it detects an error. Nevertheless, it still leaves the application program with the responsibility of detecting the error. The application program may bypass the test and use the value obtained by the third parameter! After all, the third parameter will certainly have some value or the other. The library function has no way of forcing the application program to take notice of the error condition!

To conclude, we should note that these C-style solutions are extreme in nature. They are either too strict (simply abort the program without allowing the application to take corrective action) or too lenient (merely return an error value without forcing the application program to take corrective action). What we need is a well-balanced solution by which the library function forces and at the same time allows its caller to take corrective action. Such a well-balanced solution is the exception-handling mechanism provided by C++.

11.3 C++-Style Solution—the try/throw/catch Construct

C++ offers the mechanism of exception handling as a superior solution to the problem of handling unexpected situations during run time. Listing 11.5 illustrates the use of `try`, `throw`, and `catch` keywords for implementing exception handling. The advantages and limitations of this feature are discussed later.

Listing 11.5   The try–throw–catch mechanism

```
/*Beginning of hmean.h*/
float hmean(const float, const float);
/*End of hmean.h*/

/*Beginning of hmean.cpp*/
#include"hmean.h"
float hmean(const float a, const float b)
```

```
{
    if(a==-b)
        throw "bad arguments to hmean()" ;
    return 2.0*a*b /(a+b) ;
}
/*End of hmean.cpp*/

/*Beginning of hmeanmain.cpp*/
#include<iostream.h>
#include"hmean.h"
void main()
{
    char choice='y' ;
    double x,y,z ;
    while(choice=='y')
    {
        cout<<"Enter a number: " ;
        cin>>x;
        cout<<"Enter another number: " ;
        cin >>y ;
        try
        {
            z=hmean(x,y);
        }
        catch(char * s)
        {
            cout<<s<<endl ;
            cout<<"Enter a new pair of numbers\n";
            continue;
        }
        cout<<"Harmonic mean of "<<x<< "and "<<y<< " is "<<z<<endl;
        cout<<"continue ? (y/n) ";
        cin>>choice;
    }
    cout<<"Bye\n";
}
/*End of hmeanmain.cpp*/
```

Output
Enter a number: **4** <*enter*>
Enter another number: **-4** <*enter*>
bad arguments to hmean()
Enter a new pair of numbers
Enter a number: **2** <*enter*>
Enter another number: **6** <*enter*>
Harmonic mean of 2 and 6 is 8
continue ? (y/n) **n** <*enter*>
Bye

Exception handling provides a way to transfer control from the library to the application. Handling an exception has three components. They are:
* throwing an exception,
* catching an exception with a handler, and
* using a try block.

The throw keyword is used to throw an exception. It is followed by a value, such as character string or an object, indicating the nature of the exception. The library function notifies the user program about the error by throwing an exception.

The catch keyword is used to catch an exception. A catch-handler block begins with the keyword catch followed, in parentheses, by a type declaration indicating the type of exception that it catches. That, in turn, is followed by a brace enclosed block of code indicating the actions to take. The catch keyword, along with the exception types, is the point to which control should jump when an exception is thrown.

A try block encloses the block of code that is likely to throw an exception. Such a code generally consists of calls to library functions that are designed to throw errors in the manner described herein. One or more catch blocks follow the try block. The 'try' block is itself indicated by the keyword try followed by a brace—enclosed block of code indicating the code within which exception will be caught.

The try block looks like this:

```
try  // start of try block
{
    z=hmean(x,y);
} // end of try block
```

If any statement in the try block causes an exception, the catch blocks after this block will handle the exception.

Exceptions are thrown as follows:

```
if(a==-b)
    throw "bad hmean() arguments : a = -b not allowed";
```

In this case, the thrown exception is the string bad hmean() arguments : a = -b not allowed. The throw statement resembles the return statement because it terminates function execution. However, instead of merely returning control to the calling program, a throw causes the control to back up through the sequence of current function calls until it finds the try block. In this case, the throw passes program control back to main(). There, the program looks for an exception handler (following the try block) that matches the type of exception thrown.

```
catch (char * s)                        // start of exception handler
{
    cout<<s<<"\n";
    cout<<"Enter a new pair of numbers : ";
    continue;
}                                       // end of handler
```

The keyword catch identifies the handler and the char * s means that this handler catches a string-type exception. The thrown exception is assigned to 's'. Since the exception matches this handler, the program executes the code within the braces.

If a program completes executing statements in a try block without any exceptions being thrown, it skips the catch block or blocks after the try block and goes to the first statement following the handlers.

Let us follow the flow of control when the values '10' and '–10' are passed to the hmean() function. The if test succeeds and the exception (of char * type) is thrown. The hmean() function terminates. The control goes back to the point from where the hmean() function was called and determines whether the call was embedded within a try block or not. It finds that the hmean() function was called from the main() function and that the call was embedded within a try block. The control then searches for a catch block that follows the try block and is of the

```
while(choice=='y')
{
    cout<<"Enter a number : ";
    cin>>x;
    cout<<"Enter another number : " ;
    cin>>y;
    try
    {
                    z=hmean(x,y);
    }
    catch(char * s)
    {
        cout<<s<<endl;
        cout<<"Enter a new pair of numbers\n";
                    continue;
    }
}
double hmean(double a, double b)
{
    if(a==-b)
        throw "bad hmean() arguments a = -b not allowed" ;
    return 2.0*a*b/(a+b);
}
```

1. The program calls **hmean()** within a try block
2. **hmean()** throws an exception, transferring execution to the **catch** block, and assigning the exception string to **s**.
3. The **catch** block transfers execution back to the **while** loop

Figure 11.1 Flow of control when exceptions are thrown

matching char * type. The one and only catch block that follows the try block is of char * type. Therefore, the statements enclosed within it are executed. Figure 11.1 illustrates this.

In the introduction of this chapter, we had realized that an ideal solution to the problem of handling run-time errors should enable the library to sense and dispatch errors and the application to trap the dispatched error and take appropriate action. The exception-handling mechanism of C++ meets this requirement perfectly.

In order to appreciate the superiority of exception handling over the C-style solutions, we should keep the following two things in mind:

- It is necessary to catch an exception if it is thrown.
- When an exception is thrown, the stack is unwound.

11.3.1 It is Necessary to Catch Exceptions

The program terminates immediately if an exception thrown by a called function is not caught by the calling function. (A point to be borne in mind is that it is illegal to have a try block without a catch block.) The program in Listing 11.6 is a case in point.

Listing 11.6   Abnormal program termination due to uncaught `exception`

```cpp
#include<iostream.h>

void abc(int);
void main()
{
    int i;
    abc(-1);
    for(i=1;i<=10;i++)
        cout<<i<<endl;
}

void abc(int x)
{
    if(x<0)
        throw "Invalid parameter";
}
```

Output
Abnormal program termination

As we can observe in Listing 11.6, the remaining part of the `main()` function after the call to the `abc()` function does not execute. Instead, the program terminates. This happens because the call to the `abc()` function has not been placed in a try block. Thus, when `abc()` function throws an exception, there is no catch handler specified by the application programmer to execute a desirable piece of code. The program simply terminates with the default error message.

Thus, if the library programmer creates functions that throw exceptions, then the application programmer who uses the functions, is compelled to place the calls to such exception throwing library functions inside a try block and to provide suitable catch handlers.

Obviously, the library programmer should indicate the kinds of exceptions his/her function might throw. The list of exceptions a function throws is indicated in its prototype that is placed in the header file. The application programmer can find out what exceptions the library function throws by reading the header file. If a function, say `abc()` function, throws exceptions of the `char *` type and `int` type and accepts an `int` type value as a parameter, then the function prototype should be as follows.

```cpp
void abc(int) throw(char *,int);
```

11.3.2 Unwinding of the Stack

The throw statement unwinds the stack, cleaning up all objects declared within the try block by calling their destructors. Next, throw calls the matching catch handler, passing the parameter object.

Listing 11.7 illustrates this fact.

Listing 11.7   Unwinding of the stack due a thrown exception

```cpp
#include<iostream.h>
class A
{
    int x ;
  public :
```

```
                    A(int p)
                    {
                        x = p ;
                        cout << "A                    "<< x << endl ;
                    }
                    ~A()
                    {
                        cout << "~A                    " << x << endl ;
                    }
                };
            void abc();

            void main()
            {
                try
                {
                    A A_main(1);
                    abc();
                }
                catch(char * s)
                {
                    cout<<s<<endl;
                }
            }
            void abc()
            {
                A A_abc(2);
                throw "Exception thrown from abc()";
            }
```

Output

A 1

A 2

~A 2

~A 1

Exception thrown from abc()

As can be seen, throw destroys all objects from the point of throw until the try block. This action of the throw statement is clearly highlighted by Listing 11.8.

Listing 11.8   Reversal of flow of control from the point of throw to the try block

```
#include<iostream.h>
class A
{
    int x;
    public:
        A(int p)
        {
            x=p;
            cout<<"A "<<x<<endl;
        }
        ~A()
        {
            cout<<"~A                    "<<x<<endl;
        }
```

```
};

void abc();
void def();
void ghi();

void main()
{
  try
  {
    A A_main(1);
    cout<<"calling abc()\n";
    abc();
  }
  catch(char * s)
  {
    cout<<s<<endl;
  }
}
void abc()
{
  A A_abc(2) ;
  cout<<"calling def()\n";
  def();
}

void def()
{
  A A_def(3) ;
  cout<<"calling ghi()\n" ;
  ghi();
}

void ghi()
{
  A A_ghi(4);
  throw "Exception from ghi()";
}
```

Output
A 1
calling abc()
A 2
calling def()
A 3
calling ghi()
A4
~A 4
~A 3
~A 2
~A 1
Exception from ghi()

In Listing 11.8, the try block does not contain a direct call to a function throwing an exception but it calls a function that throws an exception. Still, the control jumps from the

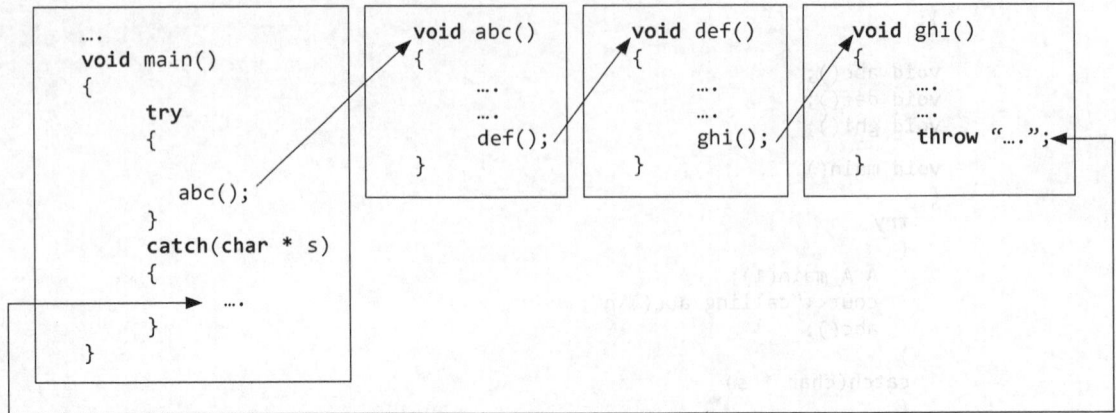

Figure 11.2 Unwinding of stack when an exception is thrown

function in which the exception is thrown to the function containing the try block and handlers. All local variables from the throw to the try block are destroyed. See Figure 11.2.

11.3.3 Need to Throw Class Objects

The problem with throwing values of fundamental data types is that the number of fundamental data types is limited. Thus, if two or more statements in a try block throw values of the same data type, then conflicts arise and it becomes difficult to detect the source of error in the catch block. The advantage with throwing objects of classes is that the library programmer can define any number of classes as exception classes. Listing 11.9 illustrates this.

Listing 11.9 Throwing objects of exception classes

```cpp
#include<iostream.h>
#include<math.h> //for sqrt()

class hmeanexcp{}; //an empty exception class
class gmeanexcp{}; //an empty exception class

double hmean(double,double);
double gmean(double,double);

void main()
{
    double x,y,z1,z2;
    char choice='y';
    while(choice=='y')
    {
        cout<<"Enter a number: ";
        cin>>x;
        cout<<"Enter another number: ";
        cin>>y;
        try
        {
            z1=hmean(x,y);
            z2=gmean(x,y);
        }
        catch(hmeanexcp)
```

```
    {
        cout<<"Exception error - a=-b not allowed\n";
        cout<<"Enter a fresh pair of numbers\n";
        continue;
    }
    catch(gmeanexcp)
    {
        cout<<"Exception error - a*b<0 not allowed\n";
        cout<<"Enter a fresh pair of numbers\n";
        continue;
    }
    cout<<"Harmonic mean = "<<z1<<endl;
    cout<<"Geometric mean = "<<z2<<endl;
    cout<<"Enter again ? (y/n)";
    cin>>choice;
  }
  cout<<"Bye\n";
}
double hmean(double a,double b)
{
  if(a==-b)
     throw hmeanexcp();//construct and throw objects!!
  return 2.0*a*b/(a+b);
}
double gmean(double a,double b)
{
  if(a*b<0)
     throw gmeanexcp();//construct and throw objects!!
  return sqrt(a*b);
}
```

Output

Enter a number: **10**<*enter*>
Enter another number: **-10**<*enter*>
Exception error – a=-b not allowed
Enter a fresh pair of numbers
Enter a number: **10**<*enter*>
Enter another number: **-6**<*enter*>
Exception error – a*b<0 not allowed
Enter a fresh pair of numbers
Enter a number: **16**<*enter*>
Enter another number: **4**<*enter*>
Harmonic mean = 6.4
Geometric mean = 8
Enter again? (y/n) **n**<*enter*>
Bye

We may note that it is not mandatory to declare an object of the exception class in the catch block. However, through the throw statements, we always throw objects (as has been done by calling constructors of the hmeanexcp and gmeanexcp classes in the hmean() and gmean() functions of Listing 11.9).

11.3.4 Accessing the Thrown Object in the Catch Block

If we declare an object of the exception class in the catch handler, then the thrown object gets copied into it. This object can then be accessed and used for further processing. Listing 11.10 illustrates this.

Listing 11.10   Accessing thrown objects

```
include<iostream.h>
#include<math.h>
#include<string.h>

double hmean(double,double);
double gmean(double,double);

class hmeanexcp
{
    char cError[30];
  public:
    hmeanexcp(char * s)
    {
        strcpy(cError,s);
    }
    char * getcError()
    {
        return cError;
    }
};

class gmeanexcp
{
    char cError[30];
  public:
    gmeanexcp(char * s)
    {
        strcpy(cError,s);
    }
    const char * getcError()
    {
        return cError;
    }
};

void main()
{
    double x,y,z1,z2;
    char choice='y';
    while(choice=='y')
    {
        cout<<"Enter a number: ";
        cin>>x;
        cout<<"Enter another number: ";
        cin>>y;
        try
        {
            z1=hmean(x,y);
            z2=gmean(x,y);
        }
```

```
        catch(hmeanexcp& e)
        {
            cout<<e.getcError()<<endl;
            cout<<"Enter a fresh pair of numbers\n";
            continue;
        }
        catch(gmeanexcp& e)
        {
            cout<<e.getcError()<<endl;
            cout<<"Enter a fresh pair of numbers\n";
            continue;
        }
        cout<<"Harmonic mean = "<<z1<<endl;
        cout<<"Geometric mean = "<<z2<<endl;
        cout<<"Enter again ? (y/n)";
        cin>>choice;
    }
    cout<<"Bye\n";
}

double hmean(double a,double b)
{
    if(a==-b)
        throw hmeanexcp("Exception error - a=-b not allowed");
    return 2.0*a*b/(a+b);
}

double gmean(double a,double b)
{
    if(a*b<0)
        throw gmeanexcp("Exception error - a*b<0 not allowed");
    return sqrt(a*b);
}
```

Output

Enter a number: **10**<*enter*>
Enter another number: **-10**<*enter*>
Exception error – a=-b not allowed
Enter a fresh pair of numbers
Enter a number: **10**<*enter*>
Enter another number: **-6**<*enter*>
Exception error – a*b<0 not allowed
Enter a fresh pair of numbers
Enter a number: **16**<*enter*>
Enter another number: **4**<*enter*>
Harmonic mean = 6.4
Geometric mean = 8
Enter again? (y/n) **n**<*enter*>
Bye

A temporary copy of the object to be thrown is created and thrown. Hence, the object in the catch handler refers to a copy of the thrown object. This is desirable because the thrown object disappears after the function from which it was thrown terminates. Thus, after the object is thrown, its three copies may be created—the object itself, its copy, and the object in the catch block. The object itself gets destroyed automatically when the function terminates.

Therefore, we are left with two copies. In order to reduce this to one, we normally create a reference to the thrown object in the catch handler (as in the catch blocks of Listing 11.10).

11.3.5 Throwing Parameterized Objects of a Nested Exception Class

Let us have a look at Listing 11.11.

Listing 11.11   Nested exception class

```cpp
#include<iostream.h>
#include<string.h>

template<class T>
class vector
{
    T * v;
    int size;
  public:
    class RangeError
    {
        char cError[30];
        int errorPos;
      public:
        RangeError(char * str,int p)
        {
            strcpy(cError,str);
            errorPos=p;
        }
        char * getcError()
        {
            return cError;
        }
        int getPos()
        {
            return errorPos;
        }
    };
    vector(int s)
    {
      v=new T[s];
      size=s;
    }
    ~vector()
    {
      delete[] v;
    }
    void setElement(T val,int p)
    {
      if(p>size-1 || p<0)
        throw RangeError("Out of range exception - could not _ write", p);
      v[p]=val;
    }
    T getElement(int p)
    {
      if(p>size-1 || p<0)
        throw RangeError("Out of range exception - could not _ read",p);
      return v[p];
    }
```

```
};
void main()
{
    vector<int> int_vector(5);
    try
    {
        int_vector.setElement(3,5);
        cout<<int_vector.getElement(3)<<endl;
    }
    catch(vector<int>::RangeError& e)
    {
        cout<<e.getcError()<<" at position "<<e.getPos()+1<<endl;
    }

    vector<float> float_vector(6);
    try
    {
        float_vector.setElement(3.14,3);
        cout<<float_vector.getElement(6)<<endl;
    }
    catch(vector<float>::RangeError& e)
    {
        cout<<e.getcError()<<" at position "<<e.getPos()+1<<endl;
    }
}
```

Output

Out of range exception – could not write at position 6

Out of range exception – could not read at position 7

We can define the exception class as a nested class of the class that throws it. This indicates the class originating an exception. It also prevents pollution of the global namespace. In the example in Listing 11.11, the class RangeError has been declared within the vector class. If the setElement() function or the getElement() function finds a bad subscript value, it throws an exception of type RangeError. The handler for this exception looks like this

```
catch(vector<int>::RangeError& e) {…}
```

it may be noted that the nested exception class is public. This allows the catch block to have access to the type.

11.3.6 Catching Uncaught Exceptions

The C++ language supports a feature to catch exceptions that were raised in a try block but not caught by any of the catch blocks. The syntax of the catch construct to handle such exceptions is as follows.

```
catch(…)
{
    //action for handling an exception
}
```

The three dots in catch(…) indicate that it catches all types of exceptions. Listing 11.12 illustrates the use of this catch block.

Listing 11.12 Catching uncaught exceptions

```cpp
#include<iostream.h>
class Sugar{};
class Spice{};
class Tasteless{};
void abc(int);

void main()
{
   try
   {
      abc(-1);
   }
   catch(Sugar)
   {
      cout<<"Caught Sugar\n";
   }
   catch(Spice)
   {
      cout<<"Caught Spice\n";
   }
   catch(…)
   {
      cout<<"Unidentified object caught\n";
   }
}
void abc(int p)
{
   if(p<0)
      throw Tasteless();
}
```

Output
Unidentified object caught

11.3.7 Re-throwing Exceptions

Suppose you are defining a function, which calls another function and the called function throws an exception. You will therefore have a try/catch mechanism in your function for handling the exception that the called function throws. Suppose that the name of your function is `test_hmean()` and that the name of the called function is `hmean()`. The overall structure of your function would look like this:

```cpp
double test_hmean(double p, double q)
{
   //Variable declaration statements.
   try
   {
      r=hmean(p,q);
   }
   catch
   {
      //Catch handler.
   }
}
```

Now, suppose that you either know only a part of what your function needs to do if it catches the exception or you do not have any idea of what your function needs to do if it catches the exception. In both cases, you would like the function that calls your function to do something about it. For this, you would like your function to re-throw the exception to the function that has called it.

Listing 11.13 shows how functions can re-throw exceptions. In this case, the main() function has called your function. Note how the throw keyword has been used below in the test_hmean() function.

Listing 11.13   Re-throwing exceptions

```
/*Beginning of Rethrowing01.cpp*/
/*
    Program to illustrate re-throwing of exceptions.
*/
#include <iostream.h>
#include <string.h>

double test_hmean(double, double);
double hmean(double, double);

class hmeanexcp
{
    char cError[30];
    public:
        hmeanexcp(char * s)
        {
            strcpy(cError, s);
        }
        char * getcError()
        {
            return cError;
        }
};

void main()
{
    double x, y, z;
    x = 10;
    y = -10;
    try
    {
        z = test_hmean(x, y);
    }
    catch(hmeanexcp& e)
    {
        cout << "Inside the catch block of main()\n";
    }
}

double test_hmean(double p, double q)
{
    double r;
    try
    {
        r = hmean(p, q);
    }
    catch(hmeanexcp& e)
```

```
    {
        cout << "Inside the catch block of test_hmean()\n";
        throw;
    }
    return r;
}

double hmean(double a, double b)
{
    if(a==-b)
        throw hmeanexcp("Exception error - a=-b not allowed");
    return 2.0*a*b/(a+b);
}
/*End of Rethrowing01.cpp*/
```

Output

Inside the catch block of `test_hmean()`
Inside the catch block of `main()`

Let us follow the execution of the `main()` function. The `main()` function calls the `test_hmean()` function from inside the try block. The `test_hmean()` function in turn calls the `hmean()` function from inside the try block. The `hmean()` function throws an error because the values passed to it are opposite to each other (10 and −10). The type of the exception is `hmeanexcp`. The `test_hmean()` has a catch block that handles exceptions of this type. Therefore, the catch block of the `test_hmean()` function executes. The first statement of this block displays the message 'Inside the catch block of `test_hmean()`'. The second statement of the catch block throws the same exception again. Thus, the exception is not consumed by the `test_hmean()` function. Instead, it gets thrown upwards to the calling function, which is `main()`.

The `main()` function in turn has a catch block that handles exceptions of the thrown type. Therefore, the catch block of the `main()` function executes. The single statement in this block displays the error message 'Inside the catch block of `main()`.

Naturally, if the throw statement is removed from the catch block of the `test_hmean()` function, then the catch handler block of the `main()` function would not execute (because the `test_hmean()` function would not be throwing any exception for it to handle). Let us remove the throw statement and see whether the output changes or not. See Listing 11.14.

Listing 11.14 Removing throw statement prevents re-throwing of exceptions

```
/*Beginning of Rethrowing02.cpp*/
/*
    Program to illustrate effect of throw statement's
    absence.
*/
#include <iostream.h>
#include <string.h>

double test_hmean(double, double);
double hmean(double, double);

class hmeanexcp
{
        char cError[30];
    public:
```

```
      hmeanexcp(char * s)
      {
         strcpy(cError, s);
      }
      char * getcError()
      {
         return cError;
      }
};
   void main()
   {
      double x, y, z;
      x = 10;
      y = -10;
      try
      {
         z = test_hmean(x, y);
      }
      catch(hmeanexcp& e)
      {
         cout << "Inside the catch block of main()\n";
      }
   }

   double test_hmean(double p, double q)
   {
      double r;
      try
      {
         r = hmean(p, q);
      }
      catch(hmeanexcp& e)
      {
         cout << "Inside the catch block of test_hmean()\n";
      }
      return r;
   }

   double hmean(double a, double b)
   {
      if(a==-b)
         throw hmeanexcp("Exception error - a=-b not allowed");
      return 2.0*a*b/(a+b);
   }
   /*End of Rethrowing.cpp*/
```

Output

Inside the catch block of test_hmean()

As can be seen, the catch handler of the `main()` function did not execute. This happened because the catch handler of the `test_hmean()` function did not re-throw the exception.

We now understand that exceptions can be re-thrown. We have seen the reasons for re-throwing exceptions. We have also studied the method for re-throwing exceptions.

11.4   Limitation of Exception Handling

The limitation of exception handling is that if a resource has been acquired (file has been opened, memory has been allocated dynamically in the heap area, etc.) and the statements to release the resource are after the throw statements, then the acquired resource may remain locked up. Listing 11.15 illustrates this.

Listing 11.15   Dynamically allocated resources remain locked after the throw statement

```cpp
#include<iostream.h>
class A
{
    public:
        A()
        {
            cout<<"Constructor\n";
        }
        ~A()
        {
            cout<<"Destructor\n";
        }
};
void abc(int);

void main()
{
    try
    {
        abc(-1);
    }
    catch(char * s)
    {
        cout<<s<<endl;
    }
}


void abc(int p)
{
    A * Aptr = new A[2];
    if(p<0)
        throw "Invalid argument to abc()";
}
```

Output
Constructor
Constructor
Invalid argument to abc()

In Listing 11.15, when the stack is unwound, memory occupied by the pointer Aptr in abc() function gets destroyed. However, the memory block at which the pointer points remains locked up. (This is evident from the fact that the destructor was not called for the objects created in the heap.)

In order to overcome this problem, classes whose objects function like pointers should be devised. Obviously, such objects will have pointers embedded in them. Memory will be allocated dynamically for these pointers during the lifetime of the objects. This memory can be deallocated through the destructor. Thus, when the object itself is destroyed, the memory locked up and referenced by the embedded pointer will also be destroyed.

Summary

Statements to detect conditions that prohibit further execution of the library function can and should be placed within the library function itself. Statements to take appropriate action when such conditions are detected can and should be placed in the functions that call these library functions.

Exception handling enables the library function to notify the detected invalid conditions to the user by using the throw statement. The program terminates prematurely if the application program ignores such notifications. Application program can catch such notifications in a try block and take appropriate action in a catch block.

Library functions can announce the list of all possible exceptions that they throw by enlisting them in their headers. Appropriately, the application program should place calls to these functions in a try block and append the try block with a series of catch blocks, one for each of the exceptions expected to be thrown.

Since the number of fundamental data types is limited, it is better to throw objects of exception classes created specifically for the purpose. These objects can be initialized with appropriate information before being thrown by the library functions. This information can then be accessed within the corresponding catch block of the application program.

Uncaught exceptions can be caught by the catch(...) {} construct. Exceptions can be re-thrown. During unwinding of the stack, memory occupied by the objects themselves is destroyed. However, the memory acquired dynamically by the pointers embedded in these objects remains locked up. This is a limitation of exception handling.

Key Terms

exception handling
C-style solutions for exception handling
try
catch

throw
catching uncaught exceptions
exception classes
unwinding of the stack

Exercises

1. What is exception handling? What is the need for exception handling?
2. What is the negative impact if the library programmer simply terminates an application upon detecting an error condition?
3. Which three keywords are provided by C++ for implementing exception handling?
4. What happens if the application does not catch the exception thrown by a library function?
5. Explain how the stack is unwound when an exception is thrown.
6. What is the need to throw class objects instead of values of fundamental types?
7. Why are nested exception classes needed?
8. How are uncaught exceptions caught?
9. What is the limitation of exception handling in C++?

10. Derive a class from another. Create two catch blocks—the first one for catching the base class-type exception and the second one for catching the derived class-type exception. Throw an exception of the base class type from the try block. Observe the result. Now, throw an exception of the derived class-type from the try block. Observe and compare the results. Repeat the above two observations by reversing the sequence of the catch blocks. What do you conclude?

11. Add a function to the class **String** that will return the character from the position that is passed as a parameter to it. If the position is out of bounds, the function should throw a user-defined exception.

12. Explain the concept and method of re-throwing exceptions with the help of an example.

Appendix A

Case Study—A Word Query System

Problem Statement

The word query system should allow us to determine whether a particular word exists in a given text file or not.

If the program finds the word being searched, it would display all the lines in which the word was found. The program would also display the number of occurrences of the word, the serial number of the line in the file, and the position of the word in the line.

A Sample Run

The file having the following lines, written by the author about his favorite game, can be taken as input:

```
Chess is the most intellectual mind sport known to mankind.
A game of chess is a war of intelligence and a clash of
wills. It is a game of kings, queens, rooks, knights,
bishops and pawns. What appears to be a two-dimensional
black and white board of 64 squares is, for the chess
master, a multidimensional multicolored wonderland of
cunning strategy and brilliant tactics. Chess has a rich
and long history. Invented in India as a war game, it has
followers all over the world. Of all the sports, it has
perhaps the largest literature. To be a true master of the
game requires years of hard labor, study and practice. The
game has been played by kings and by commoners alike. A
regular practice of the game leads to better concentration
and an improved ability to deduce facts from logic.
```

A sample run of the program is as follows (we would implement a case sensitive search):

Please enter the word to be searched (enter blank to quit): **chess** <*enter*>
Number of occurrences of 'chess' = 2
(2,4) A game of chess is a war of intelligence and a clash of
(5,11) black and white board of 64 squares is, for the chess

Please enter the word to be searched (enter blank to quit): **master** <*enter*>
Number of occurrences of 'master' = 2
(6, 1) master, a multidimensional multicolored wonderland of
(10,9) perhaps the largest literature. To be a true master of the

Please enter the word to be searched (enter blank to quit): **mind** <*enter*>
Number of occurrences of 'mind' = 1
(1,6) Chess is the most intellectual mind sport known to mankind.

Please enter the word to be searched (enter blank to quit): **golf** <*enter*>
Number of occurrences of 'golf' = 0
Please enter the word to be searched (enter blank to quit): <*enter*>
Bye!

The Source Code

The program listing to implement the word query system as described in the Problem Statement follows:

(Please note that the code calls a few of the member functions of the library string class. These simple calls have been explained in the accompanying comments.)

```cpp
/*Beginning of textQuerySearch.cpp*/
#include<string>//the library string class
#include<vector>
#include<fstream.h>
#include<map>

using namespace std;

void main()
{
    ::ifstream infile("C:\\abc.txt");

    int flag=0;
    char cVar;
    string word,line;
    int iLineNum=1;
    int iWordNum=1;

    typedef pair<int,int> location;
    location loc;
    typedef vector<location> lvec;
    lvec temp;
    vector<location>::iterator liter;

    map<string,lvec> wordmap;
    map<string,lvec>::iterator iter;

    map<int,string> linemap;

    while(infile)
    {
        infile.get(cVar);

        if(cVar==' ' || cVar=='.' || cVar==',' ||
          cVar==';' || cVar=='\n')
        {
            if(flag==0)
            {
                                loc.first=iLineNum;
                                loc.second=iWordNum;
                                iWordNum++;
                                iter=wordmap.find(word);
```

```cpp
                              if(iter!=wordmap.end())
                                  (iter->second).push_back(loc);
                              else
                              {
                                  temp.push_back(loc);
                                  wordmap[word]=temp;

                                  temp.erase(temp.begin(),
                                              temp.end());
                              }
                              word.erase(); //nullifying the string
                              flag=1;
            }

        if(cVar!='\n')
            line=line+cVar;          //adding a character to
                                     //the string
        else
        {
            linemap[iLineNum]=line;
            line.erase(); //nullifying the string
            iLineNum++;
            iWordNum=1;
        }
        continue;
    }
    else
        flag=0;
    word=word+cVar; //adding a character to the
                    //string
    line=line+cVar;
}

while(1)
{
    cout<<"Please enter the word to be searched "
        <<(enter blank to quit): ";
    word.erase();
    while(cin)
    {
        cin.get(cVar);
        if(cVar=='\n')
            break;
        word=word+cVar;
    }
    if(word.empty()) //if string is empty
        break;
    iter=wordmap.find(word);
    //string::c_str()returns the contained string
    cout<<"\nNumber of occurrences of '"
        <<word.c_str()<<"' = "
        <<iter->second.size()<<endl<<endl;
    for(liter=iter->second.begin();
        liter!=iter->second.end();liter++)
        cout<<"("<<liter->first<<","
            <<liter->second<<") "
            <<linemap[liter->first].c_str();
    cout<<endl<<endl;
}
```

```
      cout<<"\nBye!\n\n";
    }
    /*End of textQuerySearch.cpp*/
```

Explanation of the Code

The code can be broadly divided in two steps as follows:

Step 1: Create a map of words with their locations.

```
64 (5,6)
A (2,1) (12,11)
Chess (1,1) (7,6)
India (8,6)
Invented (8,4)
It (3,2)
Of (9,6)
The (11,10)
To (10,5)
What (4,4)
a (2,6) (2,11) (3,4) (4,8) (6,2) (7,8) (8,8) (10,7)
ability (14,4)
alike (12,10)
all (9,2) (9,7)
an (14,2)
and (2,10) (4,2) (5,2) (7,3) (8,1) (11,8) (12,7) (14,1)
appears (4,5)
as (8,7)
be (4,7) (10,6)
been (12,3)
better (13,8)
bishops (4,1)
black (5,1)
board (5,4)
brilliant (7,4)
by (12,5) (12,8)
chess (2,4) (5,11)
clash (2,12)
commoners (12,9)
concentration (13,9)
cunning (7,1)
deduce (14,6)
dimensional (4,10)
facts (14,7)
followers (9,1)
for (5,9)
from (14,8)
game (2,2) (3,5) (8,10) (11,1) (12,1) (13,5)
hard (11,5)
has (7,7) (8,12) (9,11) (12,2)
history (8,3)
improved (14,3)
in (8,5)
intellectual (1,5)
intelligence (2,9)
is (1,2) (2,5) (3,3) (5,8)
it (8,11) (9,10)
kings (3,7) (12,6)
```

```
knights (3,10)
known (1,8)
labor (11,6)
largest (10,3)
leads (13,6)
literature (10,4)
logic (14,9)
long (8,2)
mankind (1,10)
master (6,1) (10,9)
mind (1,6)
most (1,4)
multicolored (6,4)
multidimensional (6,3)
of (2,3) (2,8) (2,13) (3,6) (5,5) (6,6) (10,10) (11,4) (13,3)
over (9,3)
pawns (4,3)
perhaps (10,1)
played (12,4)
practice (11,9) (13,2)
queens (3,8)
regular (13,1)
requires (11,2)
rich (7,9)
rooks (3,9)
sport (1,7)
sports (9,9)
squares (5,7)
strategy (7,2)
study (11,7)
tactics (7,5)
the (1,3) (5,10) (9,4) (9,8) (10,2) (10,11) (13,4)
to (1,9) (4,6) (13,7) (14,5)
true (10,8)
two (4,9)
war (2,7) (8,9)
white (5,3)
wills (3,1)
wonderland (6,5)
world (9,5)
years (11,3)
```

Step 2: Create a map of lines.

1 Chess is the most intellectual mind sport known to mankind.

2 A game of chess is a war of intelligence and a clash of

3 wills. It is a game of kings, queens, rooks, knights,

4 bishops and pawns. What appears to be a two dimensional

5 black and white board of 64 squares is, for the chess

6 master, a multidimensional multicolored wonderland of

7 cunning strategy and brilliant tactics. Chess has a rich

8 and long history. Invented in India as a war game, it has

9 followers all over the world. Of all the sports, it has

```
10 perhaps the largest literature. To be a true master of the
11 game requires years of hard labor, study and practice. The
12 game has been played by kings and by commoners alike. A
13 regular practice of the game leads to better concentration
14 and an improved ability to deduce facts from logic.
```

The detailed explanation

Let us go straight to the while loop. The loop reads the characters from the file one by one. If the first character is neither a punctuation mark nor the new line character, we simply add it to the string representing a word (second last line of the while loop).

```
word=word+cVar;
```

When a punctuation mark or the end of line is encountered,

```
if(cVar==' ' || cVar=='.' || cVar==',' || cVar==';' ||
   cVar=='\n')
```

we reckon that we have *finished* loading a word. We populate an object 'loc' with the line number and word number of the word.

```
loc.first=iLineNum;
loc.second=iWordNum;
```

We also increment 'iWordNum' because the position of the next word would be one greater than the previous one.

For the time being, ignore the test

```
if(flag==0)
```

Since our word map (see *Step 1* above) should keep a vector of all positions of each word, we must first find whether the word already exists in our word map or not.

```
iter=wordmap.find(word);
```

This statement returns an iterator. If the word *is* found in any of the first members of the word map, it points at that element whose first member is the word itself. If the word is *not* found in any of the first members of the word map, the iterator points past its end.

If the word is found in any of the first members of the word map,

```
if(iter!=wordmap.end())
```

we append the location object 'loc', which we have already populated, into the location vector, which is the second member of the element pointed at by the iterator.

```
(iter->second).push_back(loc);
```

If the word is not found in any of the first members of the word map, we populate a temporary vector of locations with only one element—the location object 'loc'.

```
temp.push_back(loc);
```

Next, we insert the word and its location vector into the word map.

```
wordmap[word]=temp;
```

We ensure that the temporary vector of locations remains vacant by writing the following line of code.

```
temp.erase(temp.begin(),temp.end());
```

Next, we discard the contents of the string object that is holding the just read word so that the next word can be loaded from the file.

```
word.erase();
```

The test

```
if(flag==0)
```

ensures that if more than one punctuation mark or new line character are encountered one after another, then all of them are ignored while building the word map.

On the first occasion, this test returns true. Therefore, the location of the loaded word updates the word map. The value of 'flag' has been set to '1' within this if block. This ensures that this test returns false if the next character of the text file is also a punctuation mark or the new line character since the value of the 'flag' is reset to '0' only if the character encountered is neither a punctuation mark nor the new line character.

After loading the word, if the end of line character is encountered, we increment the value of line number and reset the value of word number to '1'.

```
if(cVar!='\n')
    line=line+cVar;
else
{
    . . . . .
    . . . .
    iLineNum++;
    iWordNum=1;
}
```

Also, we would like to straight away read the next character from the file without any further processing. Therefore, the continue keyword has been used.

This finishes the explanation of how the word map has been created. Let us now focus our attention on the creation of the line map.

As we read the characters from the file, we append them into the string that represents a line.

```
line=line+cVar;
```

If the read character is a punctuation mark but not the new line character, we simply continue to append it to the line string object line (punctuation marks are a part of the line).

```
if(cVar==' ' || cVar=='.' || cVar==',' || cVar==';' ||
   cVar=='\n')
{
    . . . .
        if(cVar!='\n')
            line=line+cVar;
```

If the read character is the new line character, we reckon that we have loaded one complete line into the line string object line, and therefore simply insert the line number and the contents of the line into the line map.

```
if(cVar!='\n')
    line=line+cVar;
else
{
```

```
linemap[iLineNum]=line;
line.erase();
. . . .
```

We also erase the contents of the line string object so that the next line can be loaded afresh.

Now, we come to the last portion of the code wherein the loop accepts the word to be searched from the user and returns the results.

After prompting the user, we first clean up the variable in which the word entered by the user would be stored. The read characters are appended to the word variable till the user presses the enter key.

The test that breaks the potentially infinite loop is as follows:

```
if(word.empty())
```

It has been inserted in the middle since we don't want the rest of the loop to execute. If the user enters a blank string, the loop breaks and the program terminates.

If the user does not enter a blank string, we try to find it in the word map.

```
iter=wordmap.find(word);
```

If the word is found in the word map, this iterator points at the element whose first member is the word itself and whose second element is a vector of locations of the found word. The size of this vector gives us the number of occurrences of the found word.

The for loop

```
for(witer=iter->second.begin();
    witer!=iter->second.end();witer++)
```

iterates through the vector of locations of the found word. Each element of the vector is a pair of line position and word position. The locations are displayed by enclosing these positions in brackets and separating them by commas.

```
cout<<"("<<witer->first<<","<<witer->second<<") ". . .
```

Passing the line position to the line vector returns the corresponding line. This is also displayed in the for loop.

```
cout<<. . .<<linemap[witer->first].c_str()<<endl;
```

Appendix B

Comparison of C++ with C

C++ is an extension of C language. It is a proper superset of C language. This means that a C++ compiler can compile programs written in C language. But, the reverse is not true. A C++ compiler can understand *all* of the keywords that a C compiler can understand. Again, the reverse is not true. Decision making constructs, looping constructs, structures, functions etc. are written in *exactly* the same way in C++ as they are in C language. Apart from the keywords that implement these common programming constructs, C++ provides a number of additional keywords and language constructs that enable it to implement the object-oriented paradigm.

Differences between C++ and C can be divided into two categories:

- Non-object-oriented features provided in C++ that are absent in C language.
- Object-oriented features provided in C++ to make it comply with the requirements of the Object-Oriented Programming System.

Non-object-oriented Features Provided in C++ that are Absent in C Language

Enumerated data types

An enumerated data type in C is internally treated as an integer. In C++, it is treated as a separate data type in its own right. Direct conversion from an integer to the enumerated data type is therefore prohibited.

```
enum day_of_week
{
    monday,
    tuesday,
    wednesday,
    thursday,
    friday,
    saturday,
    sunday
};

day_of_week d;
d=Monday;    //OK
d=2;         //ERROR
```

Reference variables

(Refer to Chapter 1 for a detailed discussion.)

Constants

In C, it is illegal to use an integer, which has been declared as a constant, to specify the size of an array. This is not so in C++.

```
const int size=100;
char cArr[size];                    //legal in C++ but illegal in C
```

Function prototyping

(Refer to Chapter 1 for a detailed discussion.)

Function overloading

(Refer to Chapter 1 for a detailed discussion.)

Functions with no default values for arguments

(Refer to Chapter 1 for a detailed discussion.)

Functions with no formal arguments

In C, it is reckoned that a function that has no formal arguments accepts an unspecified number of parameters. Therefore, it is legal to pass parameters to it.

In C++, it is reckoned that a function that has no formal arguments does not accept parameters. Therefore, it is illegal to pass parameters to it.

Inline functions

(Refer to Chapter 1 for a detailed discussion.)

Object-oriented Features Provided in C++ to make it Comply with the Requirements of the Object-Oriented Programming System

The following are some of the additional keywords that have been provided in C++ to make it an object-oriented programming language:
- class (Refer to Chapter 2 for a detailed discussion.)
- friend (Refer to Chapter 2 for a detailed discussion.)
- operator (Refer to Chapter 8 for a detailed discussion.)
- private (Refer to Chapter 2 for a detailed discussion.)
- protected (Refer to Chapter 5 for a detailed discussion.)
- public (Refer to Chapter 2 for a detailed discussion.)
- template (Refer to Chapter 9 for a detailed discussion.)
- this (Refer to Chapter 2 for a detailed discussion.)
- virtual (Refer to Chapter 6 for a detailed discussion.)

Appendix C

Comparison of C++ with Java

C.1 Similarities between C++ and Java

The following are some of the features that make C++ and Java similar:

- **Comments:** Comments are given in Java programs in exactly the same way as they are given in C++ programs. The multiline comments (/* … */) and single-line comments (//) of C++ are supported in Java also.

- **Control structures:** Decision-making and looping constructs of C and C++ are provided in Java also. Moreover, exactly the same syntax is used for utilizing them in Java source codes.

- **Keywords for implementing exception handling:** The keywords try, catch, and throw that are provided in C++ are provided in Java. Moreover, the same syntax is used for utilizing them in Java source codes. However, there is a slight difference between the way C++ allows all unhandled exceptions and the way Java does. This is explained in the section on 'Differences between C++ and Java'.

- **Fundamental data types:** Like C++, Java also provides a set of fundamental data types. They are:

Type	Size
byte	1 byte (signed 8-bit)
boolean	1 byte (signed 8-bit)
char	2 bytes Unicode (signed 16-bit Unicode)
short	2 bytes (signed 16-bit)
int	4 bytes (signed 32-bit)
long	8 bytes (signed 64-bit)
float	4 bytes (signed 32-bit)
double	8 bytes (signed 64-bit)

- **Declaration of objects:** Variables of primitive types are declared in exactly the same way in Java as in C++. The following statement declares an integer-type variable in both C++ and Java.

  ```
  int x;
  ```

  However, it is different in the case of classes. The section on 'Differences between C++ and Java' explains this difference.

- **Purpose of the class construct:** Like C++, Java also provides the class construct. The purpose and functionality of this construct is approximately the same in both languages. Like classes that are defined in C++, there are member functions and member data in the classes that are defined in Java. However, there are differences between the ways this construct has been implemented in the two languages. The section on 'Differences between C++ and Java' explains these differences.
- **The static keyword:** The purpose of this keyword is the same in both the languages.
- **Constructor:** Constructors in Java are defined in exactly the same way as they are defined in C++ and also serve the same purpose.

  Constructors in C++ and Java are similar to each other in the following ways: The compiler defines the constructor if we do not define one. If we define the zero-argument constructor or a parameterized constructor for a class, the compiler does not define the default constructor for the class. An access specifier can be specified to a constructor.
- **Inheritance:** Like C++, Java also supports inheritance. However, Java does not support multiple inheritance. This is explained in the section on 'Differences between C++ and Java'.
- **Static polymorphism:** Like C++, Java supports static polymorphism. Two functions with different signatures can have the same name.
- **Dynamic polymorphism:** Dynamic polymorphism is supported in both C++ and Java. If a member function of the base class has been overridden in the derived class and it is called for a base class reference that actually refers to a derived class object, then the member function of the derived class gets called.
- **Overriding member functions of a base class in its derived classes:** Base class member functions can be overridden in the derived class except when the base class function has been specified as final. This exceptional case has been explained in the section on 'Differences between C++ and Java'.

C.2 Differences between C++ and Java

The following are some of the features that make C++ and Java different:
- **Structures and unions:** There are no structures and unions in Java. Java supports only classes.
- **The main() function:** Unlike the main() function in C++, the main() function in Java is not a global function. It is instead a public static function of a class. The class that has such a main() function is executed by clients or from command line.

  Unlike the main() function in C++, which takes an array of character pointers as parameter, the main() function in Java takes an array of objects of the class String as parameter.
- **Header files versus packages:** Instead of header files, we have packages in Java. Packages in Java serve a similar purpose as header files in C++. Packages are included in Java source codes by using the import directive as follows:

```
import java.util.Date;          //importing a package
```

This statement imports the Date class, which is defined in the 'util' package, which is in turn included in the 'Java' package.

- **The zero-fill right shift operator (>>>):** Java introduces a new right shift operator—the zero-fill right shift operator. The normal right shift operator (>>), fills up the bits on the left with the value of the first bit as it shifts the bits to the right. In contrast, the zero-fill right shift operator (>>>), fills up the bits on the left with zeros as it shifts the bits to the right. This operator can be used as follows:

```
x=x>>>1;                    //shifts bits in x to the right by one place
                            //and move a zero from the left
```

There is also a complimentary zero-fill right shift assignment operator (>>>=). The foregoing statement can be rewritten as

```
x>>>=1;                     //shifts bits in x to the right by one place and
                            //move a zero from the left
```

- **Operator overloading:** Unlike C++, operator overloading is not supported by Java.
- **External functions:** There are no global functions in Java. All functions must be members of some class or the other.
- **The final keyword:** The final keyword serves the same purpose as the const keyword of C++. Member variables are declared as constants by prefixing this keyword to their declarations.
- **Declaration of objects and the new operator:** We already know that variables of primitive types are declared in exactly the same way in Java as in C++. However, the case is different in the case of classes.

  Suppose **A** is a class. The following statement creates an actual object in C++.

```
A A1;    //A1 is an object in C++ but a null reference in
         //Java
```

But in Java, the above statement would only declare a null reference. Such a reference has to be explicitly initialized by using the new operator as follows:

```
A1 = new A();
```

In C++, the new operator captures a memory block in the heap and returns a pointer to it. In Java, the new operator captures a memory block in the heap and returns a reference to it. This is the only way of declaring an object in Java whereas in C++, an object may be declared either in the stack or in the heap by using the new operator.

- **Pointers:** Java does not support pointers. In Java, apart from the variables of primitive data types, all objects are actually references.

  Listing C.1 makes it evident that variables of primitive data types are always passed by value.

Listing C.1   Variables of primitive data types are passed by value

```
class first
{
  public static void main(String args[])
  {
    int x;                        //x is of primitive type
    x=100;

    int y;
    y=x;                          //y is a separate memory
                                  //location

    //outputting to the console
```

```
                    System.out.println("Before changing:");
                    System.out.println("x=" + x + ",y=" + y);

                    x=200;                          //x changed, y unchanged

                    System.out.println("After changing:");
                    System.out.println("x=" + x + ",y=" + y);
            }
    }
```

Output

Before changing:
x=100,y=100
After changing:
x=200,y=100

Class objects are always references. Listing C.2 illustrates this.

Listing C.2   Class objects are passed by reference

```
class A
{
    public int x;                       //public member
}

class first
{
    public static void main(String args[])
    {
        A A1 = new A();                 //necessary to initialize since A1
                                        //is only a reference … now A1 is
                                        //a reference to a memory location

        A1.x=100;

        A A2;
        A2=A1;                          //A2 is also a reference to the
                                        //memory location to which A1 is a
                                        //reference

        //outputting to the console
        System.out.println("Before changing:");
        System.out.println("A1.x=" + A1.x + ",A2.x=" + A2.x);

        A1.x=200;                       //A1.x changed, A2.x also changed

        System.out.println("After changing:");
        System.out.println("A1.x=" + A1.x + ",A2.x=" + A2.x);
    }
}
```

Output

Before changing:
A1.x=100,A2.x=100
After changing:
A1.x=200,A2.x=200

- **Garbage collection:** Unlike C++, where dynamically acquired memory must be explicitly returned to the OS, garbage collection is automatic in Java. During the execution of a Java program, an automatic garbage collector runs in the background. If it finds any locked up memory that is no longer being referenced, it returns it to the OS.

- **Destructor:** There is no delete keyword in Java. Therefore, there are no destructors in Java.

In Java, the programmer can simply create an object by using the new operator. There is no need to worry about reclaiming the memory, that is the garbage collector's responsibility.

The finalize() method in Java approximates the destructor's behaviour. However, there is a difference. The garbage collector will definitely execute this method for an object that it is destroying. But the exact instance at which the garbage collector would destroy an object cannot be specified.

- **Terminating class definitions, access specifiers, defining member functions:** Class definitions are terminated by semicolon in C++. In Java, class definitions are not terminated by a semicolon.

In C++, access specifiers are specified for a group of class members. In Java, access specifiers are specified for each individual class member separately.

Class member functions may be defined outside the class in C++. In Java, class member functions are always defined inside the class.

Unlike C++, access specifiers can be specified for classes in Java. A class prefixed with the keyword public is visible to classes outside the package in which it was created. Otherwise, it is visible to classes of the same package only.

Consider the class given in Listing C.3 written in C++.

Listing C.3 Access specifiers provided to individual members in Java

```
class A
{
    private:                        //access specifiers provided to a group
                                    //of members in C++
        int x;
    public:
        void setx(int);
        int getx();
};

public class A
{
    private int x;                  //access specifiers provided to
                                    //individual members in Java

    public void setx(int p)
    {
        x=p;
    }
    public int getx()
    {
        return x;
    }
}
```

Apart from private, protected, and public access specifiers, which are also provided by C++, Java provides the package access specifier. The package access specifier makes a member or a class to which it is applied visible to other classes of the same package only. It is the default access specifier. The functionality of this access specifier is similar to that of namespaces in C++.

- **Enumerations:** Java does not support the enum keyword. However, an enumerated type can be created in Java as a class that has only static final data members (Listing C.4).

Listing C.4 Specifying and using enumerated data types in Java

```
public class Color                      //creating an enumerated type
{
    public static final int red=1;
    public static final int blue=2;
    public static final int green=3;
    public static final int yellow=4;
    public static final int brown=5;
}

. . . .
. . . .

if(fontColor==Color.red)                //using a value of the
                                        //enumerated type
. . . .
```

In C and C++, while using the values of enumerated types, we need not qualify them by the name of the enumerated type itself. This leads to potential name clashes. This drawback does not exist in Java since the value of an enumerated type is qualified by the name of the enumerated type itself.

- **The this keyword:** The this keyword provides the same functionality in Java as it does in C++ with the difference that in C++ it is a pointer whereas in Java it is a reference. Therefore the this pointer need not be dereferenced in Java (Listing C.5).

Listing C.5 this is a reference in Java

```
class A
{
    private int x;
    void setx(int x)
    {
        this.x=x;                       //'this' is a reference in Java
    }
}
```

In the above example, the this pointer was used to resolve name ambiguity. The name of the member variable of class A is the same as that of the formal argument of the setx() function of class A. Using the this keyword resolves this ambiguity and the value of the member variable gets set to that of the formal argument.

- **The syntax of inheritance:** Java provides the extends keyword for declaring a derived class. This keyword can be used as follows:

```
class B extends A                       //class B inherits from A
{
}
```

- **The default base class in Java:** If you do not specify a base class for a class you are defining, the Java compiler automatically assigns a class called `Object` as its base class. Therefore, all classes in Java inherit from the class `Object`.

- **Overriding member functions of a base class in its derived classes:** Using the `final` keyword in the declaration of the member function of a class prevents the derived class from overriding it. The compiler throws an error if a member function of the derived class overrides a final method of the base class.

- **Interfaces and abstract base classes:** An interface in Java is similar to the abstract base class in C++ but with the following differences:

  - Member functions of an interface can only be declared. They cannot be defined.

  - Member data of an interface are considered final.

  An interface is declared in Java as follows:

```java
public interface A
{
   public void abc();          //declaration only … no definition
   public void def();          //declaration only … no definition
}
```

Like the abstract base classes of C++, interfaces in Java cannot be instantiated. The following piece of code is illegal:

```java
A A1 = new A();
```

A class that implements an interface can be instantiated provided it defines all member functions of the interface. See Listing C.6.

Listing C.6   Declaring and implementing an interface in Java

```java
public class B implements A          //syntax for implementing an
                                     //interface
{
   public void abc()
   {
      /*
         definition of the function
      */
   }
}
```

If not all member functions of the interface are defined in the class that implements them, the class becomes an abstract base class and cannot be instantiated.

Multiple inheritance is not supported in Java. However, Java provides interfaces. A class in Java can inherit from only one class but implement an unlimited number of interfaces. In the following definition, class X inherits from class P but implements the interfaces A and B.

```java
//implementing more than one interface
public class X extends P implements A, B
{
   /*
      definition of class X
   */
}
```

An abstract class is declared in C++ by declaring at least one of its member functions as a pure virtual function. An abstract class is declared in Java by using the abstract keyword in its declaration. As in C++, an abstract class cannot be instantiated. See Listing C.7.

Listing C.7 An abstract class in Java

```
public abstract class A            //an abstract class
{
    public abstract void abc();    //an abstract method of
                                   //an abstract class
    public void def()              //an non-abstract method
                                   //of an abstract class
    {
    /*
        definition of the function
    */
    }
}
```

As can be seen, some functions of an abstract class can be declared as abstract by using the abstract keyword in their declaration while the others can be declared as non-abstract by not using the abstract keyword in their declaration. In contrast to interfaces, member functions of an abstract class can be defined. If not all member functions of an abstract class are defined in the class that extends it, the latter class also becomes an abstract base class and cannot be instantiated.

Abstract and non-abstract member functions of the abstract base class can be overridden in the derived class. See Listing C.8.

Listing C.8 Overriding base class functions in the derived class

```
abstract class A
{
    public abstract void abc();
    public void def()
    {
        System.out.println("def() function of class A");
    }
}

public class B extends A
{
    public void abc()                    //overriding abstract function of
                                         //base class
    {
        System.out.println("abc() function of class B");
    }
    public void def()                    //overriding non-abstract function
                                         //of base class
    {
        System.out.println("def() function of class B");
    }
    public static void main(String args[])
    {
        A A1 = new B();
        A1.abc();
```

```
        A1.def();

    B B1 = new B();
    B1.abc();
    B1.def();
    }
}
```

Output

abc() function of class B
def() function of class B
abc() function of class B
def() function of class B

The foregoing output makes one thing very clear. All non-static member functions in Java are virtual functions. The abstract qualifier is used in the declaration of a member function of the base class only to force its override in the derived class.

An overridden member function of the base class can be called from the member function of the derived class by using the keyword super as illustrated in Listing C.9.

Listing C.9 Calling an overridden function of the base class in a member function of the derived class

```
abstract class A
{
    public abstract void abc();
    public void def()
    {
        System.out.println("def() function of class A");
    }
}
public class B extends A
{
    public void abc()
    {
        System.out.println("abc() function of class B");
    }
    public void def()
    {
        super.def();                    //calling an overridden function of the
                                        //base class
        System.out.println("def() function of class B");
    }
    public static void main(String args[])
    {
        A A1 = new B();
        A1.abc();
        A1.def();
    }
}
```

Output

abc() function of class B
def() function of class A
def() function of class B

- **Base class initialization:** Base class member data are initialized in C++ by the member initialization list. In Java, using the super keyword achieves this objective. See Listing C.10.

Listing C.10 Initializing base class members from the derived class constructor

```
class A
{
   private int x;
   public A(int p)
   {
      x=p;
   }
}
class B extends A
{
   int y;
   public B(int p, int q)
   {
      super(p);                        //calling the base class constructor
      y=q;
   }
}
```

- **Exception handling:** The exception handling mechanism provided in Java is very similar to C++ with the following differences:

  - In Java, the classes of all thrown objects must inherit from the class Throwable. Therefore, the block catch(Throwable) in a try … catch construct in Java is equivalent to the catch(…) block in C++.

  - Java introduces a new keyword finally to be used in the try … catch block. The block labeled finally is always executed at the end of a try … catch block.

Appendix D

Object-Oriented Analysis and Design

D.1 Introduction

This appendix gives a brief but comprehensive overview of Object-Oriented Analysis and Design (OOAD). OOAD is a design methodology. It is used to model solutions of software engineering problems. Models can be translated into actual code written in object-oriented languages.

Why Build Models?

Software engineering problems are usually quite complex. Different aspects of the solution need to be modeled using standard notations. After these models have been verified for correctness, they are implemented in actual code.

Models serve several purposes. Some of them are as follows:

- The solution can be tested for correctness and completeness before actually building it.
- Models help the developers in communicating clearly and precisely with customers and also among themselves. This ensures that all parties are in sync with each other.
- Models help developers in visualizing the solution clearly.
- Complexity of the problem gets reduced since the entire system can be broken down into successively smaller portions.

Overview of OOAD

What is OOAD?

OOAD has the following stages:

1. **Analysis:** In this phase, a model of the solution is built. The analysis model contains classes with their members, their relationships, etc. The analysis model shows *what* the desired solution must do, not *how* it will be done. It does not contain any implementation details.
2. **System design:** In this phase, the analysis model is divided into manageable sub-systems. Relationships amongst these sub-systems are also modeled. A strategy of attacking the problem is formulated. Performance optimization is also finalized.
3. **Object design:** In this phase, implementation details are added to the model built during the analysis phase.
4. **Implementation:** The object model thus created is finally translated into a particular programming language.

Overall development time is not always less in OOAD as compared to the conventional methodology. But the benefit is that the resulting model is better suited for future reuse. Downstream errors and maintenance efforts also get reduced.

D.2 Object-Oriented Model

An object-oriented model consists of the following three kinds of models:
- Object model
- Dynamic model
- Functional model

The object model describes the objects in the system and the relationships amongst these objects. It consists of object diagrams.

The dynamic model describes how objects in the system interact with each other. It consists of state diagrams. A state diagram depicts states and transitions between states that are caused by events.

The functional model describes how data gets transformed in the system. It consists of data flow diagrams. A data flow diagram depicts processes and data flow among the processes.

The three models complement each other. They are linked to each other. The object model is described first. It is necessary to describe what is changing or transforming before describing when and how it changes.

The object model describes classes upon whom the dynamic and functional models operate. The operations in the object model relate to events in the dynamic model and functions in the functional model.

Object Model

Object diagrams are of two types: class diagrams and instance diagrams.

As its name suggests, a class diagram describes classes and relationships amongst classes.

An instance diagram depicts the relationship amongst a particular set of objects that exist together at a given instance of time. A large number of instance diagrams can be generated from a single class diagram.

Boxes are used to depict objects and classes. Different object-oriented design tools use slightly different variations of these boxes. A sample is shown in Figure D.1.

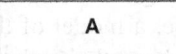

Figure D.1   A class is depicted in an object model as a box with sharp corners; name is in bold

Attributes

Attributes are nothing but data members of classes. They are listed in the second part of the class box. Each attribute name may be followed by a colon and its type. This, in turn, may be followed by an equality symbol and the default value of the data member. A line is drawn between the class names and attributes (see Figure D.2). No such line exists in object boxes (see Figure D.3).

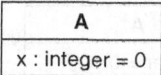

Figure D.2   Depicting attributes in class box

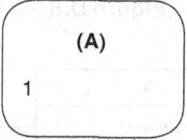

Figure D.3   An object is depicted in an `object model` as a box with rounded corners; class name is in bold but is surrounded by parentheses

Operations

Operations are nothing but member functions of classes. They are listed in the third part of the class box. The name of the operation is followed by a list of formal arguments in parentheses. The arguments are mentioned in the same way as the attributes. These parentheses may be followed by a colon and the result type of the operation (see Figure D.4).

A
x : integer = 0
setx(p : integer)
getx() : integer

Figure D.4   A class with operations

Links and associations

An association depicts a conceptual or physical relationship between two classes. A link is an instance of an association. Associations may be bidirectional or unidirectional. An association may be implemented as a pointer from one object to another. The notation for an association is a line between the associated classes. See Figure D.5.

A		B
x : integer = 0		y : integer = 0
setx(p : integer) getx() : integer		sety(p : integer) gety() : integer

Figure D.5   Association

Multiplicity

Multiplicity signifies the number of instances of one class that may relate to a single instance of an associated class. An association may be:

- One-to-one (Figure D.6)
- One-to-many (Figures D.7 and D.8)
- Many-to-many

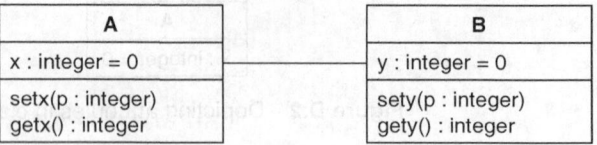

Figure D.6   A one to-one association

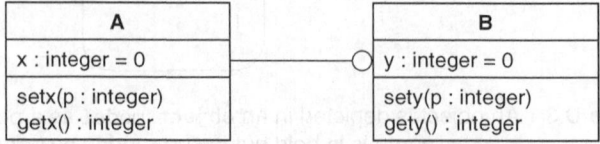

Figure D.7   A one-to-many association (zero or one instance of class B may be associated with an instance of class A)

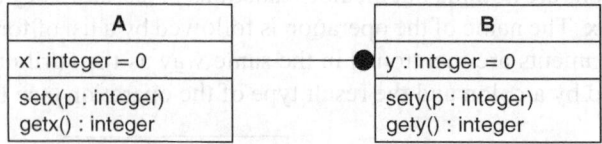

Figure D.8   A one-to-many association (exactly two instances of class B may be associated with an instance of class A)

A ball at one end of the line that depicts association between two classes indicates a 'many' side. A hollow ball indicates that zero or one instance of the class on whose side the ball appears may be associated with an instance of the associated class. A solid ball indicates that zero or many instances of the class on whose side the ball appears may be associated with an instance of the associated class. If no balls appear, it indicates a one-to-one relationship.

If possible, the exact permissible number of instances of one class that can be associated with one instance of the associated class is also specified. An exact value can be specified. An interval of values can also be specified. The interval may be a single interval or a set of disconnected intervals.

Some of the other ways of specifying the multiplicity in Figure D.8 are:

* 2+ (2 or more),
* 2–4 (2,3, or 4),
* 2,5,18 (either 2 or 5 or 18), etc.

Association attributes

An association may have its own attributes. Association attributes are depicted in boxes attached to the association by a loop (Figure D.9). Such boxes have the same characteristics as the boxes that are used to represent classes.

Attributes of a many-to-many association are always properties of the associations itself. They cannot be attached to either object. On the other hand, it is possible to insert attributes for one-to-one and one-to-many associations into the class opposite the 'one' side.

Pointers are embedded either in one or both of the associated classes to implement association. Alternatively, if a separate class has been used to implement an association as in Figure D.9, pointers to both classes appear in the third class. All this is explained in the last section of this appendix.

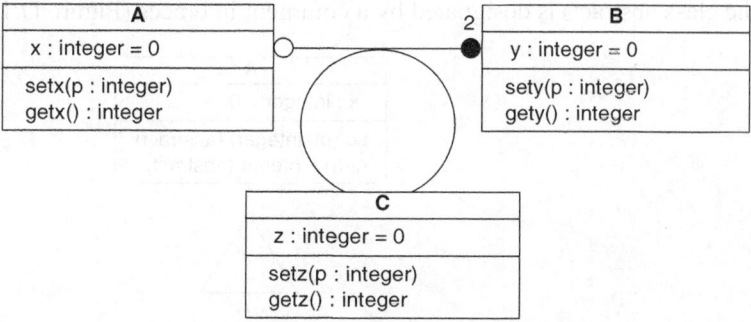

Figure D.9   Association attributes

Aggregation

In aggregation, an object of one class contains objects of other classes. Like association, a line connects two classes between whom an aggregation relationship exists. However, a diamond appears next to the container class. See Figure D.10.

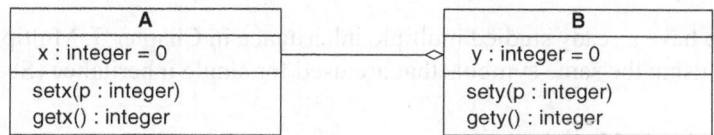

Figure D.10   Aggregation—an object of class B contains an object of class A

Inheritance

We have already studied inheritance in Chapter 5. The notation for inheritance is an upright triangle connecting a superclass to its subclasses. The superclass is connected by a line to the apex of the triangle. See Figure D.11.

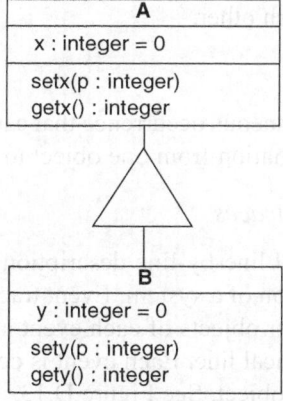

Figure D.11   Inheritance—class B derives from class A

Abstract classes

Abstract classes have already been explained in Chapter 6. An abstract function (that makes the class abstract) is designated by a comment in braces (Figure D.12).

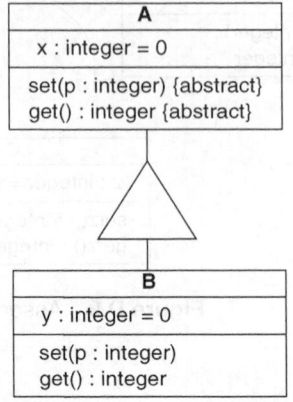

Figure D.12   Depicting an abstract base class

Multiple inheritance

We have already studied multiple inheritance in Chapter 5. Multiple inheritance is depicted by using the same symbols that are used for single inheritance (See Figure D.11).

Dynamic Model

The dynamic model models the sequence of changes that occur in a system.

Two important concepts in dynamic modelling are events and states. State of an object is represented by the set of values of the object at a given point of time. Events are external stimuli that cause a change of state.

A state diagram depicts the states, events, and transitions from one state to another for a given class. One state diagram is created for each class that exhibits important dynamic behaviour. The set of all such state diagrams constitutes the dynamic model. The state diagrams shared events with each other.

Events

An event is an instantaneous occurrence that causes a change of state. An event is a one-way transmission of information from one object to another.

Scenarios and event traces

A scenario is a textual line-by-line description of the sequence of events that occur during one particular execution of a system. Event traces are created for each scenario. For this, the sender and the receiver objects of each event are identified. This event trace shows each of these objects as a vertical line. Each event is depicted as a horizontal arrow from the sender object to the receiver object. See Figure D.13.

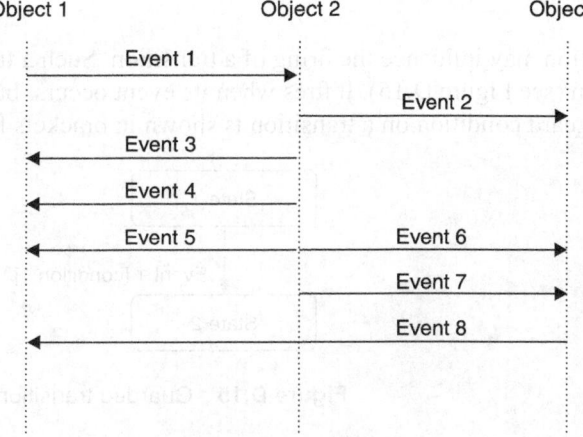

Figure D.13   An event trace

States

A state is a set of attribute values and links of an object that can be grouped together because they occur together at a given point of time. An object remains in the same state during the interval between two events.

State diagrams

A state diagram depicts the relation between events and states. Upon receiving an event, the state the recipient object attains depends on its current state as well as the event. Transition is the change of state caused by an event.

The symbol for a state is a rounded box that may contain a name for the state. A transition is depicted as an arrow from the receiving state to the target state.

A sequence of events on the event trace corresponds to a path through the state diagram. See Figure D.14.

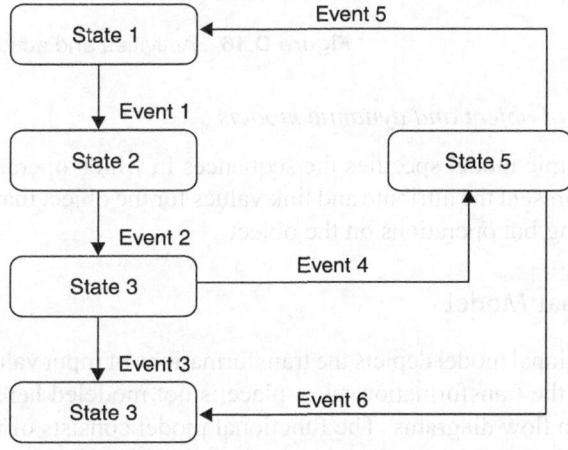

Figure D.14   A state diagram

Conditions

A condition may influence the firing of a transition. Such a transition is known as a guarded transition (see Figure D.15). It fires when its event occurs, but only if the guard condition is true. A guard condition on a transition is shown in brackets following the event name.

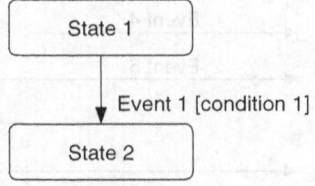

Figure D.15   Guarded transitions

Activity

An activity is an operation that executes over a period of time. An activity may continue to execute as long as an object remains in a particular state. Activities may run continuously or terminate on their own after an interval of time. The notation for specifying that an activity A executes as long as the state remains is "*do: A*" within the state box.

Actions

An action is an instantaneous occurrence that occurs when an event occurs. An action on a transition is denoted by a slash ('/') and its name, following the name of the event that causes it. Figure D.16 shows activities and actions.

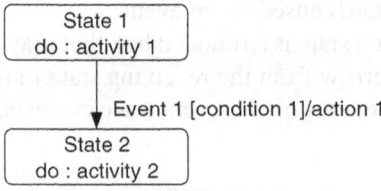

Figure D.16   Activities and actions

Relation of object and dynamic models

The dynamic model specifies the sequences in which operations of an object can be called. States represent the attribute and link values for the object that may exist concurrently. Events are nothing but operations on the object.

Functional Model

The functional model depicts the transformations of input values into output values. The order in which the transformation takes place is not modeled here. Transformations are depicted using data flow diagrams. The functional model consists of multiple data flow diagrams.

Data flow diagrams

A data flow diagram depicts the flow of data values from source objects through processes to their destinations objects.

A data flow diagram contains processes and data flows. Processes transform data. Data flows depict the flow of data amongst processes, actor objects, and data store objects. Actor objects are passive objects that enter data and use the data produced by the system. Data store objects merely store data and do not transform the data in any way.

Processes

A process is depicted as an ellipse in the data flow diagram. A descriptive name of the transformation appears as its label. The input and output data for each process are also depicted. See Figure D.17.

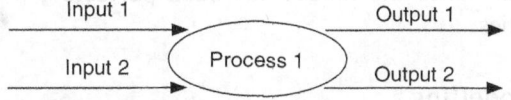

Figure D.17   A process in a data flow diagram

Data flows

A data flow connects the output of one object or process to the input of another object or process. The value is not changed by the data flow.

Actors

An actor initiates the data flow by inputting values. Values output by a data flow diagram may also terminate with an actor. Actors may be data-entry operators or timed devices. An actor is depicted as a rectangle since an actor is inherently an object.

Data stores

A data store merely stores data for later use. It does not have any operations defined. It is depicted as a pair of parallel lines with its name in between the lines (Figure D.18). Data stores are inherently objects. Figure D.19 shows a data flow diagram.

Data store 1

Figure D.18   A data store

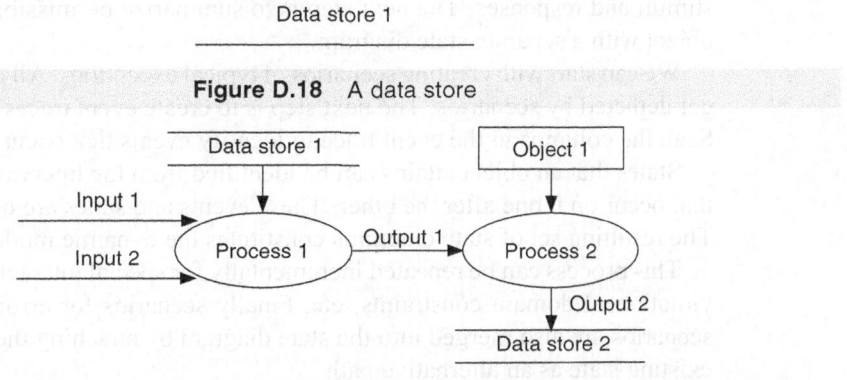

Figure D.19   A data flow diagram with data flows, processes, actors, and data stores

D.3 Analysis

Now we know the three models that constitute an object-oriented model. This section will teach us how we can create a model from the requirement document. The last section will teach us how to implement the model.

Overview of Analysis

Requests generated by users, developers, and managers are first collected and consolidated. A problem statement is created from this consolidated list. Models are built by analyzing the problem statement and by taking inputs from users, from domain experts, and from the developer's knowledge of the real world.

Large models are built up iteratively. A small model to achieve only the core requirement is built first. Once the model has been perfected, it is expanded to add all ancillary functionalities.

Object Modelling

The steps for object modelling are as follows:
1. Identify classes
2. Identify associations and aggregations
3. Add attributes to classes and associations
4. Combine classes using inheritance
5. Add operations to classes *after* constructing the dynamic and functional models

Classes often appear as nouns in the problem statement.

Associations often appear as verbs or verb phrases.

Attributes often appear as nouns followed by possessive phrases.

Identify classes that share common features and designate them as base classes. Look for nouns that appear with different adjectives. The common noun can usually be modeled as a base class whereas each of the nouns with an adjective can be modeled as its derived class.

Dynamic Modelling

Briefly, the first step in dynamic modelling is to identify events. Events appear as external stimuli and responses. The next step is to summarize permissible event sequences for each object with a separate state diagram.

We can start with creating scenarios of typical executions. All common interactions should get depicted by scenarios. The next step is to create event traces for each of these scenarios. Scan the columns in the event trace to identify events that occur on each object.

States that an object attains can be identified from the interval between all pairs of events that occur on it one after the other. These events and states are organized in a state diagram. The resulting set of state diagrams constitutes the dynamic model.

This process can be repeated incrementally for special interactions such as omitted inputs, violation of domain constraints, etc. Finally scenarios for error cases are prepared. These scenarios are also merged into the state diagram by attaching the new event sequence to the existing state as an alternative path.

Functional Modelling

Activities or actions in the state diagrams of classes can be modeled as processes on the data flow diagram. Objects and attribute values of an object diagram can be modeled as flows on a data flow diagram.

Parameters of events from the dynamic model appear as input and output values of processes. The data flow diagram can be constructed by inserting processes between corresponding input and output values.

Processes in the top-level data flow diagram may be quite complex. Create a simplified and detailed lower-level data flow diagram for each such process. If this level still contains complicated processes, repeat the process till you reach a data flow diagram with very simple processes.

Finally, write a textual description of each lowest-level process. The description should emphasize the objective of the process and not how the process would get implemented.

Identify and model actors and internal storage also.

D.4 System Design

System design is the high-level strategy for solving a problem and building a solution. The system is organized into sub-systems. Sub-systems are allocated to hardware and software components. Major conceptual and policy decisions that form the guidelines for the detail design are also taken. The overall organization of the system is called the system architecture. During system design, overall high-level implementation decisions are made. This is followed by similar decisions for successively lower levels.

Breaking the System into Sub-systems

A system is divided into sub-systems based on the similarity of *services*. A service is a set of functions that have a common objective.

Each sub-system provides a well-defined well-abstracted interface. The interface data can be exchanged with the sub-system. It does not specify how the sub-system is implemented internally. Thus, the internal design of each sub-system can be created and modified while other sub-systems that interact with it remain unchanged.

Layers

A system can be divided into sub-systems and these sub-systems can be horizontally layered one on top of another. Each layer is built to provide services to the ones above it. Thus each layer provides the basis of designing the one above it. Layers are thus strongly coupled.

Partitions

Sub-systems can be vertically placed next to each other as partitions also (see Figure D.20). Partitions are independent or weakly-coupled sub-systems.

A combination of layers and partitions can be used to divide a system.

We should also identify which activities may execute concurrently and which are mutually exclusive. The latter set of activities can be put together in a single thread of control.

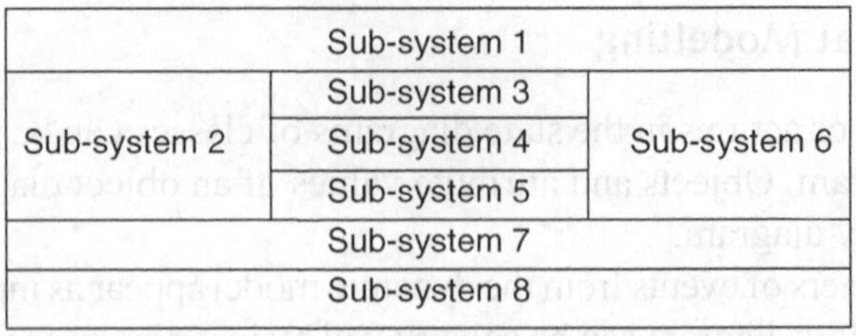

	Sub-system 1	
	Sub-system 3	
Sub-system 2	Sub-system 4	Sub-system 6
	Sub-system 5	
	Sub-system 7	
	Sub-system 8	

Figure D.20   Dividing a system into sub-systems

D.5 Object Design

Definitions of the classes and associations modeled earlier are completed in the object design phase. Algorithms to be used in the operations are also finalized.

Overview of Object Design

The list of objects found out during analysis is revised with an intention to minimize execution time and memory.

The object model describes the classes of objects in the system, including their attributes and the operations they support.

The functional model describes the operations that the system must implement. During design we must decide how each operation must be implemented.

The dynamic model describes how the system responds to external events. The control structure for a program is primarily derived from the dynamic model.

Actions and activities of the dynamic model and the processes of the functional model are converted to operations.

While designing classes we must decide when to use values of fundamental types for data members and when to use another object. Classes can contain objects of other classes, but eventually everything must be implemented in terms of built-in primitive data types.

D.6 Implementation

Writing code is an extension of the design process. Writing code should be straightforward, almost mechanical, because all the difficult decisions should already have been made during design. The code should be a simple translation of the design into code written in a particular programming language.

Classes are declared first. Attributes and operations mentioned in the object diagram are declared as private, protected, or public members.

We have already studied how a class can be defined in C++, how members can be declared in these classes, how objects of these classes can be declared and how member functions can be called with respect to the declared objects. We have also studied how inheritance can be implemented in C++. Now is the time to carry out these activities with respect to the object design just created.

There are two general approaches for implementing associations—buried pointers and distinct association objects.

A binary association is frequently implemented as a buried pointer in each of the associated objects that point at the related object or the set of related objects of the associated class. Updating one pointer in the implementation of an association implies that the other pointer must be updated as well to keep the implementation consistent.

Association can also be implemented as an associative container class (maps and sets).

Appendix E

Glossary

Abstract Base Class A class that has at least one pure virtual function. Abstract base classes cannot be instantiated. They only serve as base classes for other classes to derive from. (*see also* pure virtual functions)

Arrow Operator (->) An operator to access data members of an object or call member functions through a pointer that points at the object.

Base Class A class from which another class inherits. (*see also* inheritance)

Binary Search Tree A binary search tree is a special form of binary tree. In a binary search tree, for any given node, the value contained in its left child is less than the value contained in the node and the value contained in the node is less than the value contained in its right child.

Binary Tree A binary tree is a tree in which each node is linked to a maximum of 2 nodes.

Call by Reference The formal argument of the called function is of reference type. (*see also* reference variables)

Call by Value The formal argument of the called function is of non-reference type. (*see also* reference variables)

catch The keyword used to catch a thrown exception. (*see also* exception handling, try, throw)

Child Class A class that inherits from another class. (*see also* inheritance)

Class A language construct provided by C++ that enables the implementation of object-oriented concepts like data security, guaranteed initialization of data, data abstraction, data hiding, etc. A class has member functions and member data.

Class Template A template for a class definition. Data type of data members is undefined.

Clone Functions A function that creates an object of the same type at which a base class pointer points and returns its address.

Command Line Arguments Command line arguments are values that are passed to executables when they are run from the command line.

const_cast Operator This operator is used to cast away the constness of a value.

Constant Member Functions A member function that can only read the value of data members but not modify them.

Constructor A class member function that gets called automatically with respect to each object at the time of its creation. It is used to guarantee the initialization of data members of the object. (*see also* Guaranteed Initialization of Data)

Copy Constructor A constructor that gets called whenever an object is created and simultaneously equated to another existing object. It is called with respect to the object that is getting created while the existing object is passed as a parameter to it.

Data Member A class member that would contain the values of class objects. Each object of the class has its own copy of the data member.

Data Security An object-oriented feature that refers to preventing unauthorized functions from accessing data.

Default Constructor The constructor that gets defined by default by the compiler if we do not. It does not take parameters. (*see also* Zero-argument Constructor)

Default Values for Function Arguments Default values can be assigned for function arguments. These values are assigned to the arguments if no values are passed to them when the function is called.

delete Operator An operator that allows us to return a dynamically allocated block of memory to the operating system. (*see also* dynamic memory deallocation)

Derived Class (*see* child class)

Destructor A function that gets called automatically for each object at the time of its destruction. It is used to release resources held by objects.

Dot Operator (.) An operator that allows us to access data members of an object or call member functions with respect to an object.

dynamic_cast Operator A cast operator used for downcasting a pointer of base class type to a pointer of a particular derived class. If the base class pointer being typecast actually points at an object of the target type, the dynamic_cast operator returns the address of the object pointed at, else it returns NULL. If the dynamic_cast operator is used with references instead of pointers, it returns the reference to the target object or throws an exception of the type Bad_cast.

Dynamic Binding In dynamic binding, if an overridden function of the base class is called with respect to a pointer or a reference of the base class type, then which of the functions (base class function or one of the derived class versions) will actually be called, is decided based on the type of the object pointed at or referred to at run time. The same function has more than one form (in the base class and the derived classes). Its call can lead to the execution of a particular version depending upon circumstances arising during run time.

Dynamic Memory Allocation In this type of memory allocation, more memory is allocated in response to requirements arising during run time.

Dynamic Memory Deallocation Once it is not required, memory allocated dynamically can be retuned to the operating system. This is dynamic memory deallocation.

Dynamic Polymorphism (*see* dynamic binding)

Early Binding In early binding which version of a called function that has multiple forms will be called at run time is decided during compile time itself.

Enclosing Class A class that contains the definition of another class is known as an enclosing class. (*see also* nested class)

Exception Handling Exception handling is a facility that enables the library code to notify error conditions, which it is incapable of handling, to the calling client. The client can catch the exception and decide upon a suitable error-handling strategy. Alternatively, the client can choose to re-throw exceptions. (*see also* catch, throw, try)

Explicit Constructor Explicit constructors do not allow implicit conversions when an object is instantiated. Constructors are declared explicit by prefixing their declarations with the explicit keyword. We need to mention the explicit keyword in the declaration of the constructor only. It is not necessary to prefix the definition of the constructor with the explicit keyword. Explicit constructors can prove to be useful for the programmer if he/she is creating a class for which an implicit conversion by the constructor is undesirable.

Friend Function A non-member function that has been granted special rights to access private data members of the class of which it has been declared a friend.

Friend Class A class whose entire set of member functions has been granted special rights to access private data members of the class of which it has been declared a friend.

Function Member A function that is a member of a class. It is declared within the class. It has the right to access the private data members of all objects of the class.

Function Overloading A facility that enables the programmer to create two functions with the same name.

Function Prototype A function declaration that tells the compiler the return type of the function and the type and number of its formal arguments.

Function Template A template for a function definition. The type of its formal arguments is undefined. An actual definition of the function gets generated only when the function is called. The types of the corresponding passed parameters replace the undefined data types of formal arguments.

Generic Class (same as class template)

Guaranteed Initialization of Data The data members of a structure variable in C language may attain invalid values at its time of creation. C++ enables programmers to guarantee initialization of data members of objects by defining constructors. (*see also* constructor)

Inheritance A feature provided by all object-oriented languages that enables a class to inherit the data and function members of an existing class. (*see also* base class, parent class, super class, derived class, child class, sub class)

Inline Function A function that is expanded inline with its call by the compiler.

Late Binding (*see* dynamic binding)

Linked Lists Linked lists consist of nodes that are linked to each other in a linear fashion. Each node in a linked list is an object that is made up of two parts. The first part is the data carried by the node. The second part of each node is a pointer that carries the address of the next node in the list. This is a description of a single linked list. Alternatively, each node may have an additional pointer, a pointer to the previous node. Such linked lists are called double linked lists.

Manipulators Manipulators are operators that enable the C++ programmer to format the output from their programs.

Multiple Inheritance A type of inheritance where a class inherits the features of more than one base class.

Mutable Data Members Data members that are never constant. Even constant member functions can modify their values. (*see also* constant member functions)

Namespace A language construct in C++ that allows us to divide the source code into logical parts. This helps in preventing clashes of names. Two classes with the same name can be defined if they belong to different namespace.

Nested Class A class that is defined within another class is known as a nested class. (*see also* enclosing class)

New Handler Function A function that gets called whenever an out-of-memory condition is encountered. We can define our own new handler function.

new Operator An operator that enables us to capture more memory in response to conditions arising during run time (*see also* dynamic memory allocation)

New Style Casts C++ provides the following four new style cast operators to replace the use of the old error-prone and difficult-to-detect C style casts:
- dynamic_cast
- static_cast
- reinterpret_cast
- const_cast

Object An instance of a class is known as an object.

Object-Oriented Programming System A programming system that enables programmers to model real-world objects. Data and procedures that work upon the data are bound together in a single construct called class.

Operator Overloading A feature of most object-oriented languages that enables programmers to provide additional definitions to operators so that they can take class objects as operands.

Parameterized Class (*see* Class Template)

Parameterized Constructor A constructor that takes parameters.

Parent Class (*see* Base Class)

Polymorphism A feature of object-oriented languages that allows programmers to create two functions with identical names. Polymorphism is of two types—static and dynamic. (*see also* Static Binding, Static Polymorphism, Early Binding, Dynamic Binding, Dynamic Polymorphism, Late Binding)

Private Class Members Function and data members of a class that have been declared under the private section of a class. Private class members can be accessed by member functions of the same class only.

Procedure-Oriented Programming System In this system, code is divided into procedures. Data and procedures that work upon the data are not bound together.

Protected Class Members Function and data members of a class that have been declared under the protected section of a class. Protected class members can be accessed by member functions of the same class and those of the derived class only.

Public Class Members Function and data members of a class that have been declared under the public section of a class. Public class members can be accessed by not only the member functions of the same class and those of the derived class. They can be accessed by global non-member functions also.

Pure Virtual Functions A special type of virtual function whose declaration is suffixed by '=0'. Presence of a pure virtual function makes its class an abstract base class. A derived class that does not override the pure virtual functions of the base becomes an abstract base class. (*see* abstract base class, virtual functions)

Queues Queues are very similar to linked lists. However, in a queue, we can add a node only to the end. Moreover, in a queue, we can delete a node only from the beginning.

Reference Variables A reference variable is a reference to another variable. It does not occupy its own memory. It shares the memory occupied by the variable of which it is a reference.

reinterpret_cast Operator A new style cast operator that allows the conversion of one type to another.

Scope Resolution Operator An operator that enables the C++ programmer to define a member function outside the class.

Stacks Stacks are very similar to linked lists. However, in a stack, we can add a node only to the beginning. Moreover, in a stack, we can delete a node only from the beginning.

static_cast Operator The only difference between the static_cast operator and the dynamic_cast operator is that while the dynamic_cast operator carries out a run-time check to ensure a valid conversion, the static_cast operator caries out no such check.

Static Binding (*see* early binding)

Static Data Member Static data members hold global data that is common to all objects of the class. Static data members are members of the class and not of any object of the class, that is, they are not contained inside any object.

Static Function Member Static member functions are not called with respect to an existing object. This function's sole purpose is to access and/or modify static data members of the class.

Static Memory Allocation In this method of memory allocation, the amount of memory to be allocated and the time at which it would get allocated during run-time are both decided during compile time itself.

Static Memory Deallocation In this method of memory allocation, the amount of memory to be deallocated and the time at which it would get deallocated during run-time are both decided during compile time itself.

Static Polymorphism (*see* early binding)

Structure A language construct in C language that enables the programmer to put together data that influence each others' values and should therefore be put together. C language does not allow the programmer to define member functions inside structures. This leads to lack of data security.

Subclass (*see* child class, derived class, inheritance)

SuperClass (*see* parent class, base class, inheritance)

this pointer A constant pointer that gets passed to each member function as a leading formal argument. It points at the object for which the function is called.

throw A keyword in C++ that allows the library programmer to throw an exception whenever an invalid condition is encountered that cannot be handled in the library code itself. (*see also* exception handling, try, throw)

Trees Trees, unlike linked lists, stacks, and queues, do not have a linear structure. In a tree, each of the nodes may be connected to more than one node.

try A keyword in C++ that allows a client to place calls to library functions that are likely to throw exceptions. (*see also* exception handling, try, throw)

typeid Operator An operator that enables us to determine the type of object at which a pointer points.

Virtual Base Class A base class that is derived by using the virtual keyword while declaring the derived class. If a class derives from two classes that in turn inherit from a virtual base class, the final derived class gets only one copy of the features of the virtual base class.

Virtual Function A class member function can be declared as a virtual function by prefixing its declaration with the virtual keyword. Virtual functions enable dynamic polymorphism. If a virtual function is overridden in a derived class and called with respect to a pointer of base class type that points at an object of the same derived class, then the function called would be of the derived class and not of the base class. (*see also* Dynamic Binding, Dynamic Polymorphism, Late Binding)

Zero-argument Constructor A constructor that does not take any arguments is called a zero-argument constructor. The constructor that is created by default by the compiler is also a zero-argument constructor. Therefore, the two terms zero-argument constructor and default constructor are used interchangeably. (*see also* constructor, default constructor)

Appendix F

Self Tests

Time: 1 hour
Max Marks: 50

True/False

[1 × 10 = 10]

1. Variables must be declared at the beginning of the function in a C++ program code.
2. A function can modify the value of the passed parameter if the corresponding formal argument is a reference variable.
3. The presence of an inline function in a code does not impact the size of the resultant executable.
4. Structures in C++ cannot have member functions.
5. A constant member function cannot access the static data members of the class.
6. The return type of a constructor in C++ is void.
7. A function of the derived class can access the public member of the base class even if the private keyword is used for derivation.
8. A pure virtual function cannot be overloaded.
9. An actual definition is created from a function/class template during run time.
10. Each node of a single linked list can contain only integer-type values in its data part.

Fill in the Blanks

[1 × 10 = 10]

1. The process of binding together data and code that works upon the data is known as ....
2. **cout** is an object of the .... class.
3. The .... operator is used to access a class member with respect to a pointer.
4. Members declared under the private and .... sections of a class cannot be accessed by non-member functions.
5. Virtual functions enable .... polymorphism.
6. A virtual function can be specified as a pure virtual function by suffixing its declaration with ....
7. Conversion of basic type to class type can be achieved by using ....
8. The .... flag should be passed to the open( ) function to ensure that a file does not get created if it does not exist.
9. The three keywords provided by C++ for implementing exception handling are try, catch, and ....
10. The syntax for catch all block is ....

Multiple Choice Questions

(more than one choice can be correct)

[2 × 5 = 10]

1. Which of the following are features of the Object-Oriented Programming System?
   (a) Inheritance
   (b) Data persistence
   (c) Polymorphism
   (d) Data abstraction
2. Which of the following is a correct function prototype?
   (a) `int abc(int, int);`
   (b) `int abc(int a, int b);`
   (c) `int abc(int a, int b) {}`
   (d) `int abc(int a, b);`
3. The benefits of inheritance is/are
   (a) code reusability
   (b) faster executables
   (c) data hiding
   (d) smaller executables
4. A copy constructor is called when
   (a) an object is created and simultaneously equated to another existing object.
   (b) a reference is created to an existing object.
   (c) an object is passed to a function whose formal argument is an object.
   (d) an object is passed to a function whose formal argument is a reference.
5. Which of the following is/are used for outputting in text mode?
   (a) `write()` function
   (b) `insertion` operator
   (c) `put()` function
   (d) `extraction` operator

Short Answer Questions

[4 × 5 = 20]

1. Write an inline function and a macro to return the larger of two numbers. Which is better and why?
2. Explain the need for user-defined destructors with the help of examples.
3. What are the ambiguities that arise in multiple and diamond-shaped inheritance. How can they be removed?
4. Explain why read operation on a file should take place in the same mode in which the write operation has occurred?
5. Explain the function that deletes nodes from the beginning of single linked lists.

Test 2

Time: 1 hour
Max Marks: 50

True/False

[1 × 10 = 10]

1. Two functions with same names and signatures can exist together if their return types are different.
2. A function that returns a non-reference value can be placed on the left of the assignment operator.
3. Only one copy of the static data member exists for a class.
4. Class members are private by default.
5. A class can have more than one destructor.
6. A base class pointer can point at an object of the derived class.
7. All functions of a class must be declared as pure virtual functions in order to make it an abstract base class.
8. The `const_cast` operator is used to convert a pointer of base class type to a pointer of derived class type.
9. Only one function definition is generated from a single function template.
10. An unhandled exception will cause the program to terminate.

Fill in the Blanks

[1 × 10 = 10]

1. .... is a feature of the Object-Oriented Programming System that allows one function to have more than one definition.
2. The .... operator is used to define a member function outside its class.
3. The non-member function that has special rights to access private members of objects of a class is known as a .... function.
4. The formal argument of the .... constructor must always be a reference object.
5. Inheritance implements a/an .... relationship.
6. If a derived class is derived from a base class by using the protected keyword, the public members of the base class become .... with respect to member functions of the derived class.
7. Apart from the non-static data member, objects of a class that has at least one virtual function contain ....
8. Input pointer can be manipulated by using the .... function.
9. .... is the base class of all classes in the stream handling library of C++.
10. Adding a node to a stack or a queue is known as ....

Multiple Choice Questions

(more than one choice can be correct)

[2 × 5 = 10]

1. Consider the following function

```
int abc(int, int) {}
```

Which of the following overload the function?
(a) `int abc(int, int, int) {}`
(b) `float abc(int, int) {}`
(c) `int abc(float, int) {}`
(d) `int abc(int, int=0) {}`
2. Which of the following is/are true about constructors?
(a) Its name is prefixed with the tilde sign.
(b) It can be overloaded.
(c) It can access static data members of a class.
(d) It can be virtual.
3. Which of the following kinds of functions can access the protected members of a class?
(a) A global non-member friend function.
(b) A member function of a friend class.
(c) A global non-member function.
(d) A member function of a friend class that has been derived by `public` or `protected` keywords.
4. Which of the following are classes in the standard C++ stream handling library?
(a) iostream
(b) stream
(c) ostream
(d) fstream
5. Which of the following enable code reusability?
(a) Function overloading
(b) Inheritance
(c) Exception handling
(d) Templates

Short Answer Questions

[4 × 5 = 20]

1. Explain the need for user-defined copy constructors with the help of examples.
2. In which order are the constructors and destructors called when an object of the derived class is created?
3. What is the difference between `static_cast` and `dynamic_cast` operators?
4. Why are operators overloaded?
5. When and how does the C++ compiler generate an actual class definition from its template?

Test 3

Time: 1 hour
Max Marks: 50

True/False

[1 × 10 = 10]

1. The value of a mutable data member can be modified by a constant function.
2. Default value cannot be given to more than one formal argument of a function.
3. A static data member of a class can be of the same type as the class.
4. A class can have more than one constructor.
5. A base class and a derived class cannot have functions with the same name and same signature.
6. Presence of virtual functions in a class does not increase the size of its objects.
7. We can overload the increment operator to decrement the value of the objects.
8. The name of the class of the object at which a pointer points can be found out by using the typeid operator.
9. A template class can have only one template type object.
10. A single catch block can be used to catch more than one type of exception.

Fill in the Blanks

[1 × 10 = 10]

1. A class that contains another class is knows as .... class.
2. The .... pointer points at the invoking object.
3. The .... operator is used to capture memory dynamically in C++.
4. The name of the destructor is prefixed with the .... sign.
5. Deriving from more than one base class is known as .... inheritance.
6. The .... keyword is used to overload operators.
7. The two modes of input/output are .... mode and binary mode.
8. The read() and write() functions operate in .... mode.
9. The .... operator is used to cast away the constness of the operand.
10. The .... keyword is used to label the block of code from which an exception is likely to be thrown.

Multiple Choice Questions

(more than one choice can be correct)

[2 × 5 = 10]

1. Which of the following keywords is used to create a new data type?
   (a) class
   (b) inline
   (c) throw
   (d) struct
2. Which of the following occur when a class is derived from another class by using the private keyword?
   (a) Public members of the base class reappear as private members of the derived class.
   (b) Public members of the base class reappear as protected members of the derived class.
   (c) Protected members of the base class reappear as protected members of the derived class.
   (d) Protected members of the base class reappear as private members of the derived class.

3. Which of the following are not keywords in C++?
   (a) struct
   (b) abstract
   (c) constant
   (d) cast
4. Which of the following functions returns the number of elements in a list?
   (a) size()
   (b) length()
   (c) width()
   (d) index()
5. Flags that indicate state of the next byte in the associated file are
   (a) eofbit
   (b) nofilebit
   (c) failbit
   (d) badbit

Short Answer Questions

[4 × 5 = 20]

1. Explain why static data members should be explicitly declared outside the class. Why should static data members be defined in the implementation files only?
2. Why is it necessary for the derived class constructor to pass values explicitly to the base class constructor for initializing base class members?
3. What is the virtual table? How is it created? What is the virtual pointer?
4. Why does the function to overload the assignment operator receive and return by reference?
5. Explain why the stack and queue classes do private inheritance from the single linked list class.

Bibliography

- **Stanley B. Lippman and Josee Lajoie (1998),** *C++ Primer*, **3rd edn, Pearson Education, Asia.**
  This book contains an in-depth coverage of a wide range of topics in C++. An excellent book for students aiming to gain an insight into the practical aspects of C++.

- **Scott Meyers (1998),** *Effective C++*, **2nd edn, Pearson Education, Asia.**
  This book gives excellent tips and tricks for writing C++ code. An easy to follow language makes the book inviting to read and keeps the reader's attention riveted till the very end. A must read for the practical C++ programmer.

- **Bjarne Stroustrup (1991),** *The C++ Programming Language*, **2nd end, Pearson Education, Asia.**
  This book has been written by the creator of C++ himself. It is an excellent reference book on the C++ language.

- **Jesse Liberty (1998),** *C++ Unleashed*, **Sams.**
  This book contains a number of excellent case studies on the practical application areas of C++, such as CORBA, Data Structures, COM, and Data Persistence. It is highly recommended for the practical C++ programmer.

- **Al Stevens (2003),** *Teach Yourself C++*, **7th edn, Wiley Publishing Inc., Indianapolis, Indiana.**
  This is a good book for learning the fundamentals of C++. Well-arranged topics make the book easy to read. A number of advanced concepts have been included in this book.

- **Stephen Prata (2001),** *C++ Primer Plus*, **4th edn, Sams.**
  This is a good book for learning the fundamentals of C++. An easy language and plenty of solved examples are the salient features of the book.

- **E. Balagurusamy (1995),** *Object Oriented Programming with C+*, **2nd edn, Tata McGraw-Hill.**
  This is a popular book on C++ in the Indian market. The book gives a good coverage of the various aspects of programming in C++.

Index

Related Titles

PROGRAMMING IN C, 2e

[9780198065289]

Dey and Ghosh, RCC Institute of Information Technology, Kolkata

The book gives an exhaustive coverage of arrays, strings, functions, pointers, and data structures. Separate chapters on linked lists and stacks, queues, and trees, with their implementation in C, have been provided to simplify the learning of complex concepts. Some advanced features of C such as memory models, command-line arguments, and bitwise operators have also been included. Case studies demonstrating the use of C in solving mathematical as well as real-life problems have also been presented. This edition also highlights C99 features wherever relevant in the text.

PROGRAMMING WITH ANSI C++

[9780195690378]

Bhushan Trivedi, GLS Institute of Computer Technology, Ahmedabad

The book starts with an overview of C++ followed by a systematic discussion of concepts such as classes, objects, functions, constructors, destructors, overloading, standard template library, and templates. An in-depth discussion of topics such as exception handling, inheritance, polymorphism, RTTI, file handling, and namespaces has been presented with suitable examples. The text is well supported by numerous program listings and exercises in each chapter. The book also includes a case study at the end to demonstrate the use of C++ in developing real-life applications.

PROGRAMMING IN JAVA

[9780198063582]

Sachin Malhotra, Chairperson, PGDM-IT, IMS, Ghaziabad

Saurabh Choudhary, Dean, Academics, IMS, Ghaziabad

Programming in Java first provides a thorough understanding of the basic concepts of object-oriented programming principles and then moves onto explain the concepts in Java. Beginning with the history and creation of Java to its properties and applications, it gradually moves ahead to provide an exhaustive coverage of features such as operators, classes, objects, inheritance, packages, and exception handling. The book provides a comprehensive discussion of the latest features of Java such as enumerations, generics, logging API, console class, StringBuilder class, NetworkInterface class, and assertions. The inclusion of these features combined with core concepts like multithreading, applets, AWT, and swings provide a thorough understanding of the important concepts. Lastly, the book gives an insight into some advanced concepts such as servlets, RMI, and JDBC.

Other related titles

9780198006224	Roy: *Web Technologies*
9780195676846	Dey & Ghosh: *Computer Fundamentals and Programming in C*
9780198065449	Thareja: *Data: Structures using C*
9780195686289	Pudi & Krishna: *Data Mining*
9780195699616	Thareja: *Data Warehousing*
9780198071068	Nagpal: *Formal Language and Automata Theory*
9780198070887	Pal: *Systems Programming*
9780195692327	Siddiqui & Tiwary: *Natural Language Processing and Information Retrieval*
9780198061847	Chauhan: *Software Testing: Principles and Practices*
9780195694840	Jain: *Software Engineering*
9780198066231	Patil: *Data Structures Using C++*

Visit us at www.oup.co.in and www.oupinheonline.com